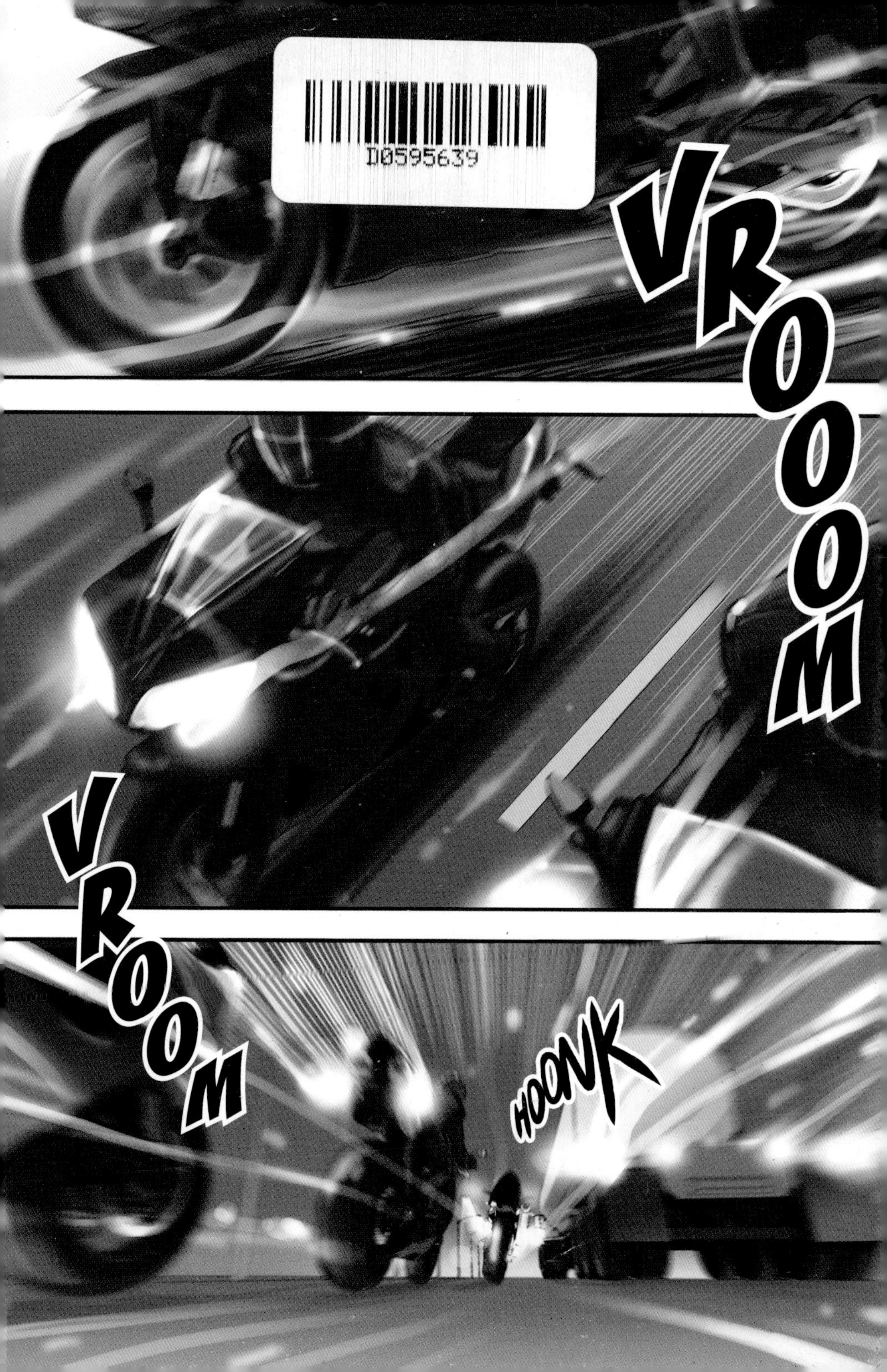
VROOOM
VROOM
HOONK

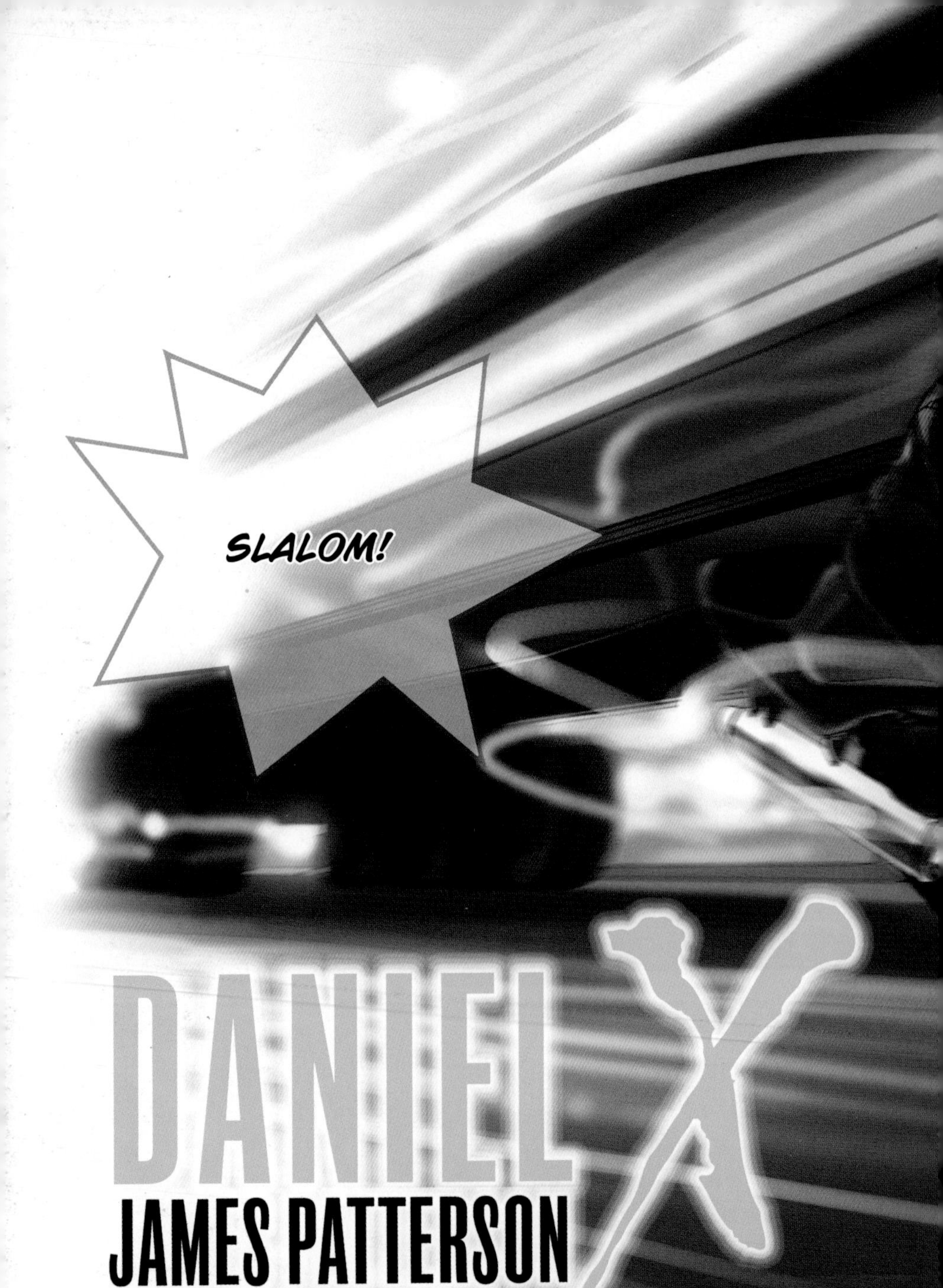
SLALOM!

DANIEL X

JAMES PATTERSON
WITH NED RUST ART: SEUNGHUI KYE

CHAPTER 7

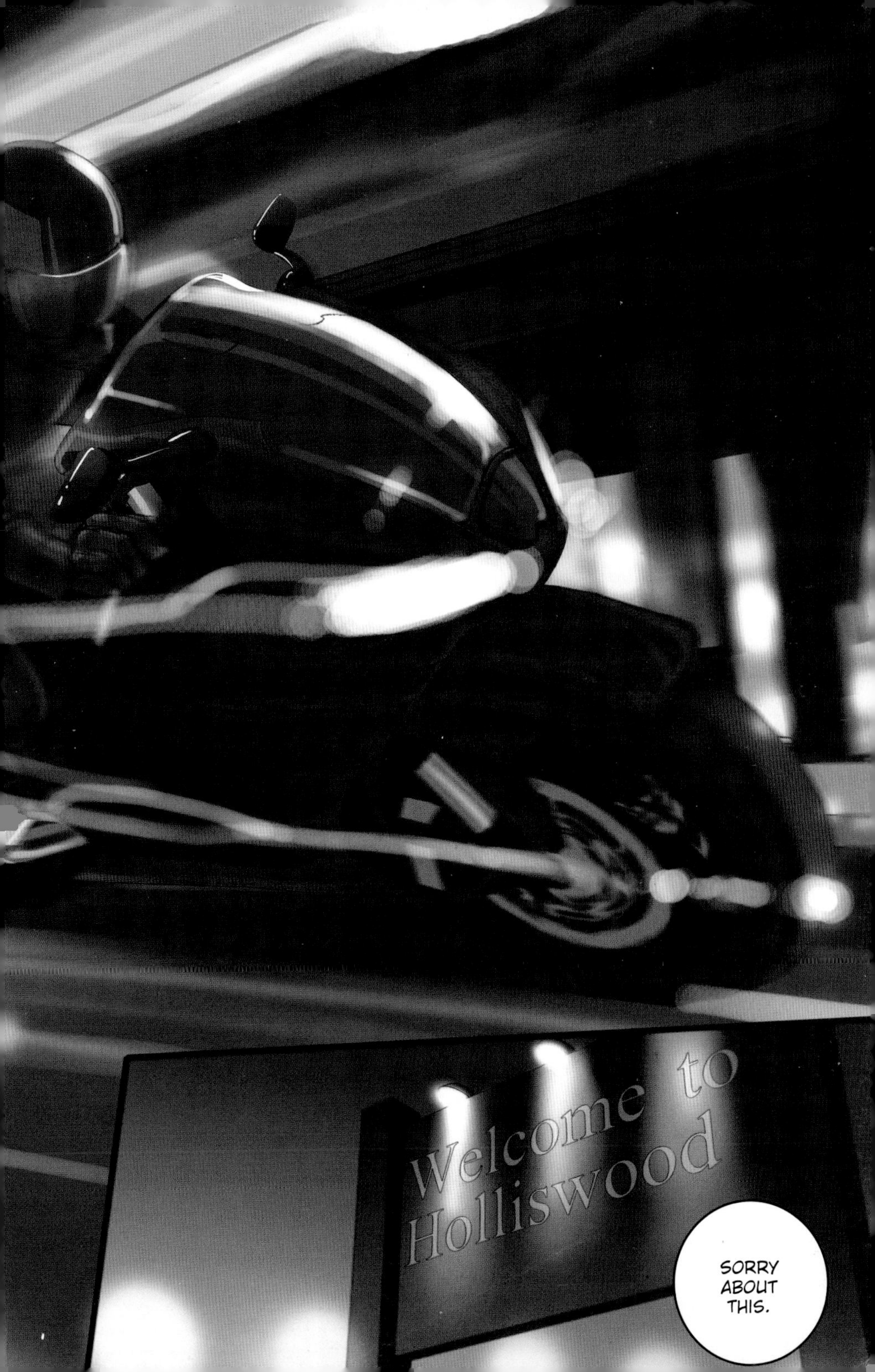
Welcome to Holliswood
SORRY ABOUT THIS.

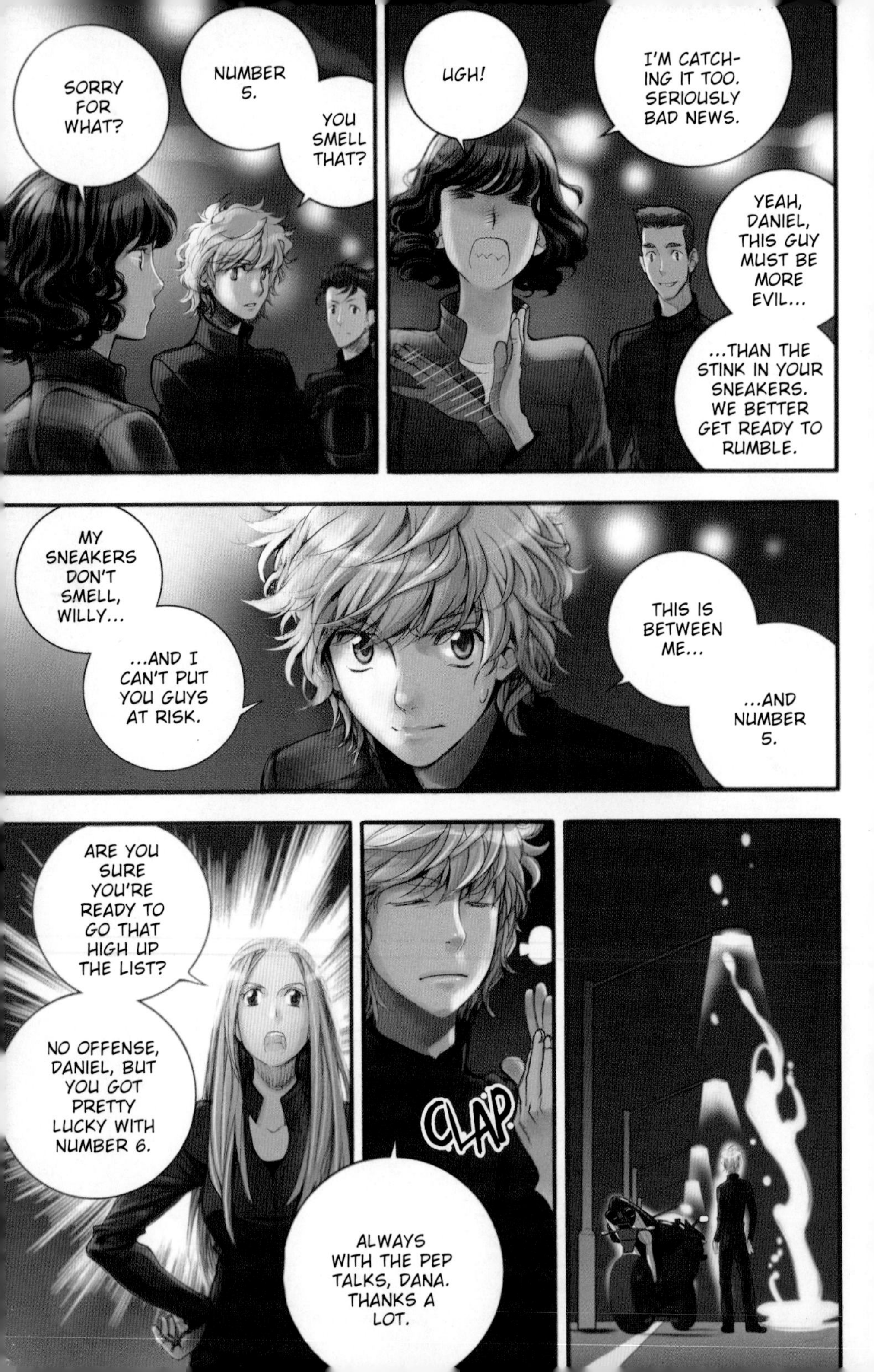
SORRY FOR WHAT?
NUMBER 5.
YOU SMELL THAT?
UGH!
I'M CATCHING IT TOO. SERIOUSLY BAD NEWS.
YEAH, DANIEL, THIS GUY MUST BE MORE EVIL...
...THAN THE STINK IN YOUR SNEAKERS. WE BETTER GET READY TO RUMBLE.
MY SNEAKERS DON'T SMELL, WILLY...
...AND I CAN'T PUT YOU GUYS AT RISK.
THIS IS BETWEEN ME...
...AND NUMBER 5.
ARE YOU SURE YOU'RE READY TO GO THAT HIGH UP THE LIST?
NO OFFENSE, DANIEL, BUT YOU GOT PRETTY LUCKY WITH NUMBER 6.
CLAP
ALWAYS WITH THE PEP TALKS, DANA. THANKS A LOT.

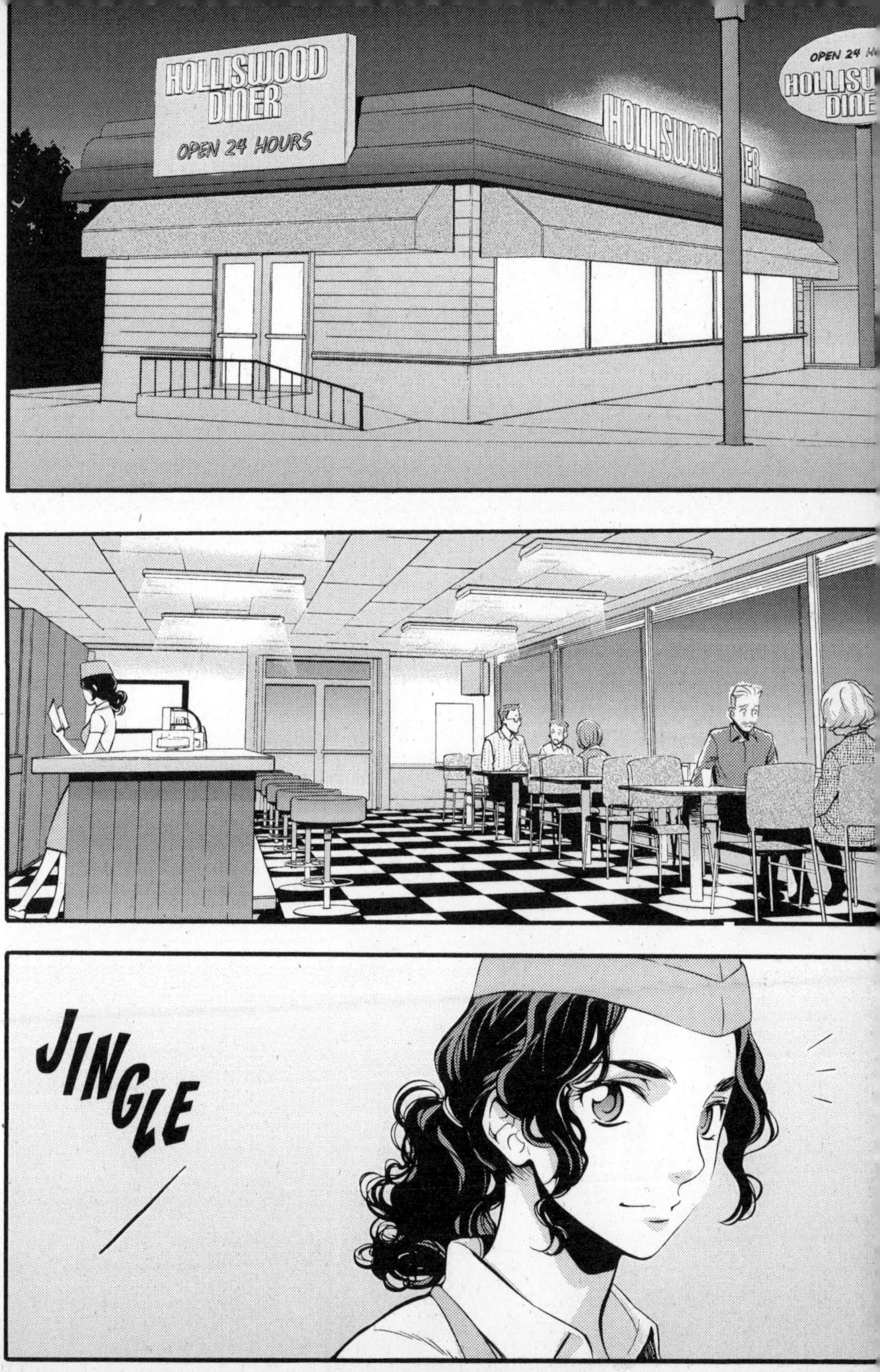
HOLLISWOOD DINER
OPEN 24 HOURS
JINGLE

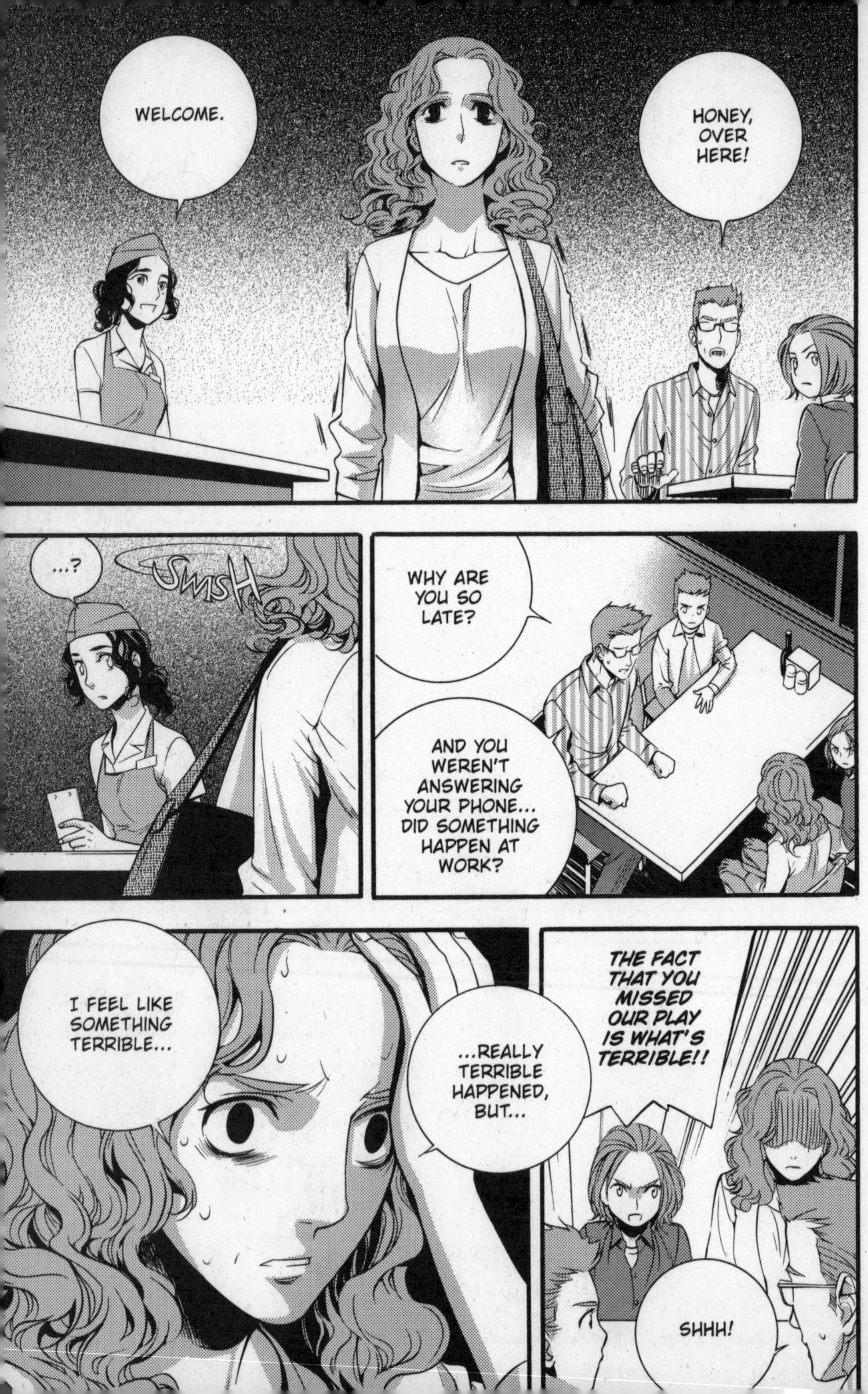
WELCOME.
HONEY, OVER HERE!
...?
SWISH
WHY ARE YOU SO LATE?
AND YOU WEREN'T ANSWERING YOUR PHONE... DID SOMETHING HAPPEN AT WORK?
I FEEL LIKE SOMETHING TERRIBLE...
...REALLY TERRIBLE HAPPENED, BUT...
THE FACT THAT YOU MISSED OUR PLAY IS WHAT'S TERRIBLE!!
SHHH!

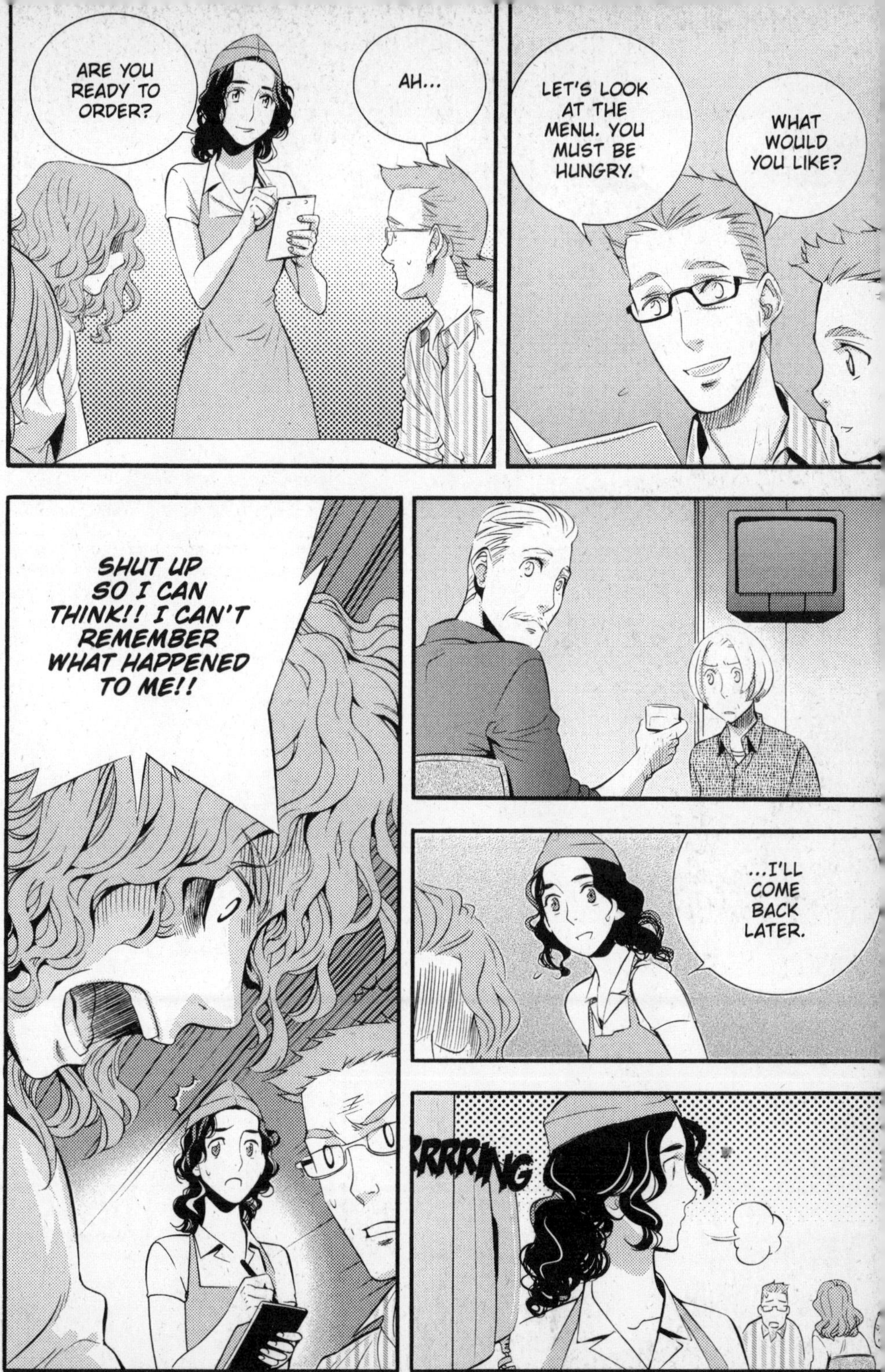
ARE YOU READY TO ORDER?
AH...
LET'S LOOK AT THE MENU. YOU MUST BE HUNGRY.
WHAT WOULD YOU LIKE?
SHUT UP SO I CAN THINK!! I CAN'T REMEMBER WHAT HAPPENED TO ME!!
...I'LL COME BACK LATER.
RRRRING

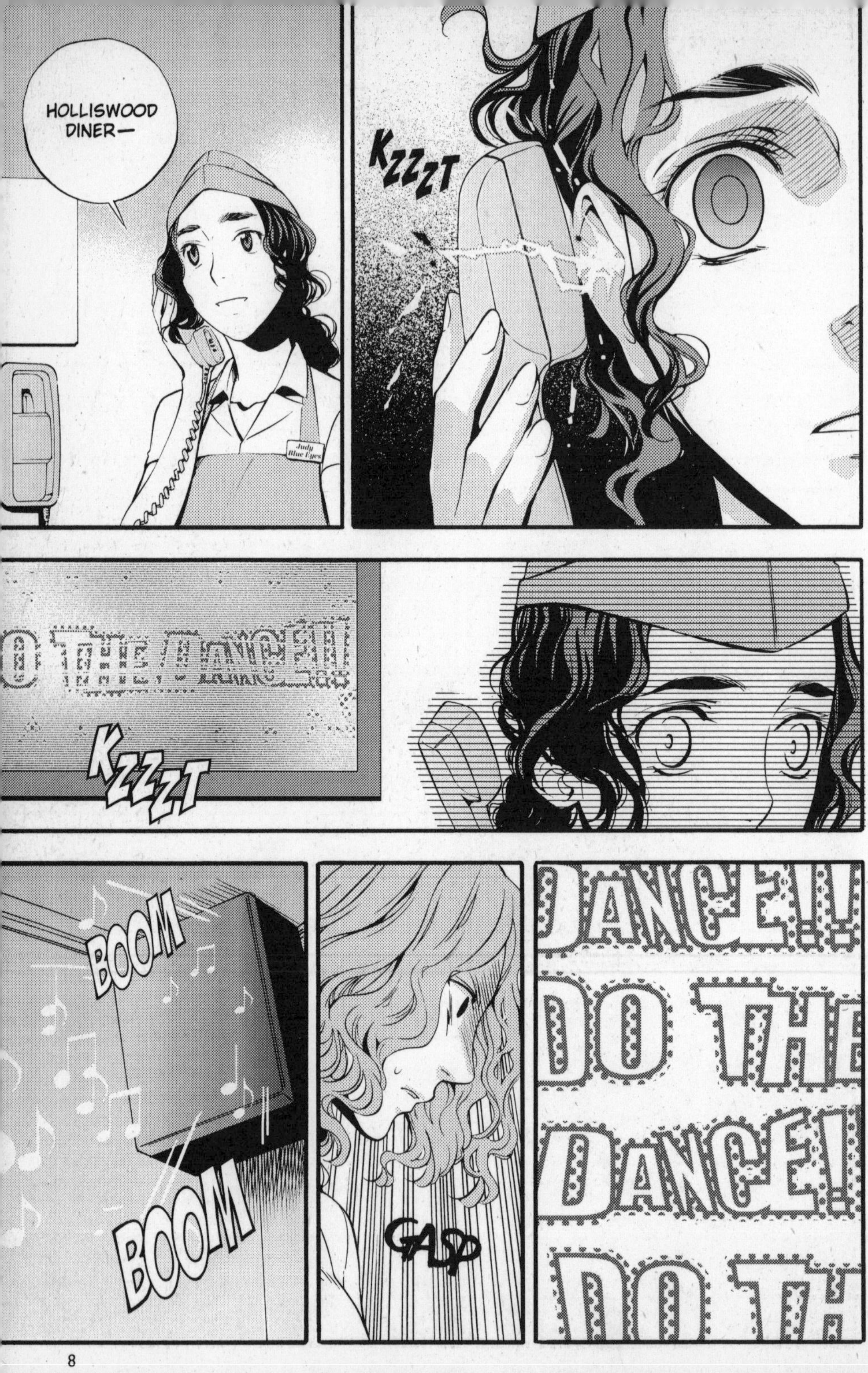
HOLLISWOOD DINER—
Judy Blue Eyes
KZZZT
O THE DANCE!!
KZZZT
BOOM
BOOM
GASP
DANCE!
DO THE
DANCE!
DO TH

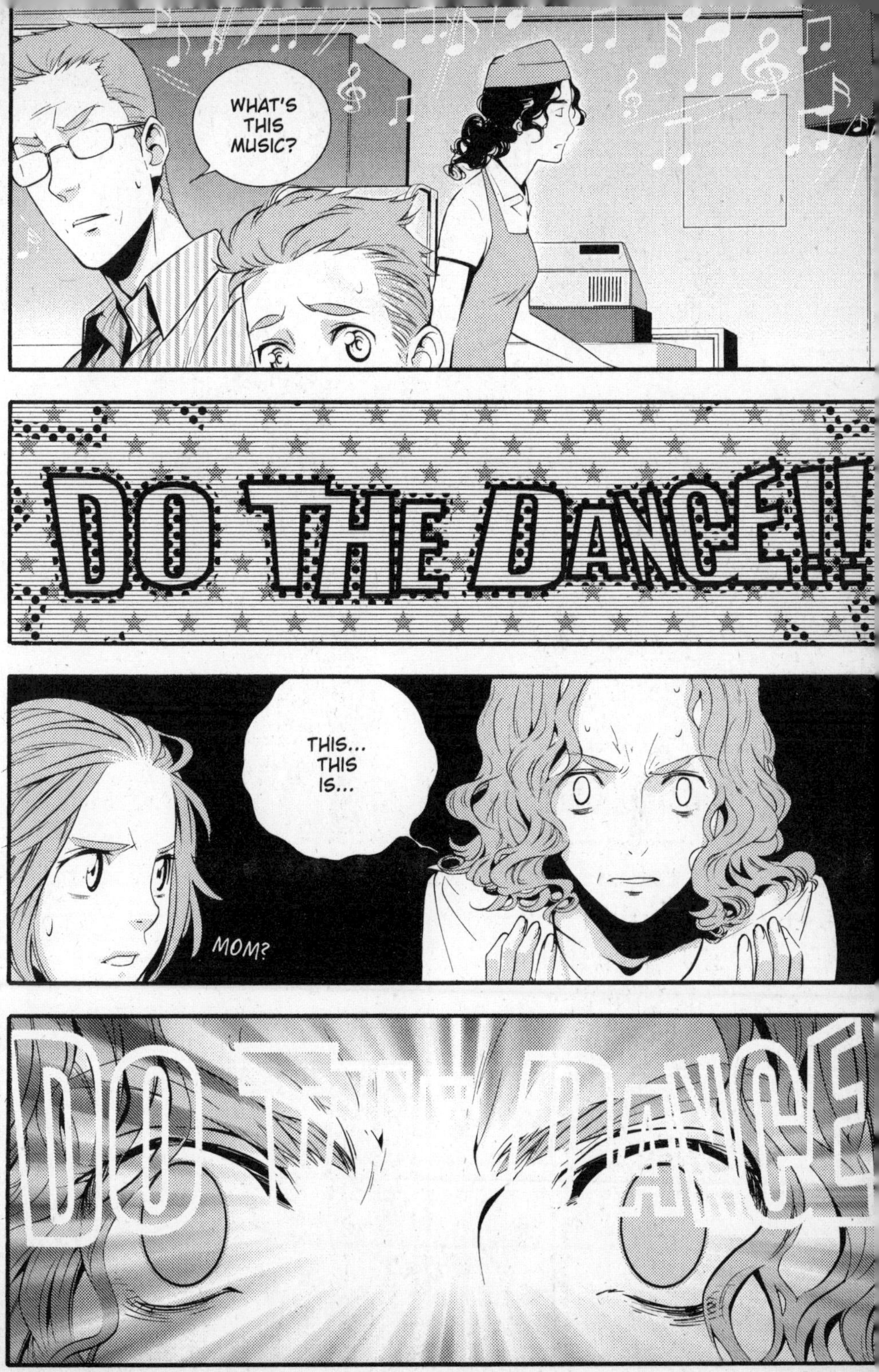
WHAT'S THIS MUSIC?
DO THE DANCE!!
THIS... THIS IS...
MOM?
DO THE DANCE

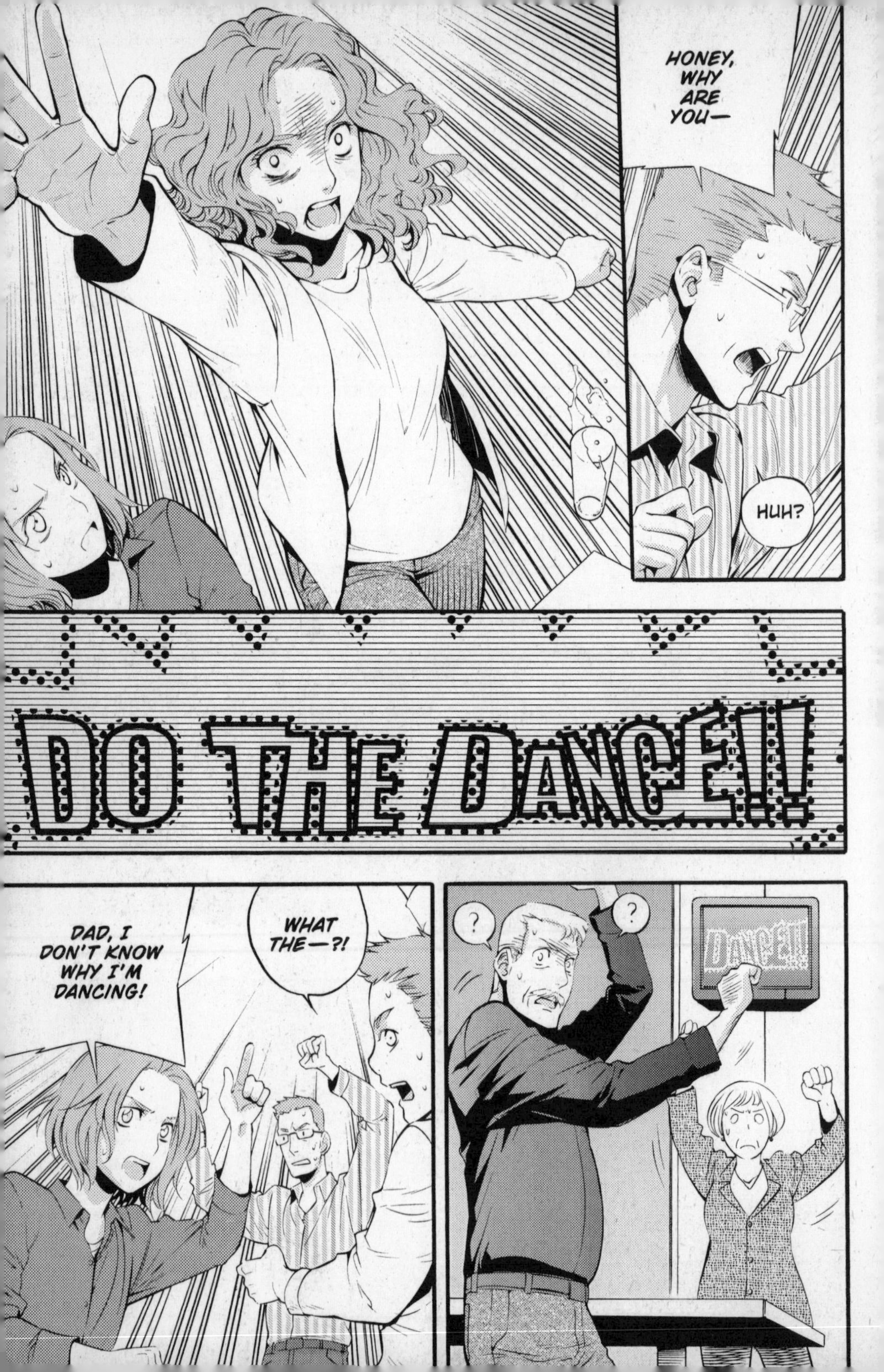
HONEY, WHY ARE YOU—
HUH?
DO THE DANCE!!
DAD, I DON'T KNOW WHY I'M DANCING!
WHAT THE—?!
?
?
DANCE!!

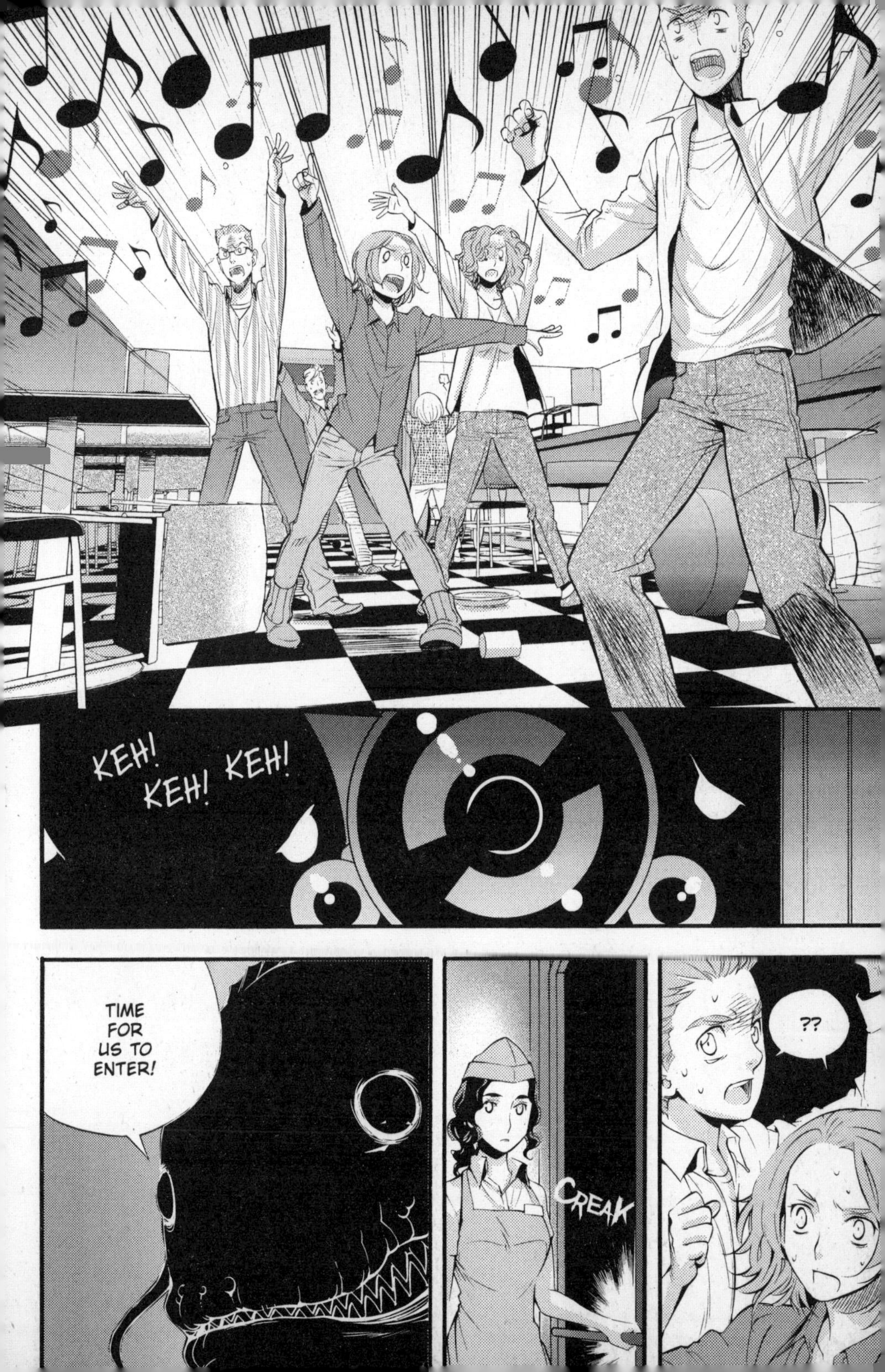
KEH! KEH! KEH!
TIME FOR US TO ENTER!
CREAK
??

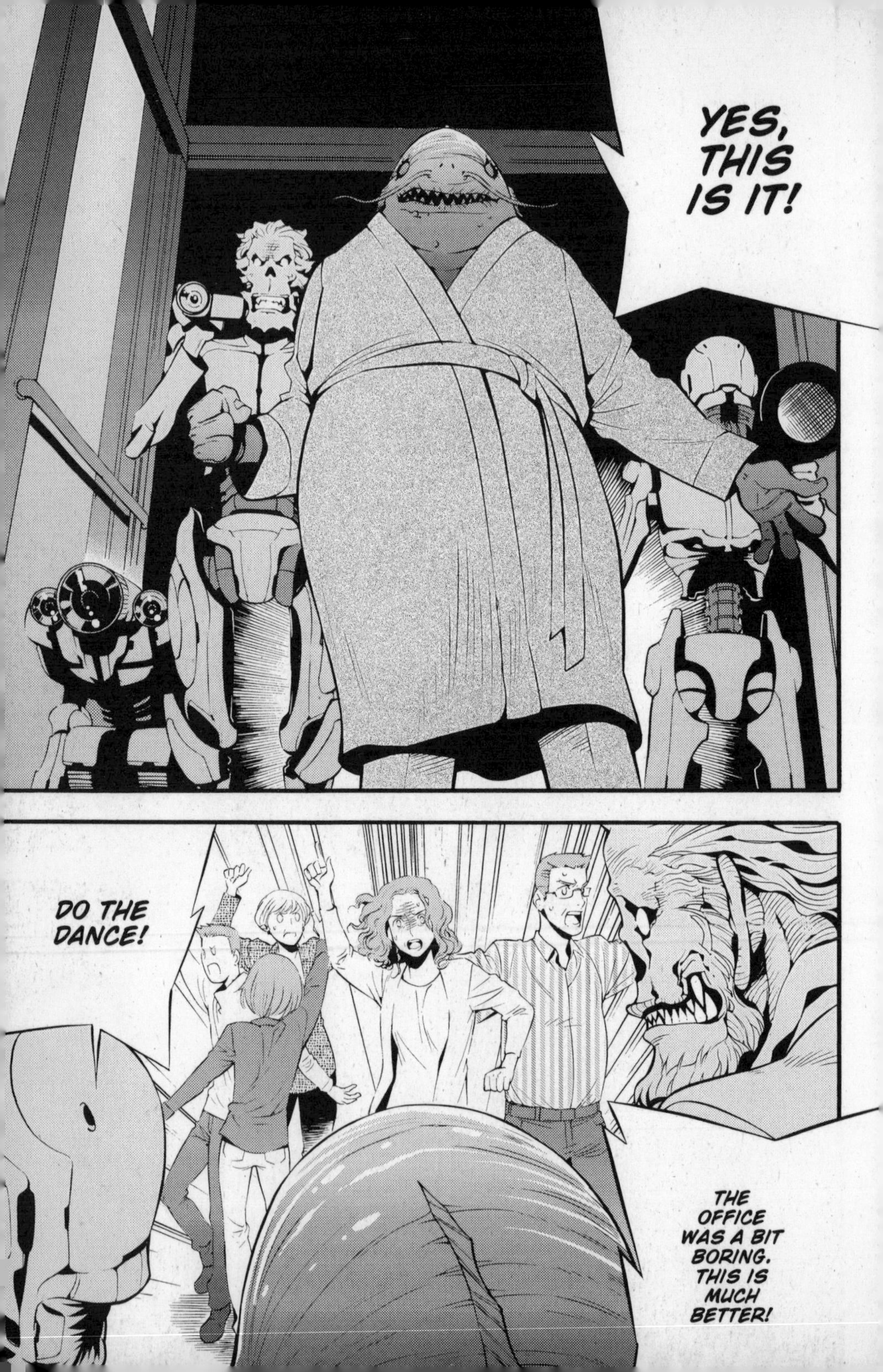
YES, THIS IS IT!
DO THE DANCE!
THE OFFICE WAS A BIT BORING. THIS IS MUCH BETTER!

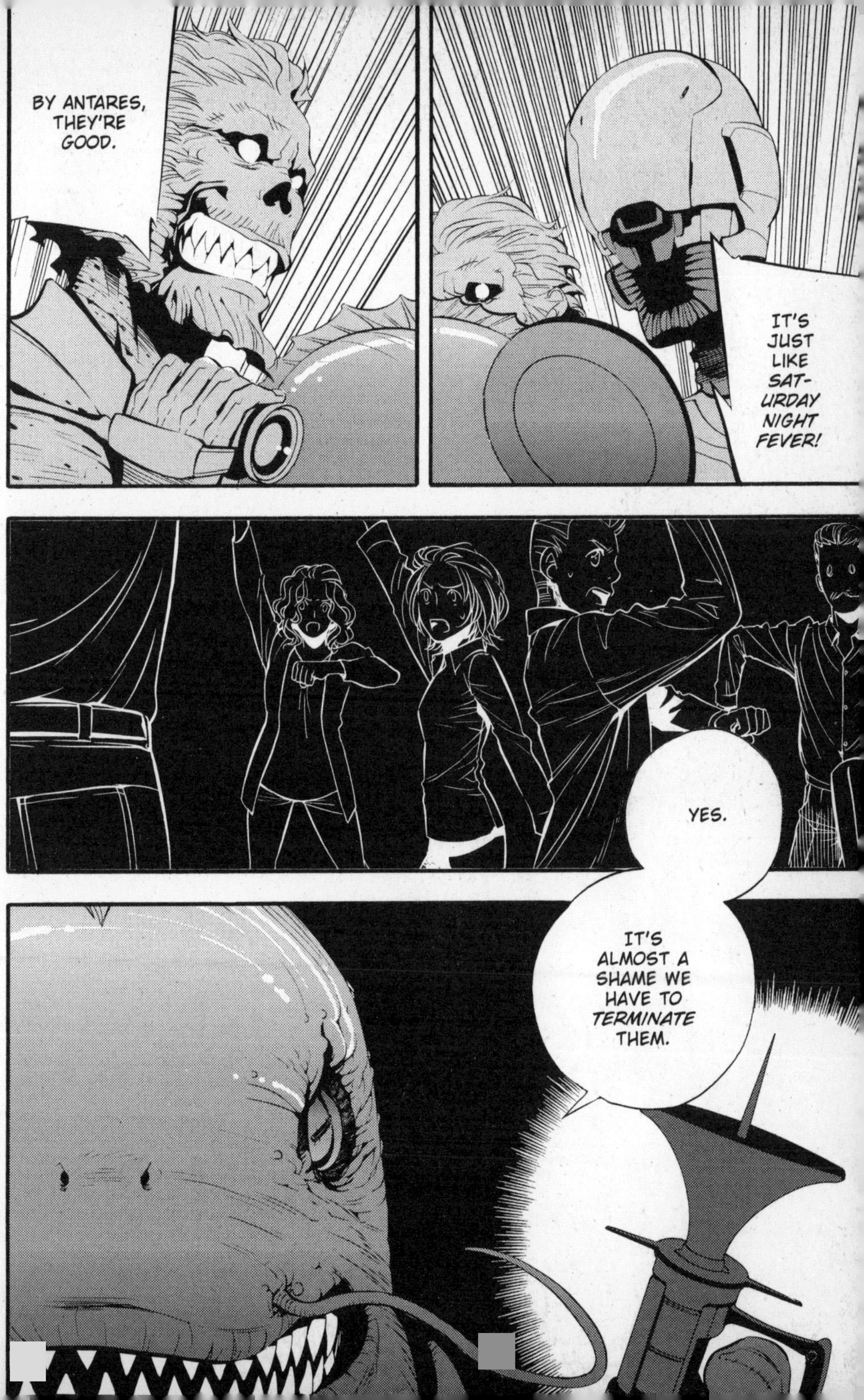
BY ANTARES, THEY'RE GOOD.
IT'S JUST LIKE SAT-URDAY NIGHT FEVER!
YES.
IT'S ALMOST A SHAME WE HAVE TO *TERMINATE* THEM.

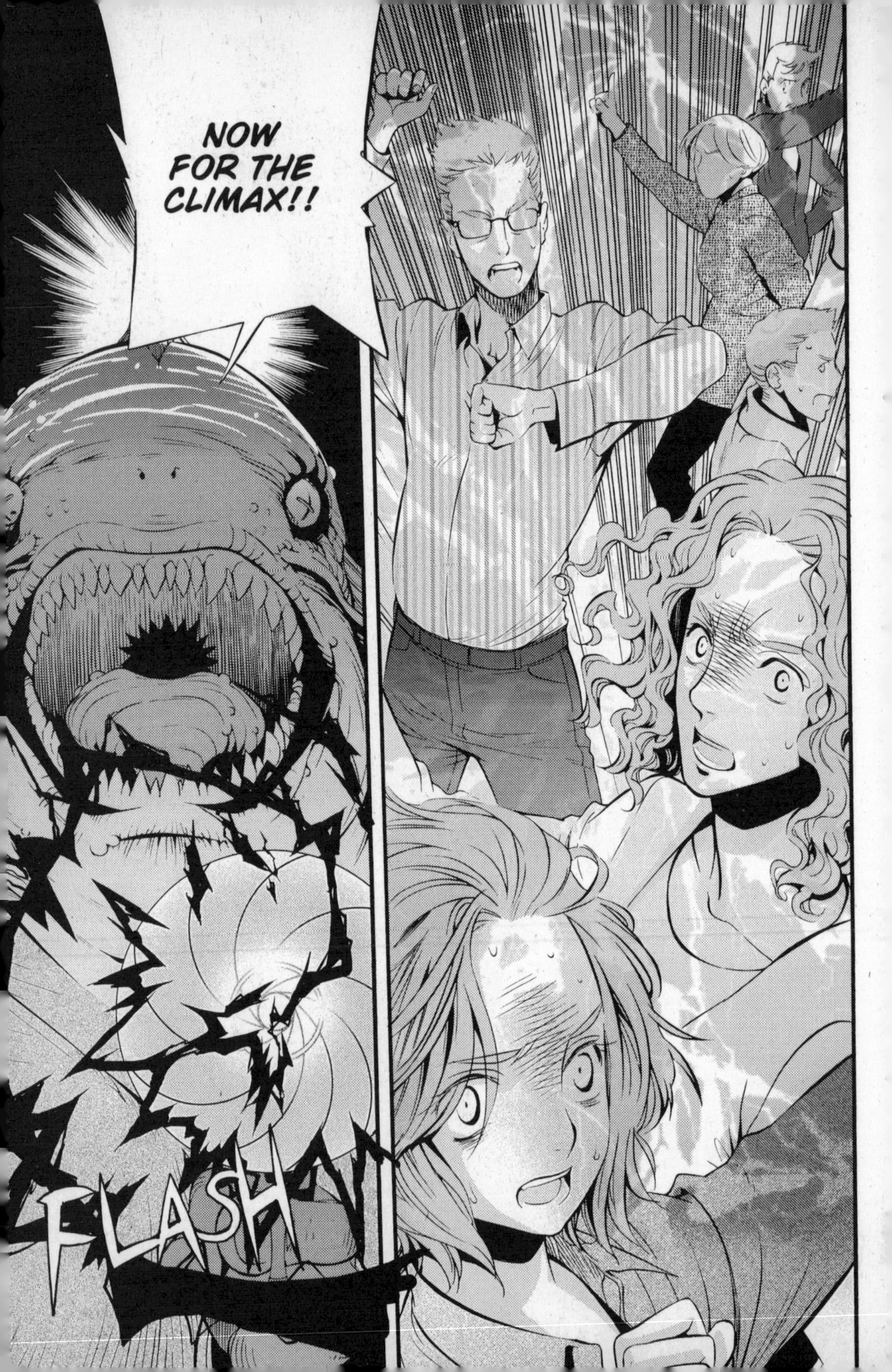
NOW FOR THE CLIMAX!!
FLASH

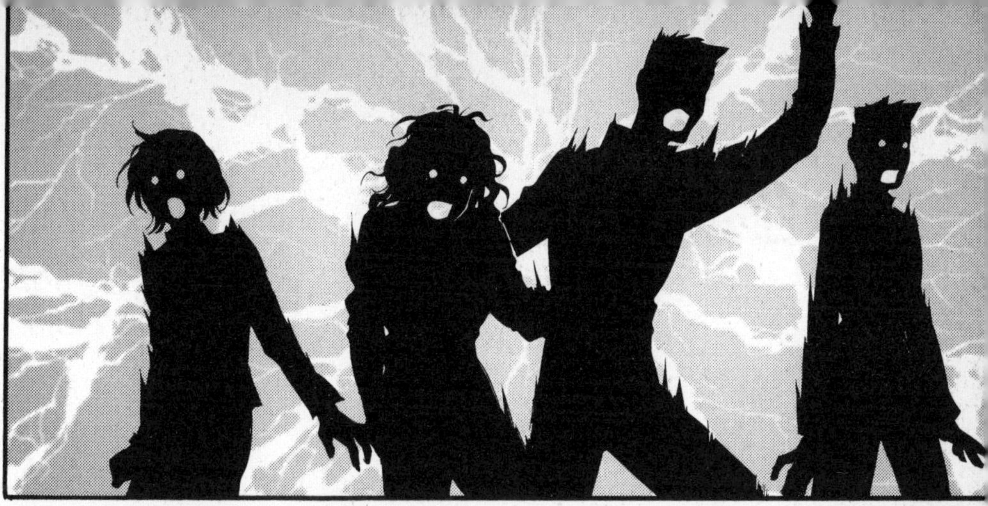

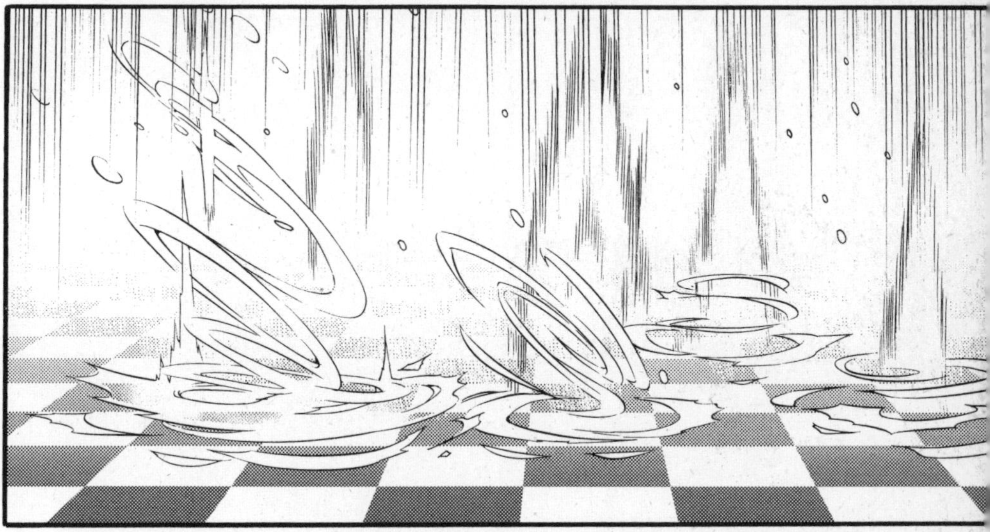

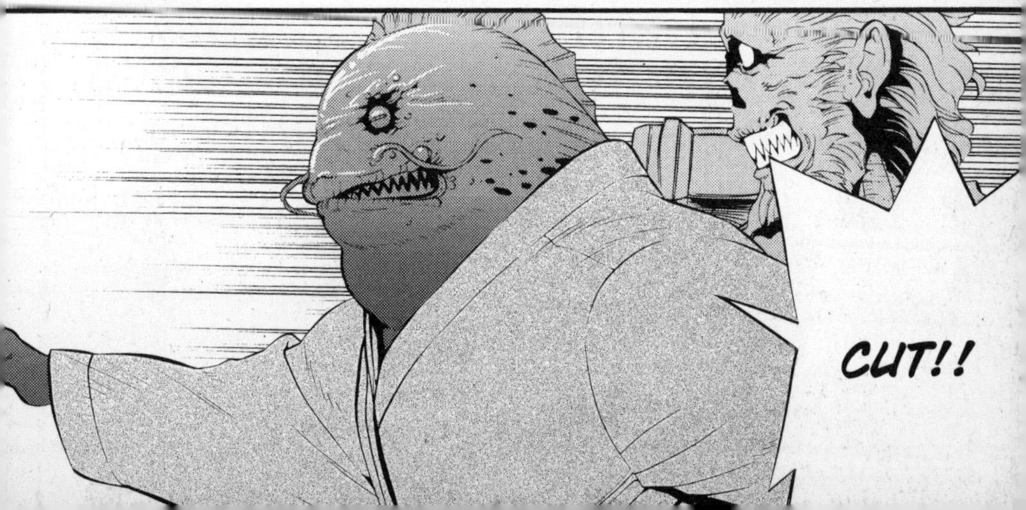
CUT!!

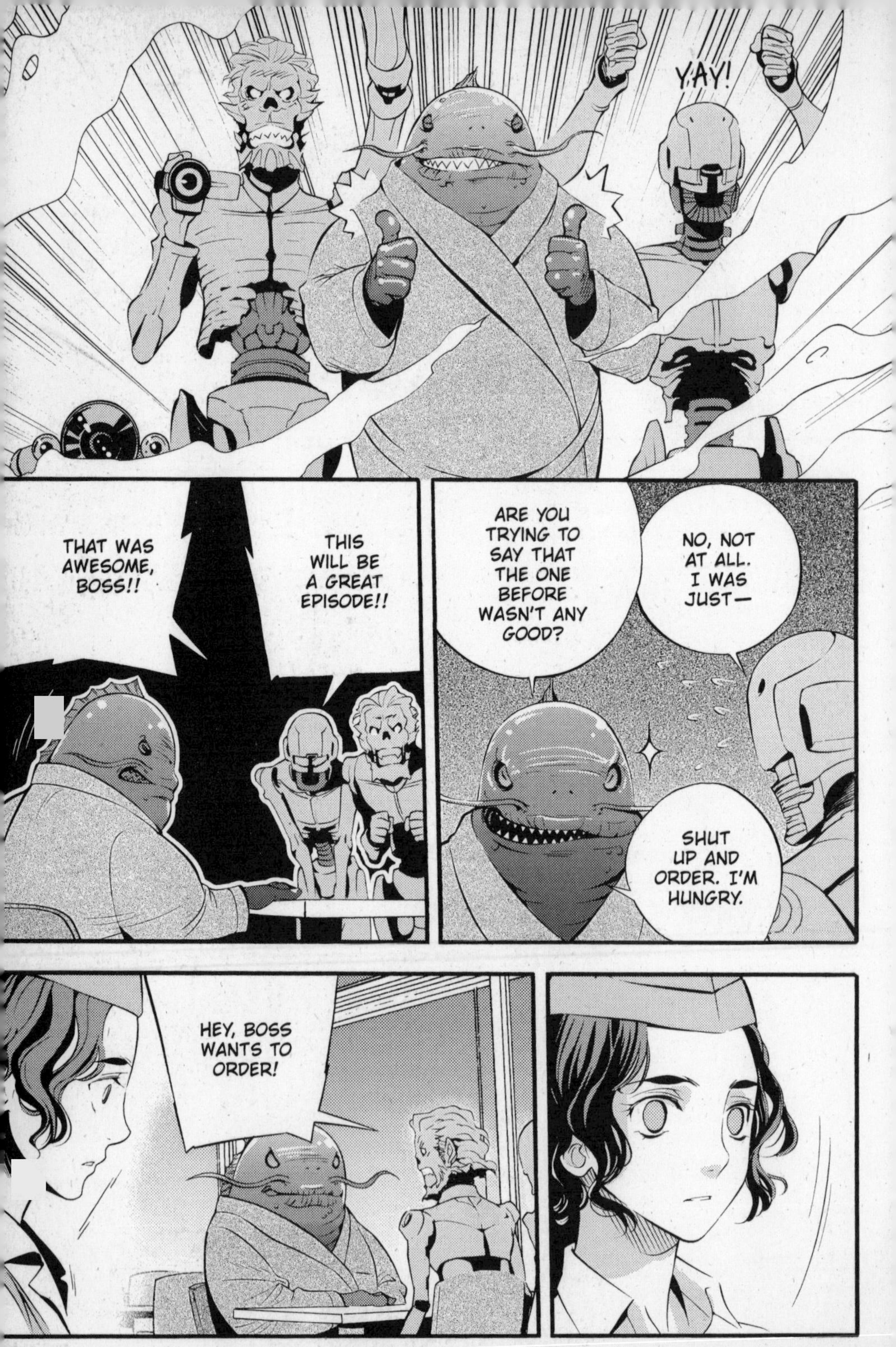
YAY!
THAT WAS AWESOME, BOSS!!
THIS WILL BE A GREAT EPISODE!!
ARE YOU TRYING TO SAY THAT THE ONE BEFORE WASN'T ANY GOOD?
NO, NOT AT ALL. I WAS JUST—
SHUT UP AND ORDER. I'M HUNGRY.
HEY, BOSS WANTS TO ORDER!

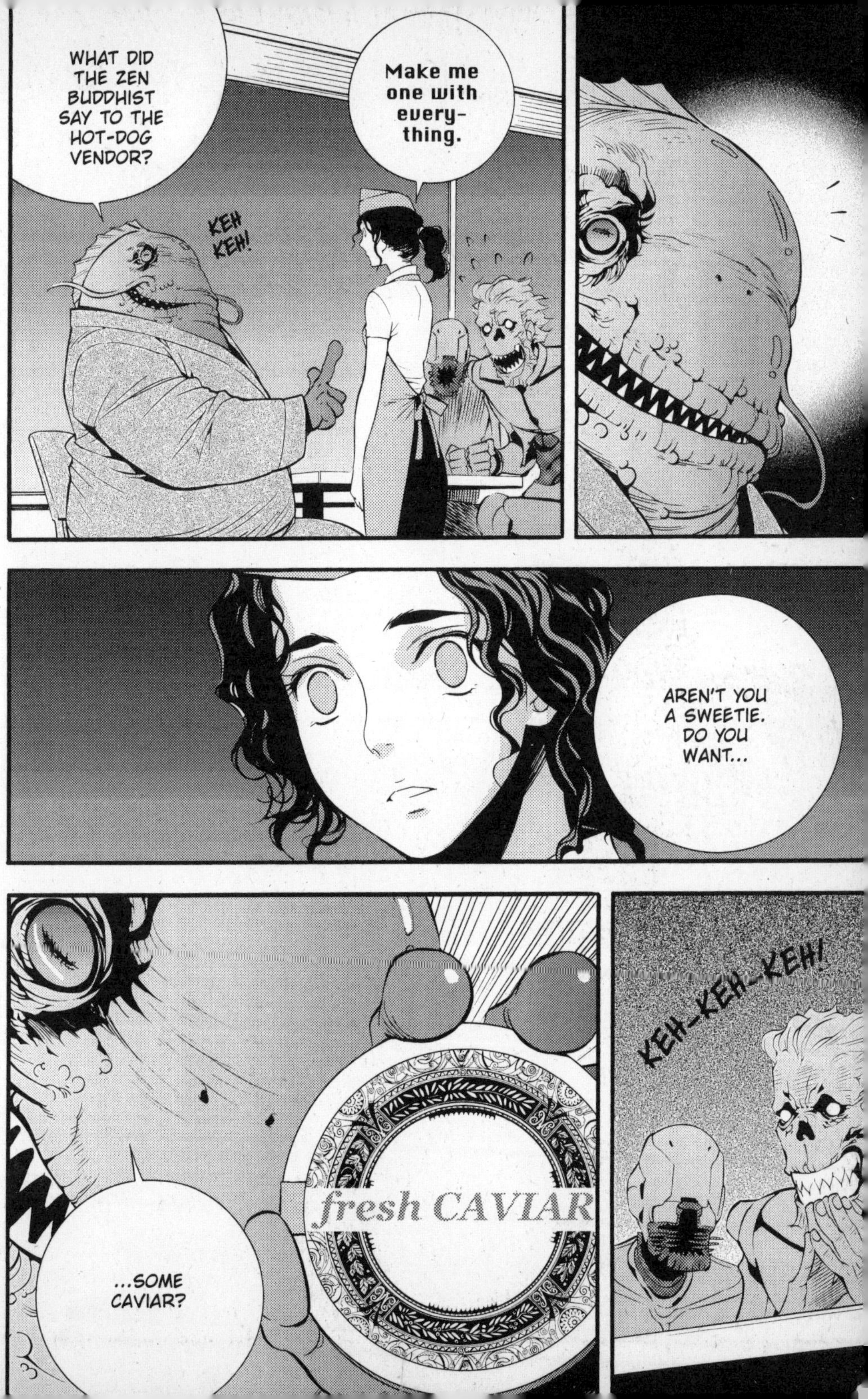
WHAT DID THE ZEN BUDDHIST SAY TO THE HOT-DOG VENDOR?
Make me one with every-thing.
KEH KEH!
AREN'T YOU A SWEETIE. DO YOU WANT...
fresh CAVIAR
...SOME CAVIAR?
KEH-KEH-KEH!

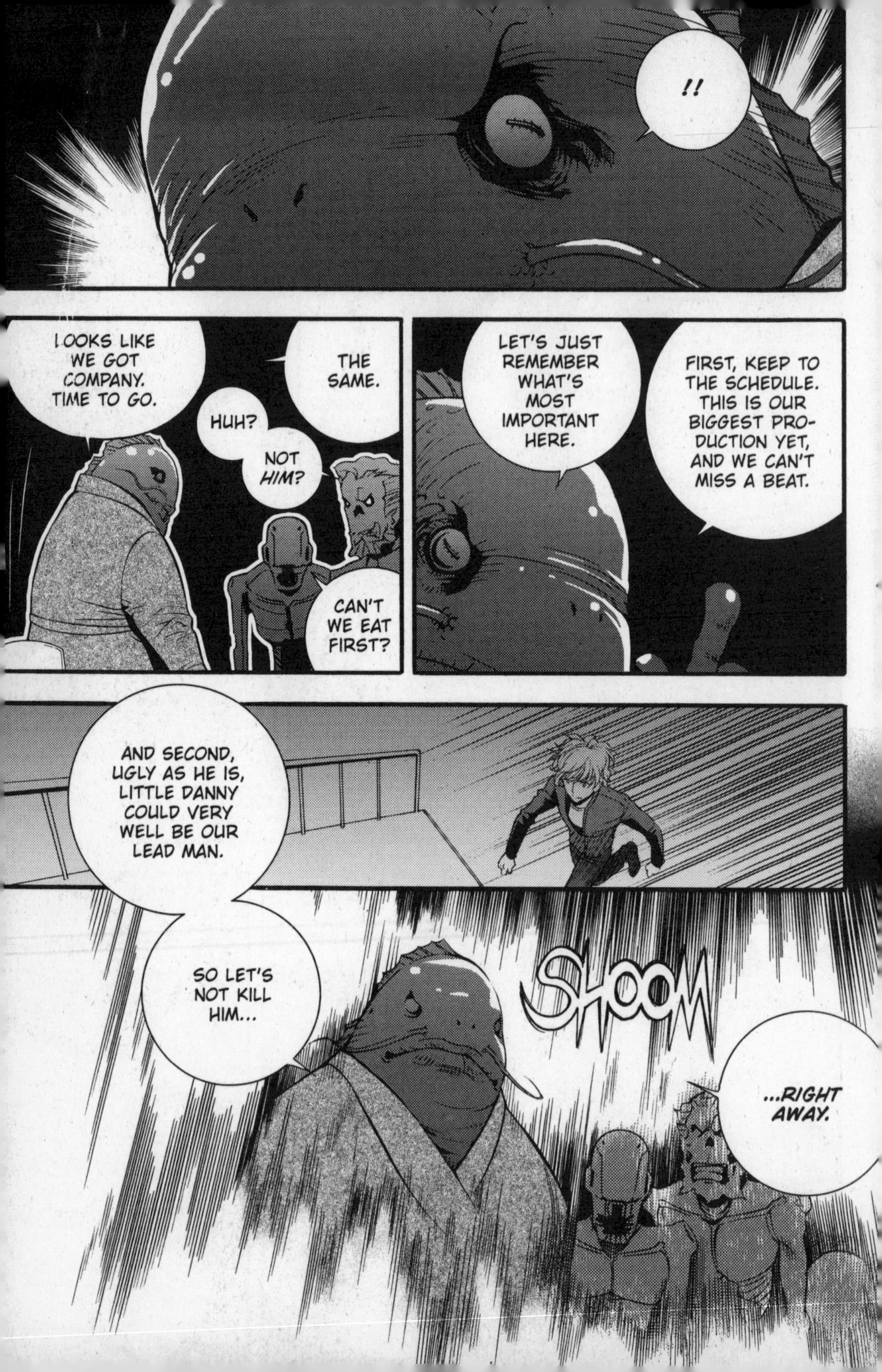
!!
LOOKS LIKE WE GOT COMPANY. TIME TO GO.
THE SAME.
HUH?
NOT *HIM?*
CAN'T WE EAT FIRST?
LET'S JUST REMEMBER WHAT'S MOST IMPORTANT HERE.
FIRST, KEEP TO THE SCHEDULE. THIS IS OUR BIGGEST PRO-DUCTION YET, AND WE CAN'T MISS A BEAT.
AND SECOND, UGLY AS HE IS, LITTLE DANNY COULD VERY WELL BE OUR LEAD MAN.
SO LET'S NOT KILL HIM...
SHOOM
...RIGHT AWAY.

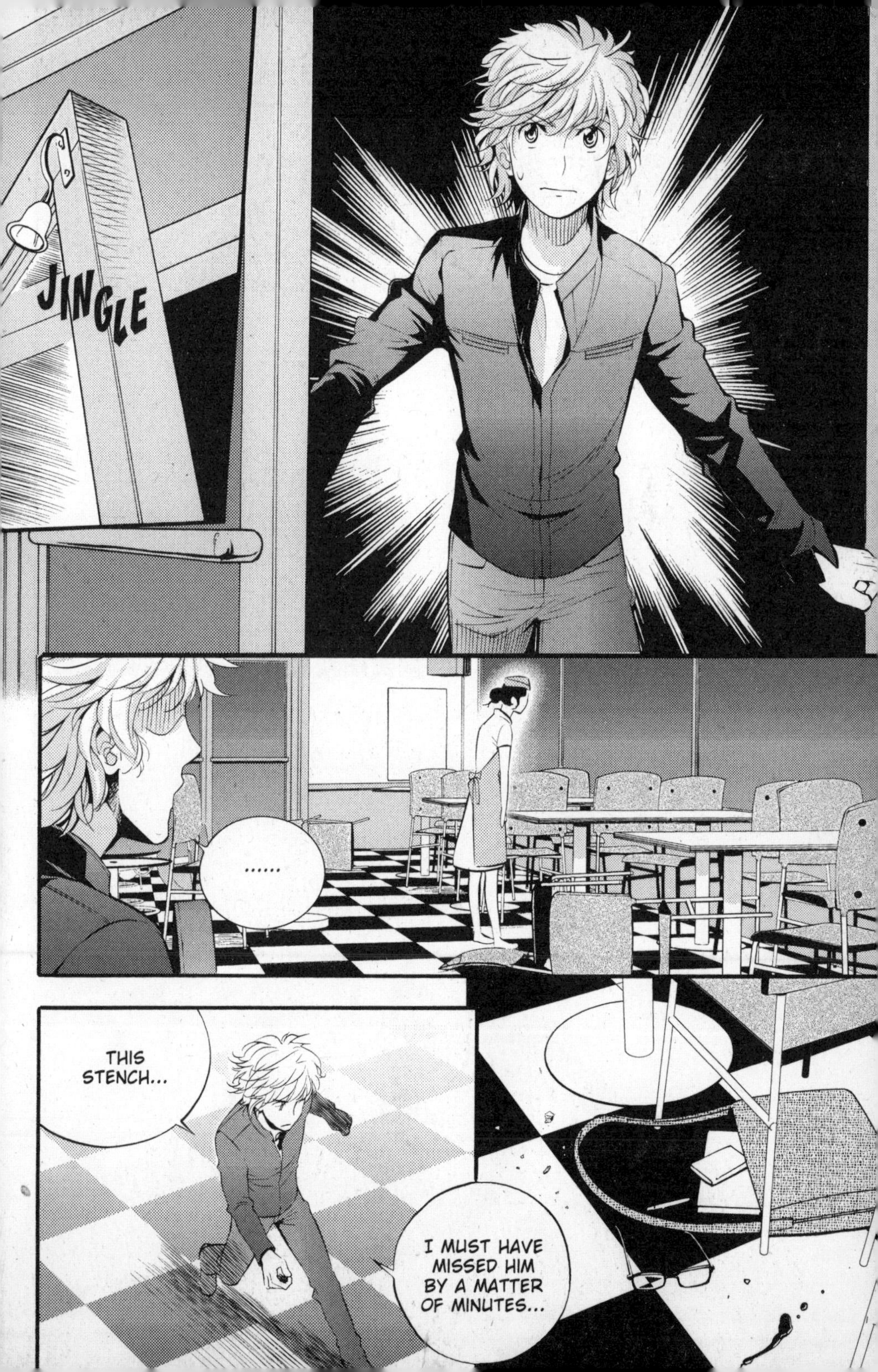
JINGLE
......
THIS STENCH...
I MUST HAVE MISSED HIM BY A MATTER OF MINUTES...

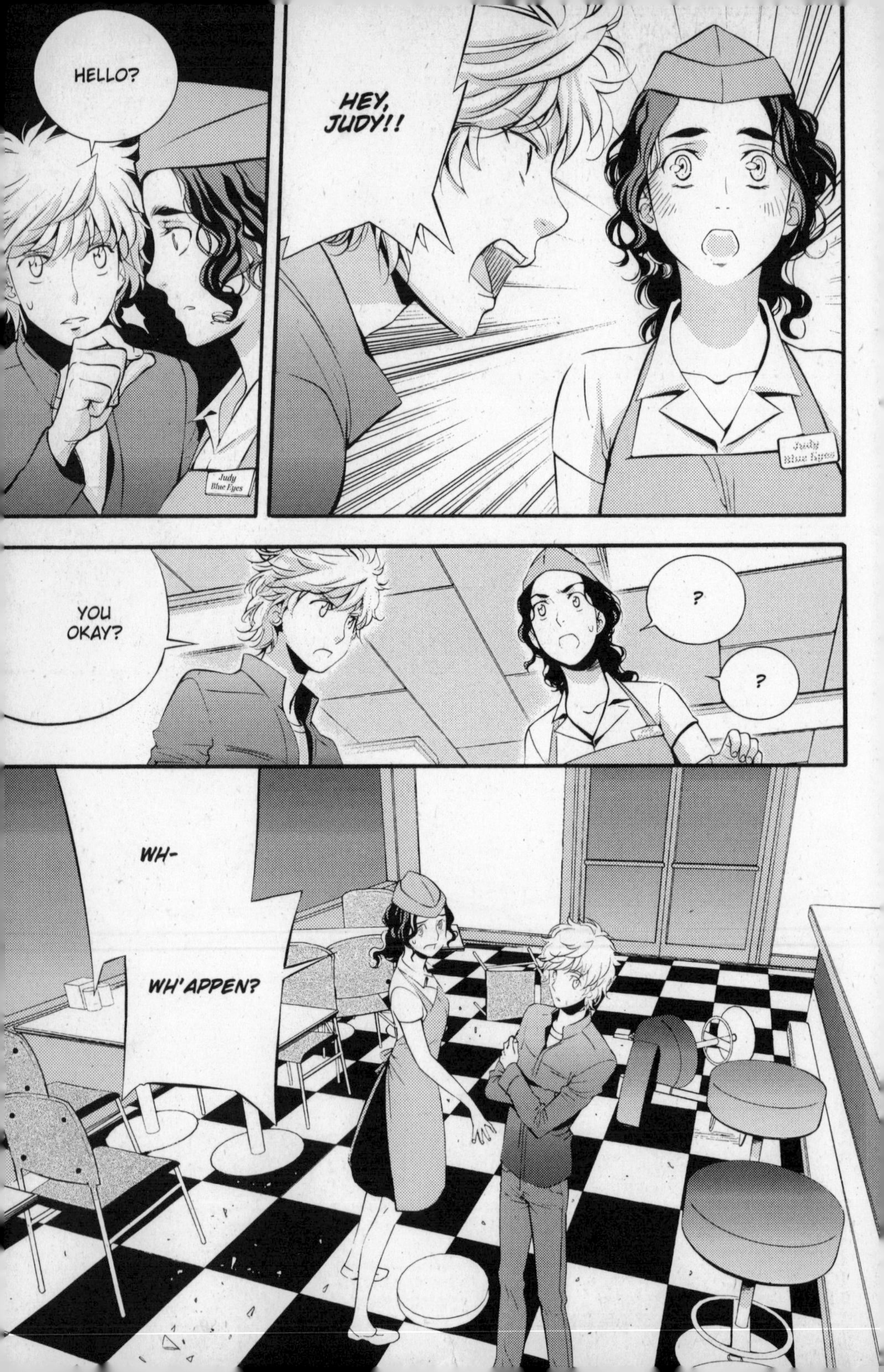
HELLO?
Judy Blue Eyes
HEY, JUDY!!
Judy Blue Eyes
YOU OKAY?
?
?
WH-
WH'APPEN?

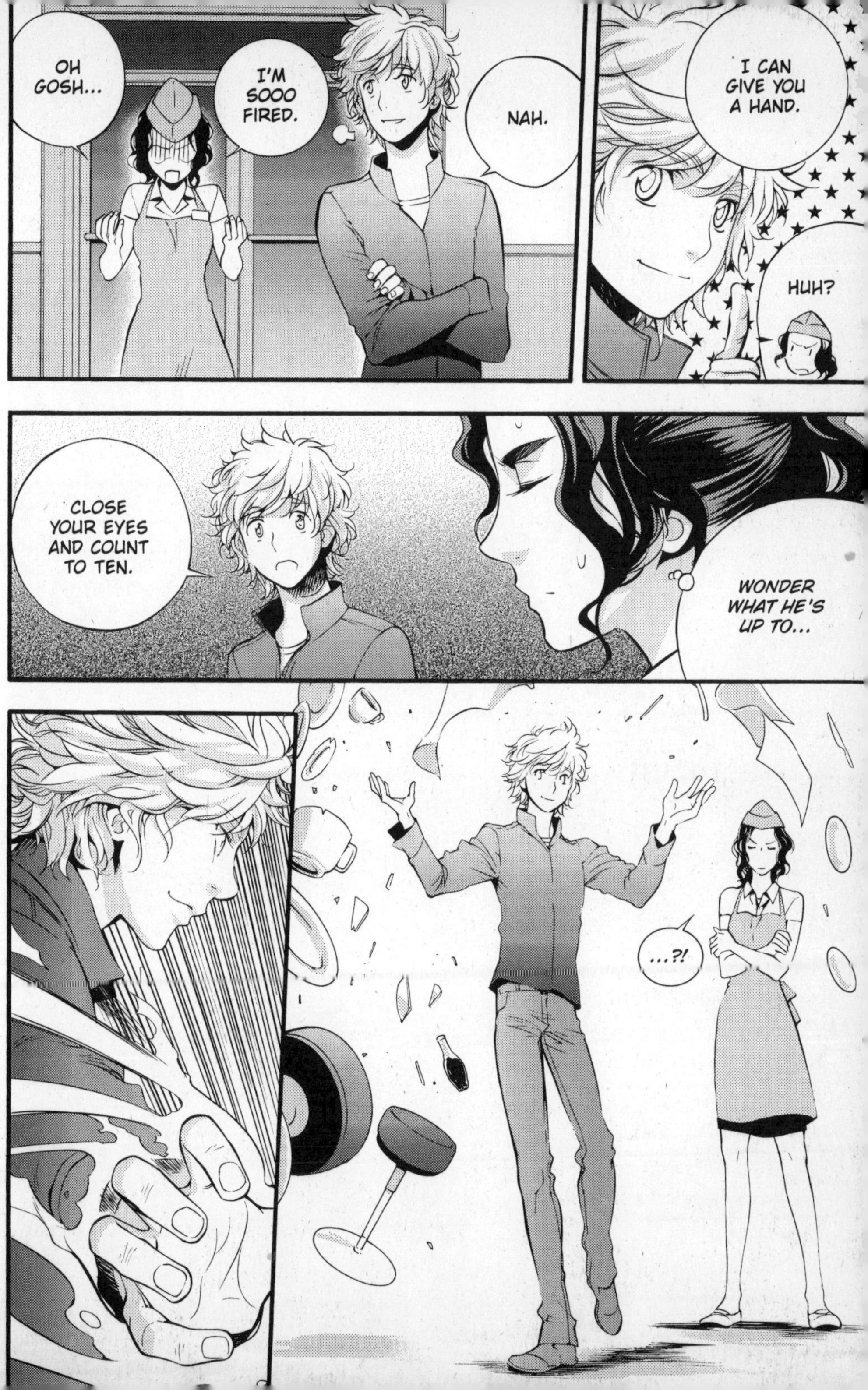
OH GOSH...
I'M SOOO FIRED.
NAH.
I CAN GIVE YOU A HAND.
HUH?
CLOSE YOUR EYES AND COUNT TO TEN.
WONDER WHAT HE'S UP TO...
...?!

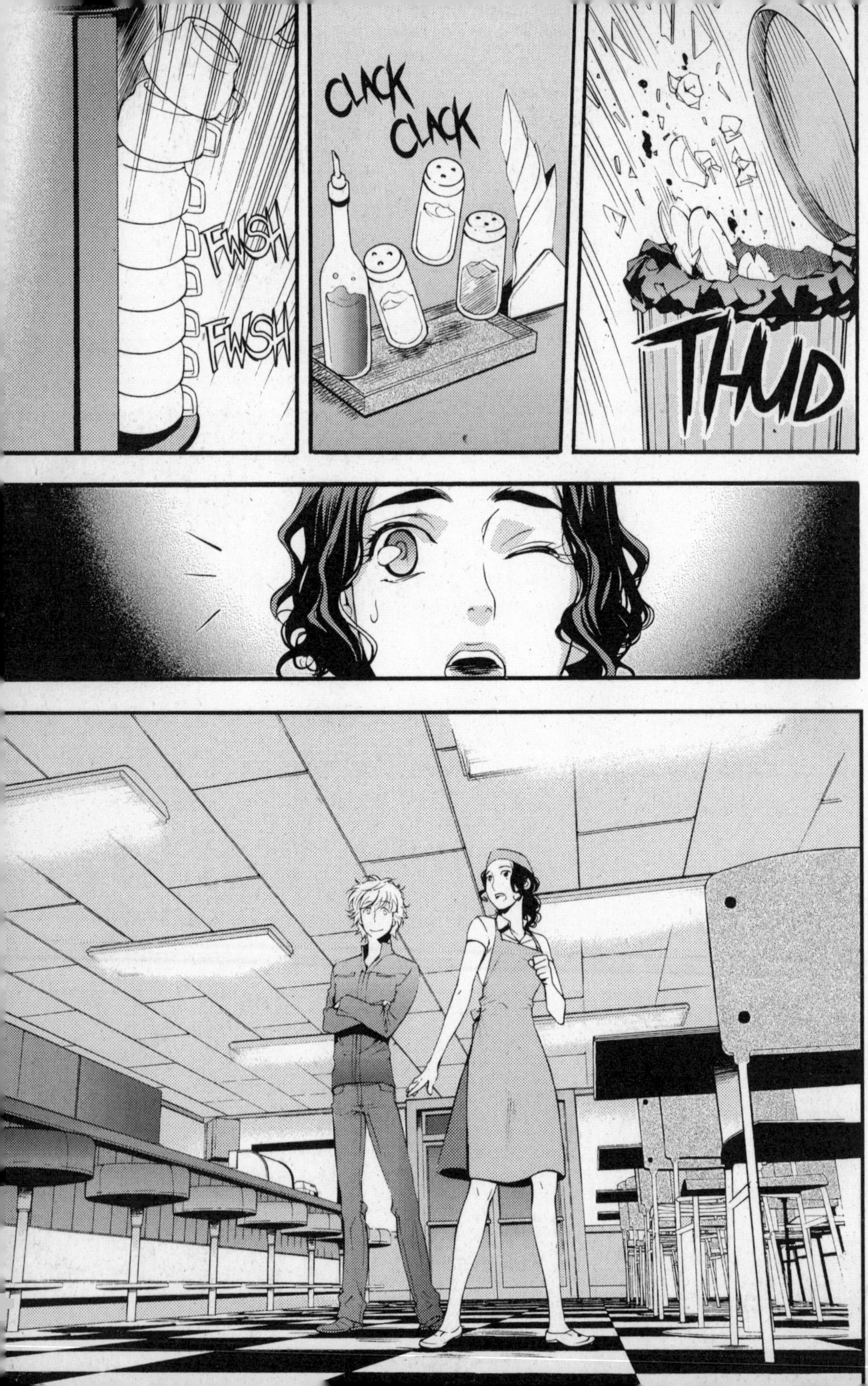
FWSH
FWSH
CLACK
CLACK
THUD

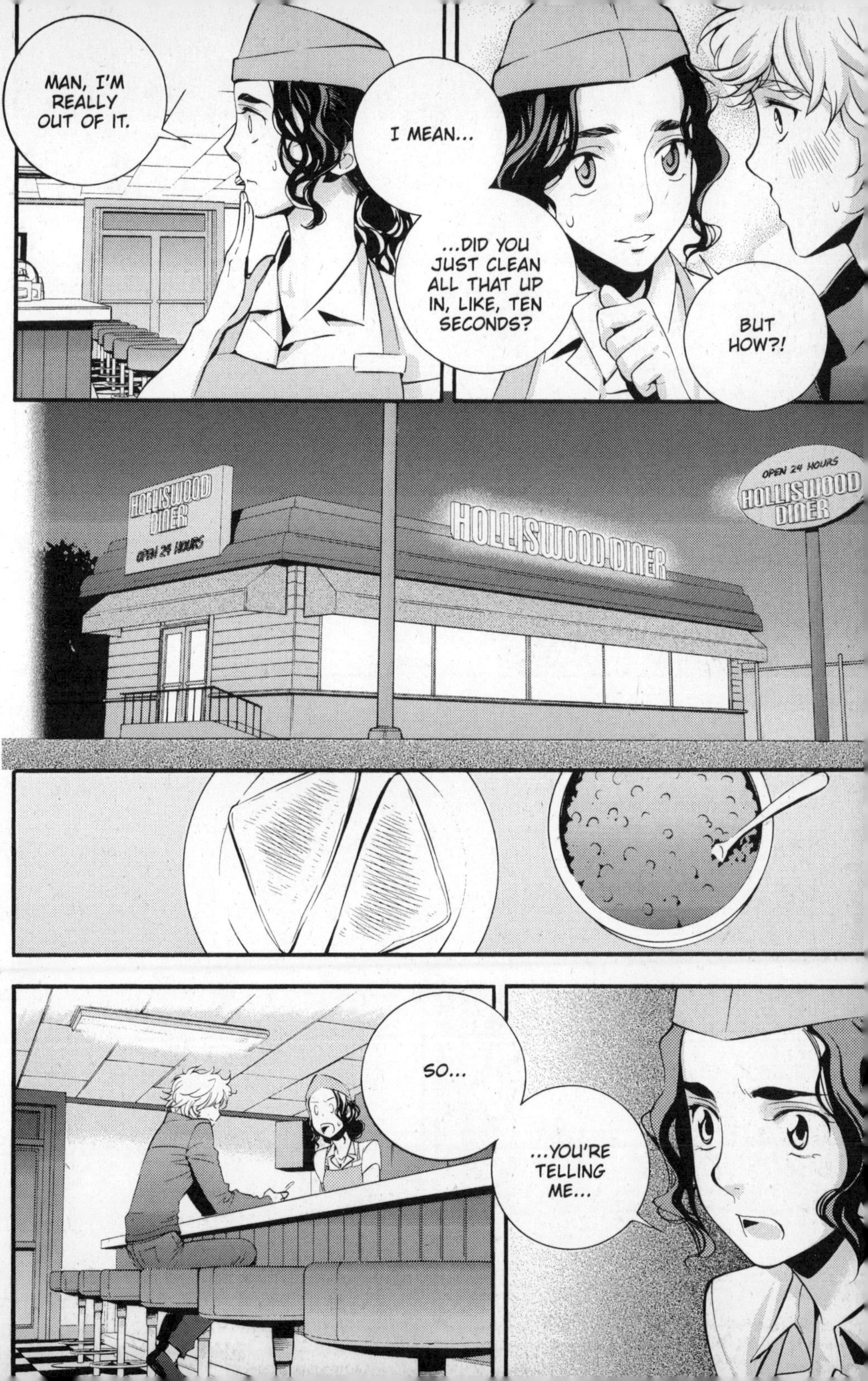
MAN, I'M REALLY OUT OF IT.
I MEAN...
...DID YOU JUST CLEAN ALL THAT UP IN, LIKE, TEN SECONDS?
BUT HOW?!
HOLLISWOOD DINER
OPEN 24 HOURS
HOLLISWOOD DINER
OPEN 24 HOURS
HOLLISWOOD DINER
SO...
...YOU'RE TELLING ME...

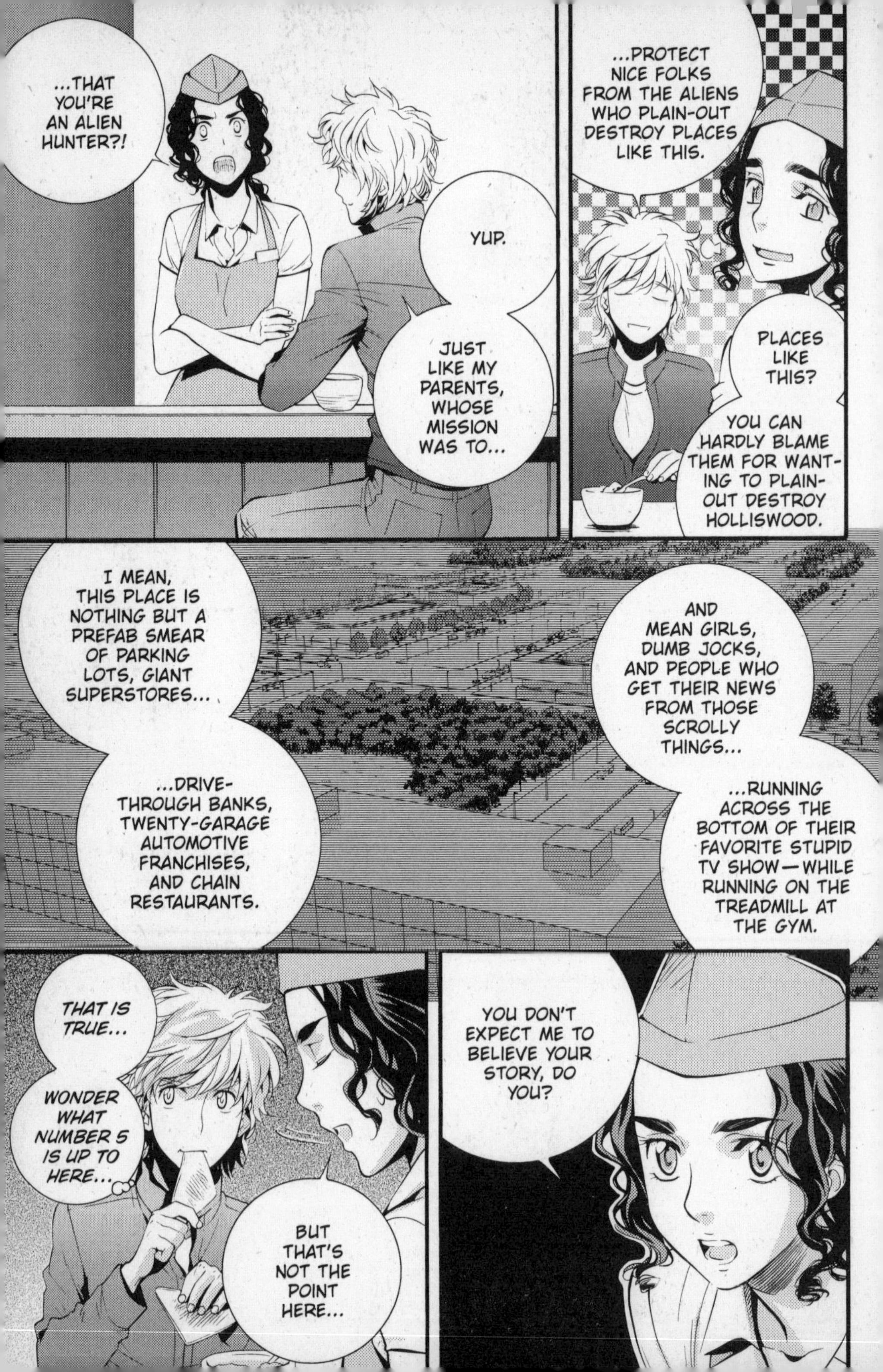
...THAT YOU'RE AN ALIEN HUNTER?!
YUP.
JUST LIKE MY PARENTS, WHOSE MISSION WAS TO...
...PROTECT NICE FOLKS FROM THE ALIENS WHO PLAIN-OUT DESTROY PLACES LIKE THIS.
PLACES LIKE THIS?
YOU CAN HARDLY BLAME THEM FOR WANT-ING TO PLAIN-OUT DESTROY HOLLISWOOD.
I MEAN, THIS PLACE IS NOTHING BUT A PREFAB SMEAR OF PARKING LOTS, GIANT SUPERSTORES...
...DRIVE-THROUGH BANKS, TWENTY-GARAGE AUTOMOTIVE FRANCHISES, AND CHAIN RESTAURANTS.
AND MEAN GIRLS, DUMB JOCKS, AND PEOPLE WHO GET THEIR NEWS FROM THOSE SCROLLY THINGS...
...RUNNING ACROSS THE BOTTOM OF THEIR FAVORITE STUPID TV SHOW—WHILE RUNNING ON THE TREADMILL AT THE GYM.
THAT IS TRUE...
WONDER WHAT NUMBER 5 IS UP TO HERE...
BUT THAT'S NOT THE POINT HERE...
YOU DON'T EXPECT ME TO BELIEVE YOUR STORY, DO YOU?

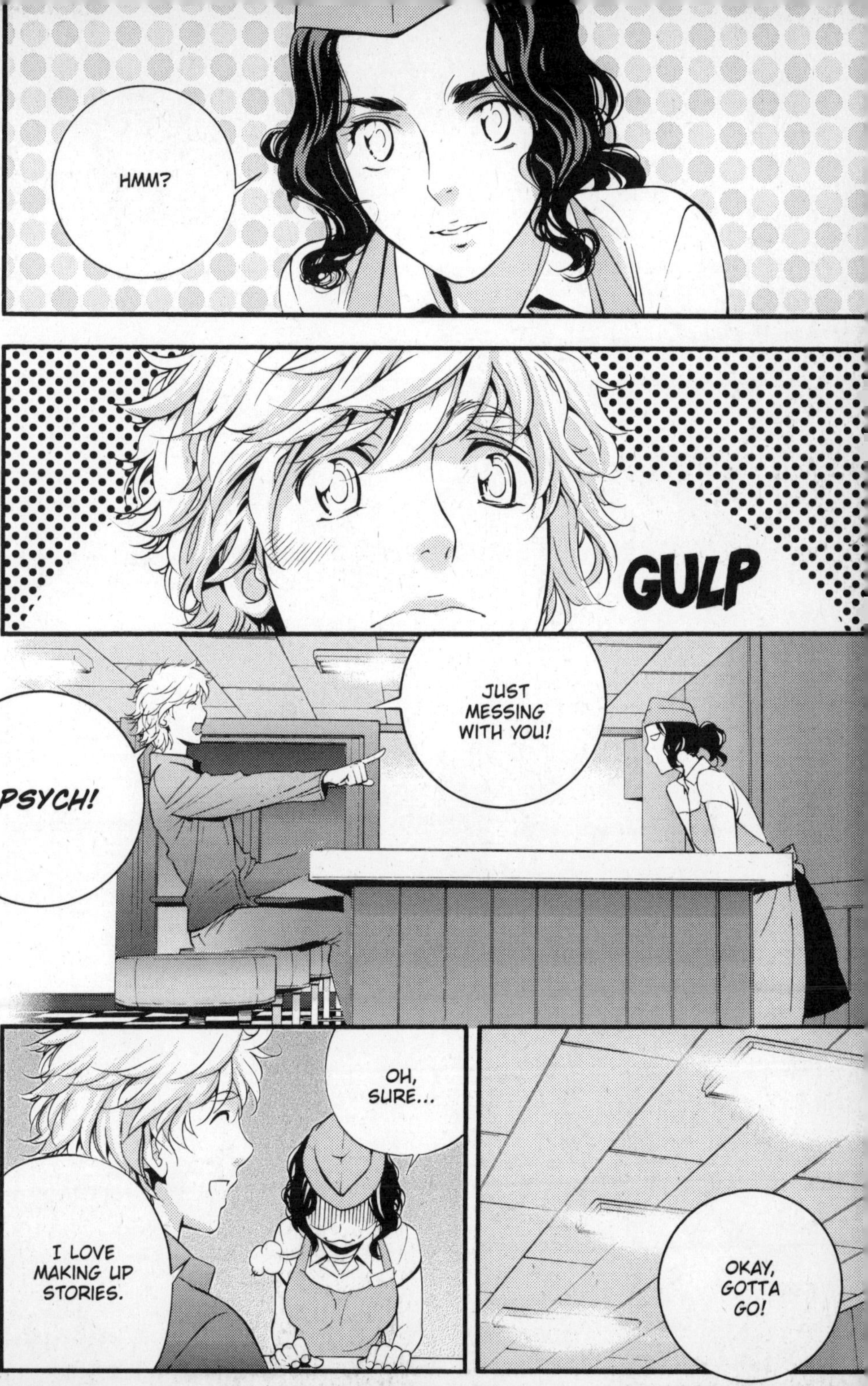
HMM?
GULP
PSYCH!
JUST MESSING WITH YOU!
I LOVE MAKING UP STORIES.
OH, SURE...
OKAY, GOTTA GO!

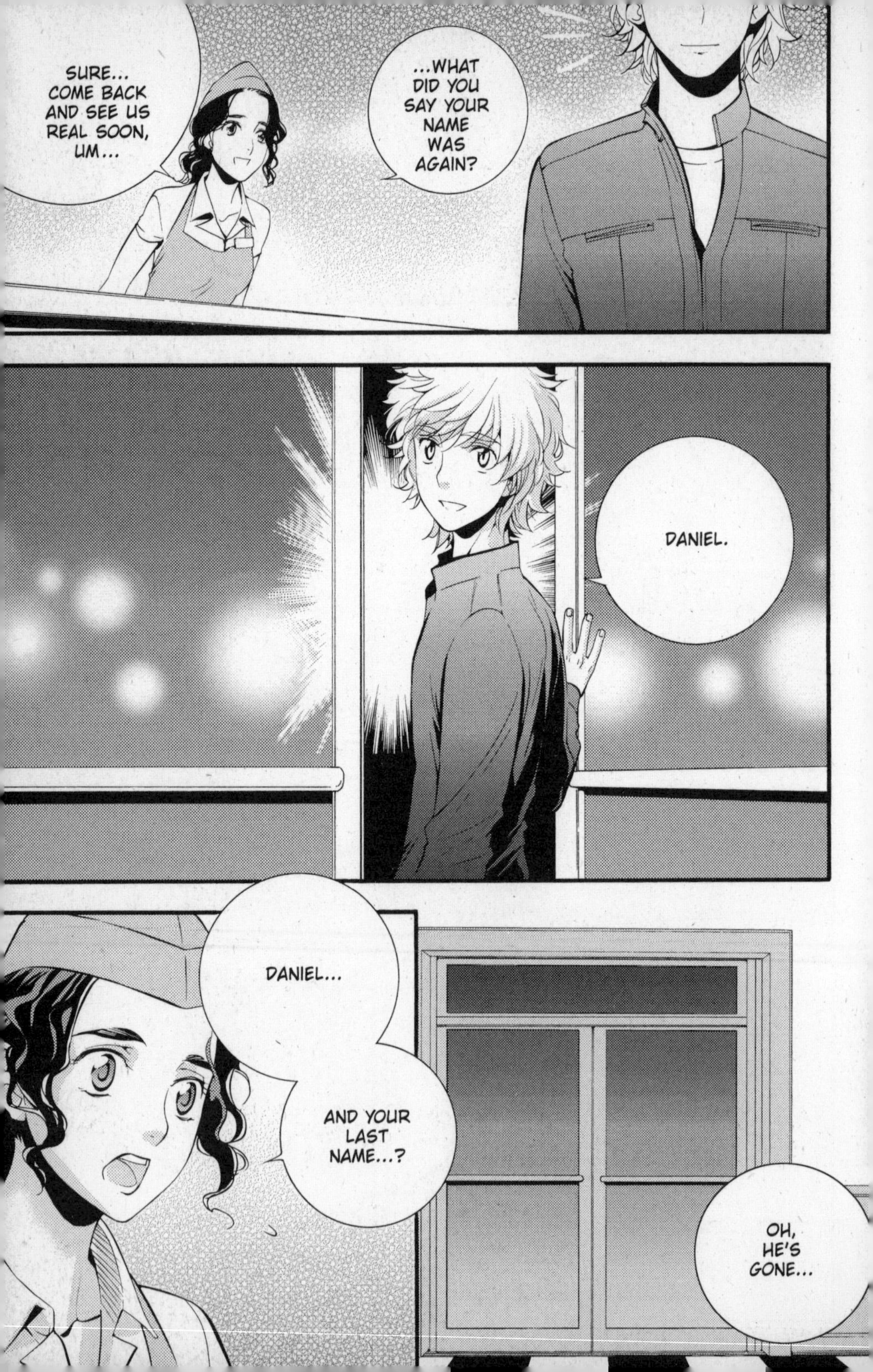
SURE... COME BACK AND SEE US REAL SOON, UM...
...WHAT DID YOU SAY YOUR NAME WAS AGAIN?
DANIEL.
DANIEL...
AND YOUR LAST NAME...?
OH, HE'S GONE...

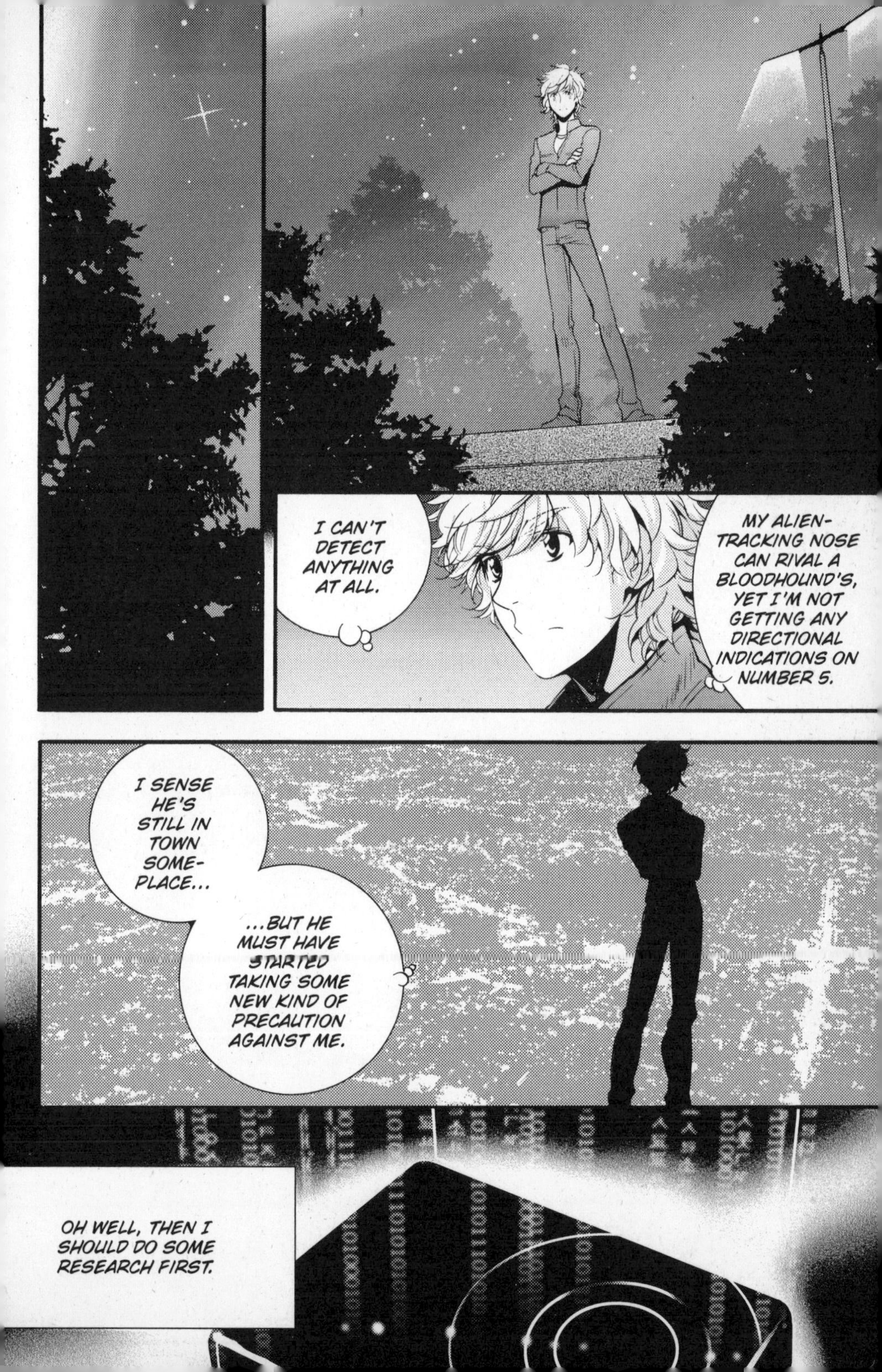
I CAN'T DETECT ANYTHING AT ALL.
MY ALIEN-TRACKING NOSE CAN RIVAL A BLOODHOUND'S, YET I'M NOT GETTING ANY DIRECTIONAL INDICATIONS ON NUMBER 5.
I SENSE HE'S STILL IN TOWN SOME-PLACE...
...BUT HE MUST HAVE STARTED TAKING SOME NEW KIND OF PRECAUTION AGAINST ME.
OH WELL, THEN I SHOULD DO SOME RESEARCH FIRST.

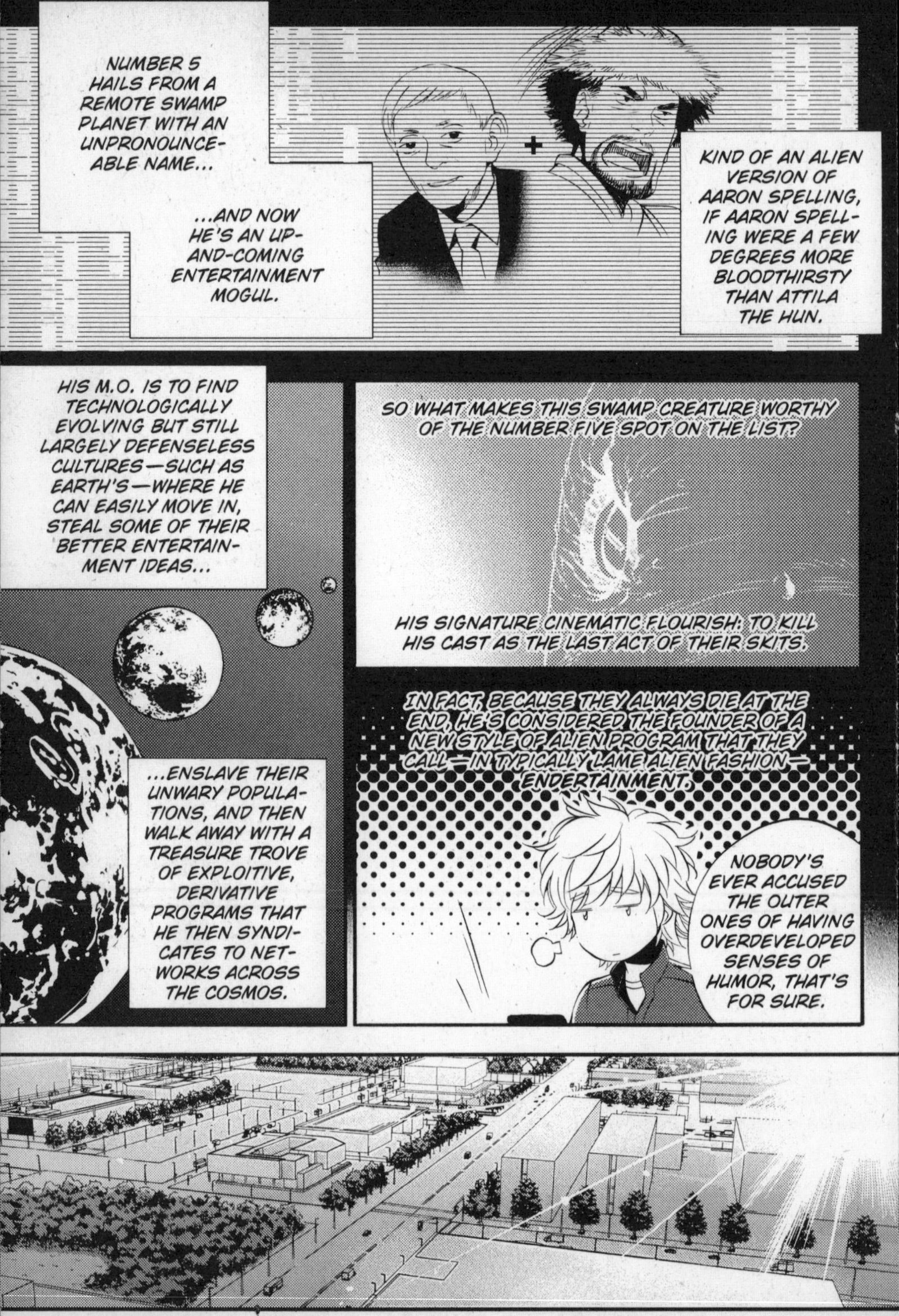

NUMBER 5 HAILS FROM A REMOTE SWAMP PLANET WITH AN UNPRONOUNCE-ABLE NAME...
...AND NOW HE'S AN UP-AND-COMING ENTERTAINMENT MOGUL.
KIND OF AN ALIEN VERSION OF AARON SPELLING, IF AARON SPELL-ING WERE A FEW DEGREES MORE BLOODTHIRSTY THAN ATTILA THE HUN.
HIS M.O. IS TO FIND TECHNOLOGICALLY EVOLVING BUT STILL LARGELY DEFENSELESS CULTURES—SUCH AS EARTH'S—WHERE HE CAN EASILY MOVE IN, STEAL SOME OF THEIR BETTER ENTERTAIN-MENT IDEAS...
...ENSLAVE THEIR UNWARY POPULA-TIONS, AND THEN WALK AWAY WITH A TREASURE TROVE OF EXPLOITIVE, DERIVATIVE PROGRAMS THAT HE THEN SYNDI-CATES TO NET-WORKS ACROSS THE COSMOS.
SO WHAT MAKES THIS SWAMP CREATURE WORTHY OF THE NUMBER FIVE SPOT ON THE LIST?
HIS SIGNATURE CINEMATIC FLOURISH: TO KILL HIS CAST AS THE LAST ACT OF THEIR SKITS.
IN FACT, BECAUSE THEY ALWAYS DIE AT THE END, HE'S CONSIDERED THE FOUNDER OF A NEW STYLE OF ALIEN PROGRAM THAT THEY CALL—IN TYPICALLY LAME ALIEN FASHION—ENDERTAINMENT.
NOBODY'S EVER ACCUSED THE OUTER ONES OF HAVING OVERDEVELOPED SENSES OF HUMOR, THAT'S FOR SURE.

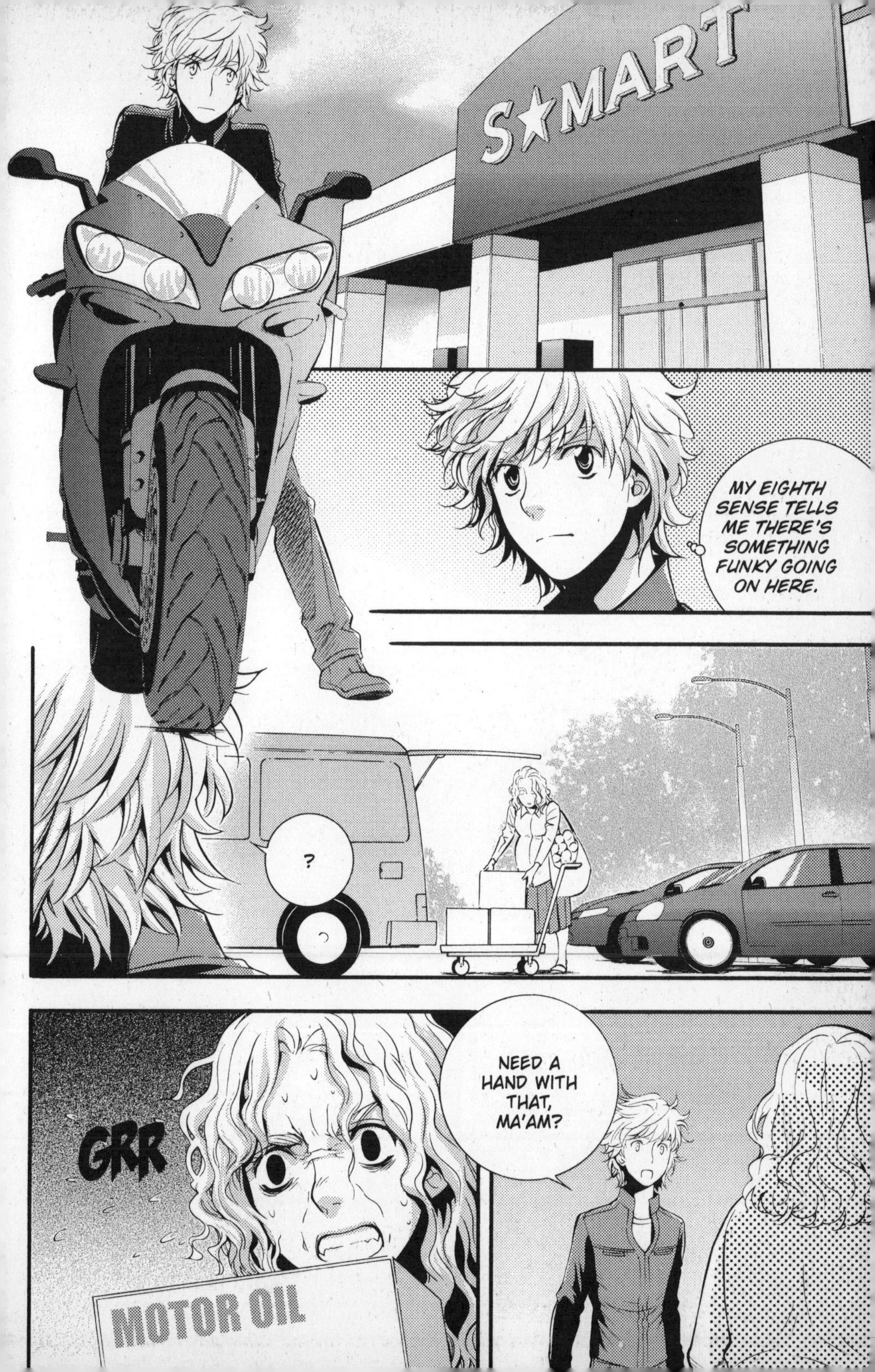
S★MART
MY EIGHTH SENSE TELLS ME THERE'S SOMETHING FUNKY GOING ON HERE.
?
GRR
MOTOR OIL
NEED A HAND WITH THAT, MA'AM?

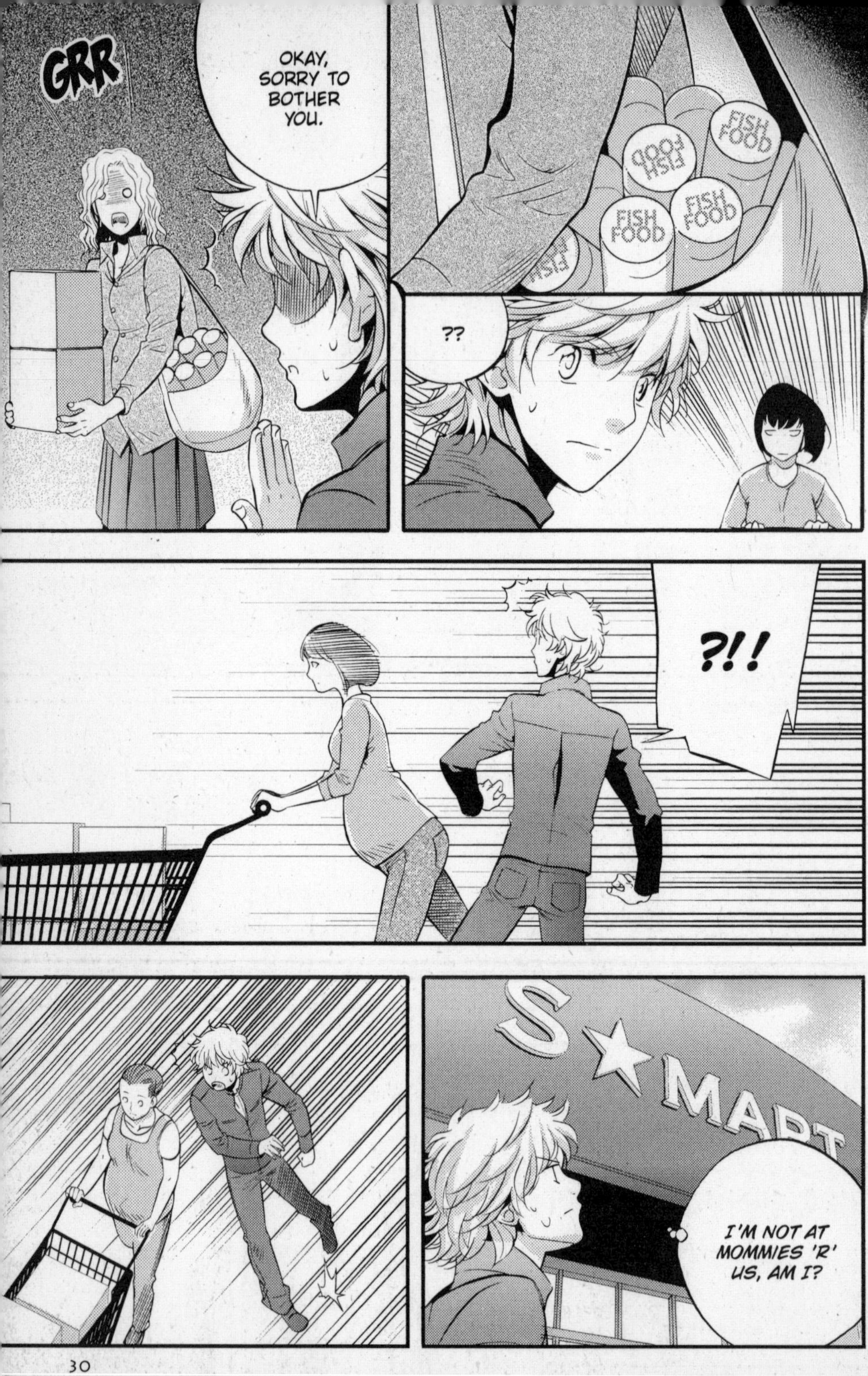
GRR
OKAY, SORRY TO BOTHER YOU.
FISH FOOD
FISH FOOD
FISH FOOD
FISH FOOD
??
?!!
S★MART
I'M NOT AT MOMMIES 'R' US, AM I?

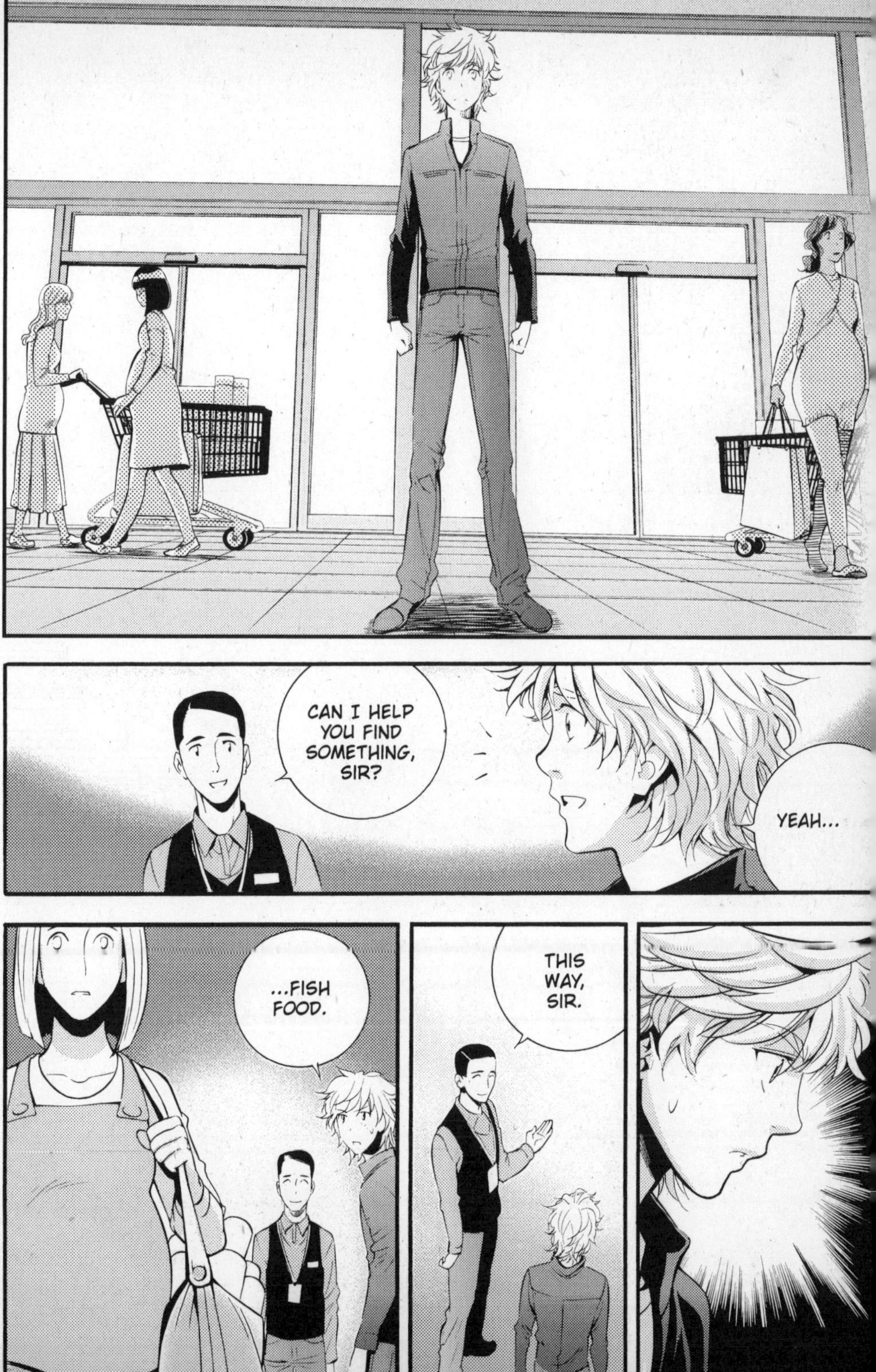
CAN I HELP YOU FIND SOMETHING, SIR?
YEAH...
...FISH FOOD.
THIS WAY, SIR.

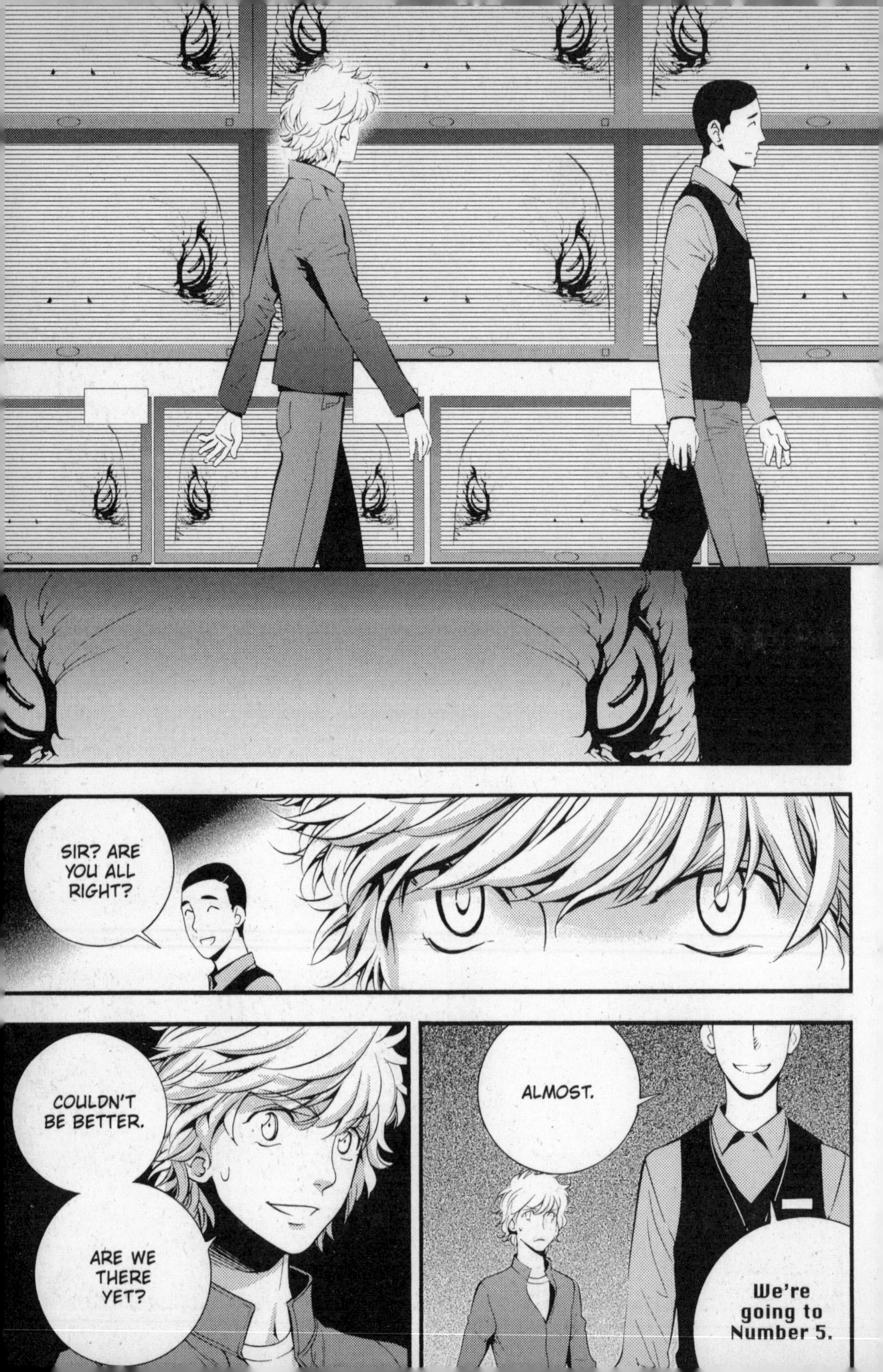
SIR? ARE YOU ALL RIGHT?
COULDN'T BE BETTER.
ARE WE THERE YET?
ALMOST.
We're going to Number 5.

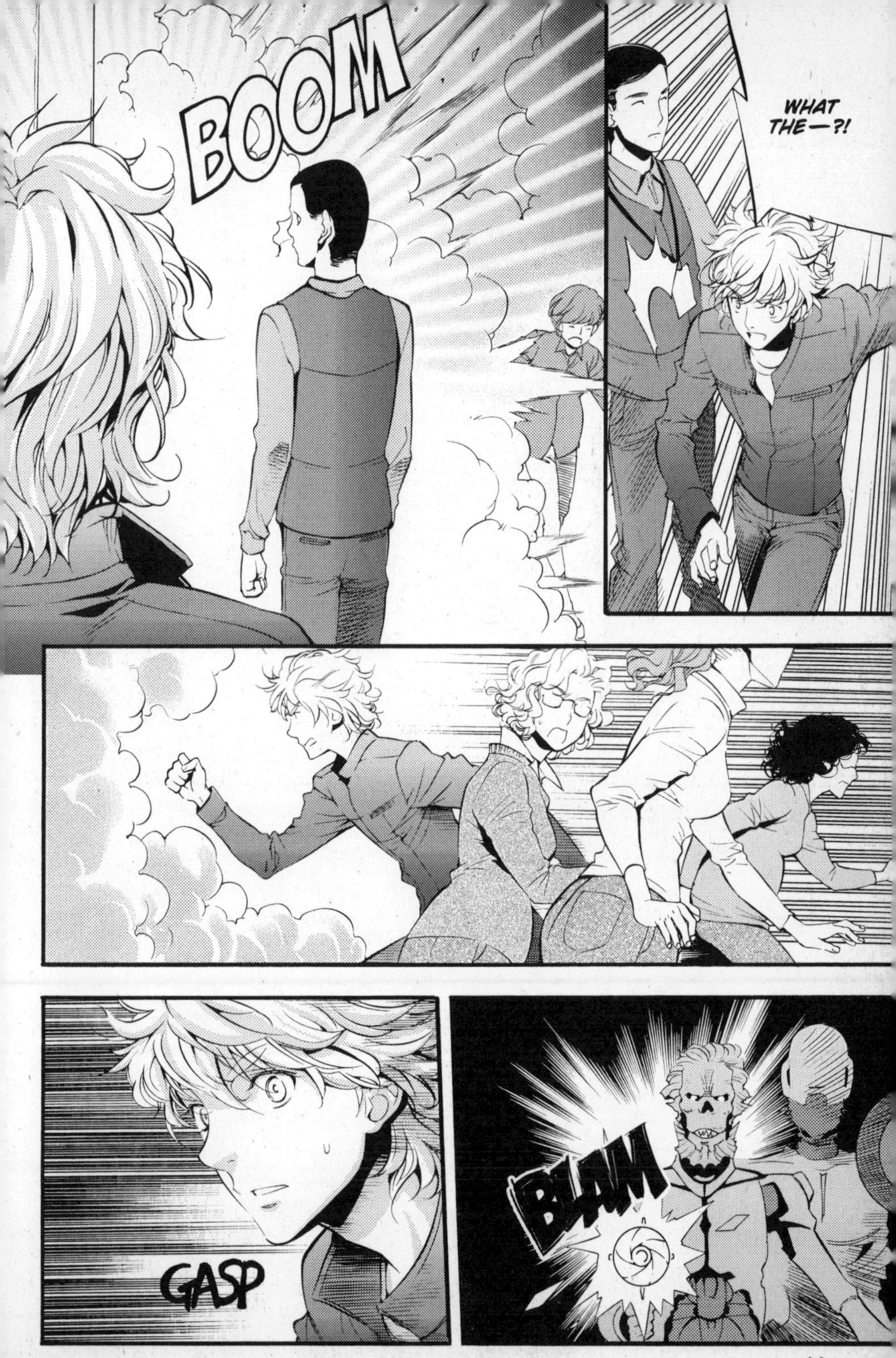
BOOM
WHAT THE—?!
GASP
BLAM

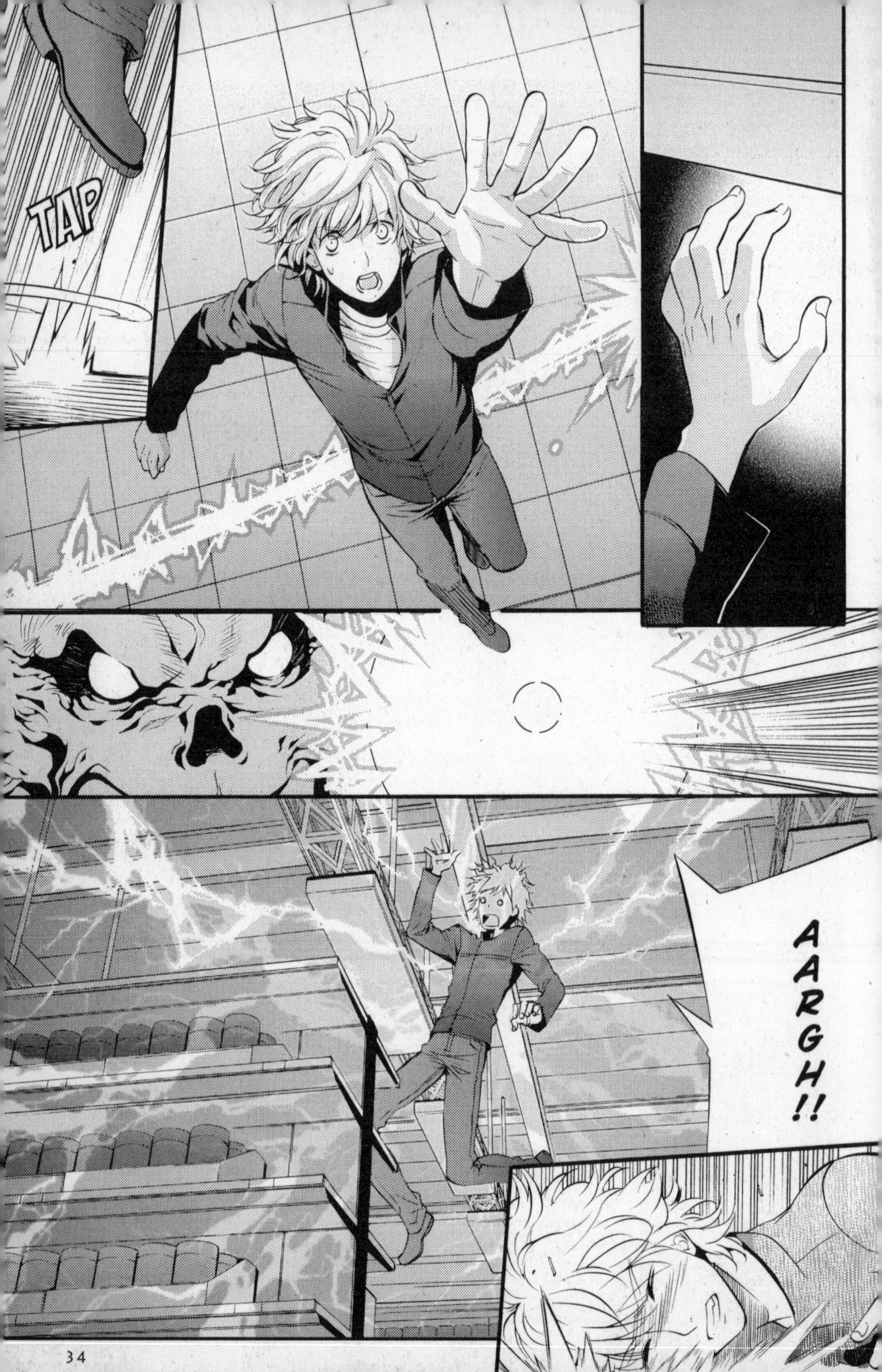
TAP
AARGH!!

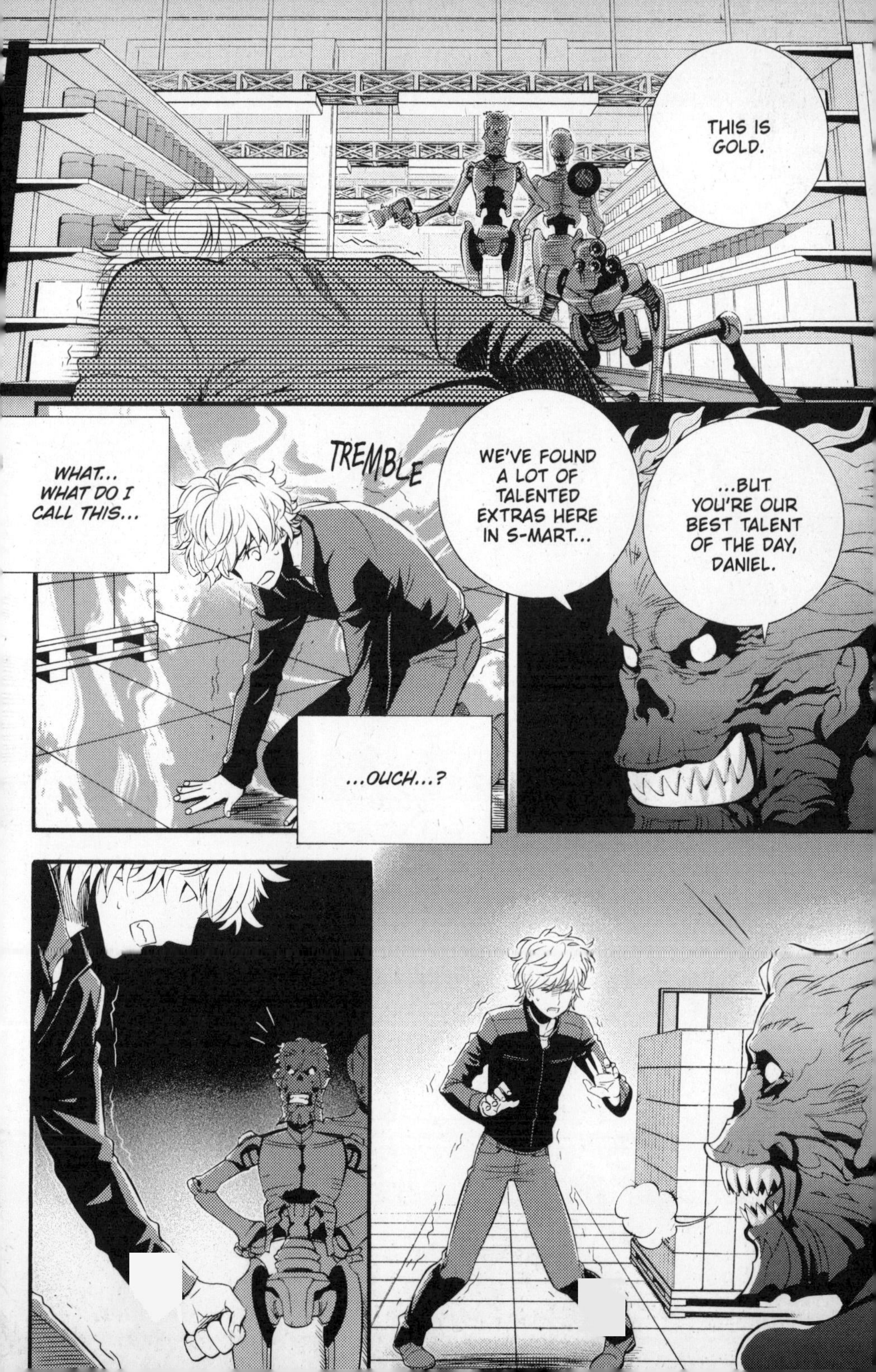
THIS IS GOLD.
WHAT... WHAT DO I CALL THIS...
TREMBLE
...OUCH...?
WE'VE FOUND A LOT OF TALENTED EXTRAS HERE IN S-MART...
...BUT YOU'RE OUR BEST TALENT OF THE DAY, DANIEL.

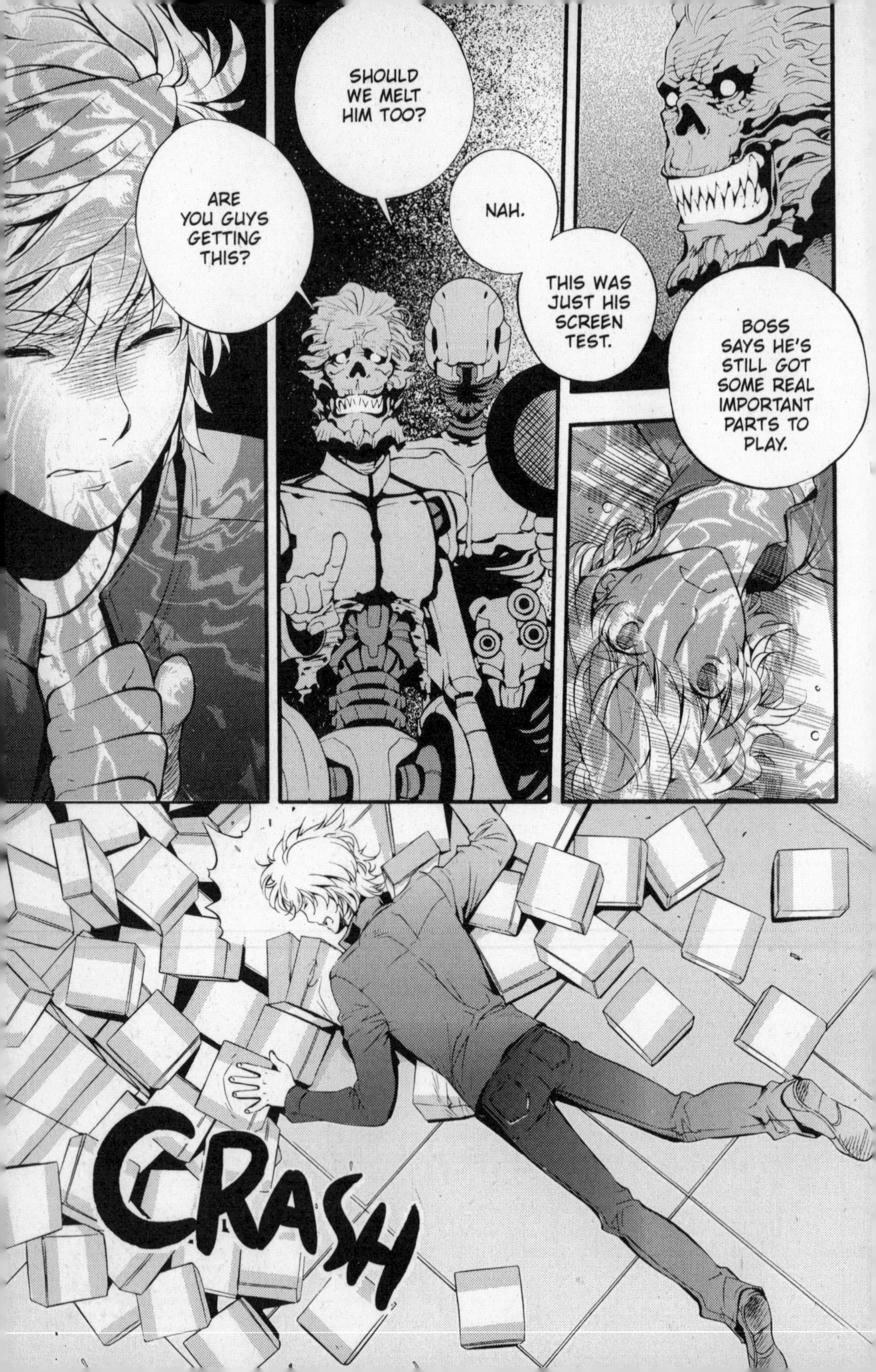
ARE YOU GUYS GETTING THIS?
SHOULD WE MELT HIM TOO?
NAH.
THIS WAS JUST HIS SCREEN TEST.
BOSS SAYS HE'S STILL GOT SOME REAL IMPORTANT PARTS TO PLAY.
CRASH

DANIEL X

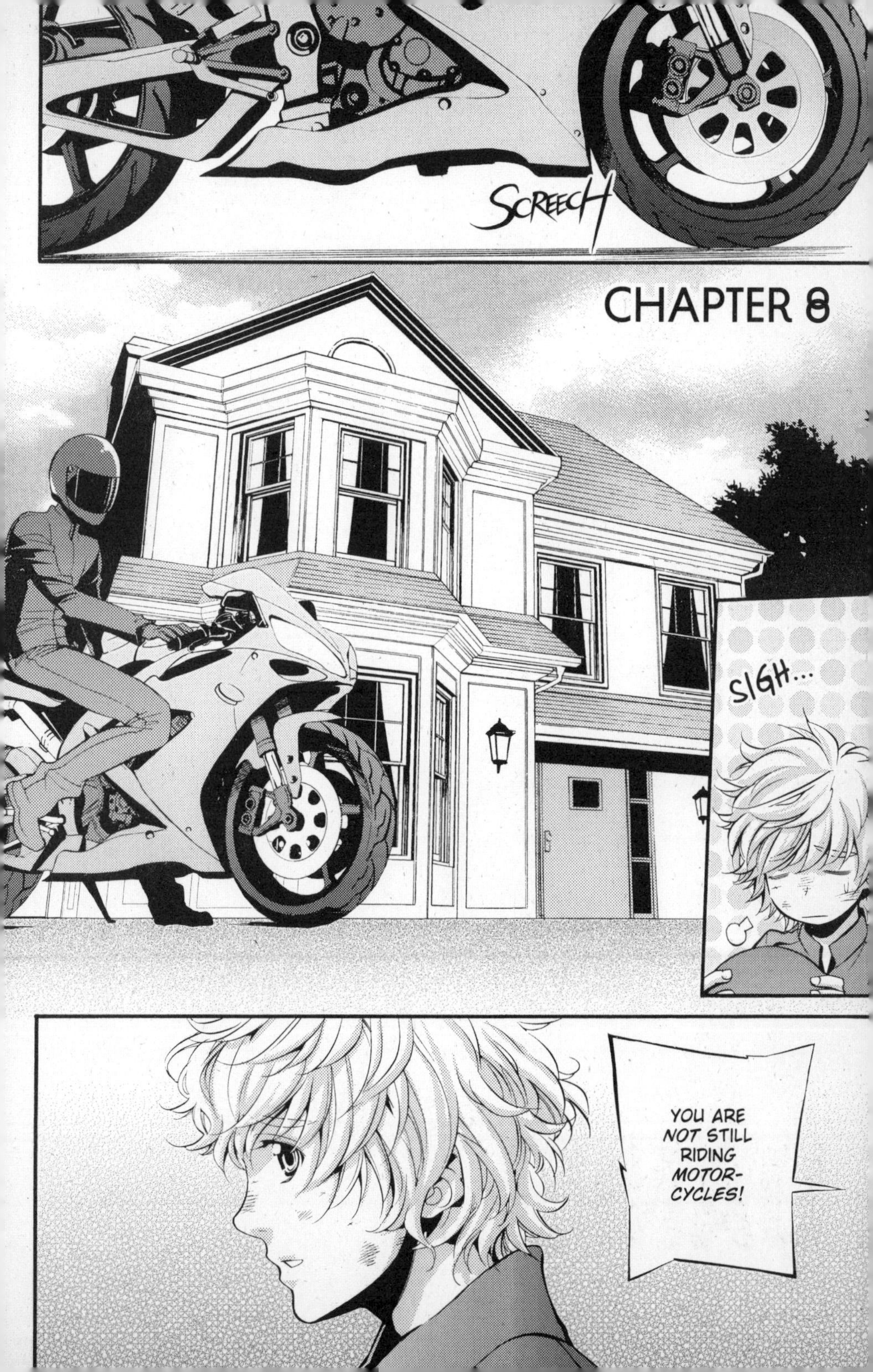
SCREECH
CHAPTER 8
SIGH...
YOU ARE NOT STILL RIDING MOTOR-CYCLES!

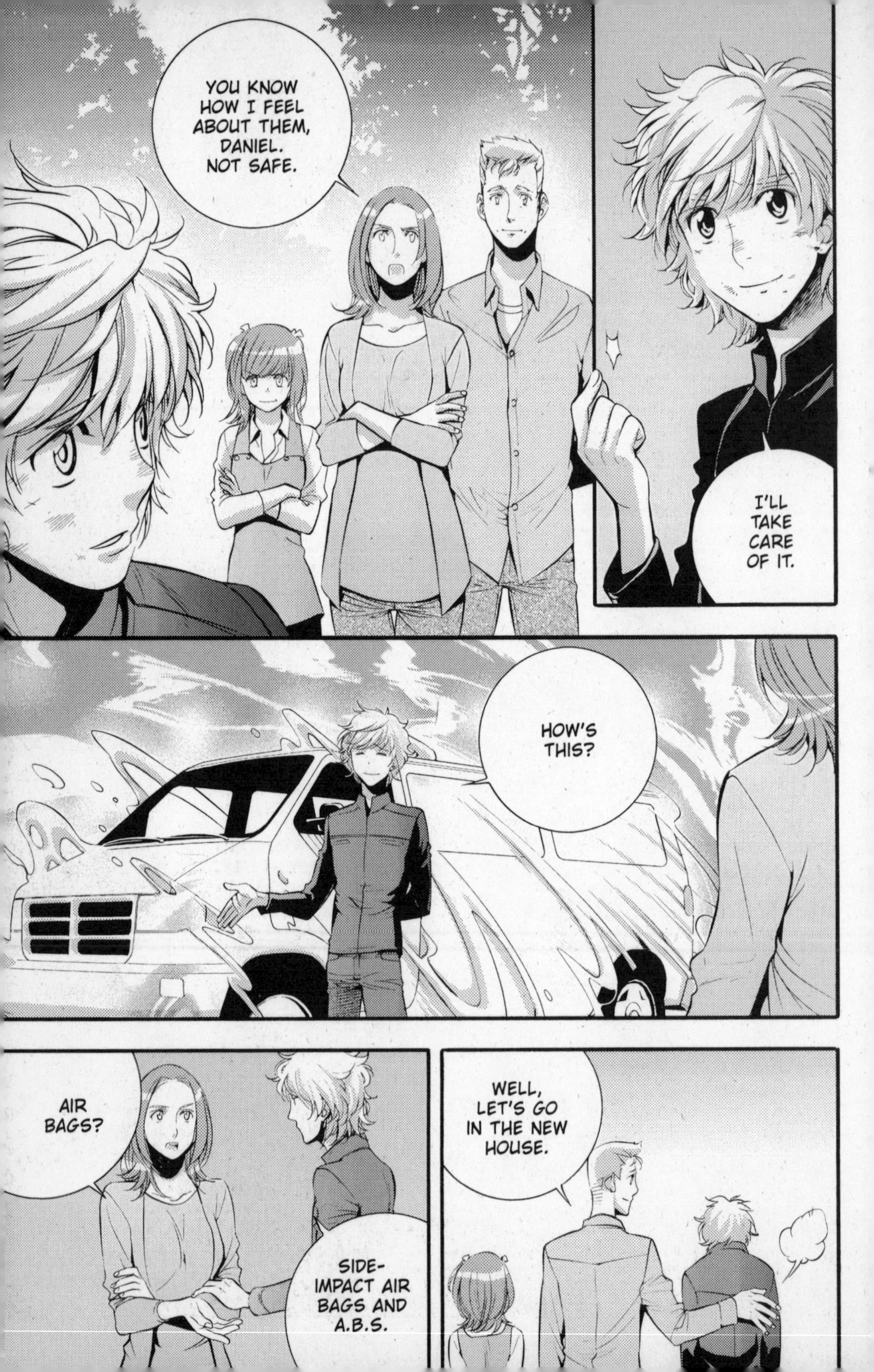
YOU KNOW HOW I FEEL ABOUT THEM, DANIEL. NOT SAFE.
I'LL TAKE CARE OF IT.
HOW'S THIS?
AIR BAGS?
SIDE-IMPACT AIR BAGS AND A.B.S.
WELL, LET'S GO IN THE NEW HOUSE.

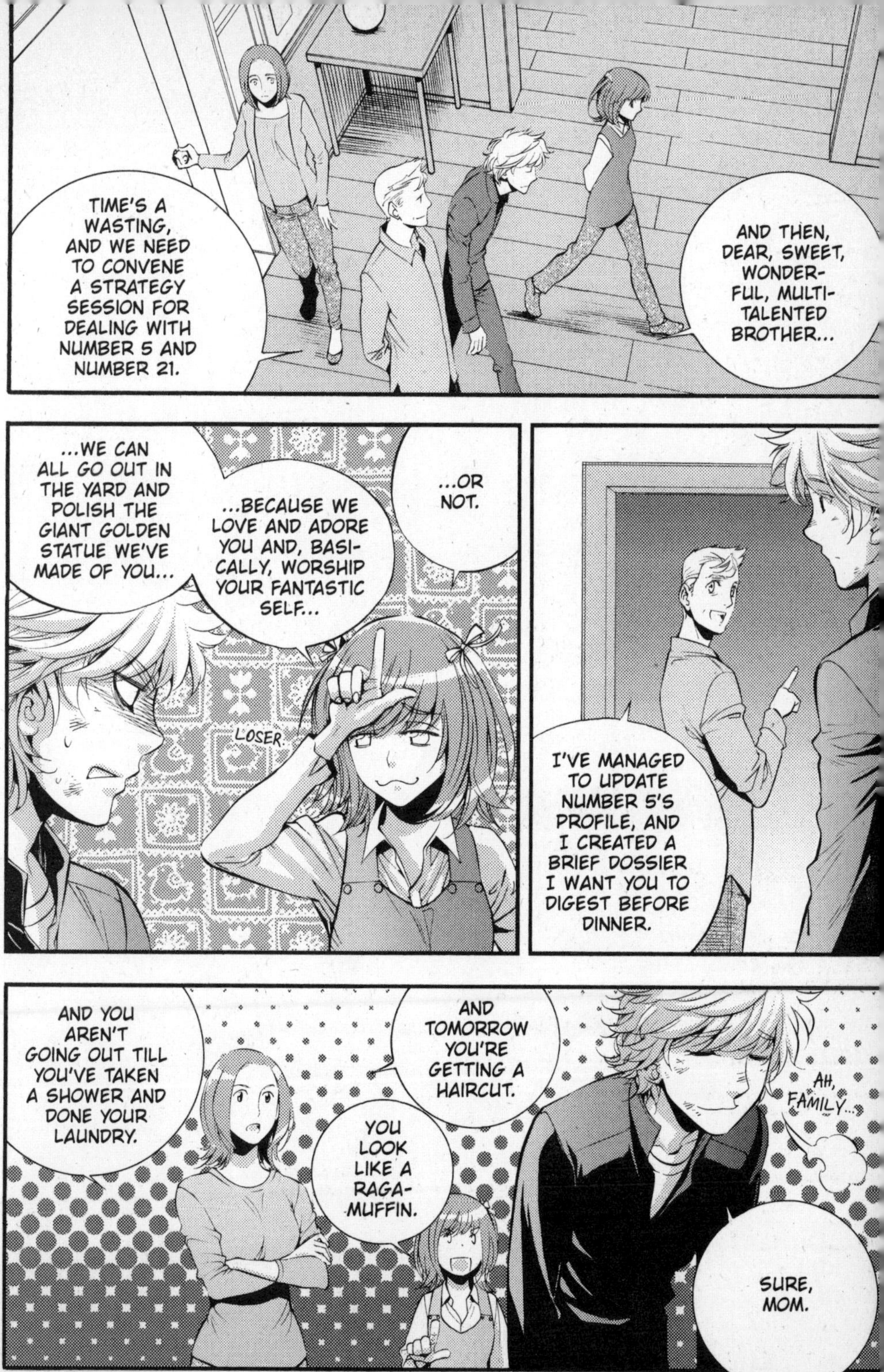
TIME'S A WASTING, AND WE NEED TO CONVENE A STRATEGY SESSION FOR DEALING WITH NUMBER 5 AND NUMBER 21.
AND THEN, DEAR, SWEET, WONDERFUL, MULTI-TALENTED BROTHER...
...WE CAN ALL GO OUT IN THE YARD AND POLISH THE GIANT GOLDEN STATUE WE'VE MADE OF YOU...
...BECAUSE WE LOVE AND ADORE YOU AND, BASICALLY, WORSHIP YOUR FANTASTIC SELF...
...OR NOT.
LOSER.
I'VE MANAGED TO UPDATE NUMBER 5'S PROFILE, AND I CREATED A BRIEF DOSSIER I WANT YOU TO DIGEST BEFORE DINNER.
AND YOU AREN'T GOING OUT TILL YOU'VE TAKEN A SHOWER AND DONE YOUR LAUNDRY.
AND TOMORROW YOU'RE GETTING A HAIRCUT.
YOU LOOK LIKE A RAGAMUFFIN.
AH, FAMILY...
SURE, MOM.

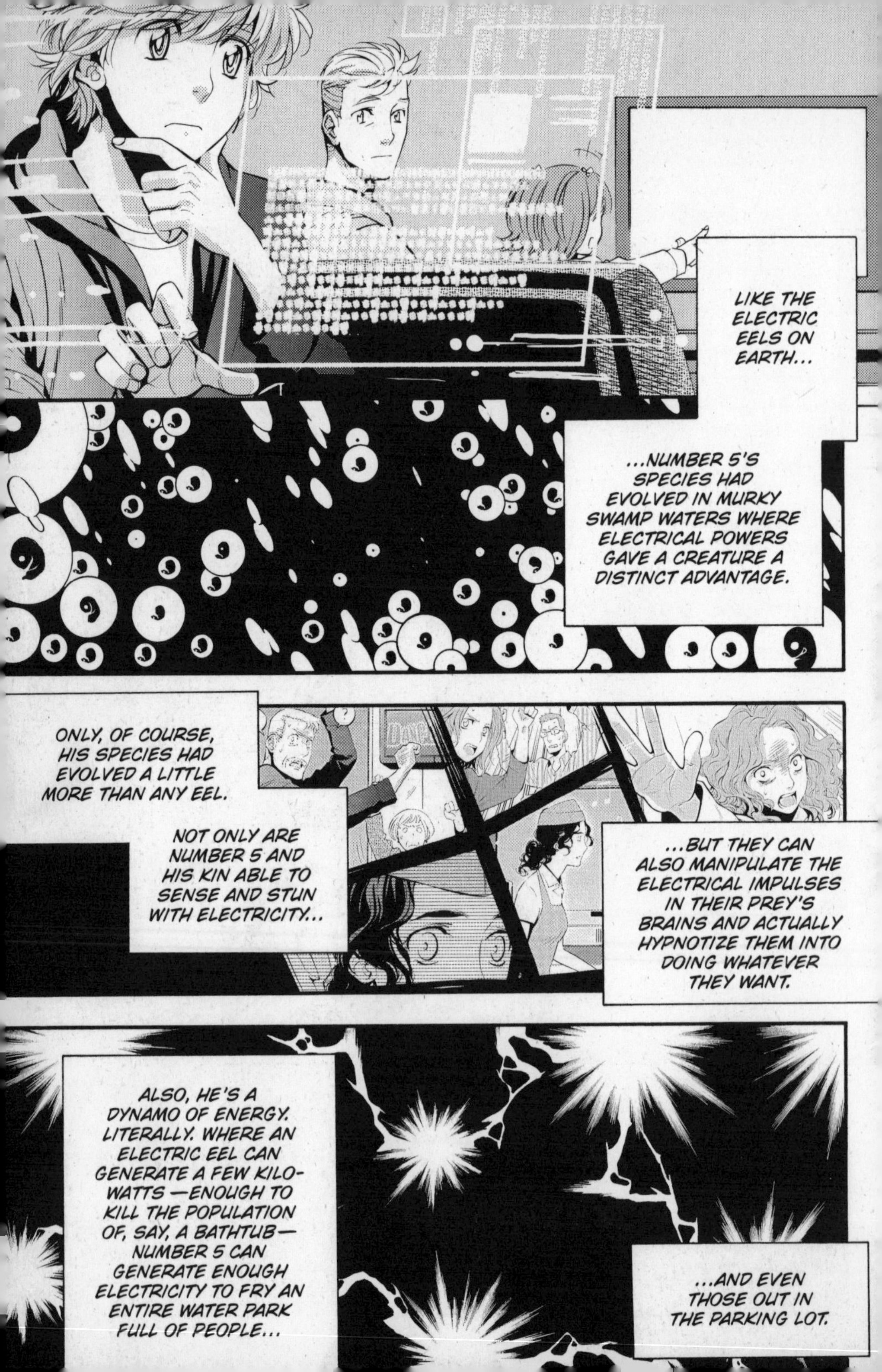
LIKE THE ELECTRIC EELS ON EARTH...
...NUMBER 5'S SPECIES HAD EVOLVED IN MURKY SWAMP WATERS WHERE ELECTRICAL POWERS GAVE A CREATURE A DISTINCT ADVANTAGE.
ONLY, OF COURSE, HIS SPECIES HAD EVOLVED A LITTLE MORE THAN ANY EEL.
NOT ONLY ARE NUMBER 5 AND HIS KIN ABLE TO SENSE AND STUN WITH ELECTRICITY...
...BUT THEY CAN ALSO MANIPULATE THE ELECTRICAL IMPULSES IN THEIR PREY'S BRAINS AND ACTUALLY HYPNOTIZE THEM INTO DOING WHATEVER THEY WANT.
ALSO, HE'S A DYNAMO OF ENERGY. LITERALLY. WHERE AN ELECTRIC EEL CAN GENERATE A FEW KILO-WATTS—ENOUGH TO KILL THE POPULATION OF, SAY, A BATHTUB—NUMBER 5 CAN GENERATE ENOUGH ELECTRICITY TO FRY AN ENTIRE WATER PARK FULL OF PEOPLE...
...AND EVEN THOSE OUT IN THE PARKING LOT.

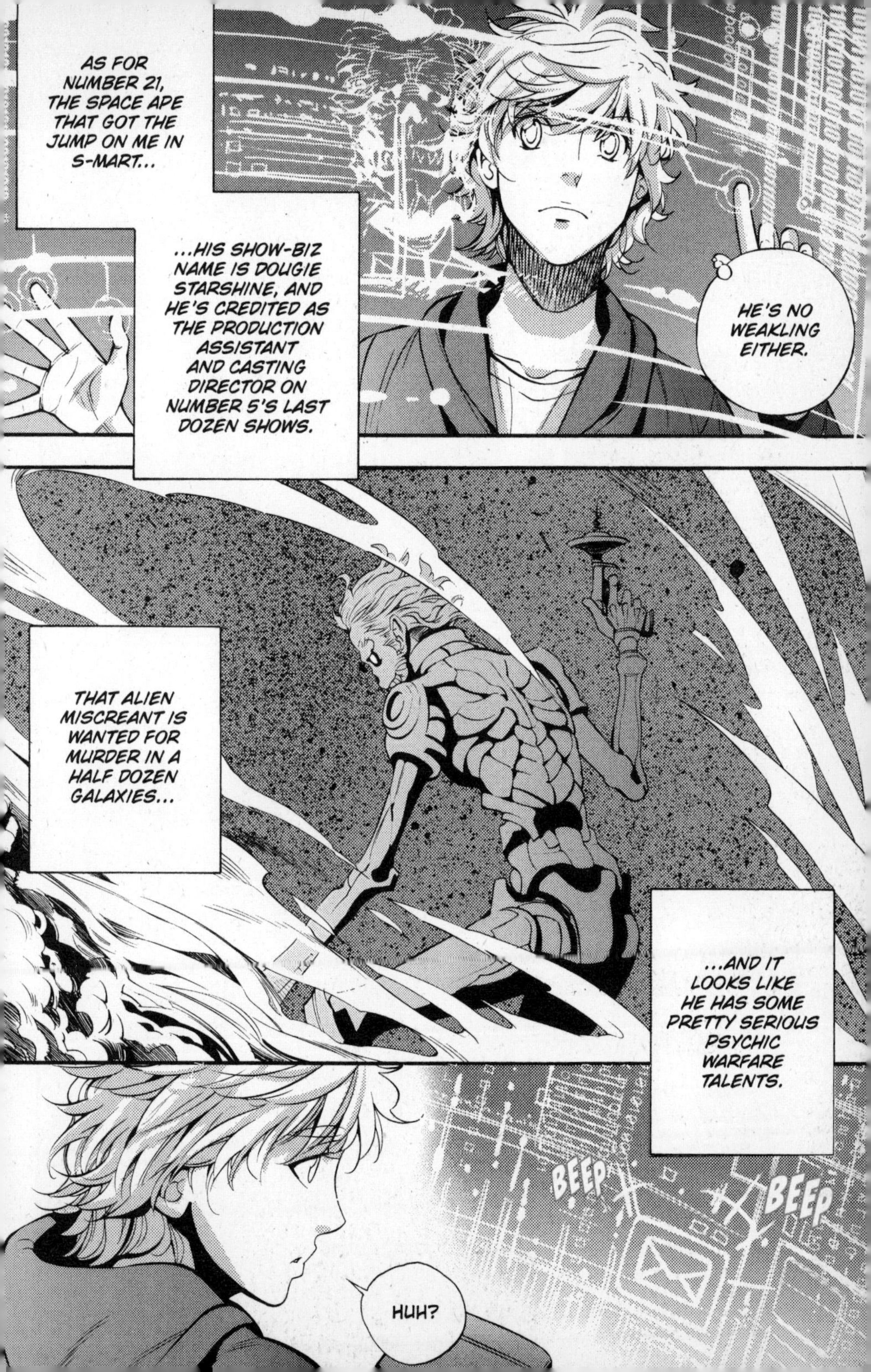
AS FOR NUMBER 21, THE SPACE APE THAT GOT THE JUMP ON ME IN S-MART...
...HIS SHOW-BIZ NAME IS DOUGIE STARSHINE, AND HE'S CREDITED AS THE PRODUCTION ASSISTANT AND CASTING DIRECTOR ON NUMBER 5'S LAST DOZEN SHOWS.
HE'S NO WEAKLING EITHER.
THAT ALIEN MISCREANT IS WANTED FOR MURDER IN A HALF DOZEN GALAXIES...
...AND IT LOOKS LIKE HE HAS SOME PRETTY SERIOUS PSYCHIC WARFARE TALENTS.
BEEP
BEEP
HUH?

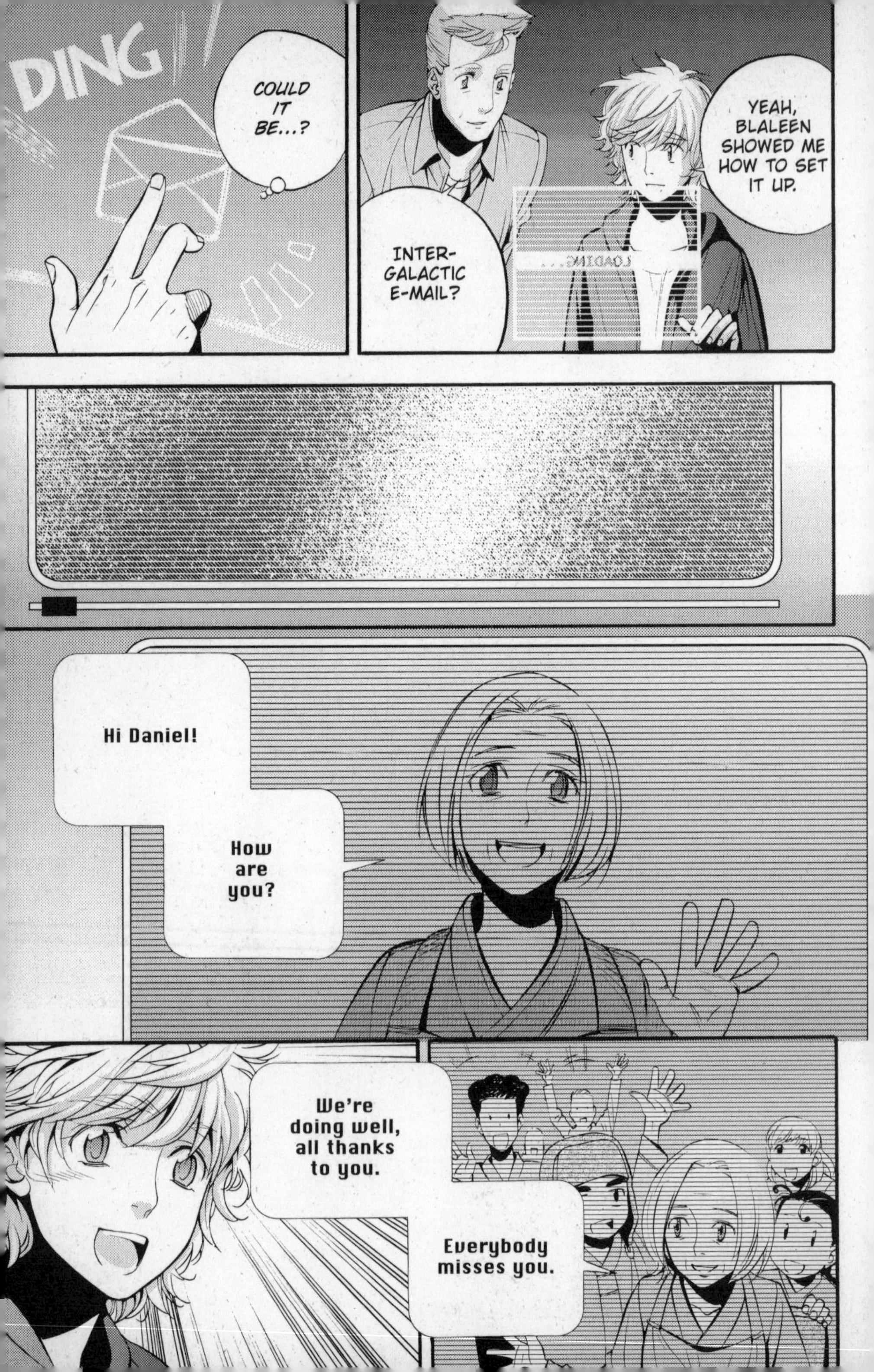
DING
COULD IT BE...?
YEAH, BLALEEN SHOWED ME HOW TO SET IT UP.
INTER-GALACTIC E-MAIL?
LOADING...
Hi Daniel!
How are you?
We're doing well, all thanks to you.
Everybody misses you.

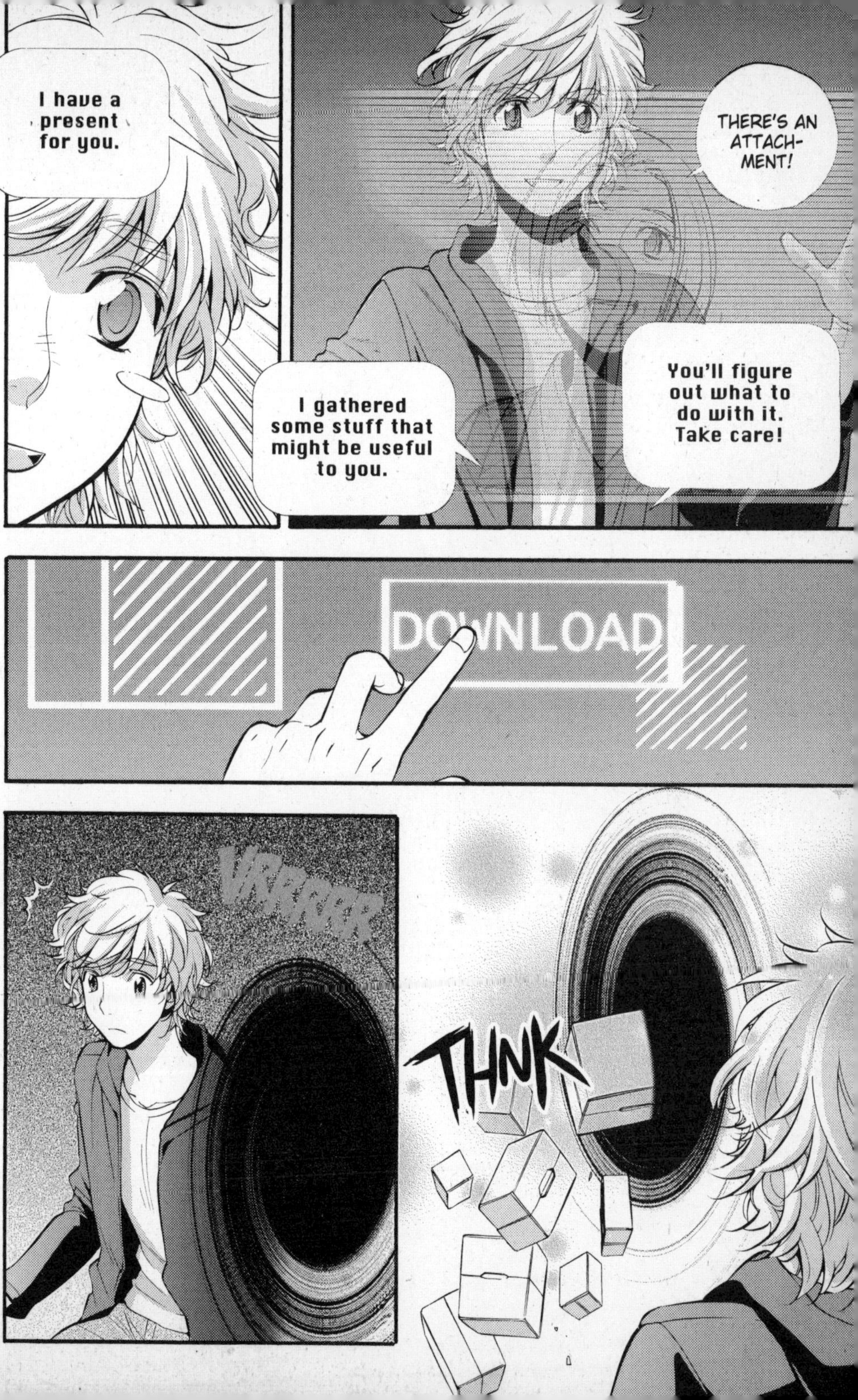
I have a present for you.
THERE'S AN ATTACH-MENT!
I gathered some stuff that might be useful to you.
You'll figure out what to do with it. Take care!
DOWNLOAD
VRRRRR
THNK

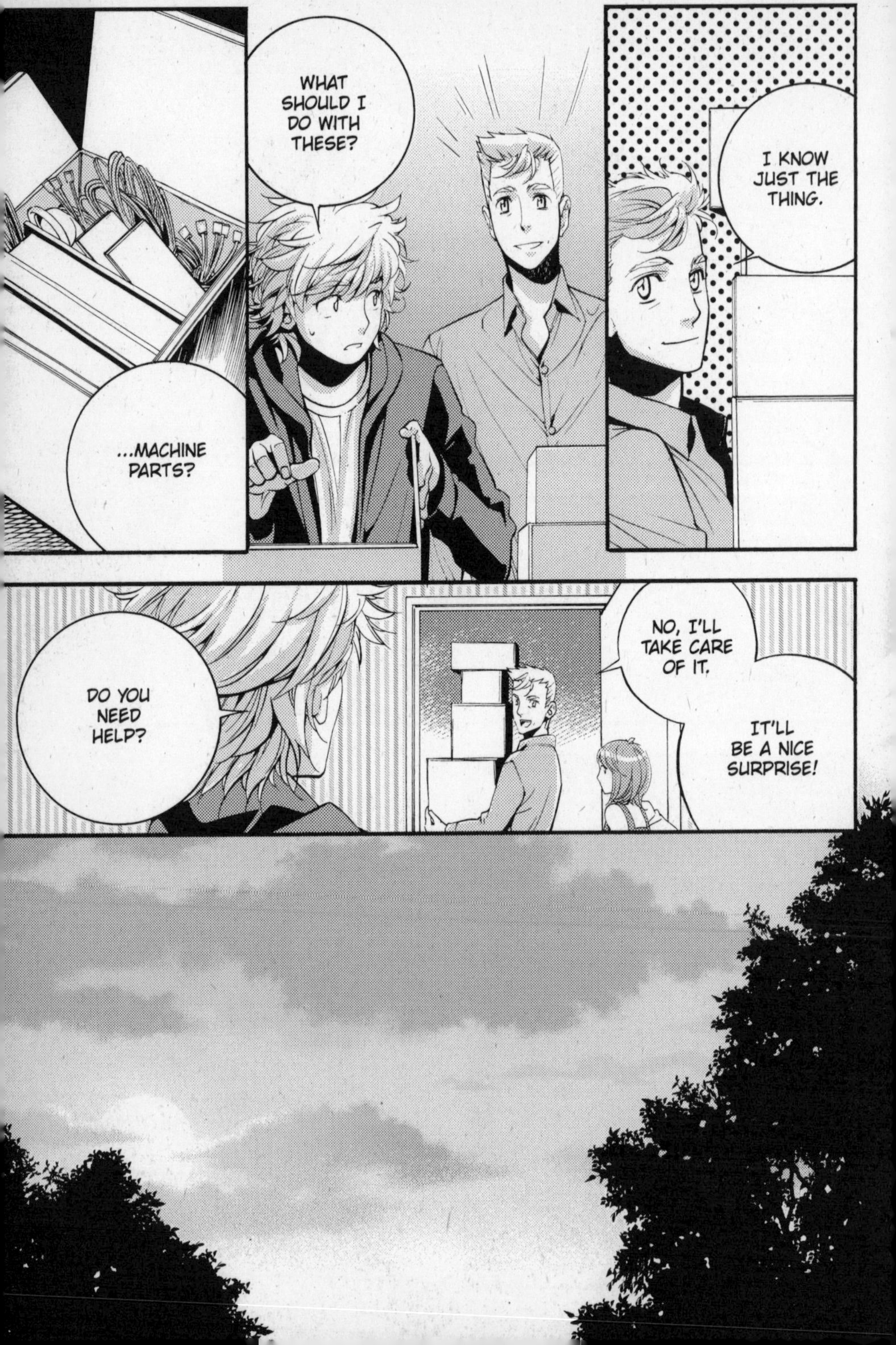
...MACHINE PARTS?
WHAT SHOULD I DO WITH THESE?
I KNOW JUST THE THING.
DO YOU NEED HELP?
NO, I'LL TAKE CARE OF IT.
IT'LL BE A NICE SURPRISE!

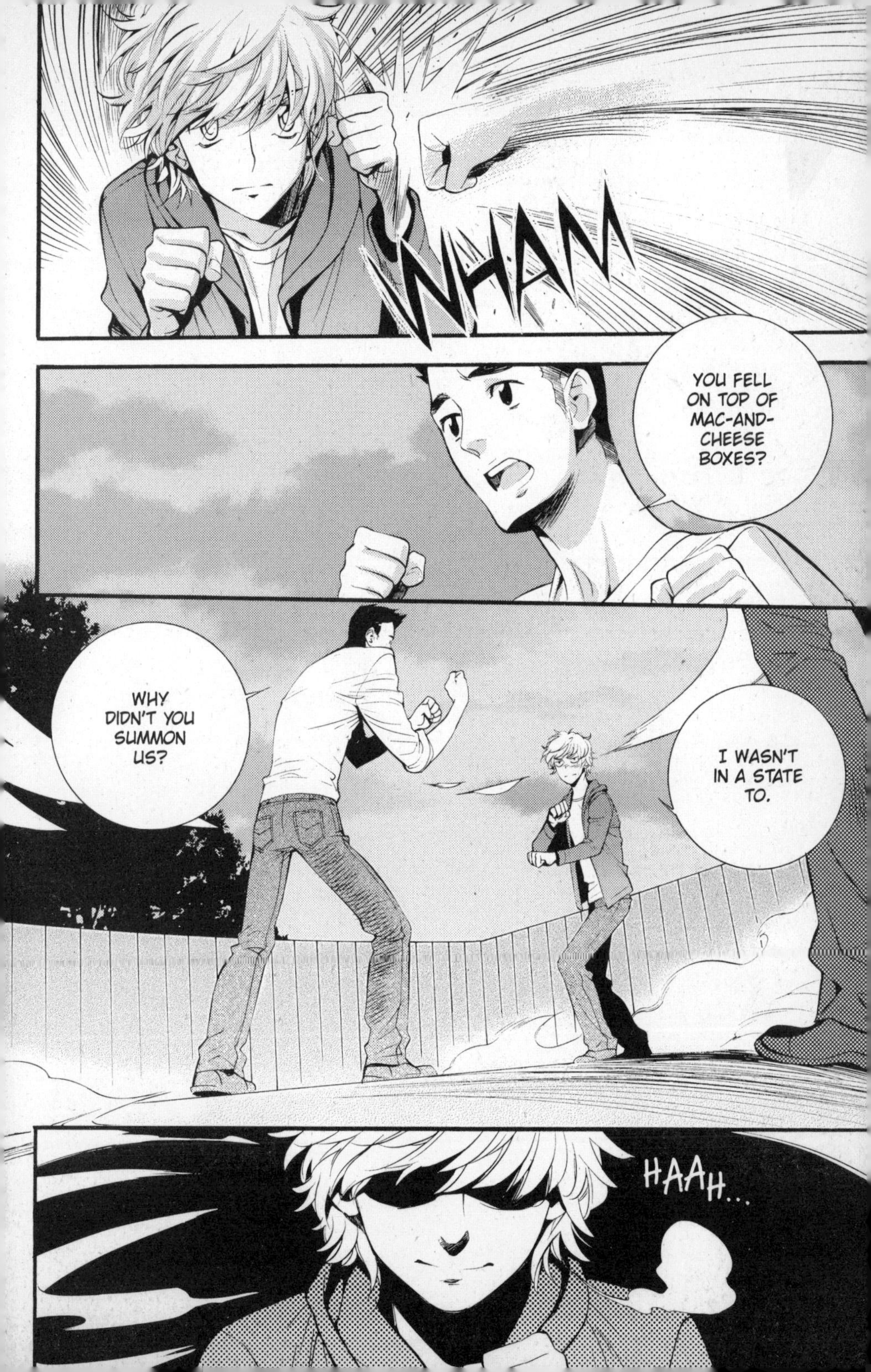
WHAM
YOU FELL ON TOP OF MAC-AND-CHEESE BOXES?
WHY DIDN'T YOU SUMMON US?
I WASN'T IN A STATE TO.
HAAH...

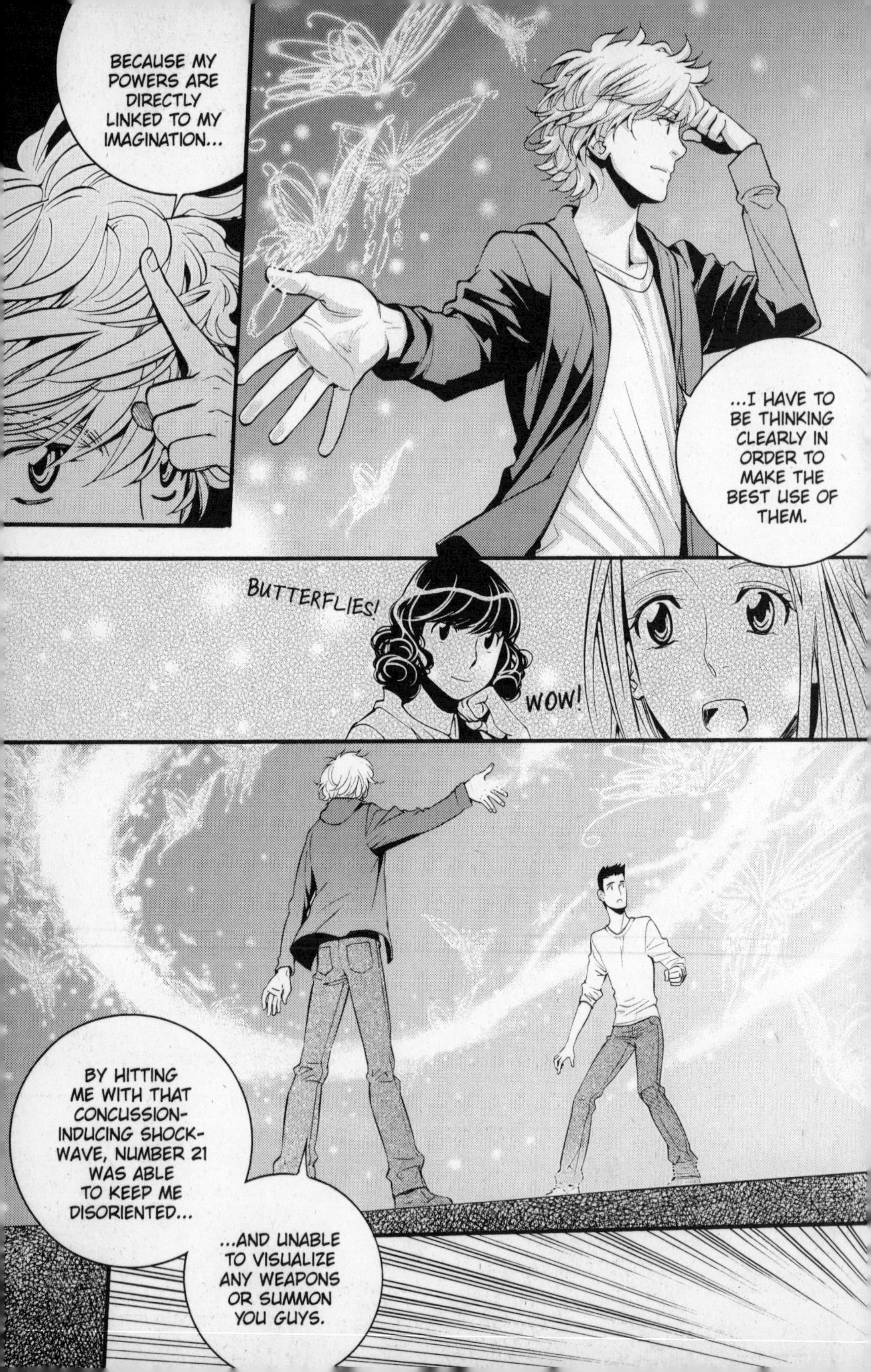
BECAUSE MY POWERS ARE DIRECTLY LINKED TO MY IMAGINATION...
...I HAVE TO BE THINKING CLEARLY IN ORDER TO MAKE THE BEST USE OF THEM.
BUTTERFLIES!
WOW!
BY HITTING ME WITH THAT CONCUSSION-INDUCING SHOCK-WAVE, NUMBER 21 WAS ABLE TO KEEP ME DISORIENTED...
...AND UNABLE TO VISUALIZE ANY WEAPONS OR SUMMON YOU GUYS.

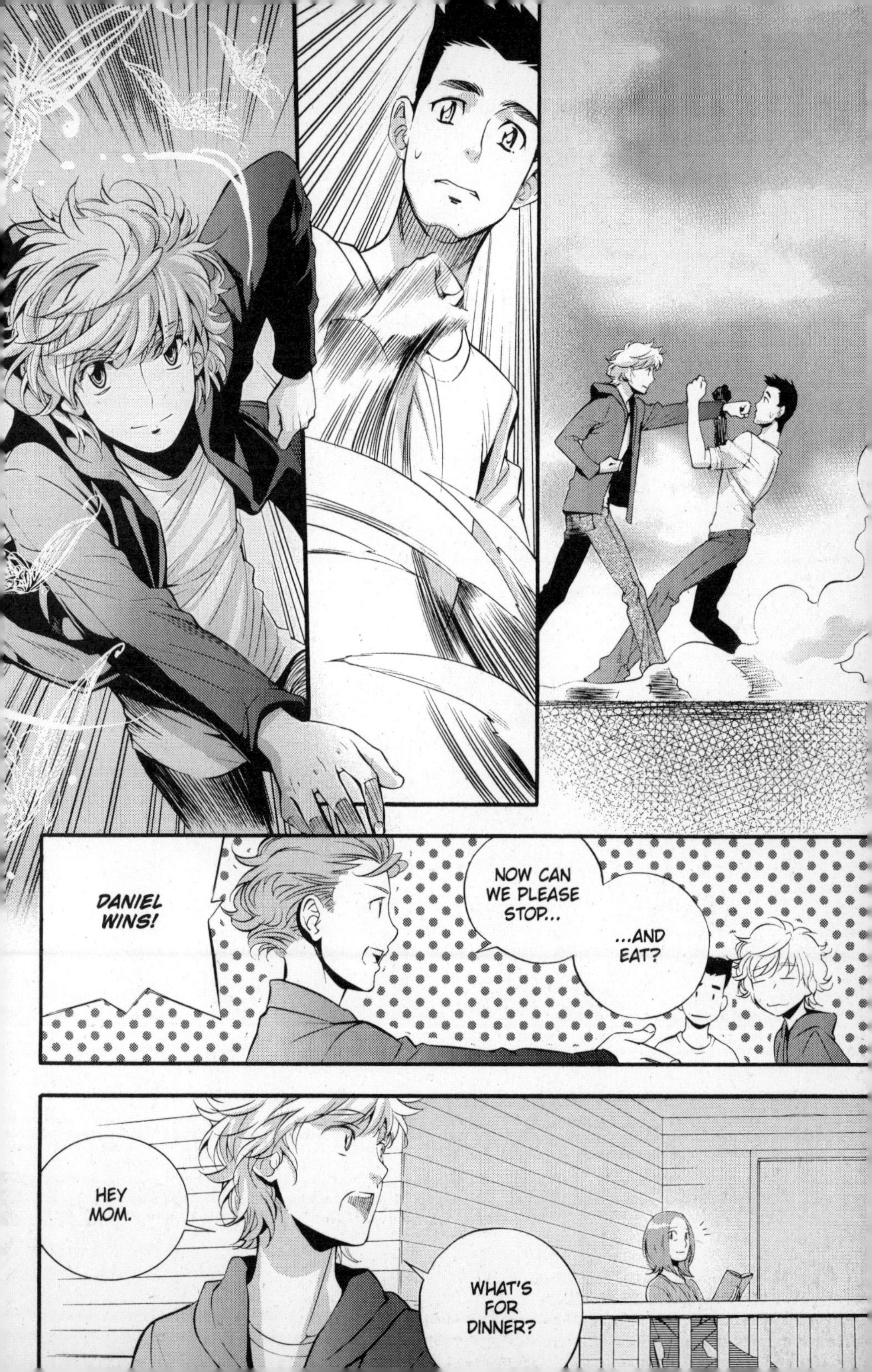
DANIEL WINS!
NOW CAN WE PLEASE STOP...
...AND EAT?
HEY MOM.
WHAT'S FOR DINNER?

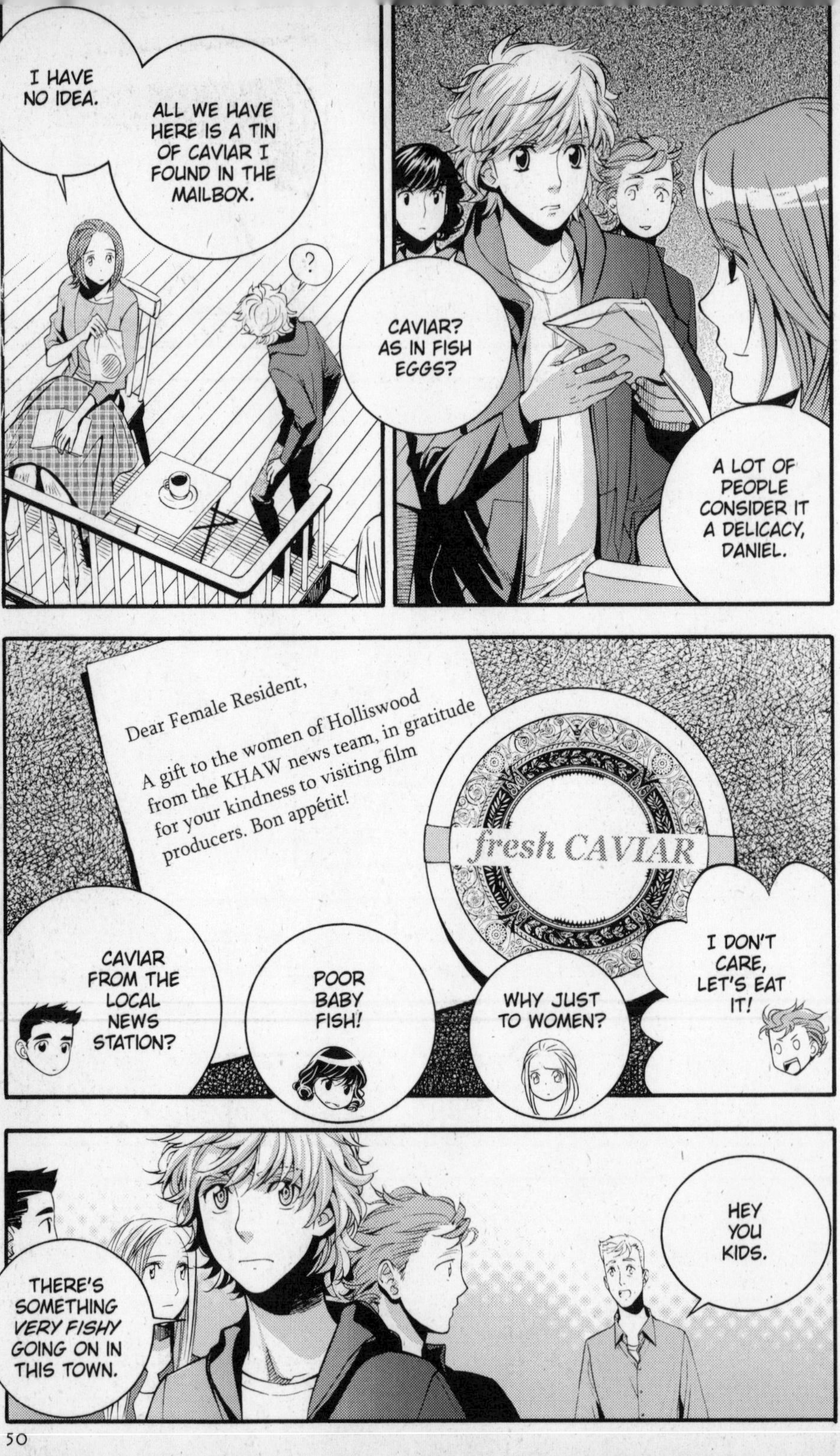
I HAVE NO IDEA.
ALL WE HAVE HERE IS A TIN OF CAVIAR I FOUND IN THE MAILBOX.
?
CAVIAR? AS IN FISH EGGS?
A LOT OF PEOPLE CONSIDER IT A DELICACY, DANIEL.
Dear Female Resident,
A gift to the women of Holliswood from the KHAW news team, in gratitude for your kindness to visiting film producers. Bon appétit!
fresh CAVIAR
CAVIAR FROM THE LOCAL NEWS STATION?
POOR BABY FISH!
WHY JUST TO WOMEN?
I DON'T CARE, LET'S EAT IT!
THERE'S SOMETHING *VERY FISHY* GOING ON IN THIS TOWN.
HEY YOU KIDS.

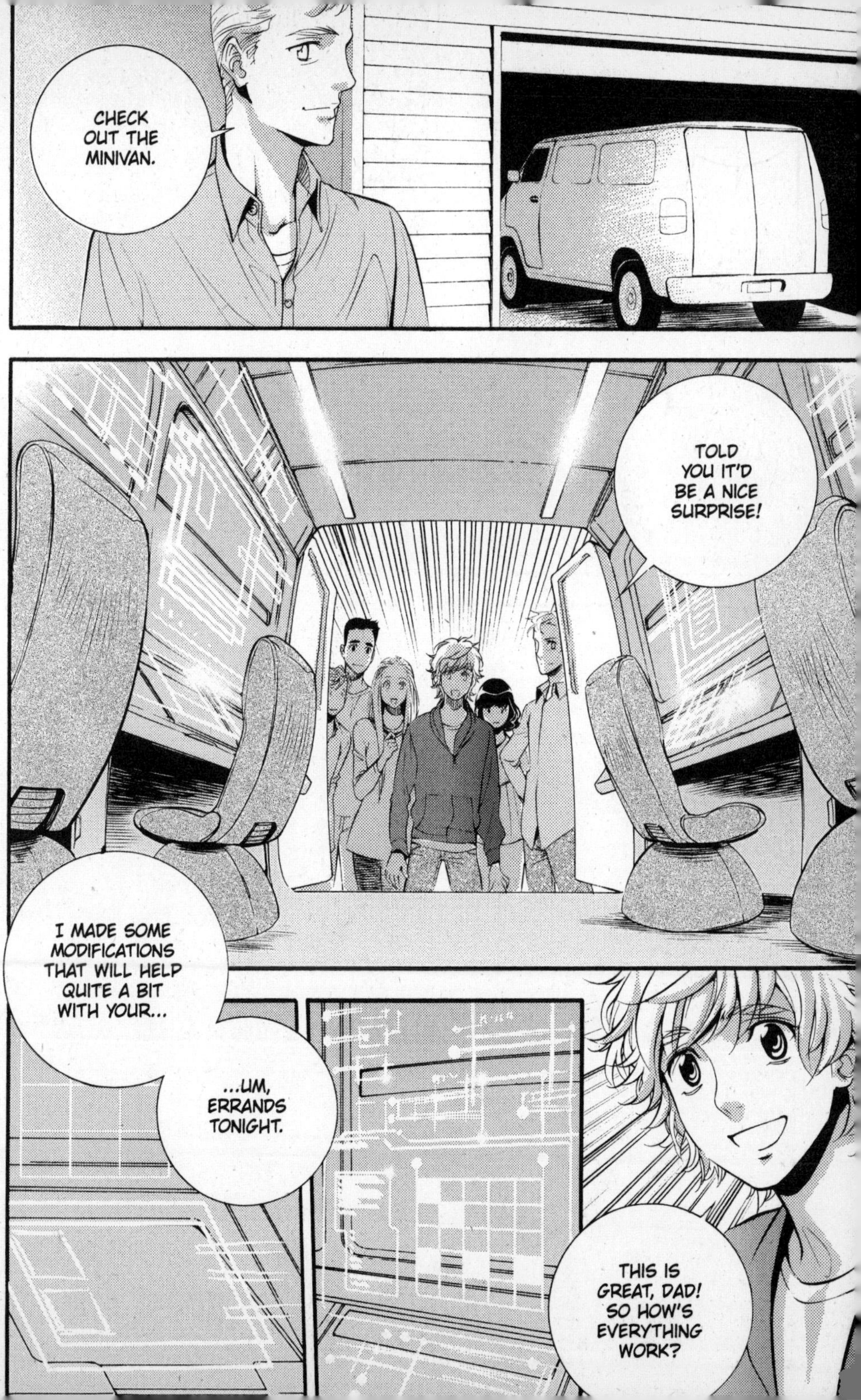
CHECK OUT THE MINIVAN.
TOLD YOU IT'D BE A NICE SURPRISE!
I MADE SOME MODIFICATIONS THAT WILL HELP QUITE A BIT WITH YOUR...
...UM, ERRANDS TONIGHT.
THIS IS GREAT, DAD! SO HOW'S EVERYTHING WORK?

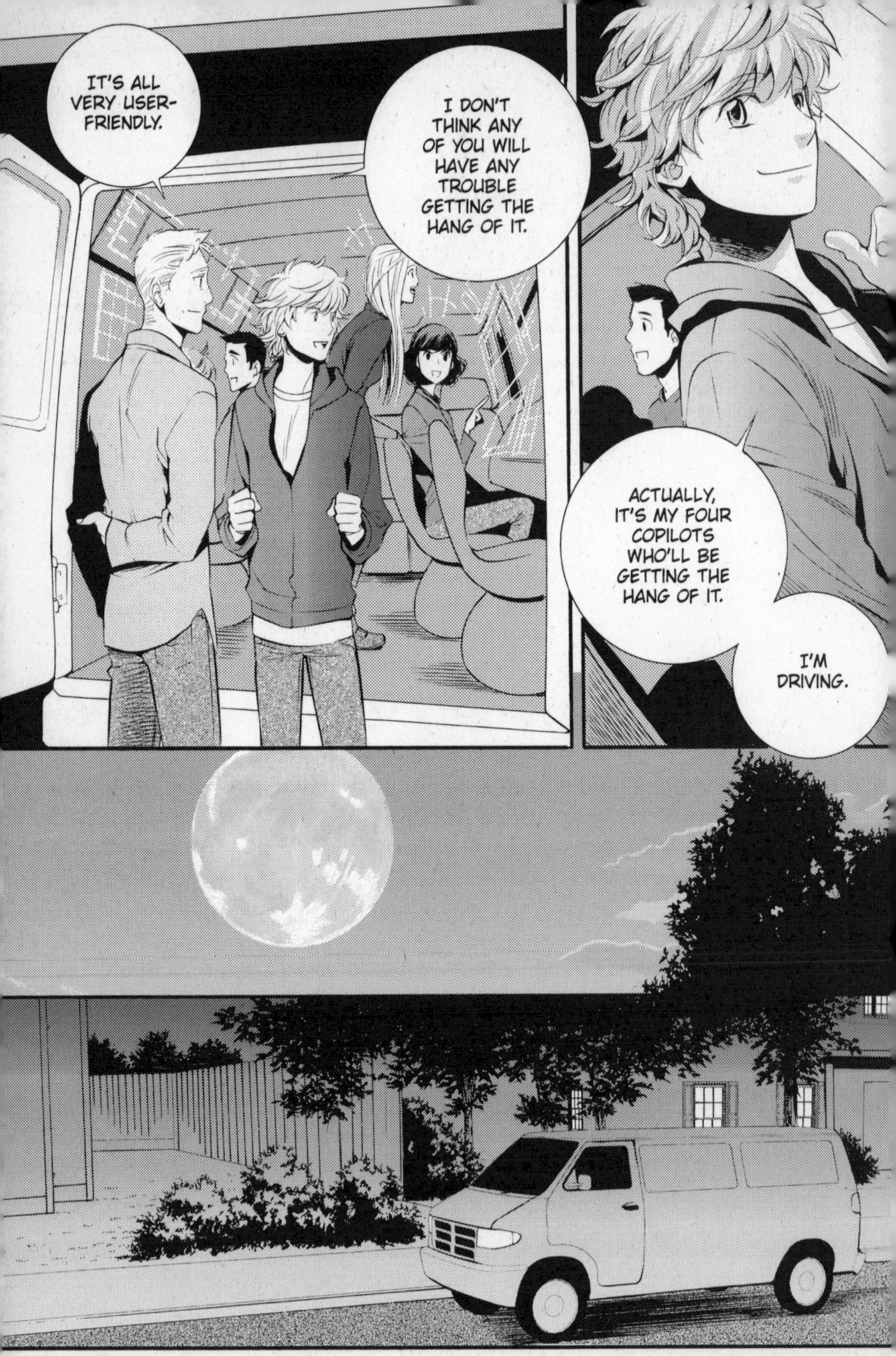
IT'S ALL VERY USER-FRIENDLY.
I DON'T THINK ANY OF YOU WILL HAVE ANY TROUBLE GETTING THE HANG OF IT.
ACTUALLY, IT'S MY FOUR COPILOTS WHO'LL BE GETTING THE HANG OF IT.
I'M DRIVING.

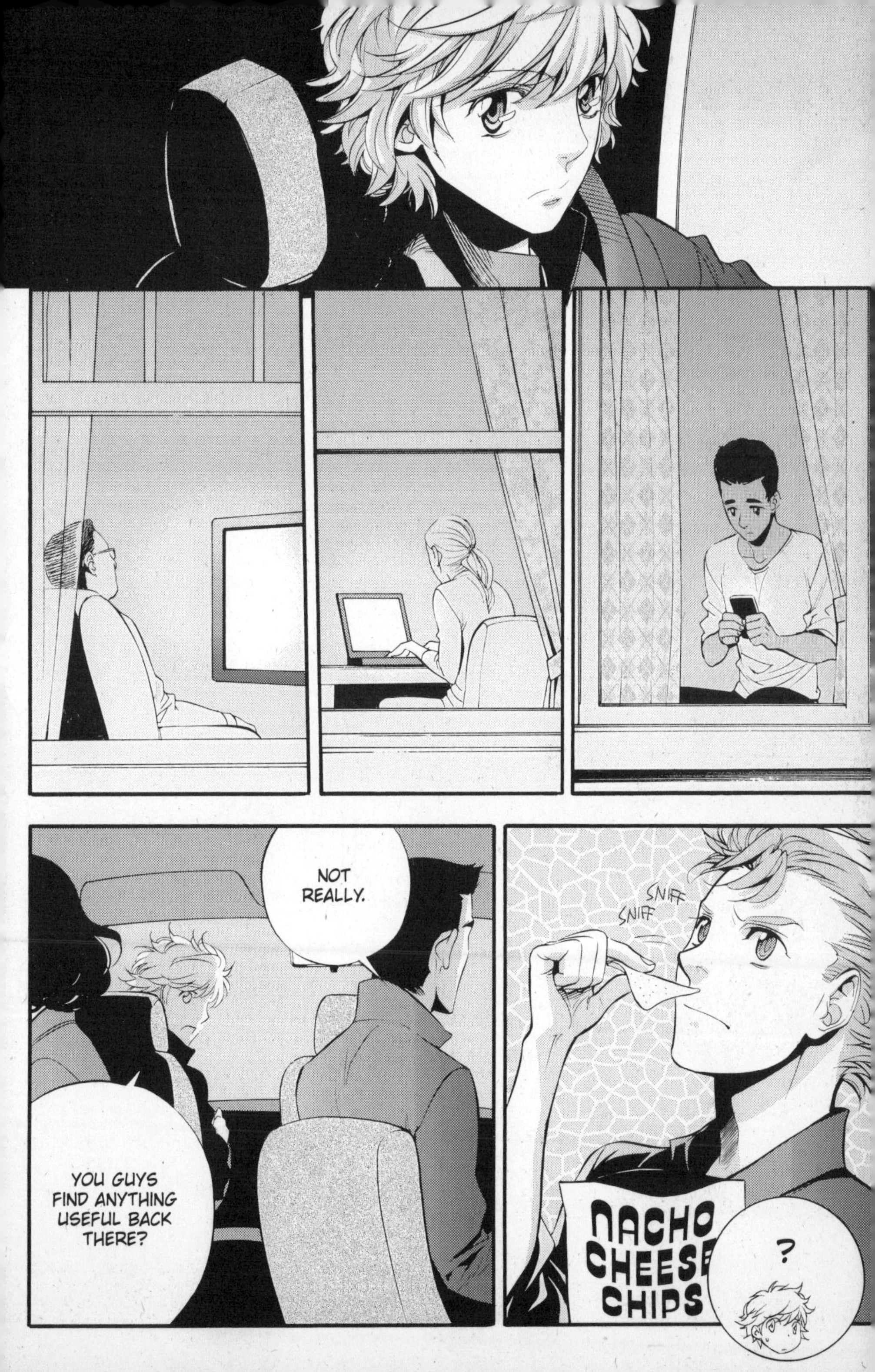
NOT REALLY.
YOU GUYS FIND ANYTHING USEFUL BACK THERE?
SNIFF SNIFF
NACHO CHEESE CHIPS
?

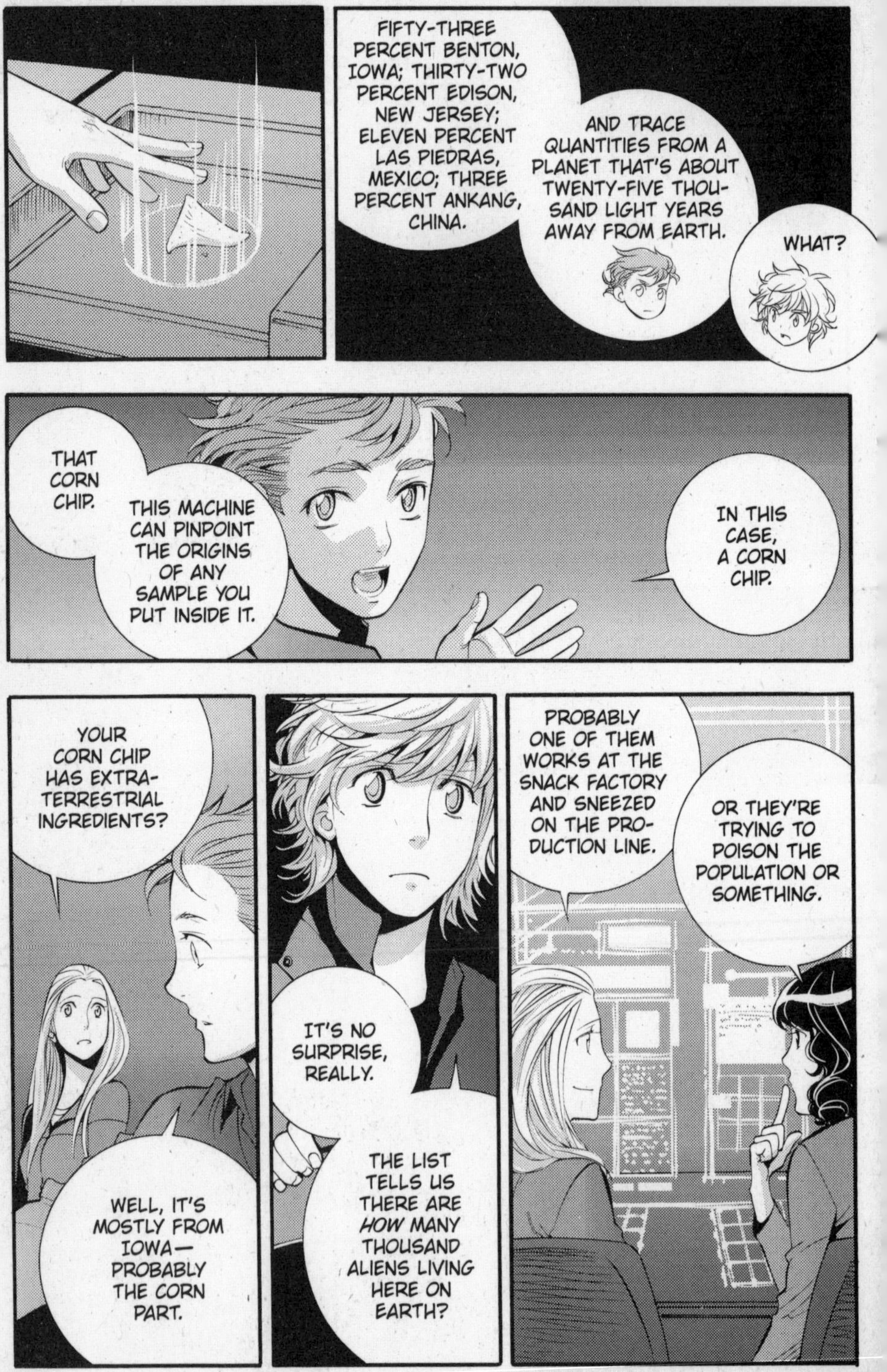
FIFTY-THREE PERCENT BENTON, IOWA; THIRTY-TWO PERCENT EDISON, NEW JERSEY; ELEVEN PERCENT LAS PIEDRAS, MEXICO; THREE PERCENT ANKANG, CHINA.
AND TRACE QUANTITIES FROM A PLANET THAT'S ABOUT TWENTY-FIVE THOU-SAND LIGHT YEARS AWAY FROM EARTH.
WHAT?
THAT CORN CHIP.
THIS MACHINE CAN PINPOINT THE ORIGINS OF ANY SAMPLE YOU PUT INSIDE IT.
IN THIS CASE, A CORN CHIP.
YOUR CORN CHIP HAS EXTRA-TERRESTRIAL INGREDIENTS?
WELL, IT'S MOSTLY FROM IOWA—PROBABLY THE CORN PART.
IT'S NO SURPRISE, REALLY.
THE LIST TELLS US THERE ARE *HOW* MANY THOUSAND ALIENS LIVING HERE ON EARTH?
PROBABLY ONE OF THEM WORKS AT THE SNACK FACTORY AND SNEEZED ON THE PRO-DUCTION LINE.
OR THEY'RE TRYING TO POISON THE POPULATION OR SOMETHING.

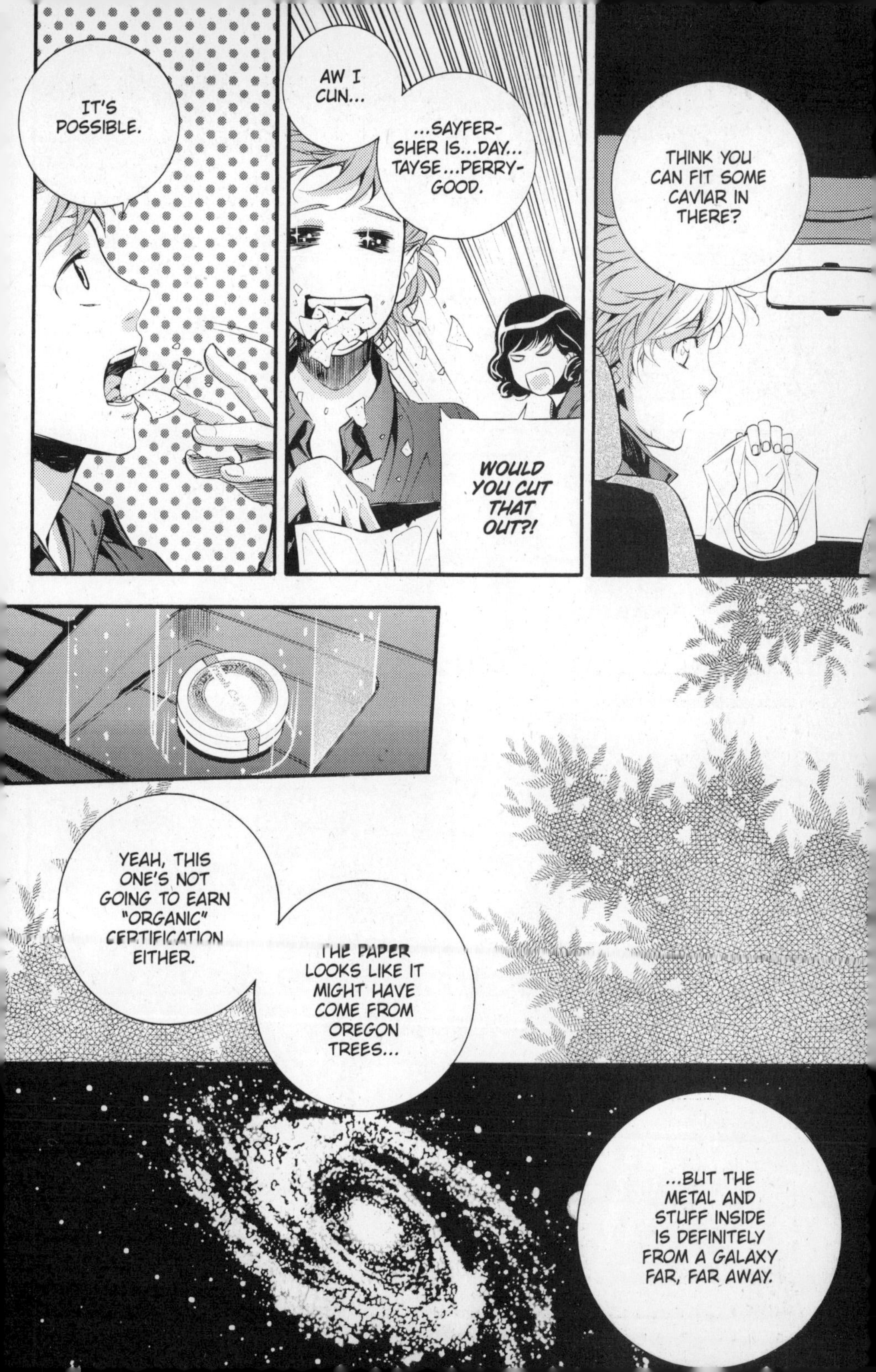
IT'S POSSIBLE.
AW I CUN...
...SAYFER-SHER IS...DAY... TAYSE...PERRY-GOOD.
WOULD YOU CUT THAT OUT?!
THINK YOU CAN FIT SOME CAVIAR IN THERE?
YEAH, THIS ONE'S NOT GOING TO EARN "ORGANIC" CERTIFICATION EITHER.
THE PAPER LOOKS LIKE IT MIGHT HAVE COME FROM OREGON TREES...
...BUT THE METAL AND STUFF INSIDE IS DEFINITELY FROM A GALAXY FAR, FAR AWAY.

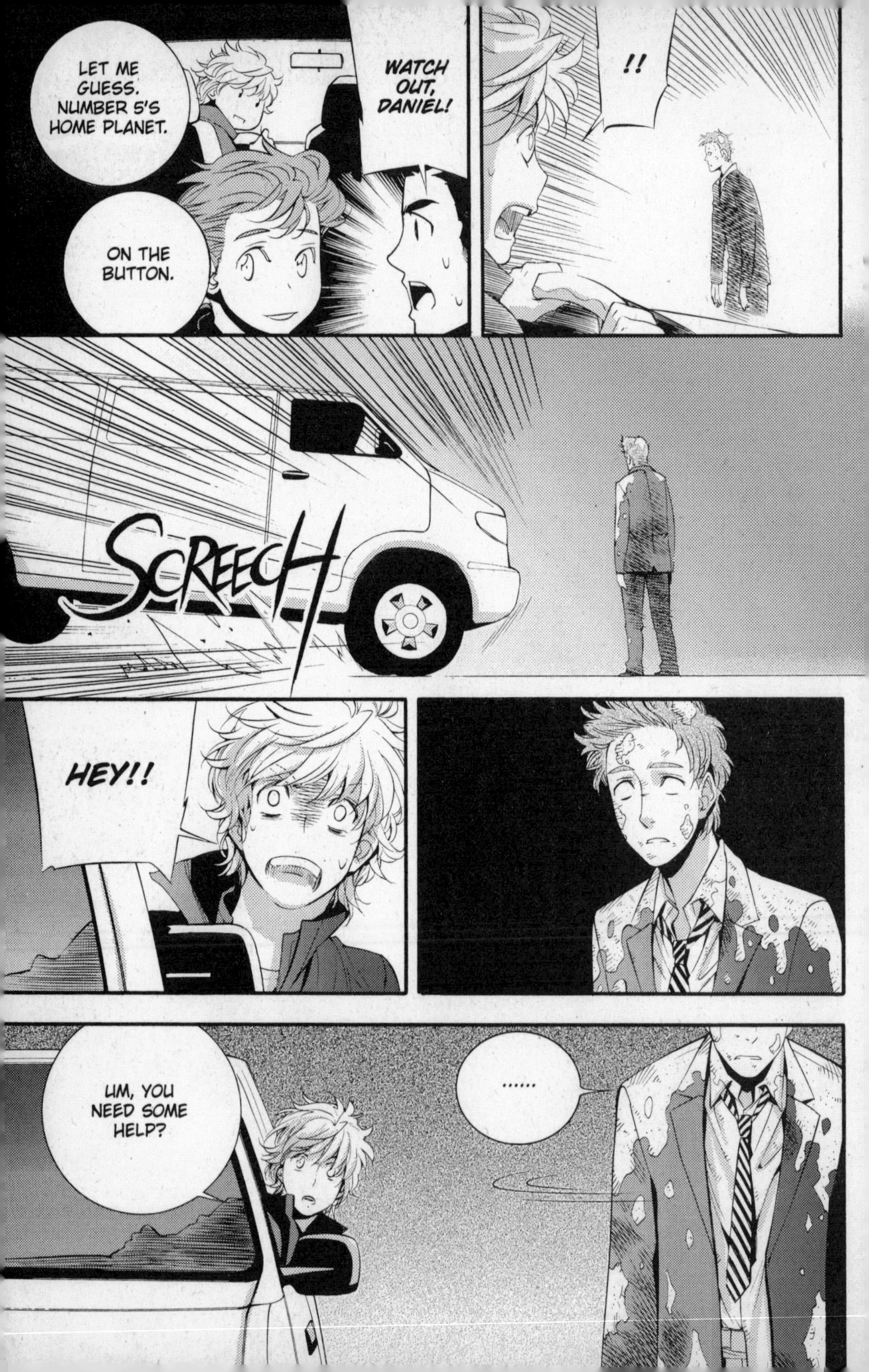
LET ME GUESS. NUMBER 5'S HOME PLANET.
ON THE BUTTON.
WATCH OUT, DANIEL!
!!
SCREECH
HEY!!
UM, YOU NEED SOME HELP?
......

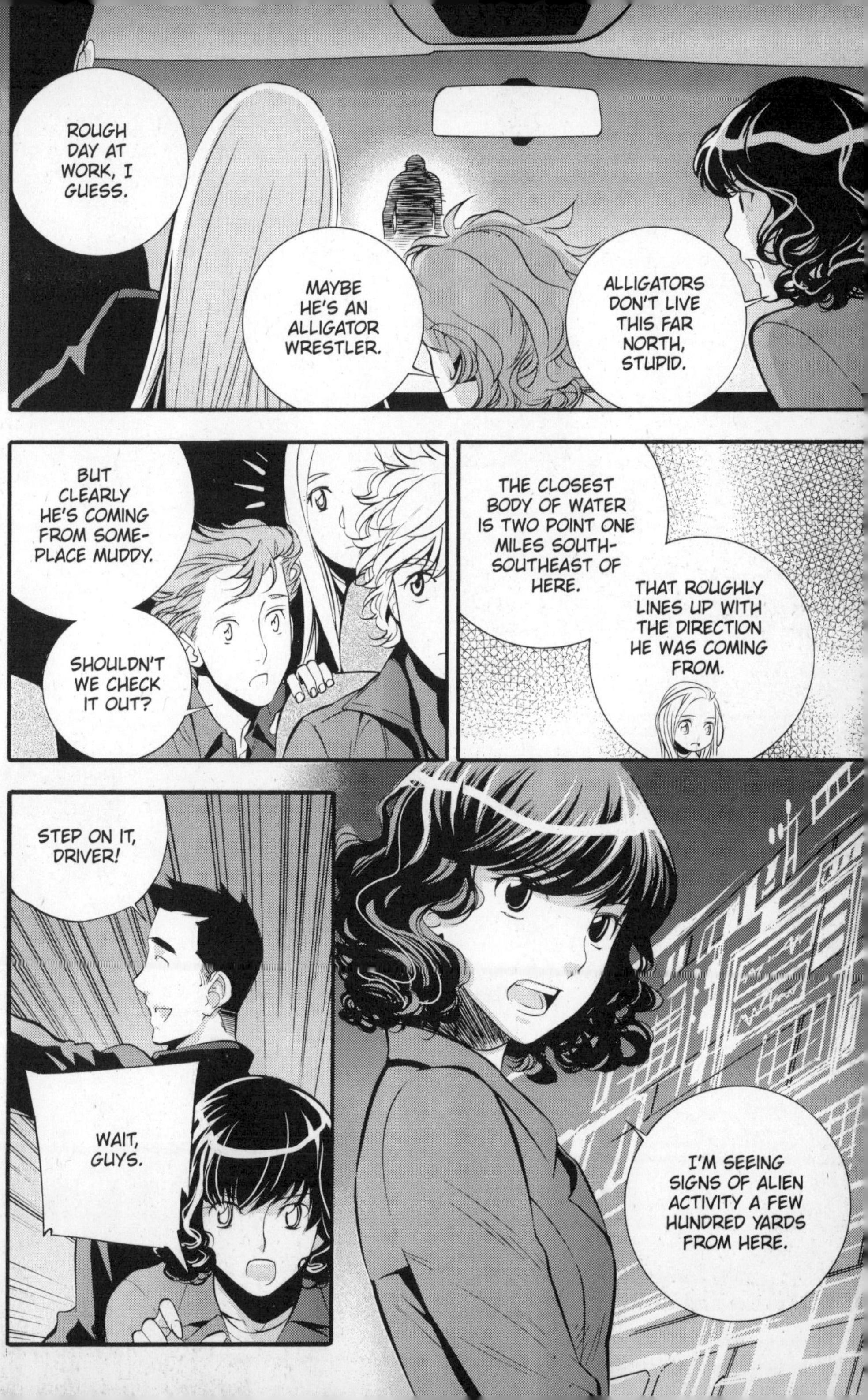
ROUGH DAY AT WORK, I GUESS.
MAYBE HE'S AN ALLIGATOR WRESTLER.
ALLIGATORS DON'T LIVE THIS FAR NORTH, STUPID.
BUT CLEARLY HE'S COMING FROM SOME-PLACE MUDDY.
SHOULDN'T WE CHECK IT OUT?
THE CLOSEST BODY OF WATER IS TWO POINT ONE MILES SOUTH-SOUTHEAST OF HERE.
THAT ROUGHLY LINES UP WITH THE DIRECTION HE WAS COMING FROM.
STEP ON IT, DRIVER!
WAIT, GUYS.
I'M SEEING SIGNS OF ALIEN ACTIVITY A FEW HUNDRED YARDS FROM HERE.

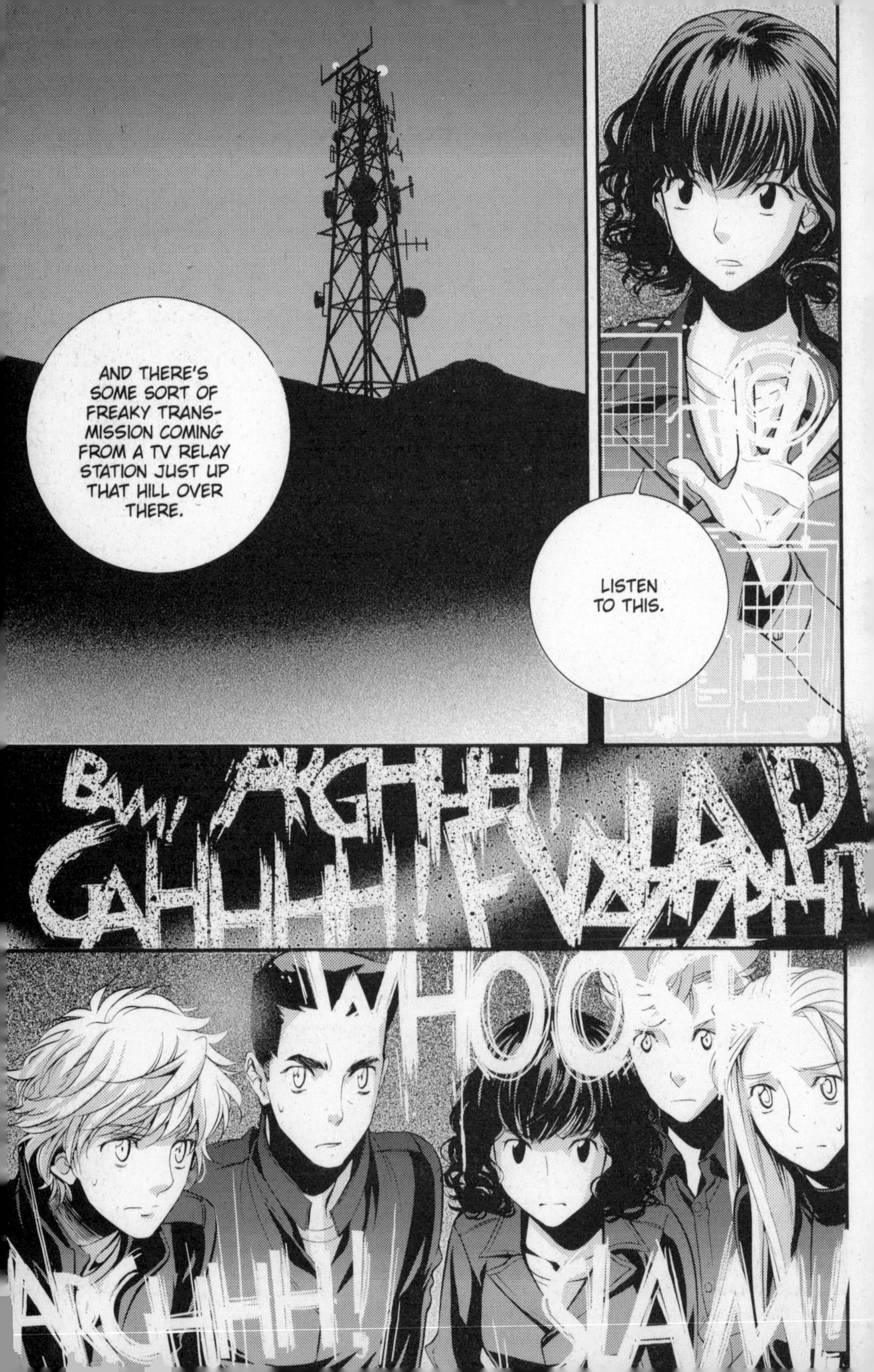
AND THERE'S SOME SORT OF FREAKY TRANS-MISSION COMING FROM A TV RELAY STATION JUST UP THAT HILL OVER THERE.
LISTEN TO THIS.
BAM!
SLAM!

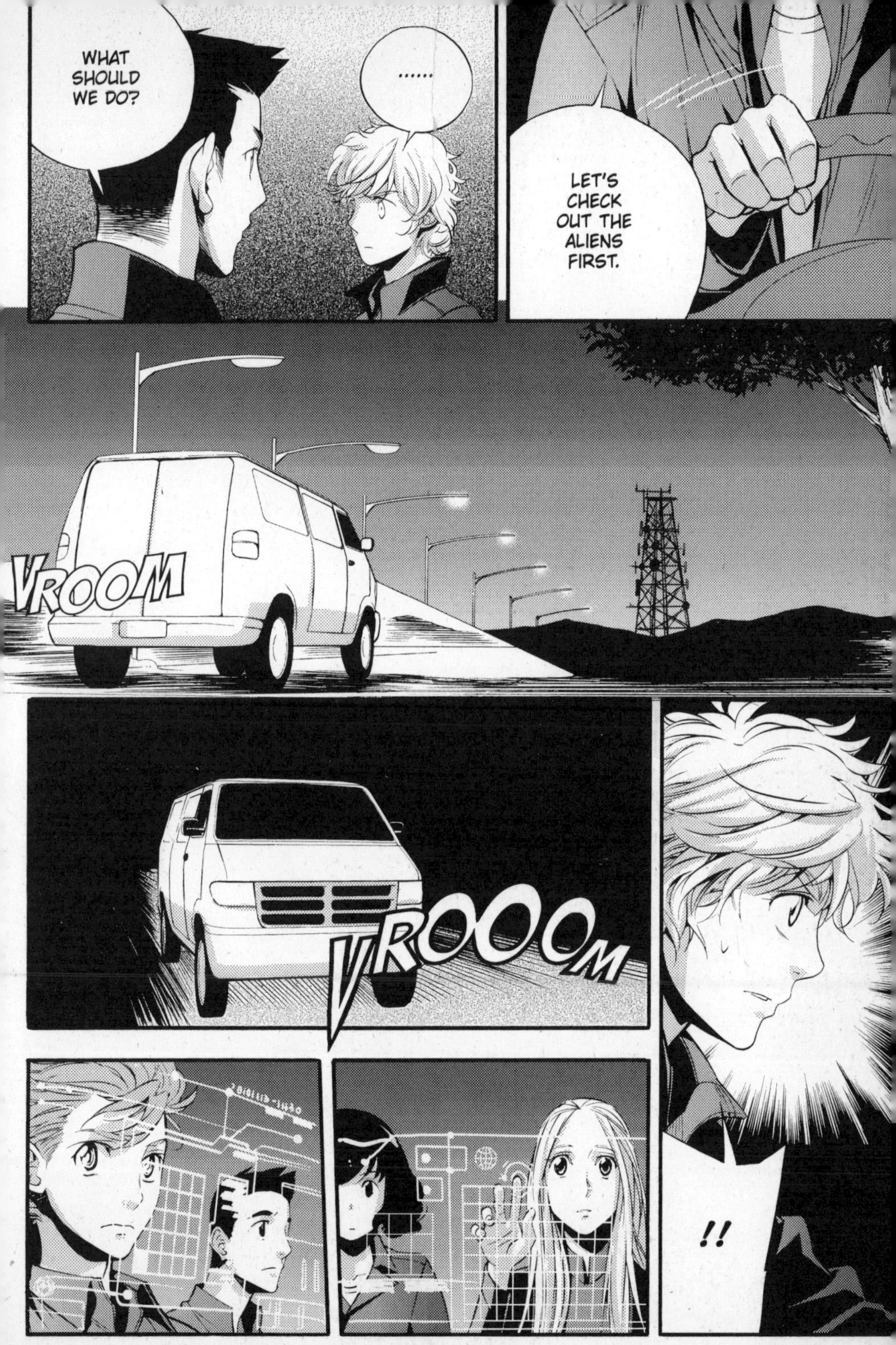
WHAT SHOULD WE DO?
......
LET'S CHECK OUT THE ALIENS FIRST.
VROOM
VROOOM
!!

DO YOU SEE SOMETHING?

WHAT IS IT?

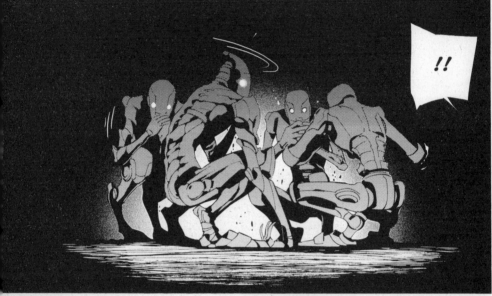

!!

?

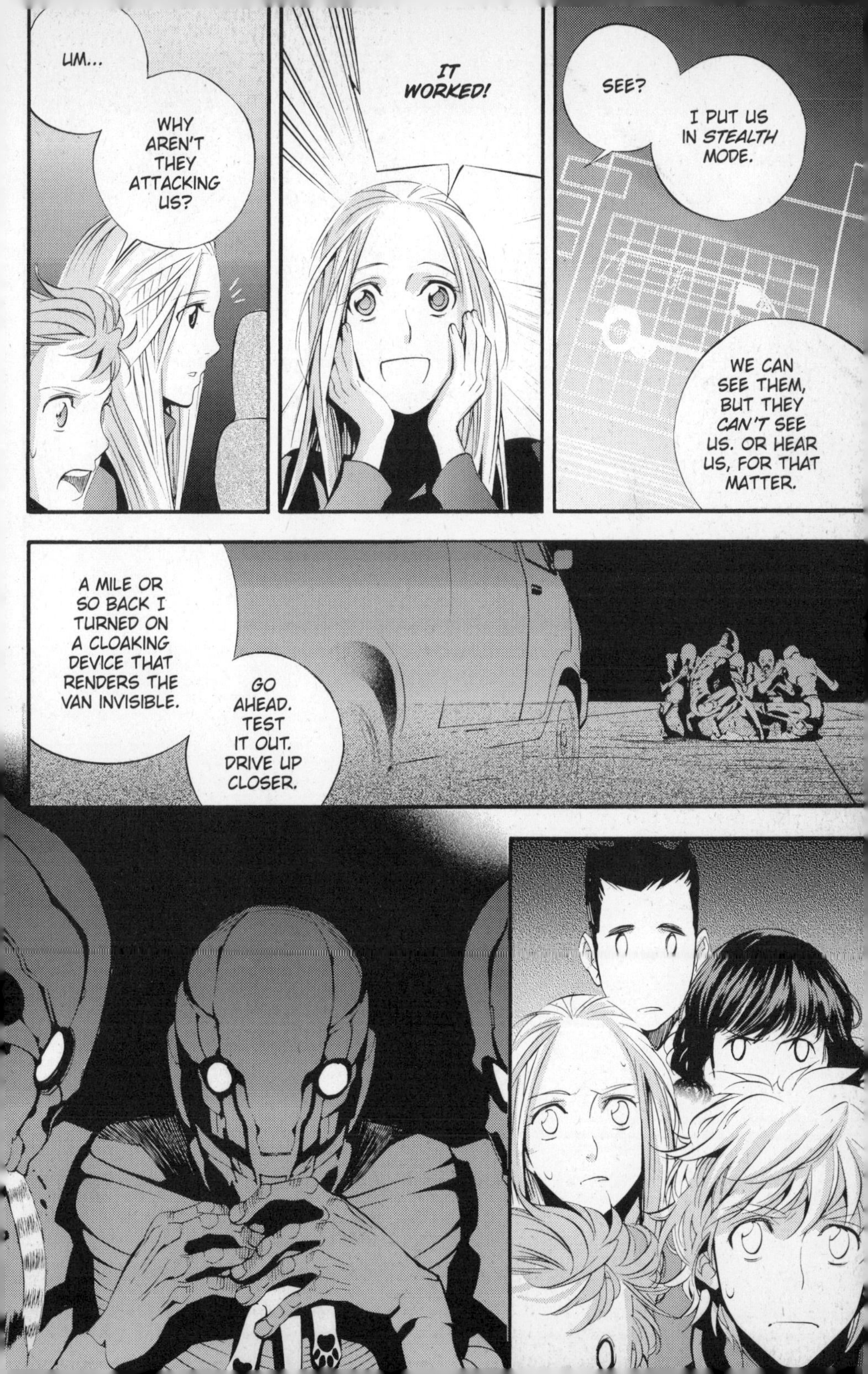
UM...
WHY AREN'T THEY ATTACKING US?
IT WORKED!
SEE?
I PUT US IN STEALTH MODE.
WE CAN SEE THEM, BUT THEY CAN'T SEE US. OR HEAR US, FOR THAT MATTER.
A MILE OR SO BACK I TURNED ON A CLOAKING DEVICE THAT RENDERS THE VAN INVISIBLE.
GO AHEAD. TEST IT OUT. DRIVE UP CLOSER.

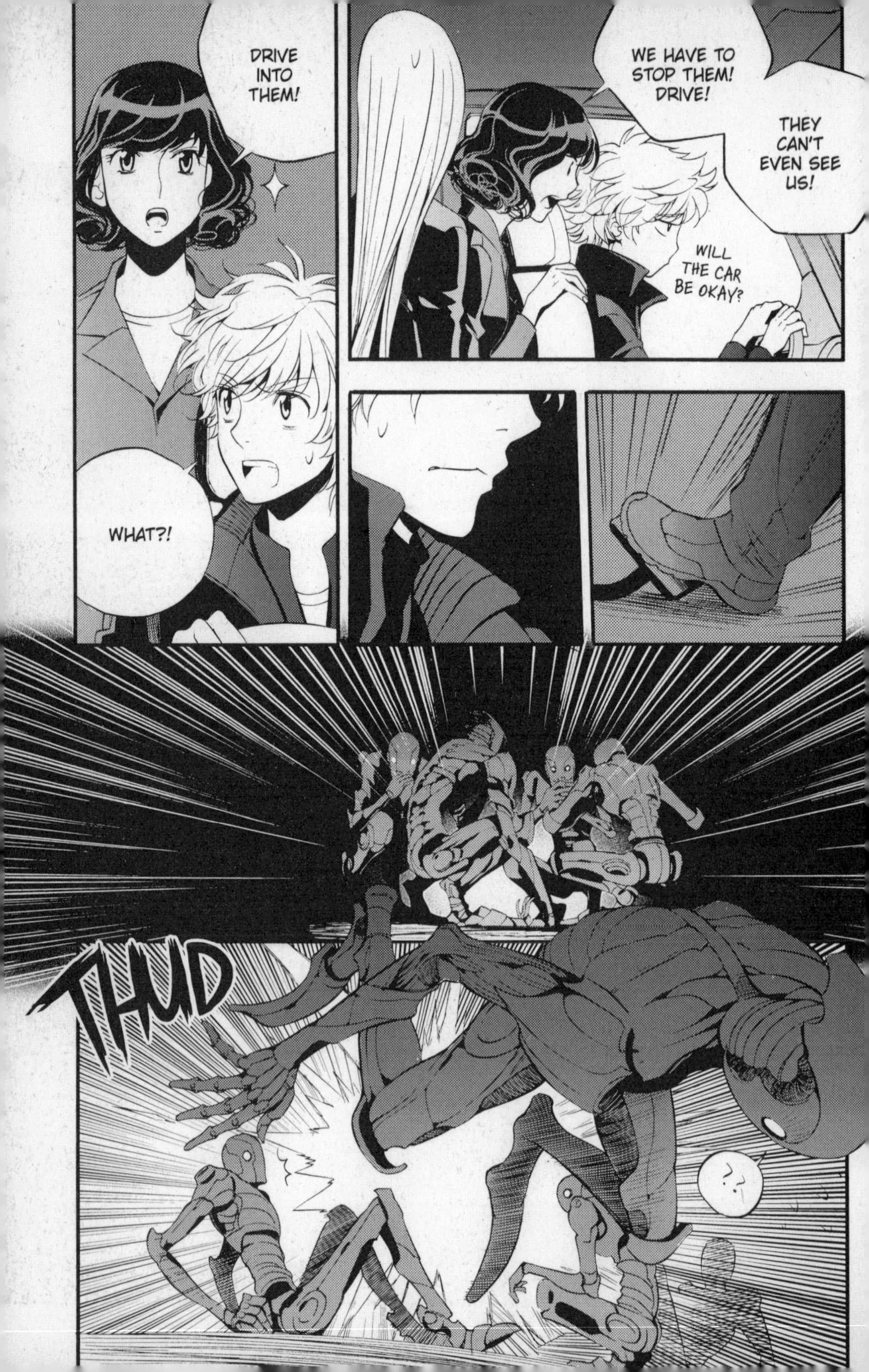
DRIVE INTO THEM!
WHAT?!
WE HAVE TO STOP THEM! DRIVE!
THEY CAN'T EVEN SEE US!
WILL THE CAR BE OKAY?
THUD
?

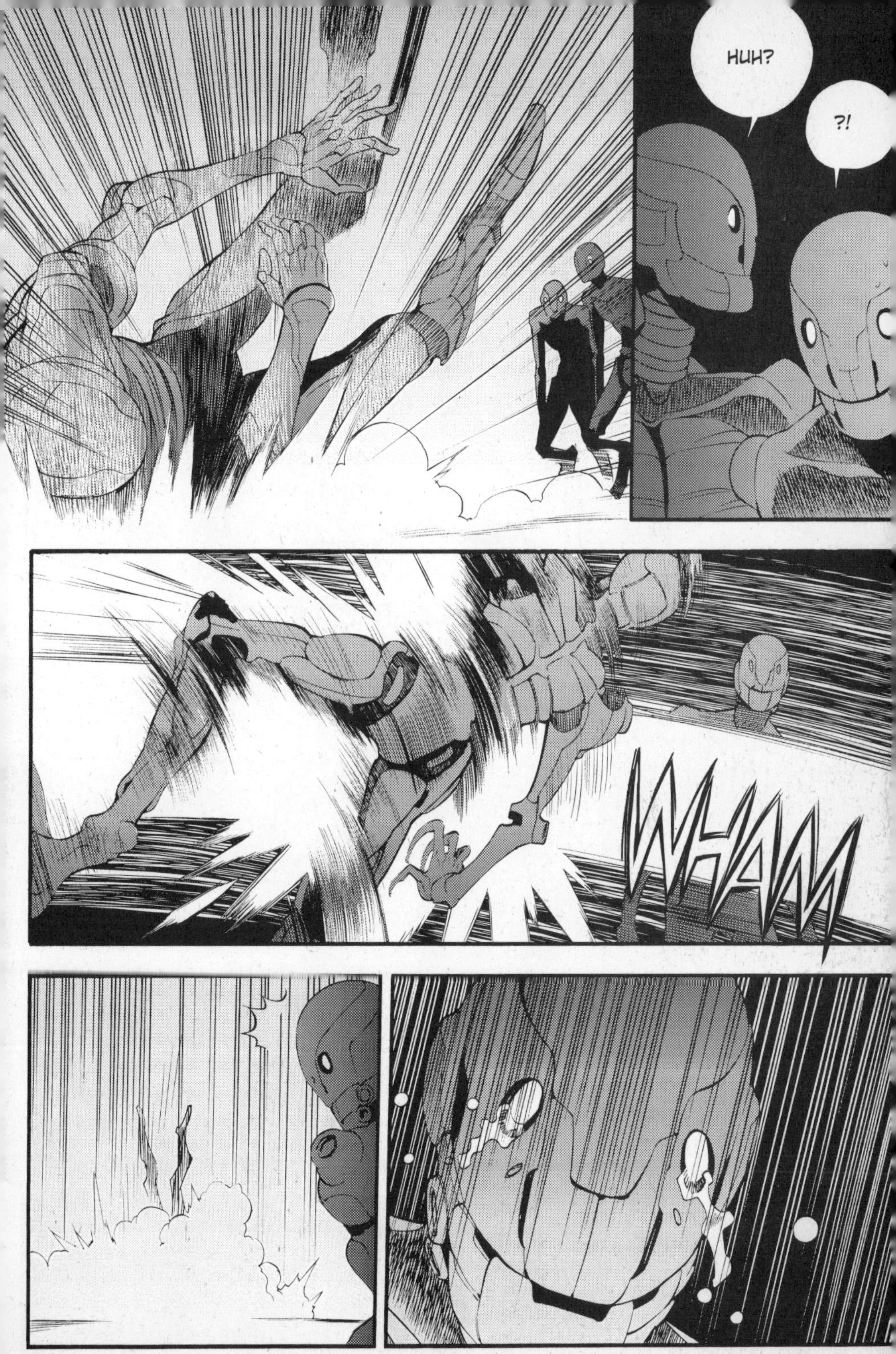
HUH?
?!
WHAM

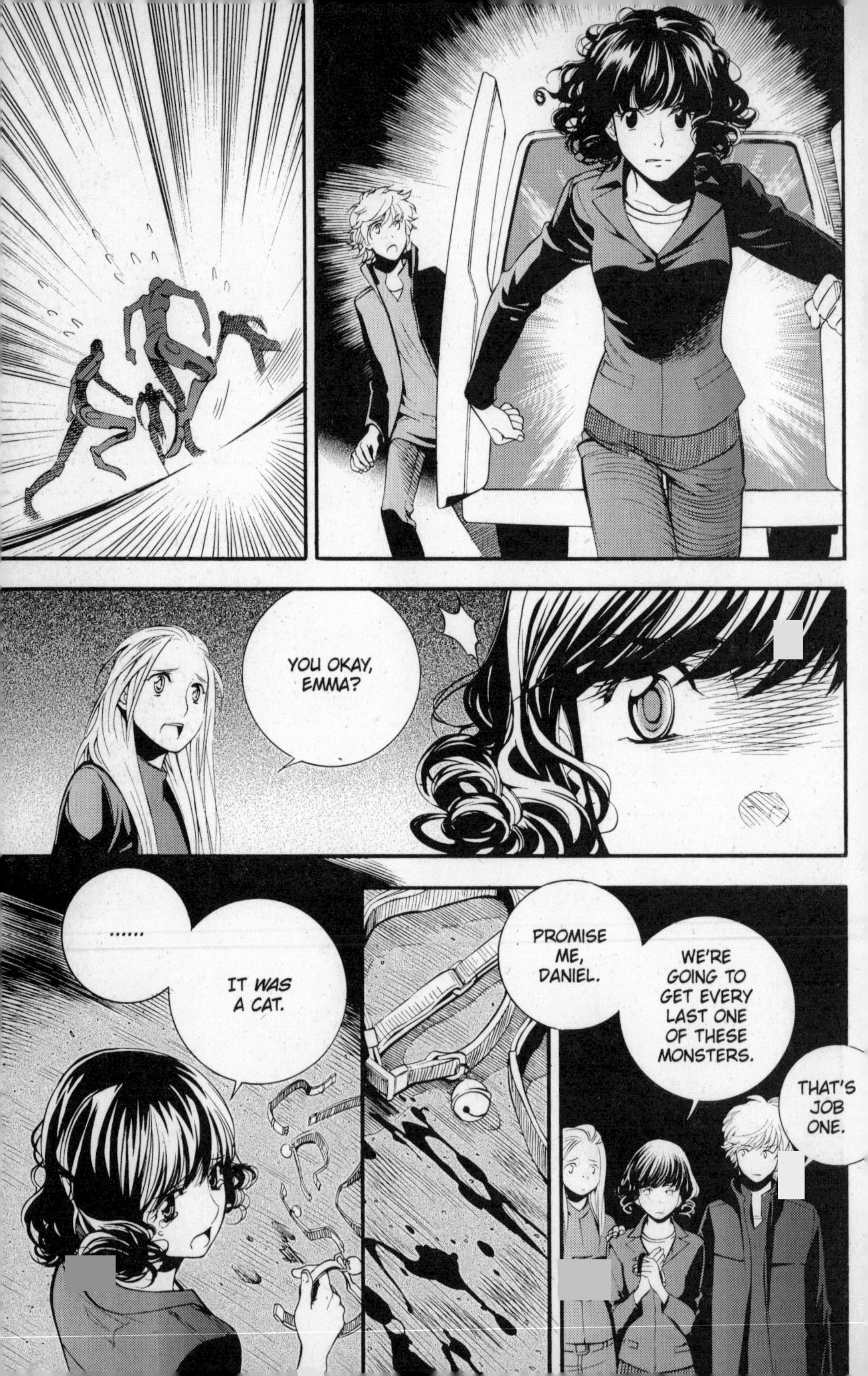
YOU OKAY, EMMA?
......
IT *WAS* A CAT.
PROMISE ME, DANIEL.
WE'RE GOING TO GET EVERY LAST ONE OF THESE MONSTERS.
THAT'S JOB ONE.

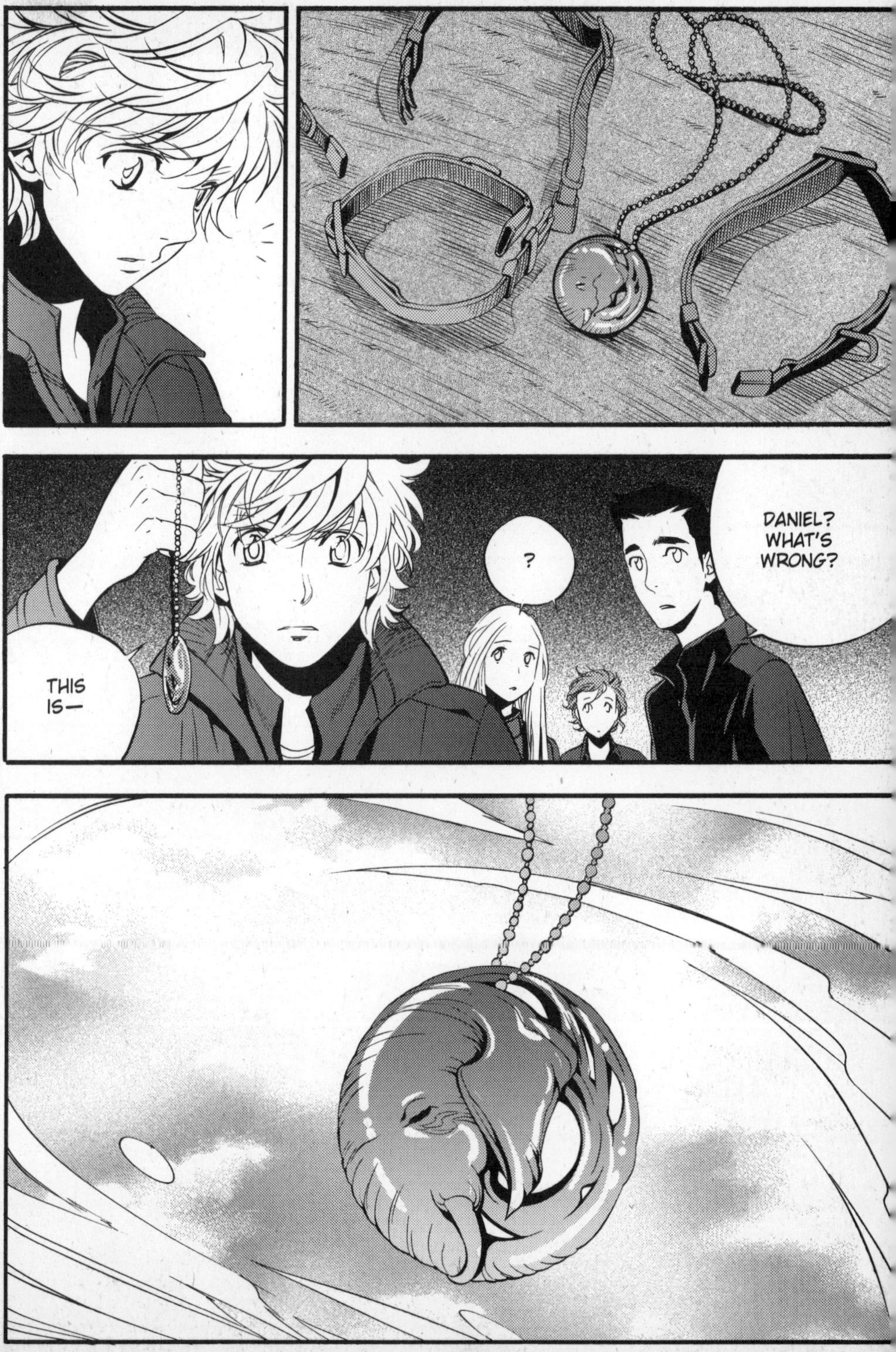
THIS IS—
?
DANIEL? WHAT'S WRONG?

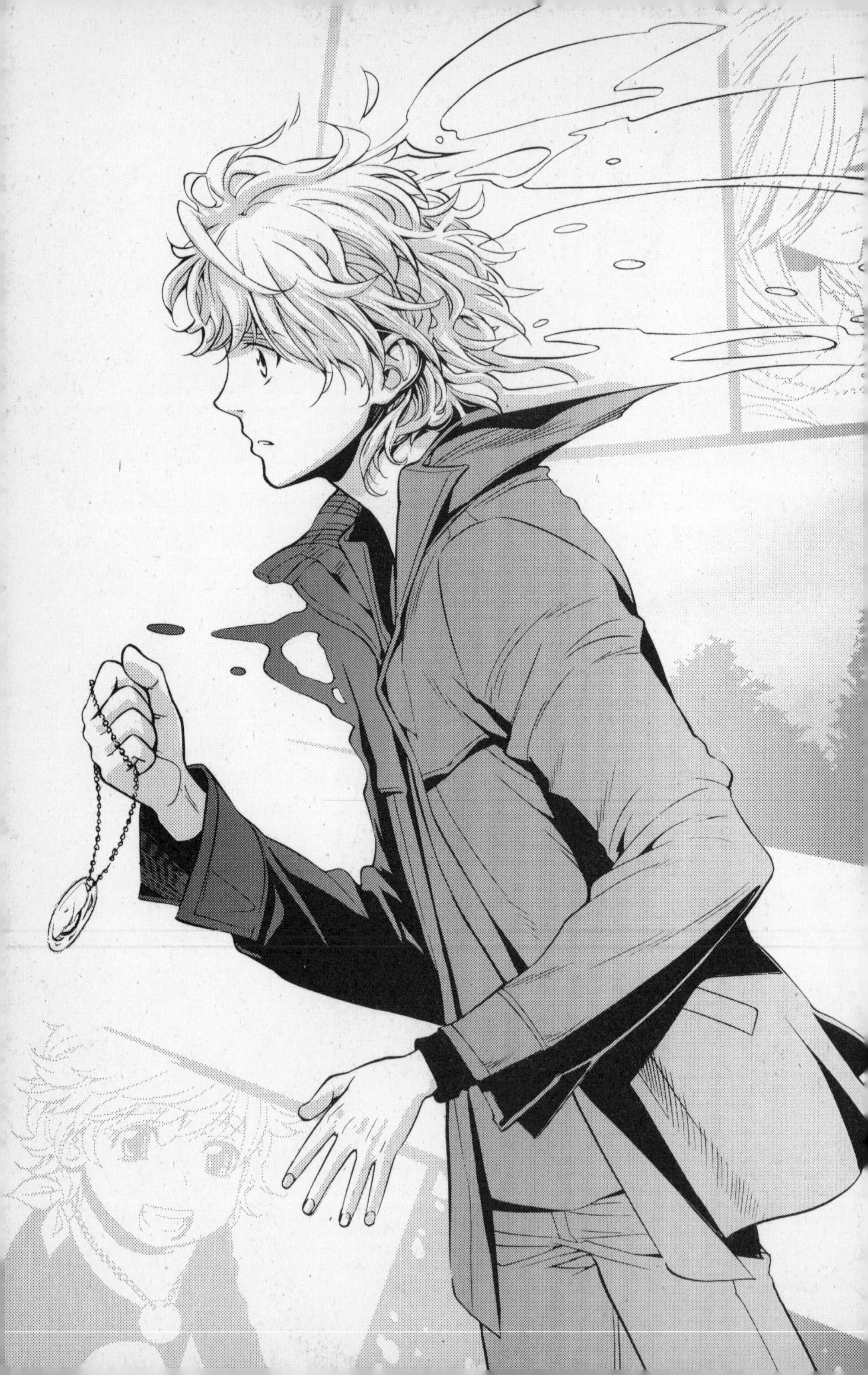

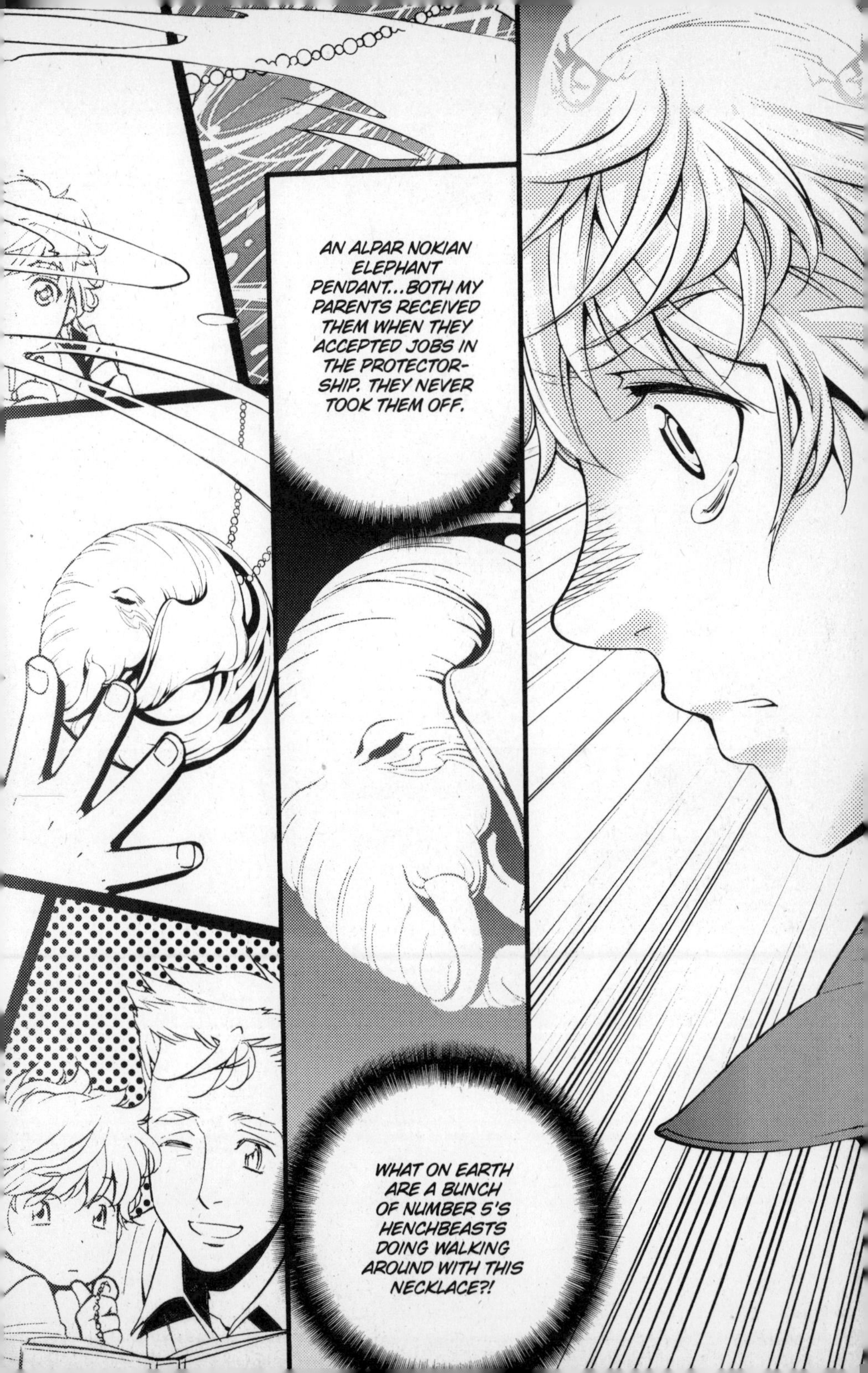
AN ALPAR NOKIAN ELEPHANT PENDANT...BOTH MY PARENTS RECEIVED THEM WHEN THEY ACCEPTED JOBS IN THE PROTECTOR-SHIP. THEY NEVER TOOK THEM OFF.
WHAT ON EARTH ARE A BUNCH OF NUMBER 5'S HENCHBEASTS DOING WALKING AROUND WITH THIS NECKLACE?!

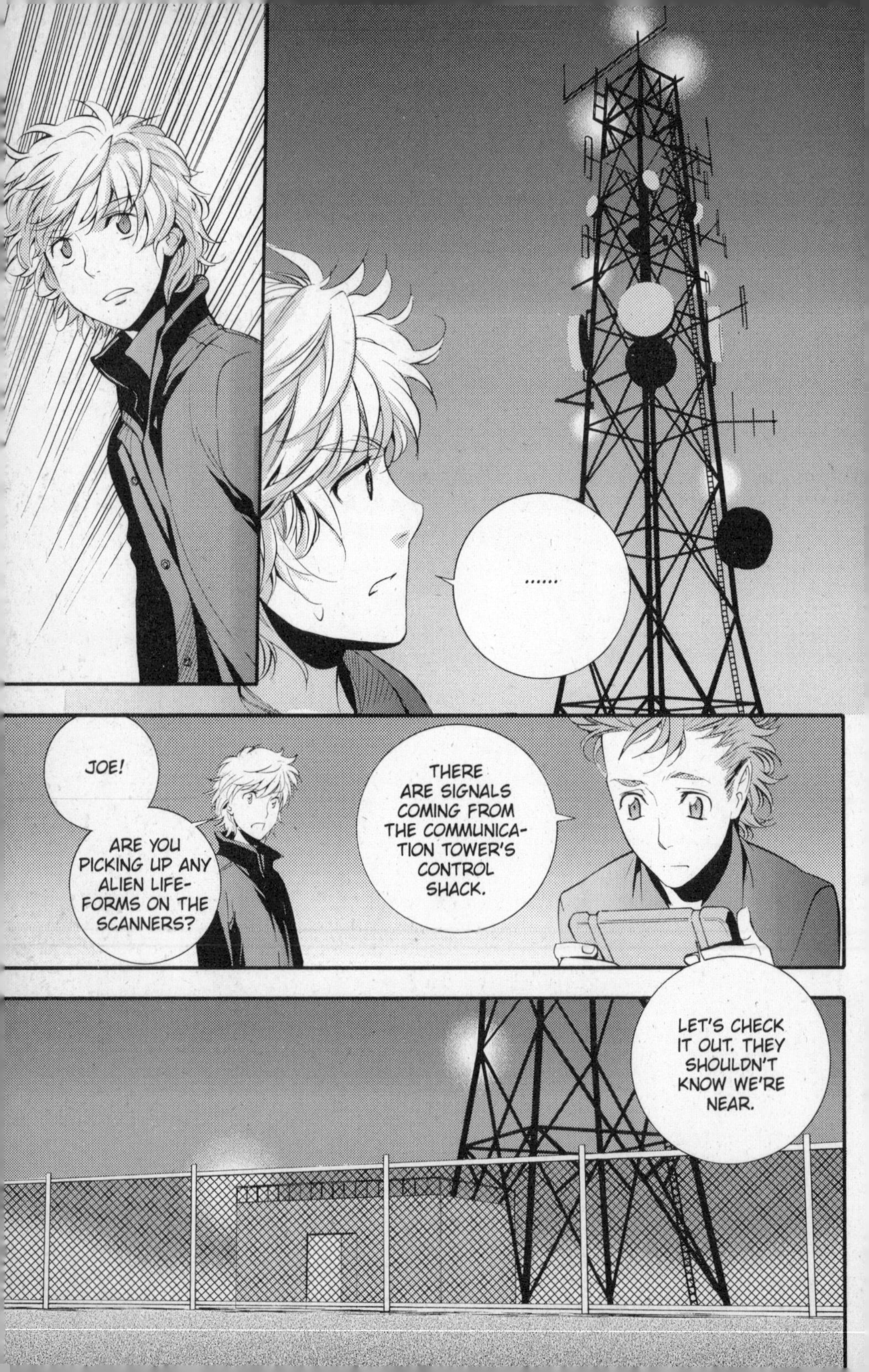

......
JOE!
ARE YOU PICKING UP ANY ALIEN LIFE-FORMS ON THE SCANNERS?
THERE ARE SIGNALS COMING FROM THE COMMUNICATION TOWER'S CONTROL SHACK.
LET'S CHECK IT OUT. THEY SHOULDN'T KNOW WE'RE NEAR.

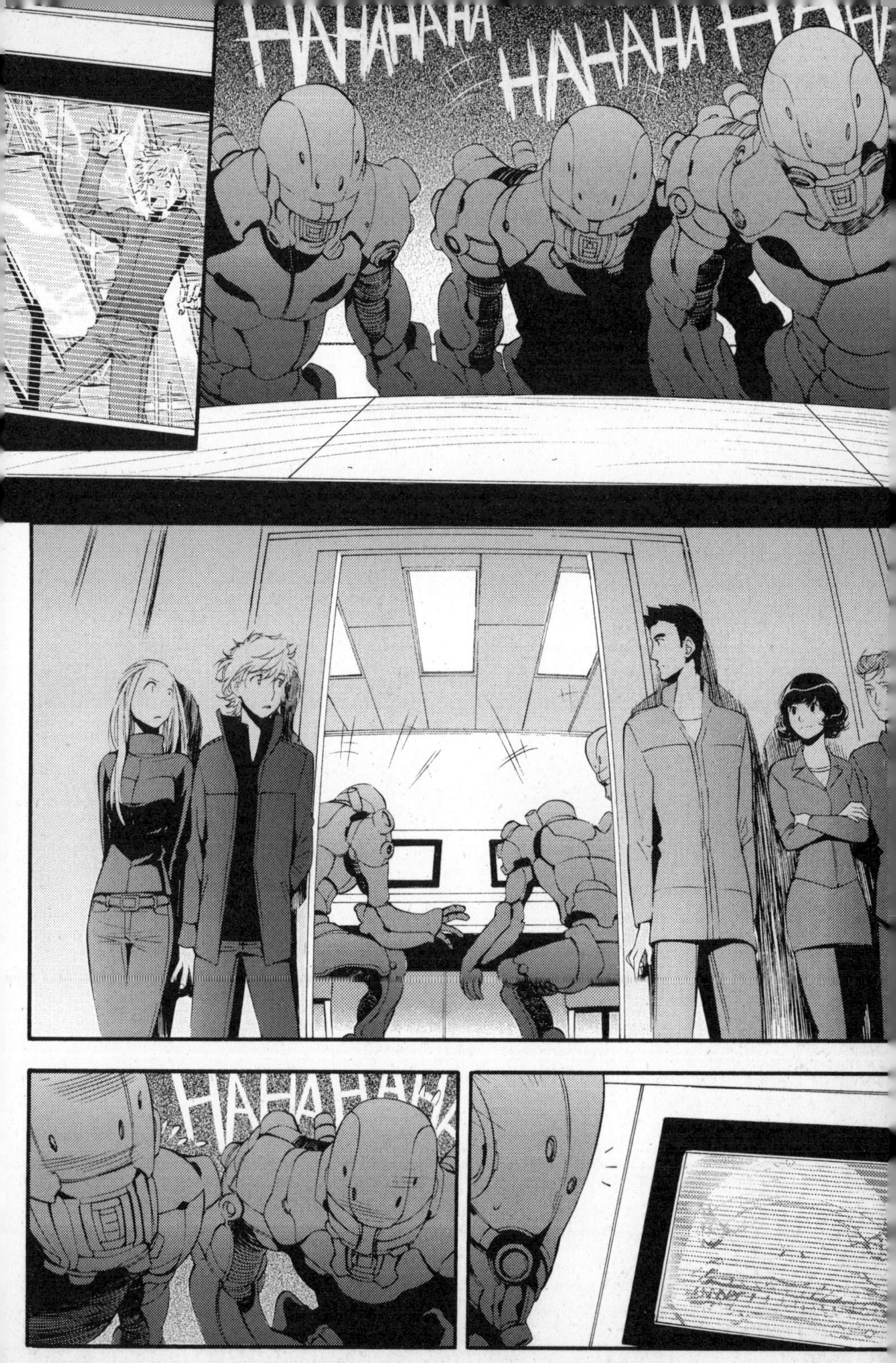
HAHAHAHA
HAHAHA
HAHAHA

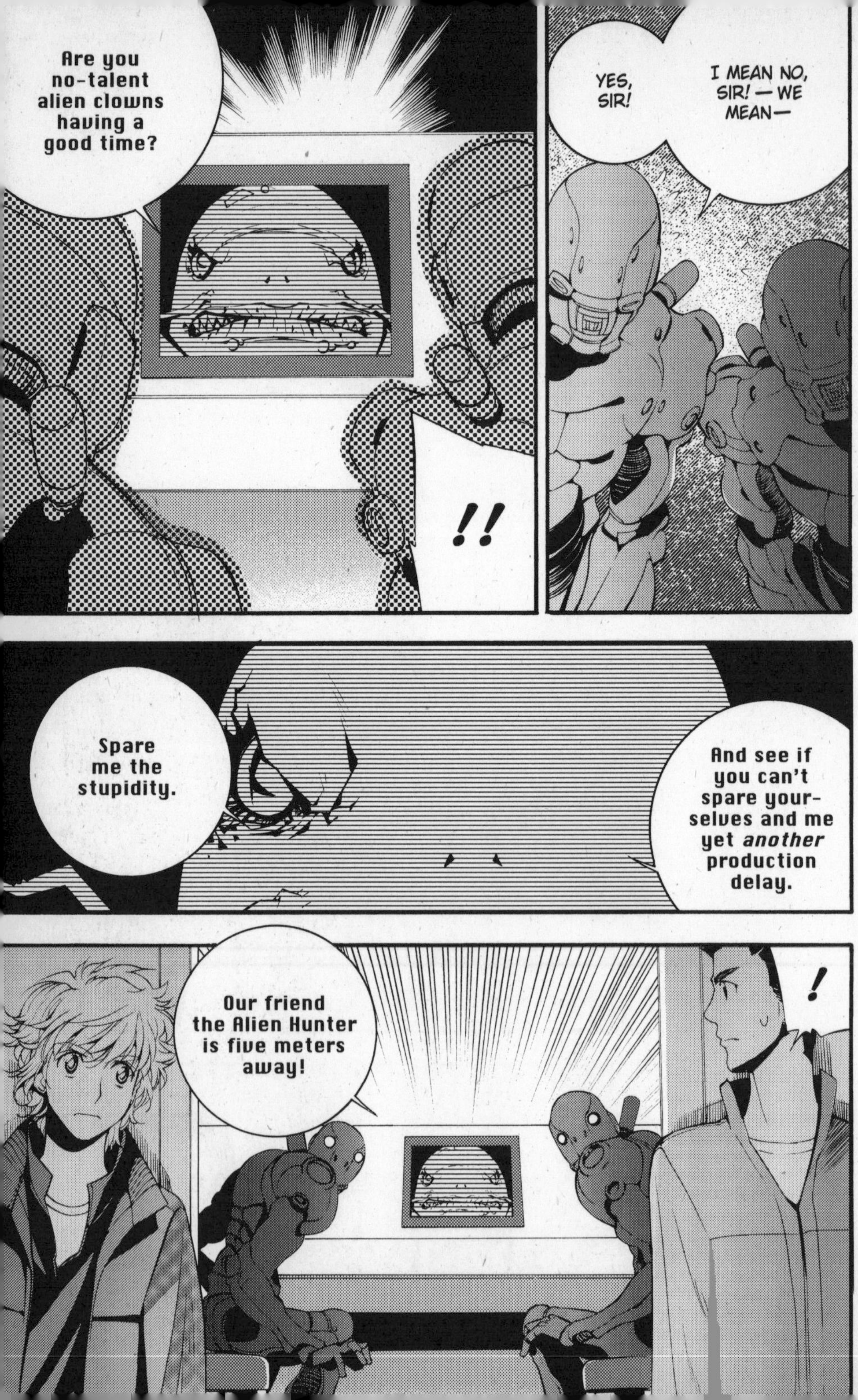
Are you no-talent alien clowns having a good time?
!!
YES, SIR!
I MEAN NO, SIR! — WE MEAN—
Spare me the stupidity.
And see if you can't spare your-selves and me yet *another* production delay.
Our friend the Alien Hunter is five meters away!
!

DANIEL X

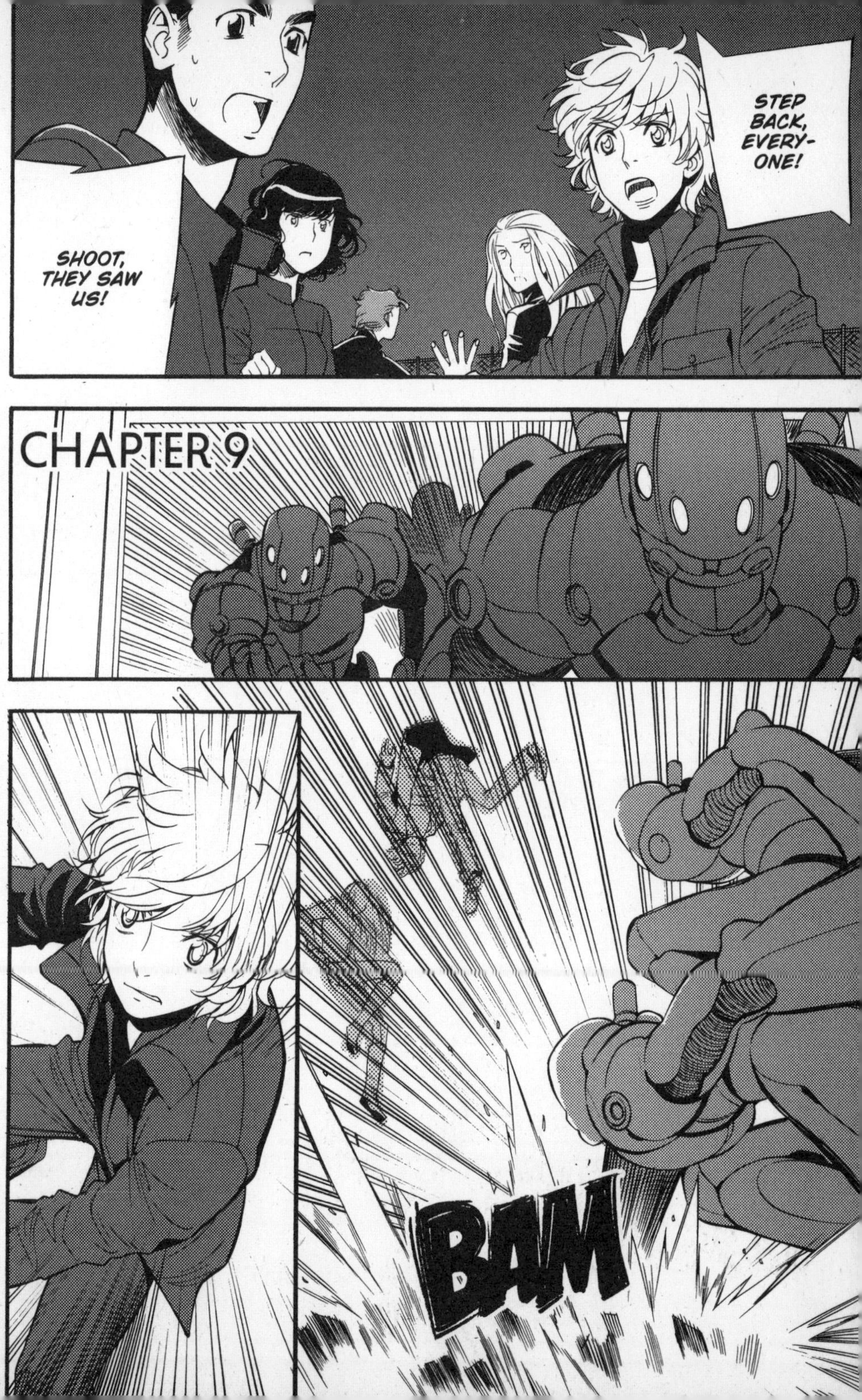
SHOOT, THEY SAW US!
STEP BACK, EVERY-ONE!
CHAPTER 9
BAM

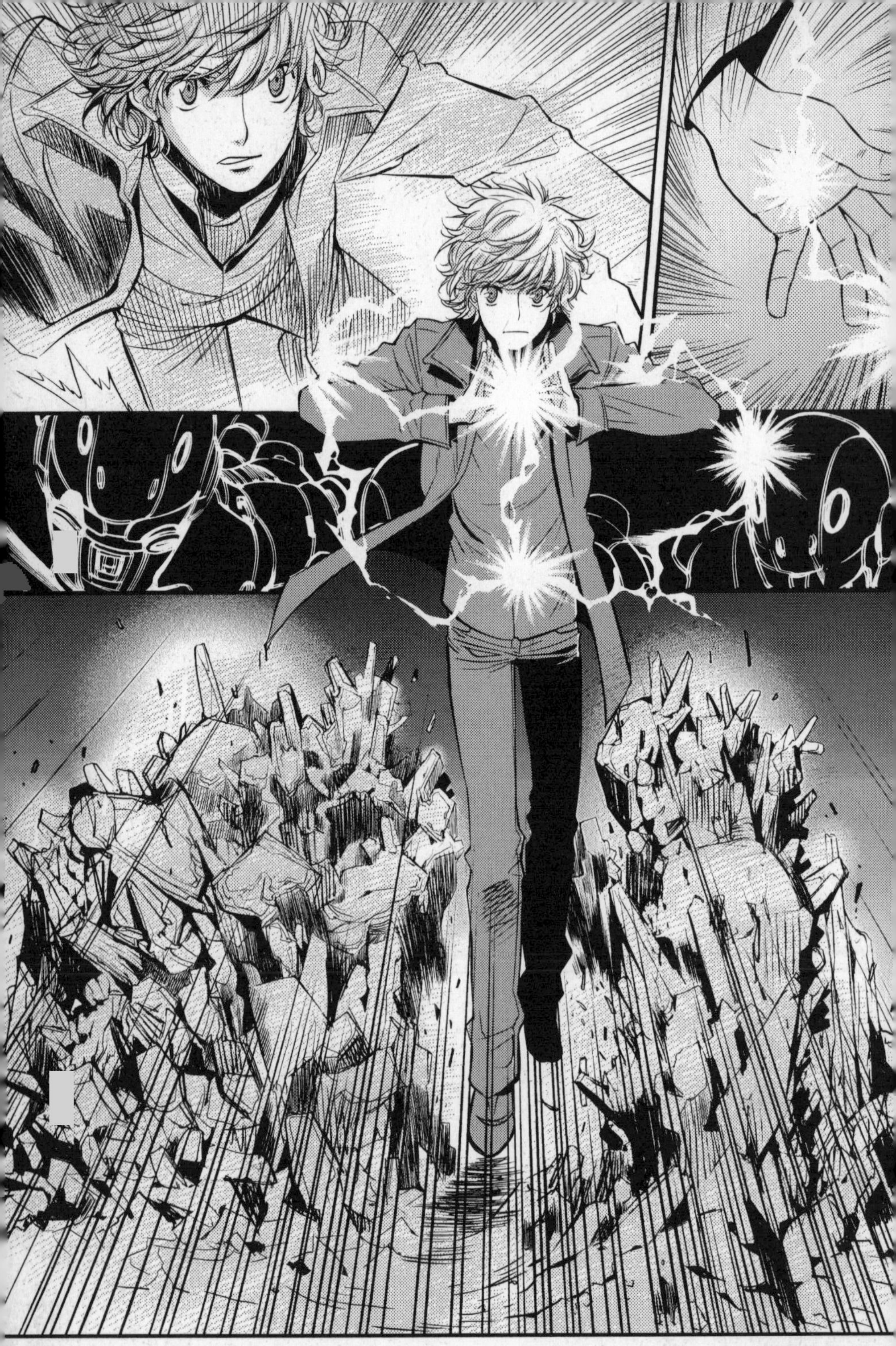

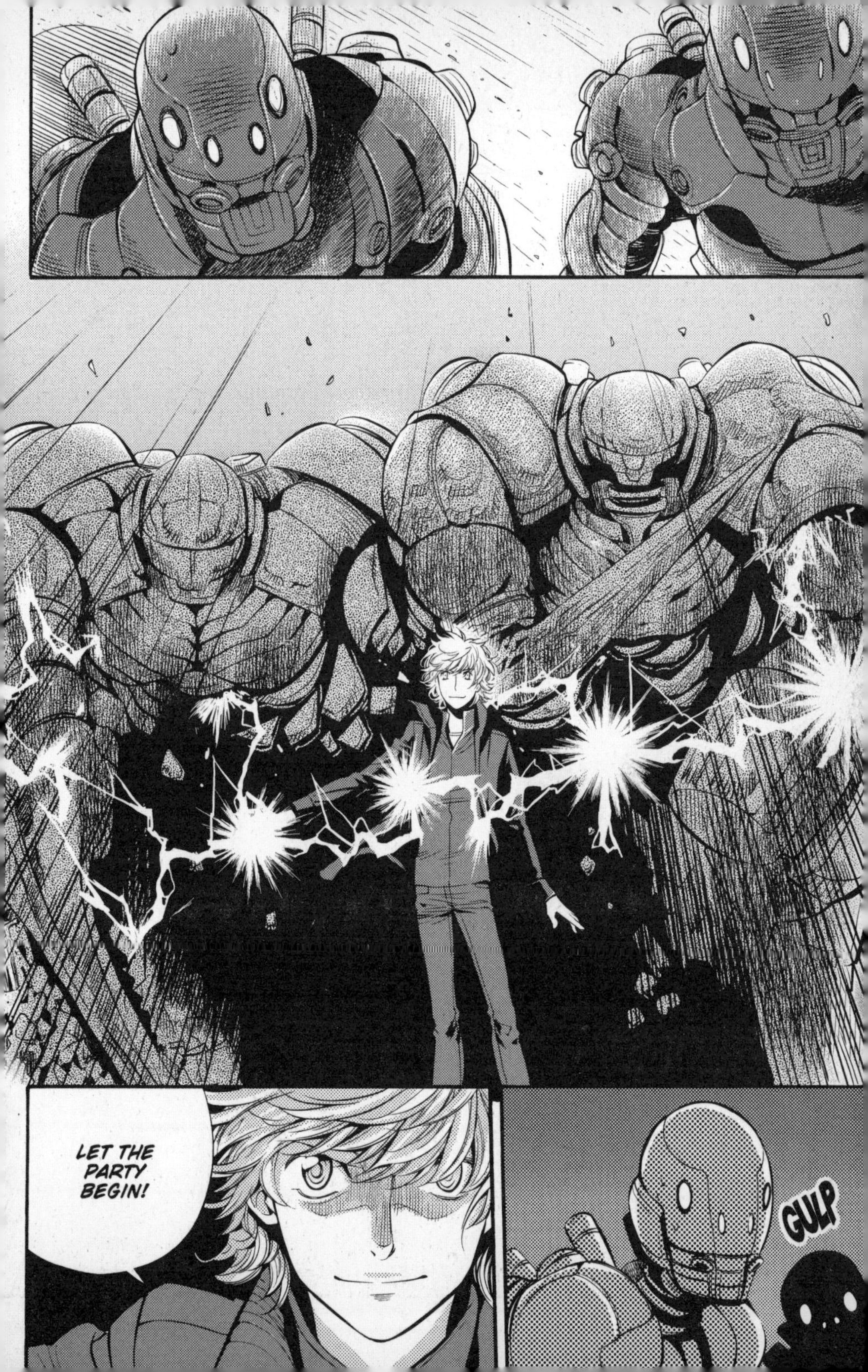
LET THE PARTY BEGIN!
GULP

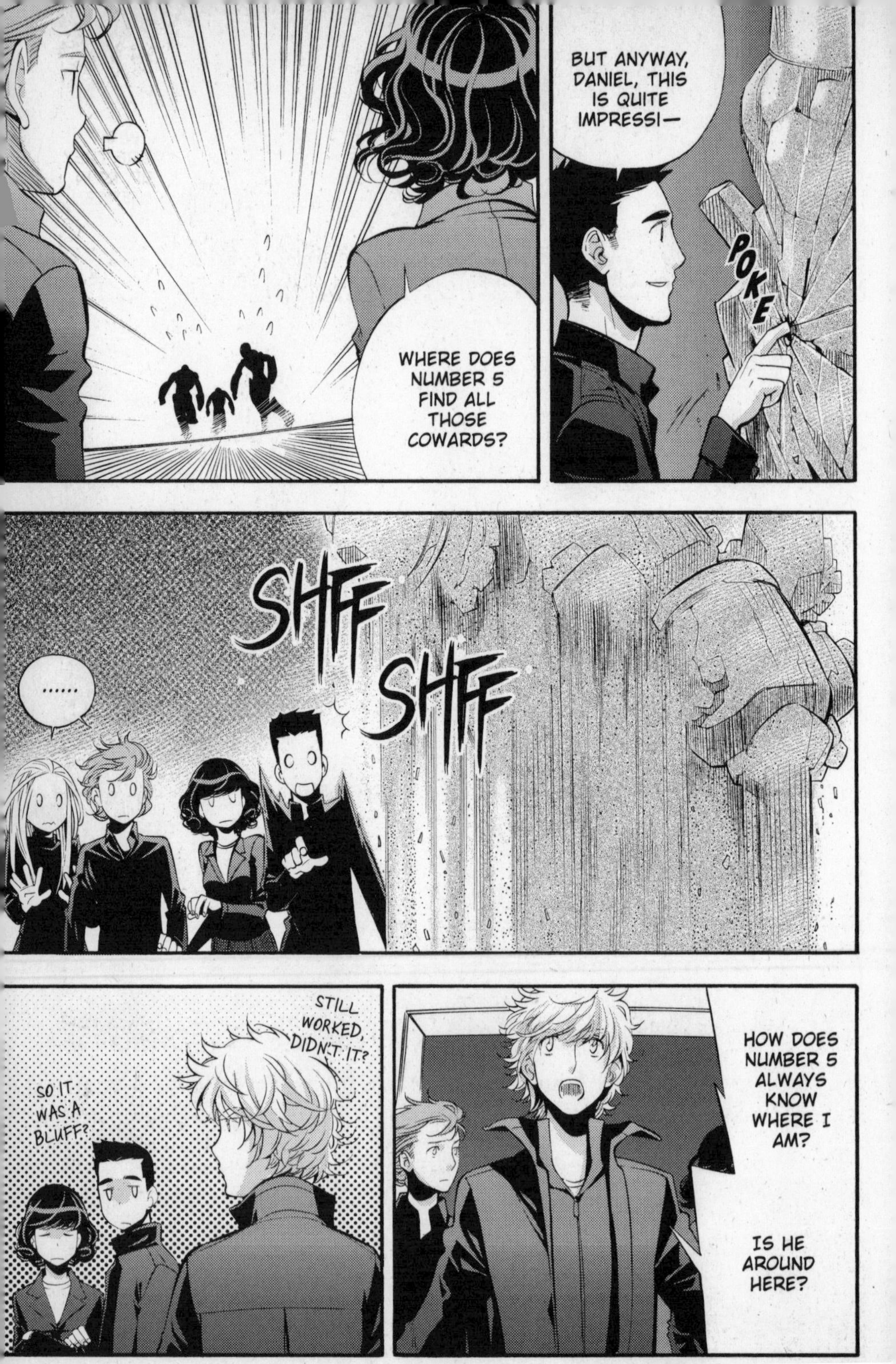

WHERE DOES NUMBER 5 FIND ALL THOSE COWARDS?
BUT ANYWAY, DANIEL, THIS IS QUITE IMPRESSI—
POKE
SHFF
SHFF
......
STILL WORKED, DIDN'T IT?
SO IT WAS A BLUFF?
HOW DOES NUMBER 5 ALWAYS KNOW WHERE I AM?
IS HE AROUND HERE?

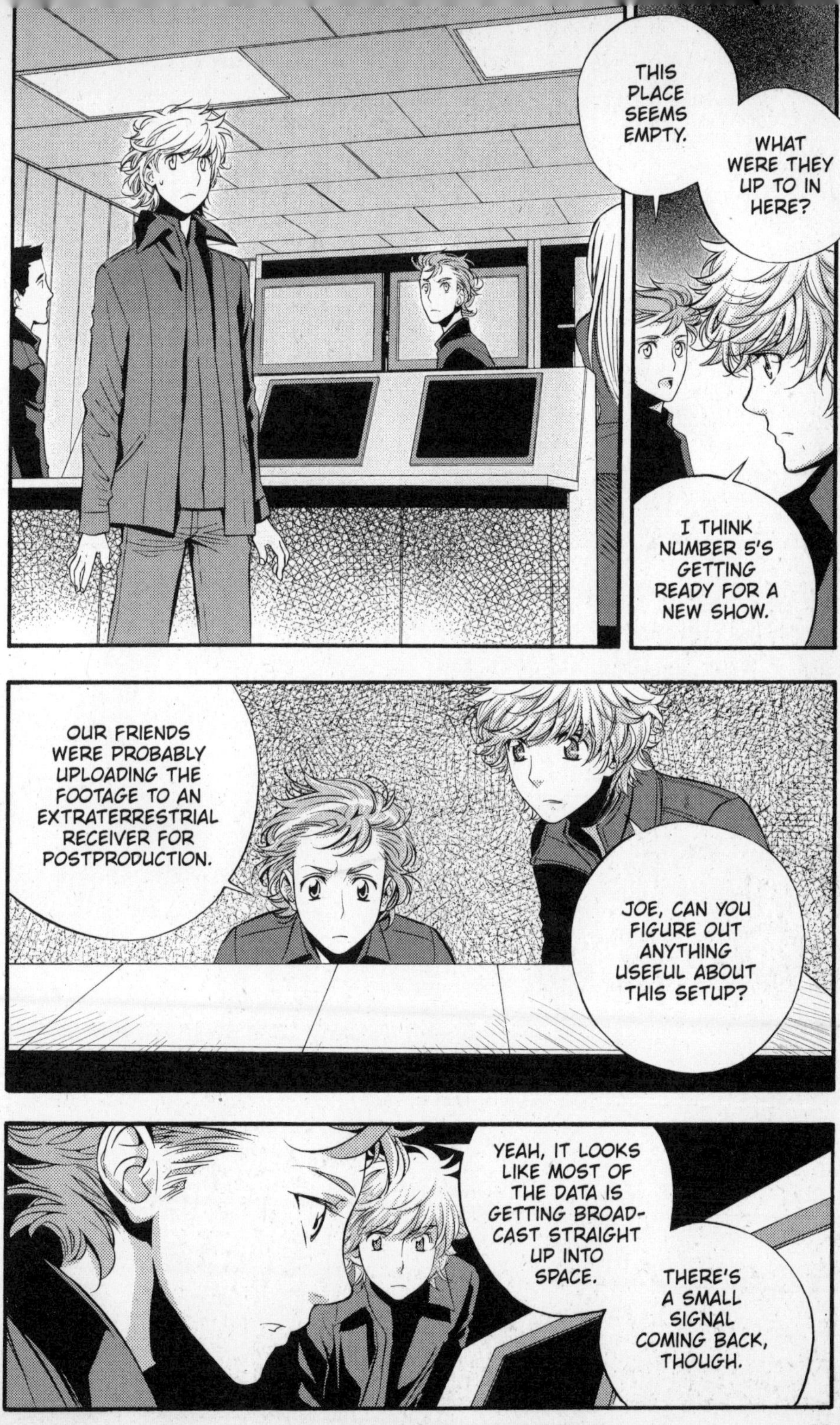
THIS PLACE SEEMS EMPTY.
WHAT WERE THEY UP TO IN HERE?
I THINK NUMBER 5'S GETTING READY FOR A NEW SHOW.
OUR FRIENDS WERE PROBABLY UPLOADING THE FOOTAGE TO AN EXTRATERRESTRIAL RECEIVER FOR POSTPRODUCTION.
JOE, CAN YOU FIGURE OUT ANYTHING USEFUL ABOUT THIS SETUP?
YEAH, IT LOOKS LIKE MOST OF THE DATA IS GETTING BROAD-CAST STRAIGHT UP INTO SPACE.
THERE'S A SMALL SIGNAL COMING BACK, THOUGH.

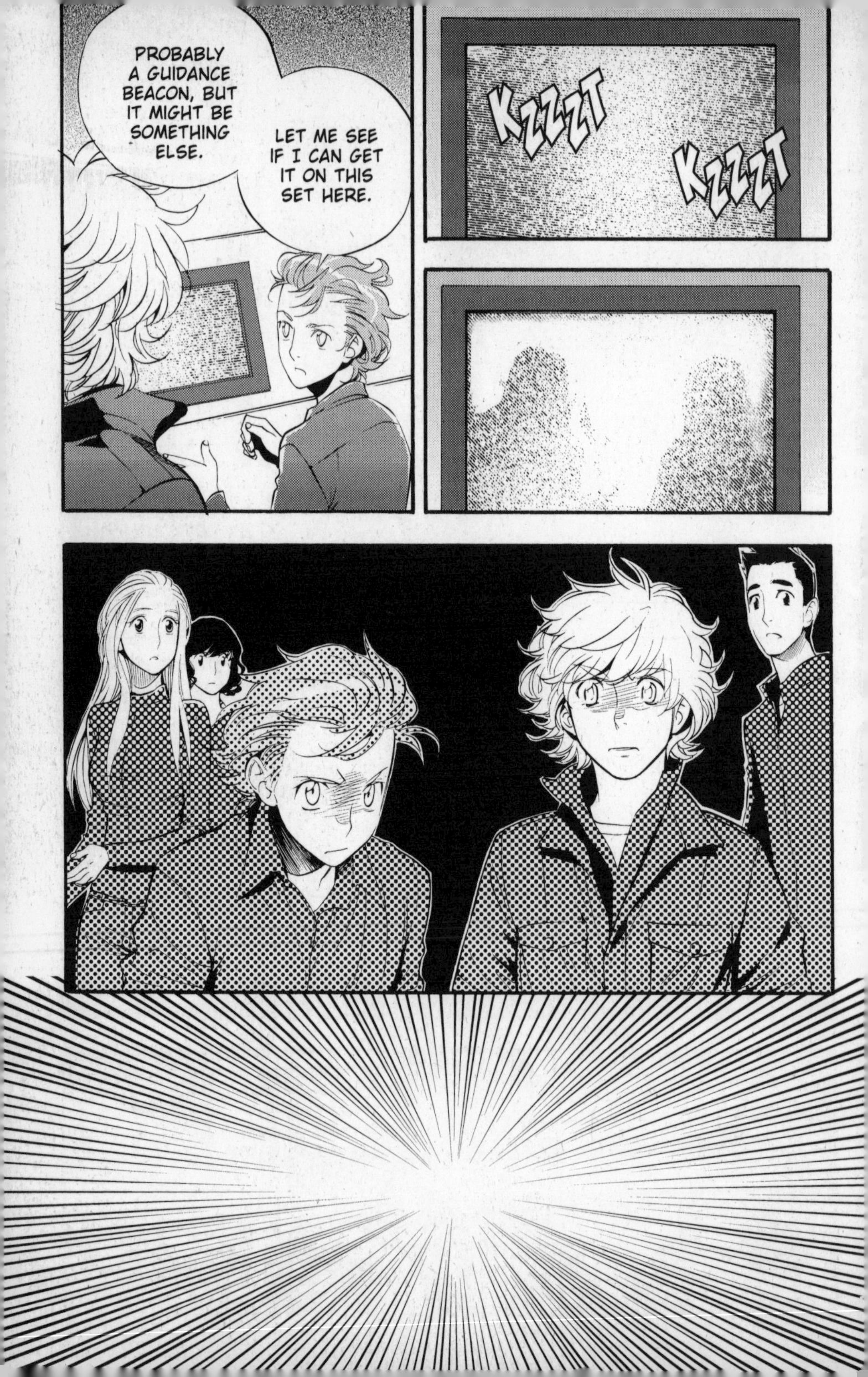
PROBABLY A GUIDANCE BEACON, BUT IT MIGHT BE SOMETHING ELSE.
LET ME SEE IF I CAN GET IT ON THIS SET HERE.
KZZZT
KZZZT

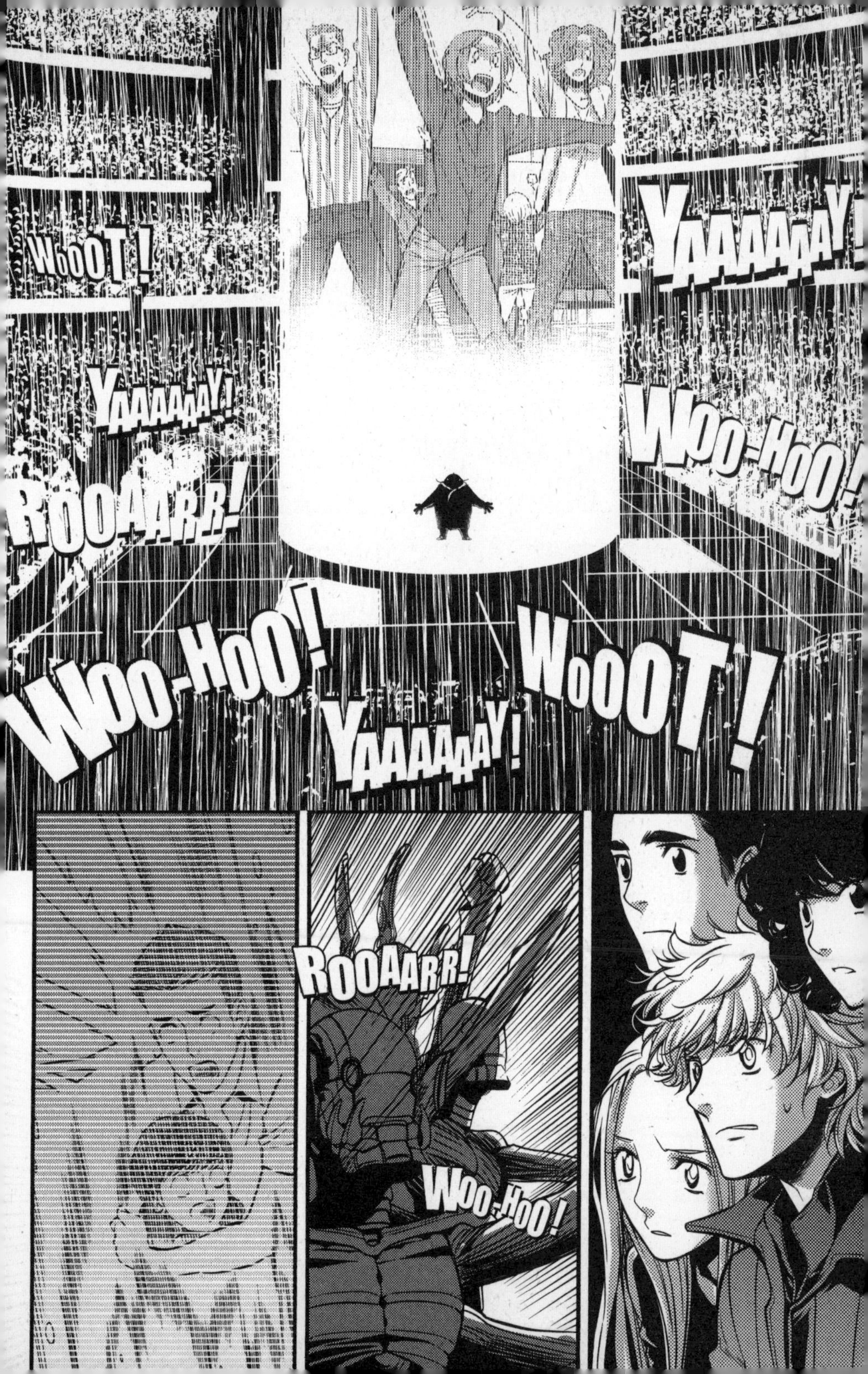
WOOOT!
YAAAAAAY!
ROOAARR!
YAAAAAAY!
WOO-HOO!
WOO-HOO!
YAAAAAAY!
WOOOT!
ROOAARR!
WOO-HOO!

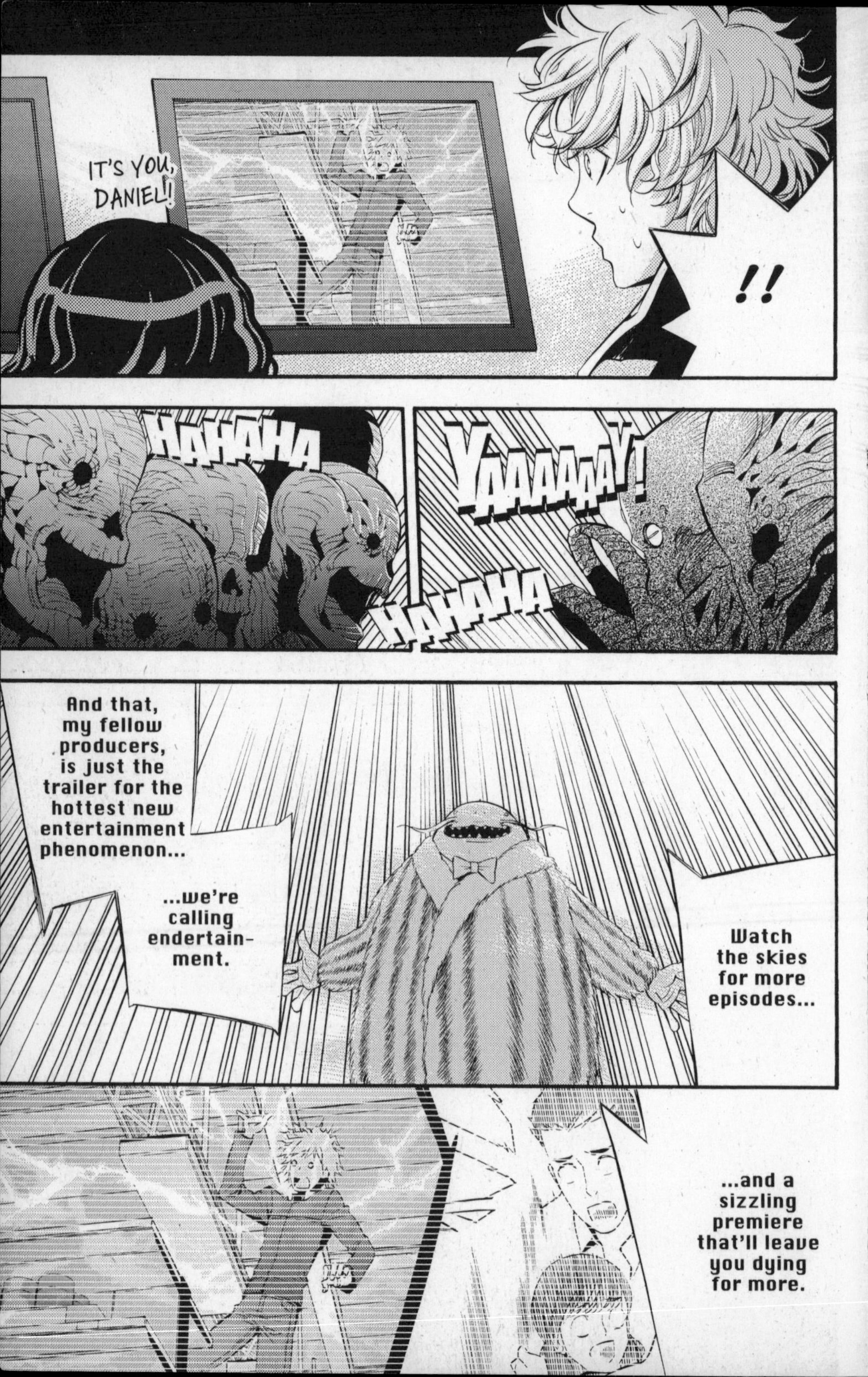
IT'S YOU, DANIEL!!
!!
HAHAHA
YAAAAAAY!
HAHAHA
And that, my fellow producers, is just the trailer for the hottest new entertainment phenomenon...
...we're calling endertainment.
Watch the skies for more episodes...
...and a sizzling premiere that'll leave you dying for more.

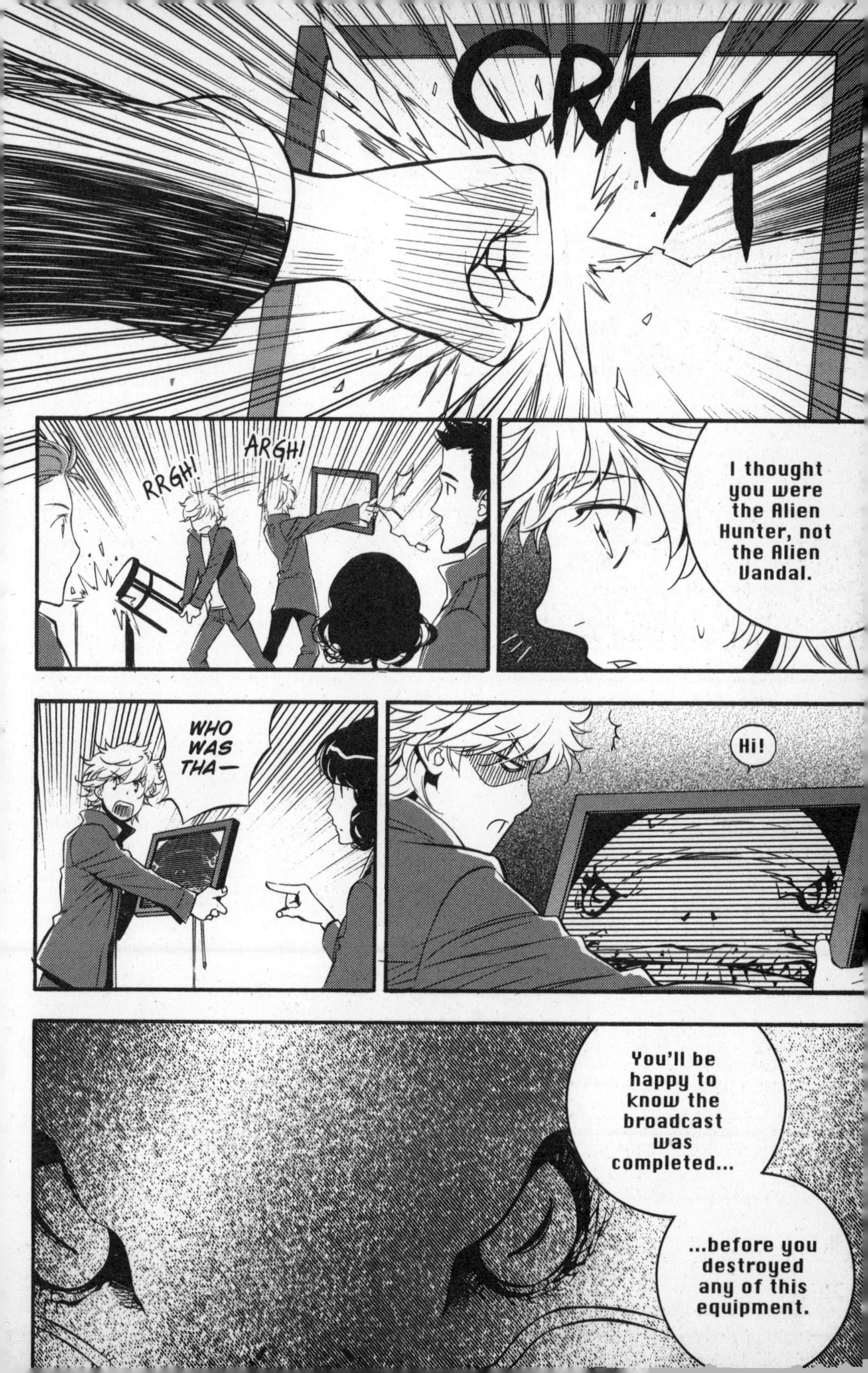
CRACK
RRGH!
ARGH!
I thought you were the Alien Hunter, not the Alien Vandal.
WHO WAS THA—
Hi!
You'll be happy to know the broadcast was completed...
...before you destroyed any of this equipment.

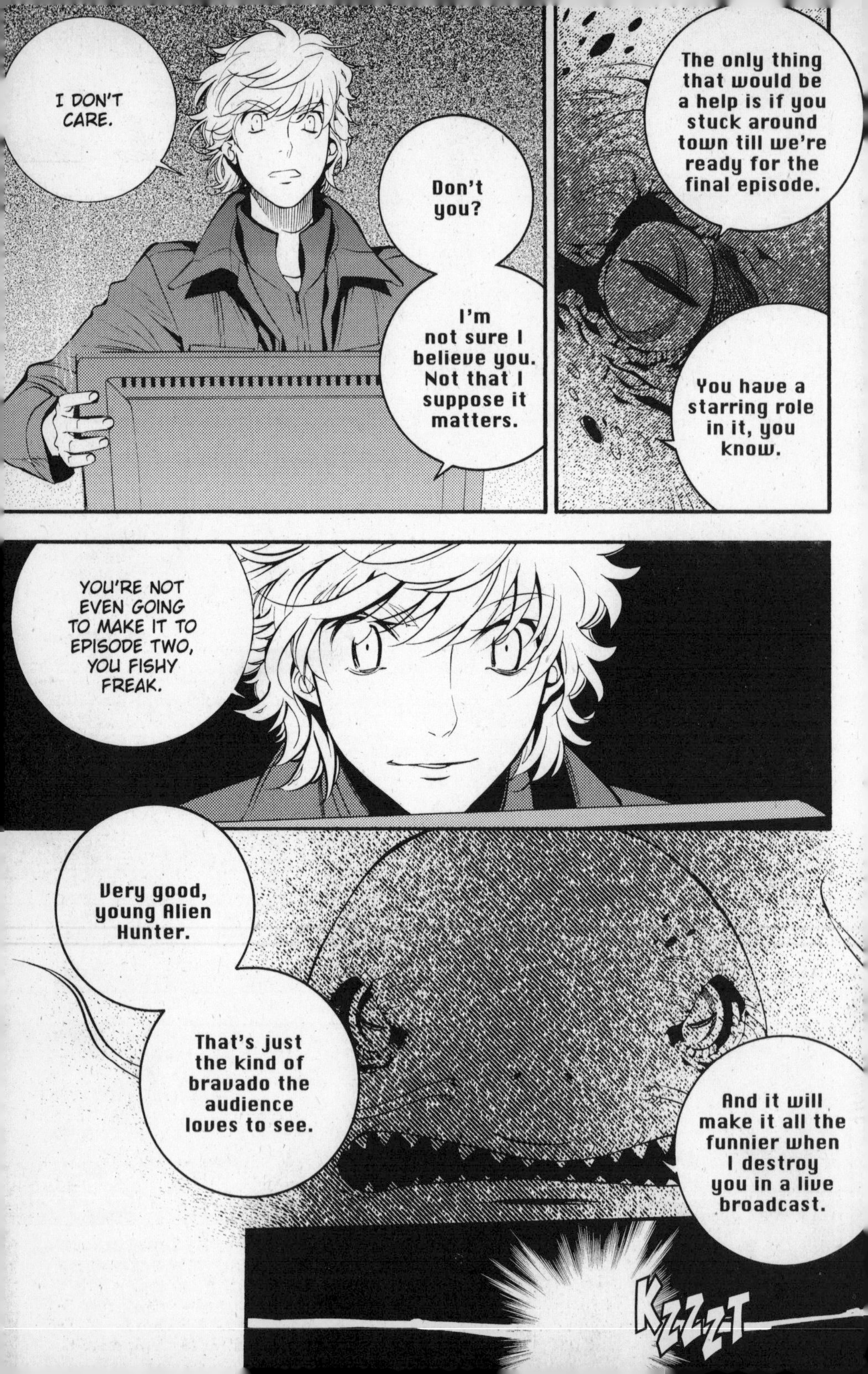
I DON'T CARE.
Don't you?
I'm not sure I believe you. Not that I suppose it matters.
The only thing that would be a help is if you stuck around town till we're ready for the final episode.
You have a starring role in it, you know.
YOU'RE NOT EVEN GOING TO MAKE IT TO EPISODE TWO, YOU FISHY FREAK.
Very good, young Alien Hunter.
That's just the kind of bravado the audience loves to see.
And it will make it all the funnier when I destroy you in a live broadcast.
KZZZZT

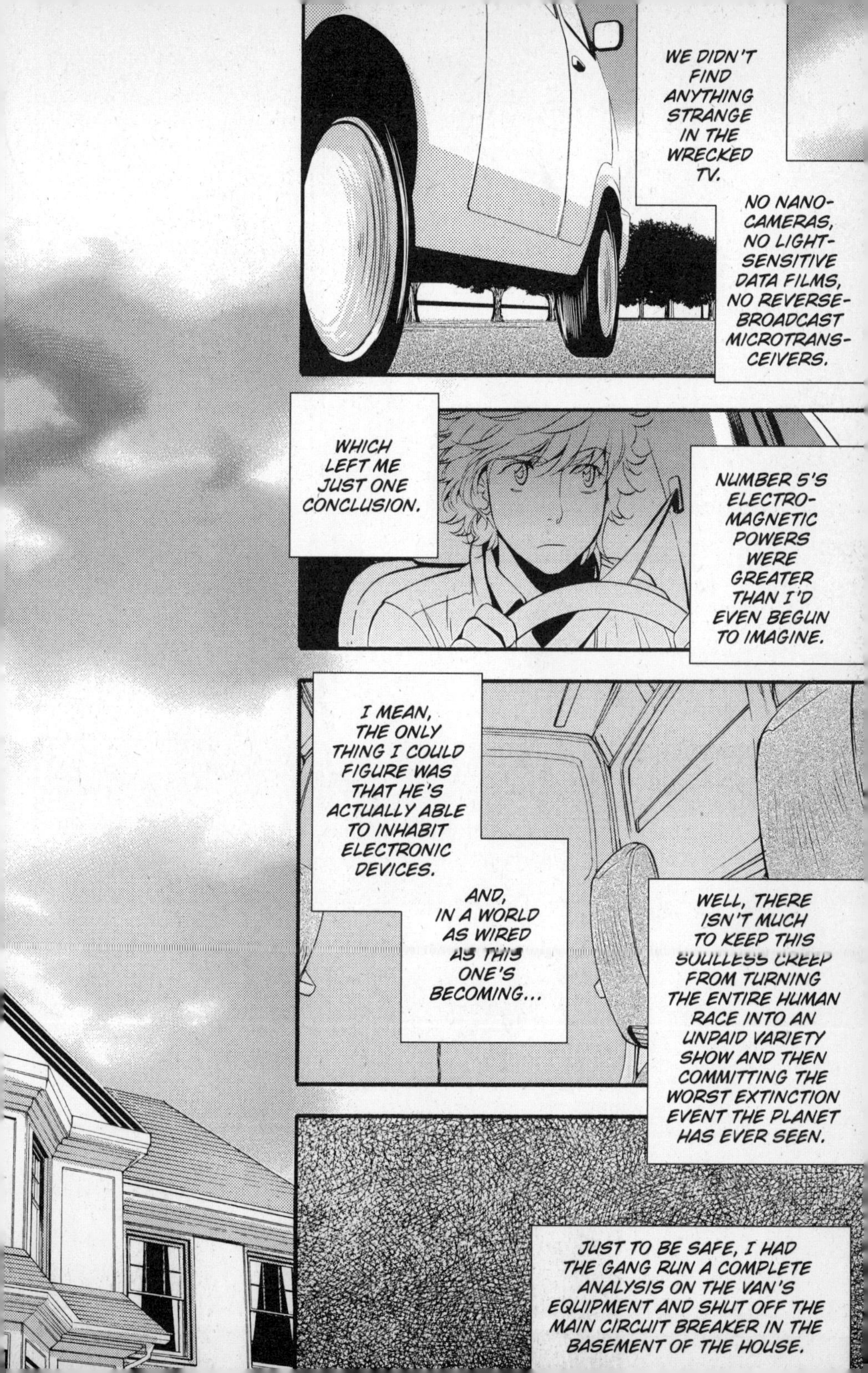
WE DIDN'T FIND ANYTHING STRANGE IN THE WRECKED TV.
NO NANO-CAMERAS, NO LIGHT-SENSITIVE DATA FILMS, NO REVERSE-BROADCAST MICROTRANS-CEIVERS.
WHICH LEFT ME JUST ONE CONCLUSION.
NUMBER 5'S ELECTRO-MAGNETIC POWERS WERE GREATER THAN I'D EVEN BEGUN TO IMAGINE.
I MEAN, THE ONLY THING I COULD FIGURE WAS THAT HE'S ACTUALLY ABLE TO INHABIT ELECTRONIC DEVICES.
AND, IN A WORLD AS WIRED AS THIS ONE'S BECOMING...
WELL, THERE ISN'T MUCH TO KEEP THIS SOULLESS CREEP FROM TURNING THE ENTIRE HUMAN RACE INTO AN UNPAID VARIETY SHOW AND THEN COMMITTING THE WORST EXTINCTION EVENT THE PLANET HAS EVER SEEN.
JUST TO BE SAFE, I HAD THE GANG RUN A COMPLETE ANALYSIS ON THE VAN'S EQUIPMENT AND SHUT OFF THE MAIN CIRCUIT BREAKER IN THE BASEMENT OF THE HOUSE.

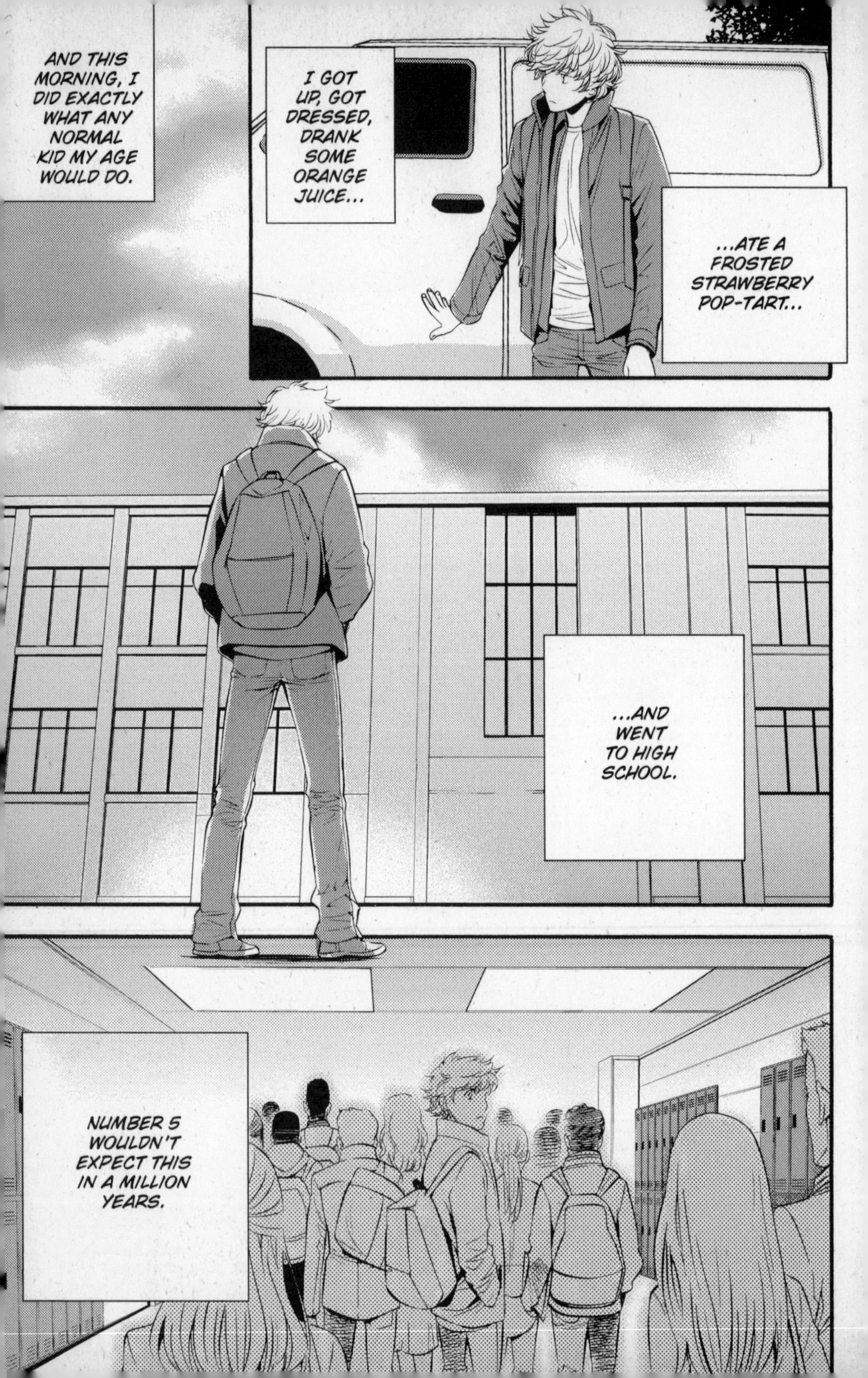
AND THIS MORNING, I DID EXACTLY WHAT ANY NORMAL KID MY AGE WOULD DO.
I GOT UP, GOT DRESSED, DRANK SOME ORANGE JUICE...
...ATE A FROSTED STRAWBERRY POP-TART...
...AND WENT TO HIGH SCHOOL.
NUMBER 5 WOULDN'T EXPECT THIS IN A MILLION YEARS.

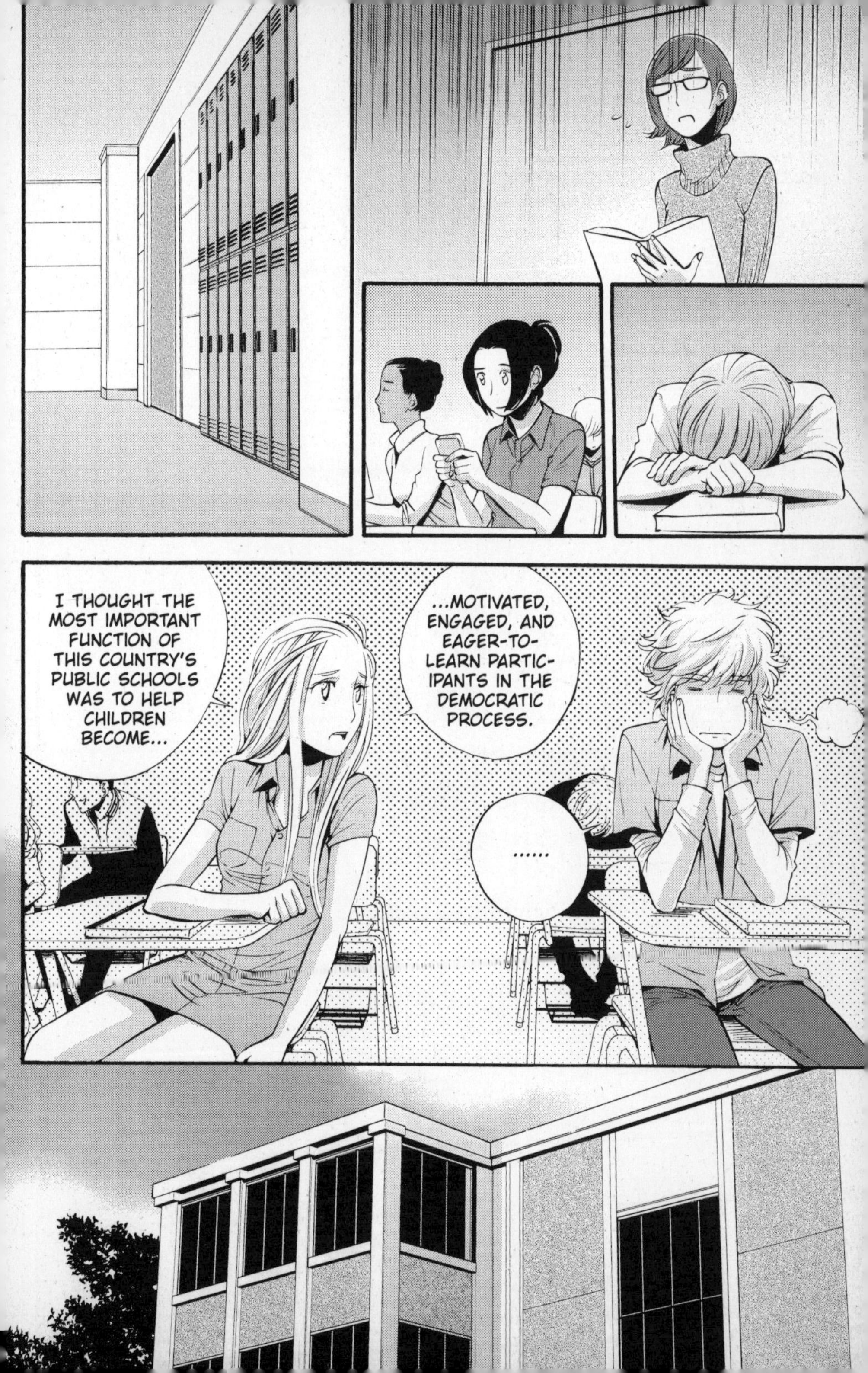
I THOUGHT THE MOST IMPORTANT FUNCTION OF THIS COUNTRY'S PUBLIC SCHOOLS WAS TO HELP CHILDREN BECOME...
...MOTIVATED, ENGAGED, AND EAGER-TO-LEARN PARTIC-IPANTS IN THE DEMOCRATIC PROCESS.
......

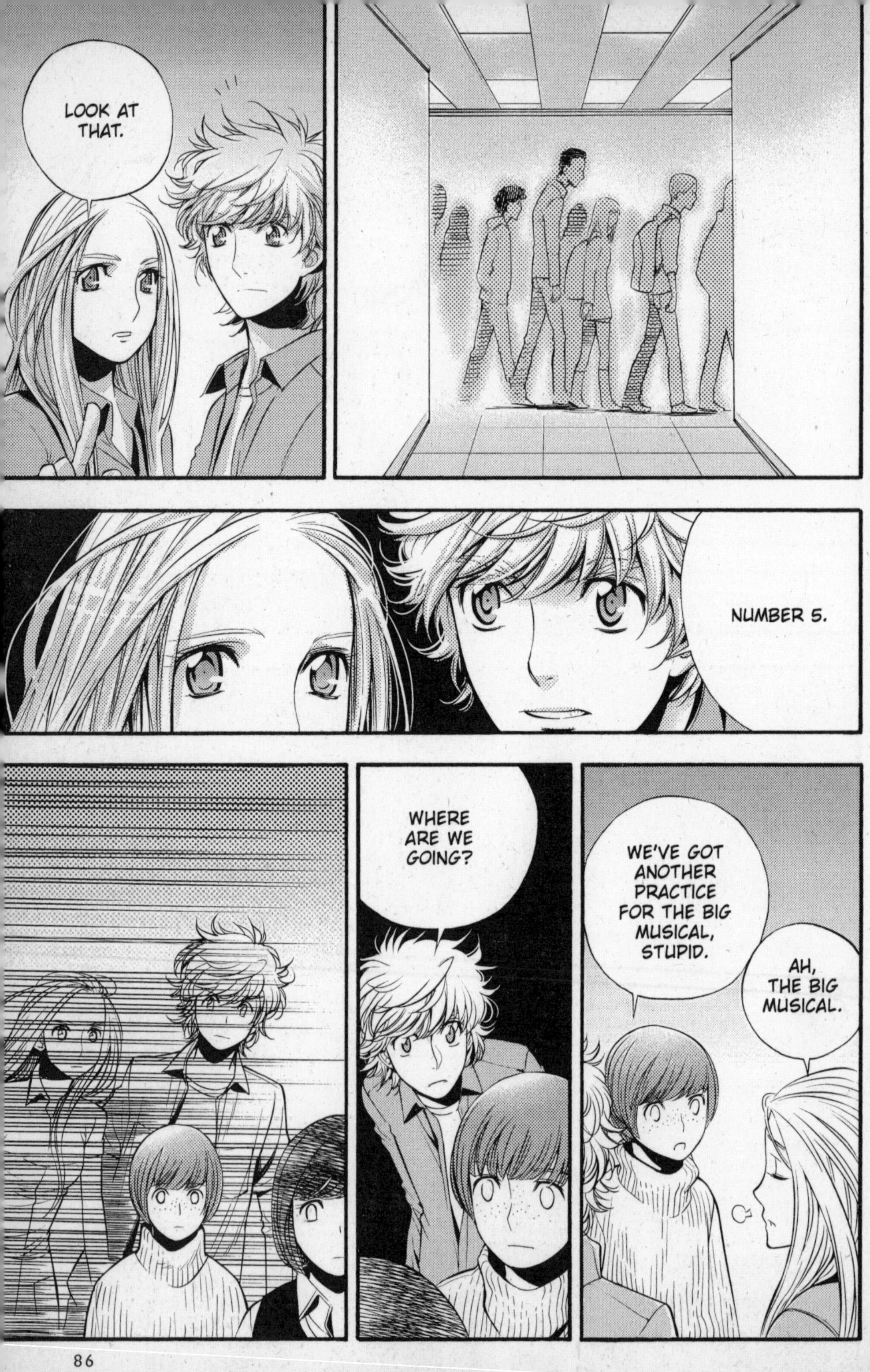
LOOK AT THAT.
NUMBER 5.
WHERE ARE WE GOING?
WE'VE GOT ANOTHER PRACTICE FOR THE BIG MUSICAL, STUPID.
AH, THE BIG MUSICAL.

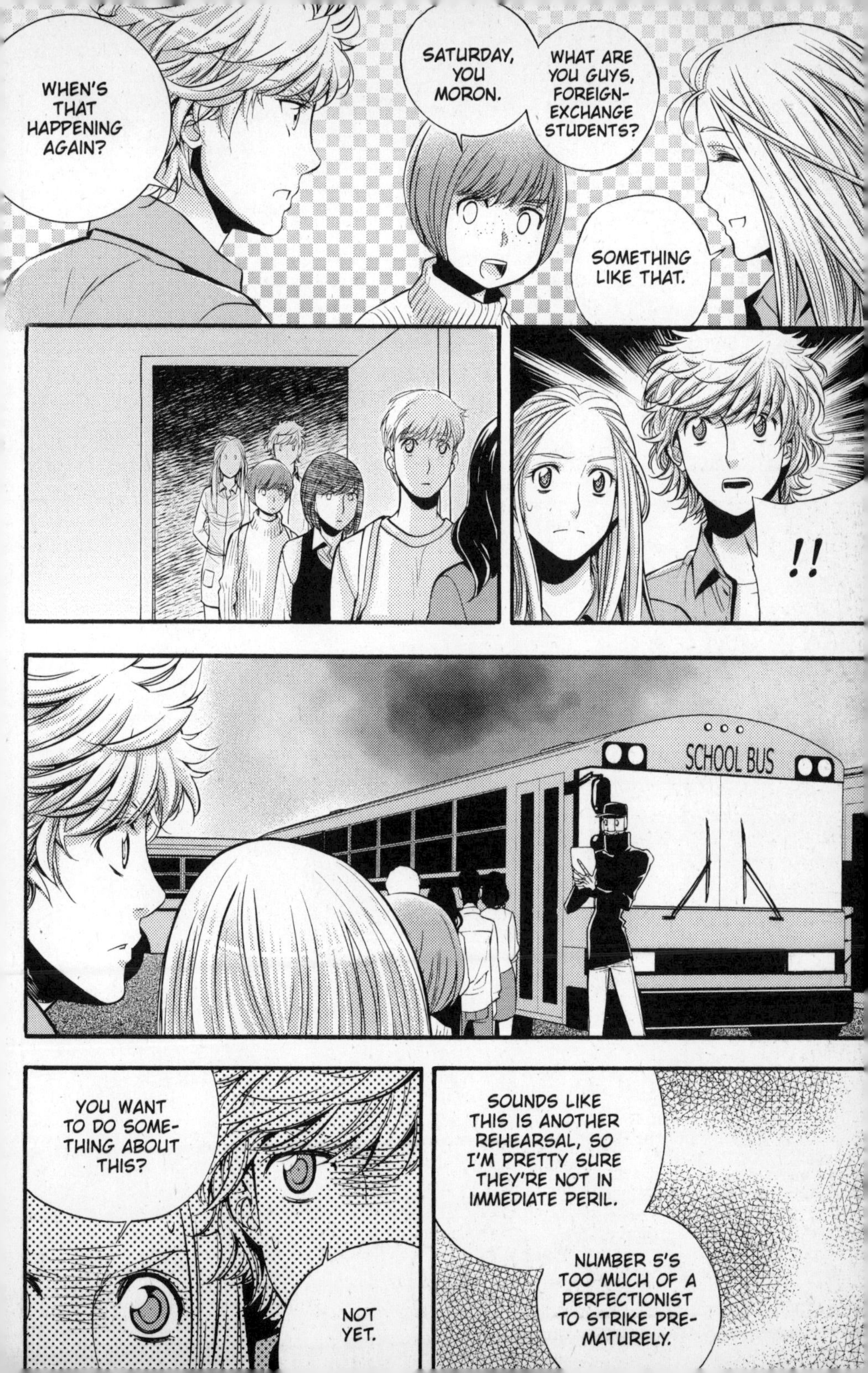
WHEN'S THAT HAPPENING AGAIN?
SATURDAY, YOU MORON.
WHAT ARE YOU GUYS, FOREIGN-EXCHANGE STUDENTS?
SOMETHING LIKE THAT.
!!
SCHOOL BUS
YOU WANT TO DO SOME-THING ABOUT THIS?
NOT YET.
SOUNDS LIKE THIS IS ANOTHER REHEARSAL, SO I'M PRETTY SURE THEY'RE NOT IN IMMEDIATE PERIL.
NUMBER 5'S TOO MUCH OF A PERFECTIONIST TO STRIKE PRE-MATURELY.

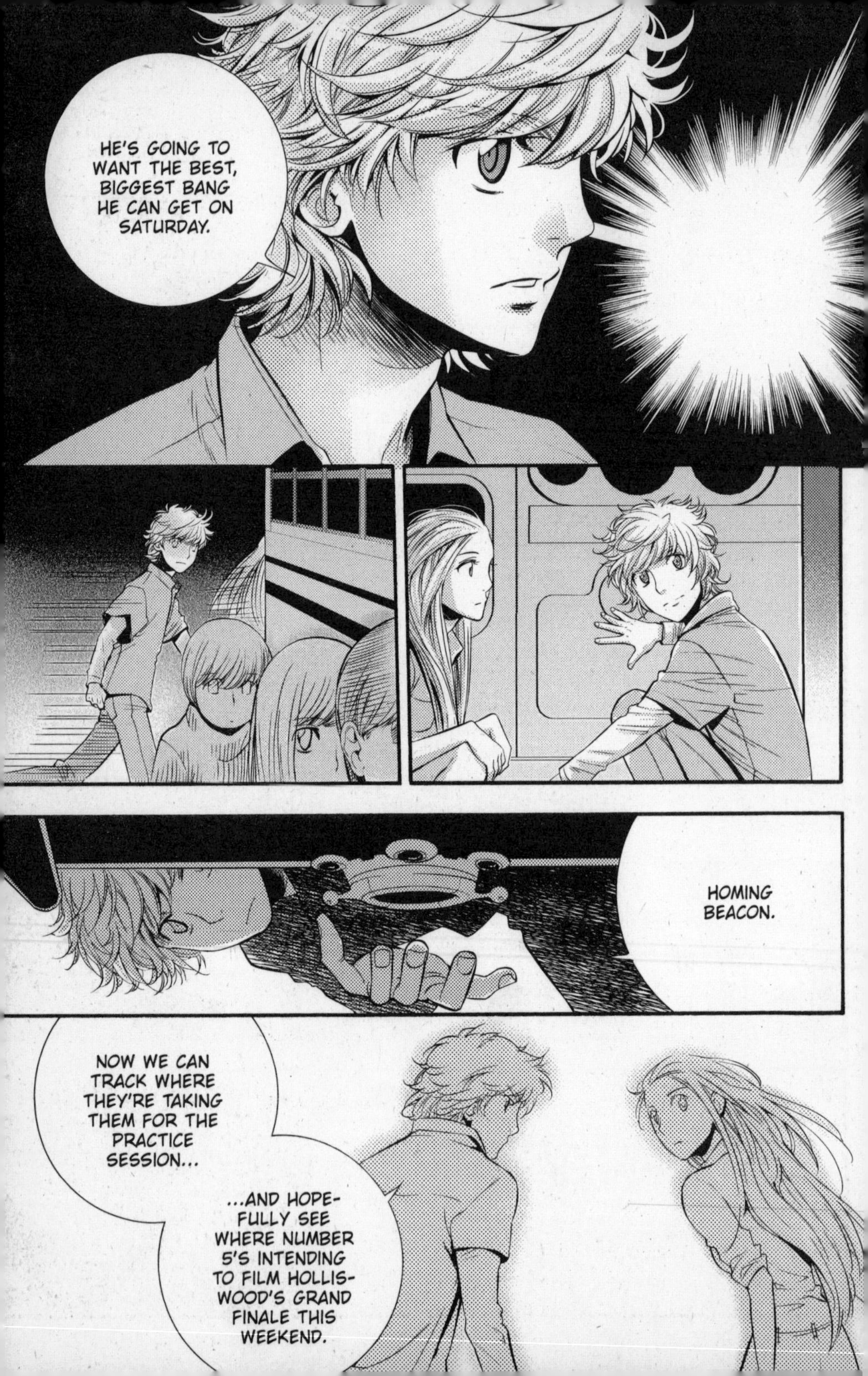
HE'S GOING TO WANT THE BEST, BIGGEST BANG HE CAN GET ON SATURDAY.
HOMING BEACON.
NOW WE CAN TRACK WHERE THEY'RE TAKING THEM FOR THE PRACTICE SESSION...
...AND HOPE-FULLY SEE WHERE NUMBER 5'S INTENDING TO FILM HOLLIS-WOOD'S GRAND FINALE THIS WEEKEND.

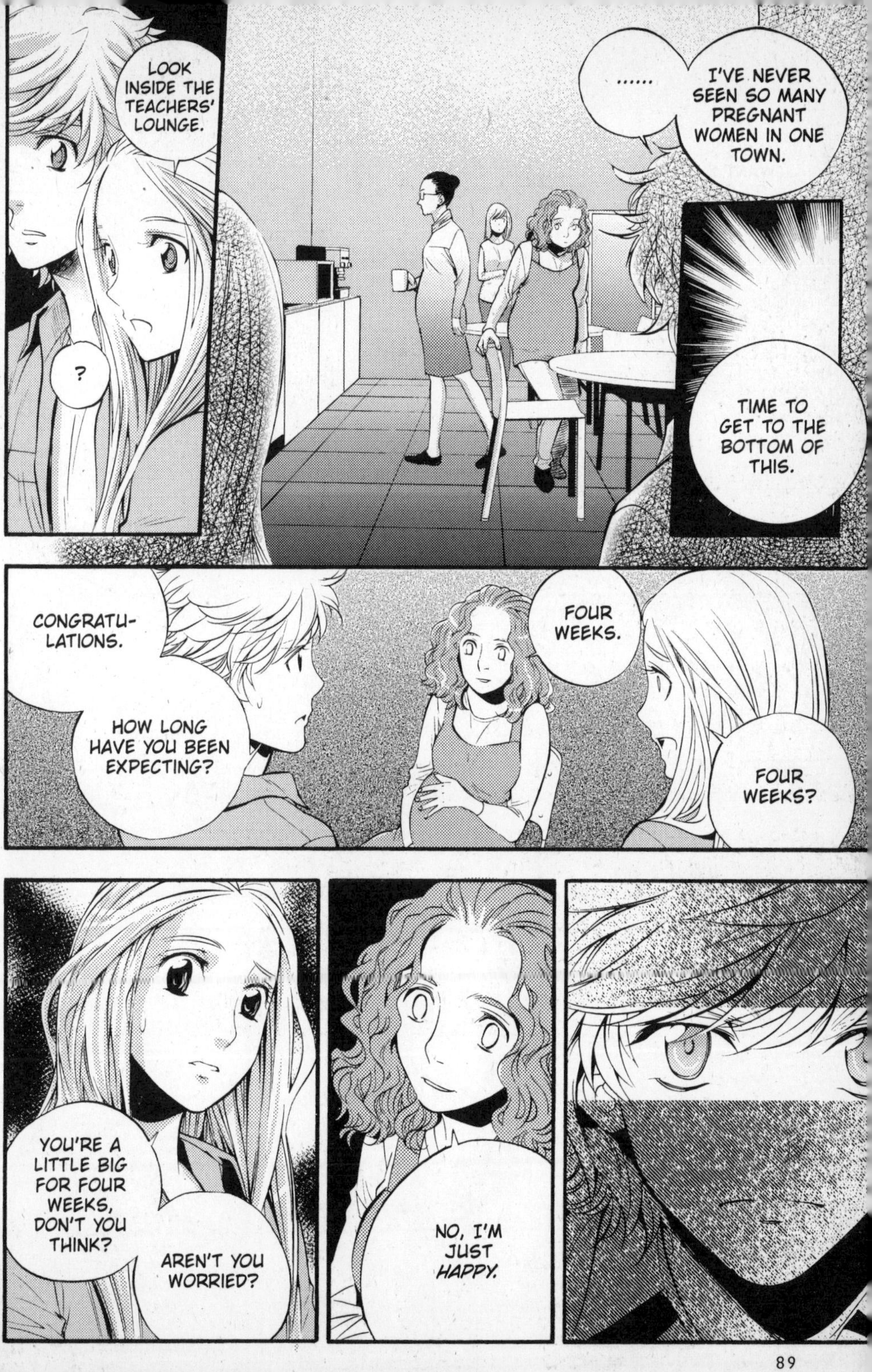
LOOK INSIDE THE TEACHERS' LOUNGE.
?
......
I'VE NEVER SEEN SO MANY PREGNANT WOMEN IN ONE TOWN.
TIME TO GET TO THE BOTTOM OF THIS.
CONGRATU-LATIONS.
HOW LONG HAVE YOU BEEN EXPECTING?
FOUR WEEKS.
FOUR WEEKS?
YOU'RE A LITTLE BIG FOR FOUR WEEKS, DON'T YOU THINK?
AREN'T YOU WORRIED?
NO, I'M JUST *HAPPY.*

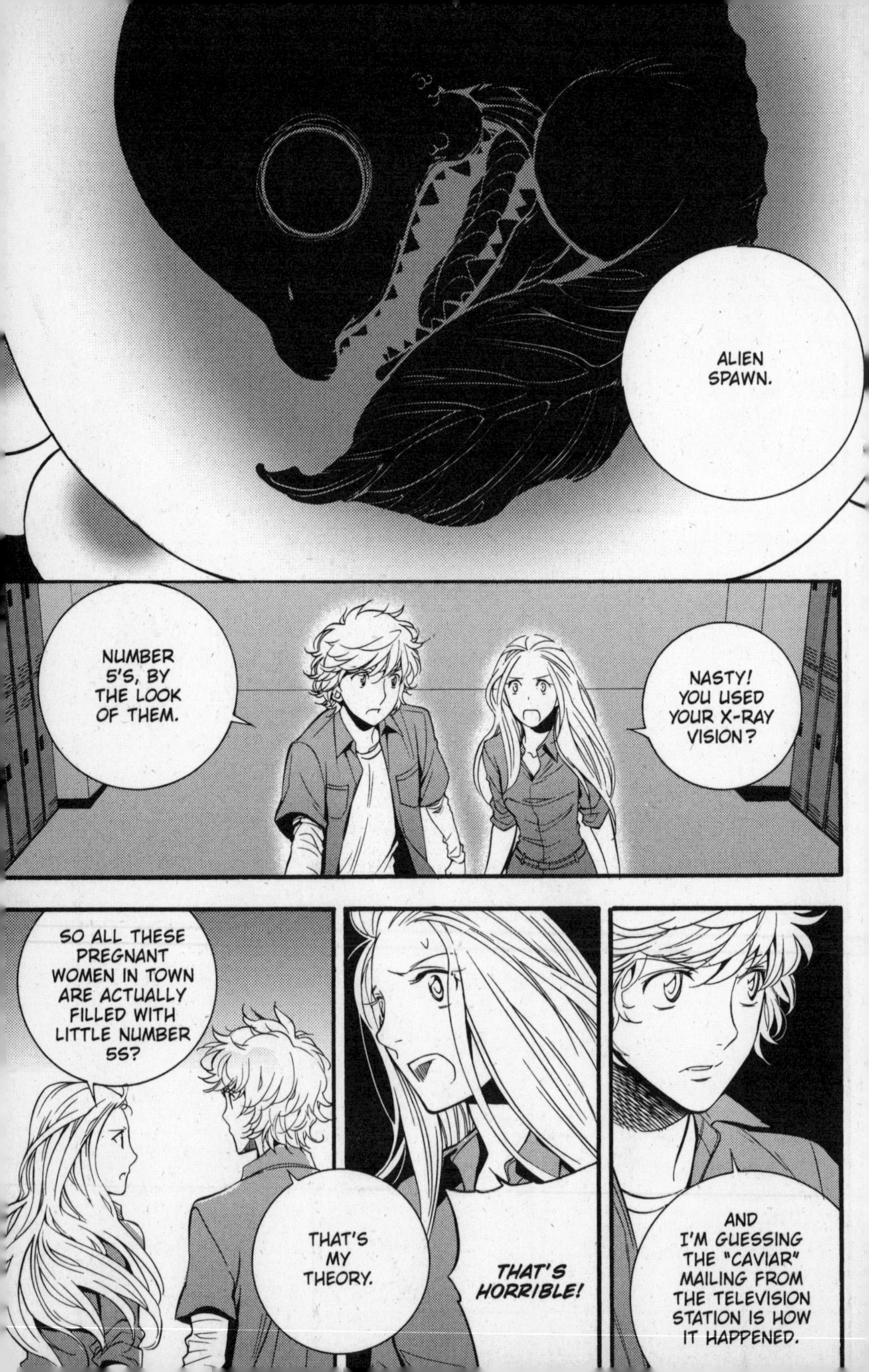
ALIEN SPAWN.
NUMBER 5'S, BY THE LOOK OF THEM.
NASTY! YOU USED YOUR X-RAY VISION?
SO ALL THESE PREGNANT WOMEN IN TOWN ARE ACTUALLY FILLED WITH LITTLE NUMBER 5S?
THAT'S MY THEORY.
THAT'S HORRIBLE!
AND I'M GUESSING THE "CAVIAR" MAILING FROM THE TELEVISION STATION IS HOW IT HAPPENED.

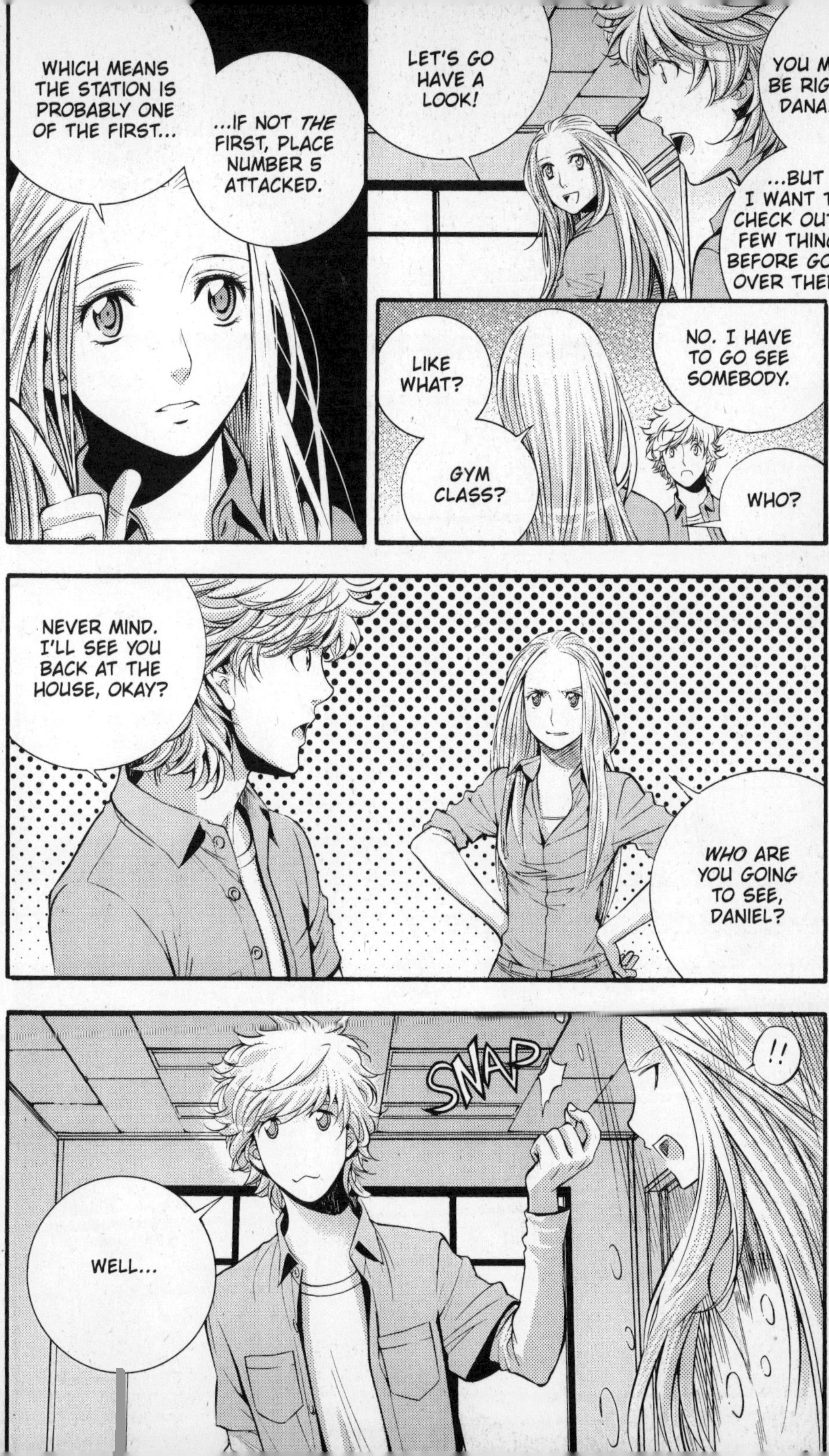
WHICH MEANS THE STATION IS PROBABLY ONE OF THE FIRST...
...IF NOT *THE* FIRST, PLACE NUMBER 5 ATTACKED.
LET'S GO HAVE A LOOK!
YOU MAY BE RIGHT, DANA...
...BUT I WANT TO CHECK OUT A FEW THINGS BEFORE GOING OVER THERE.
LIKE WHAT?
GYM CLASS?
NO. I HAVE TO GO SEE SOMEBODY.
WHO?
NEVER MIND. I'LL SEE YOU BACK AT THE HOUSE, OKAY?
WHO ARE YOU GOING TO SEE, DANIEL?
WELL...
SNAP
!!

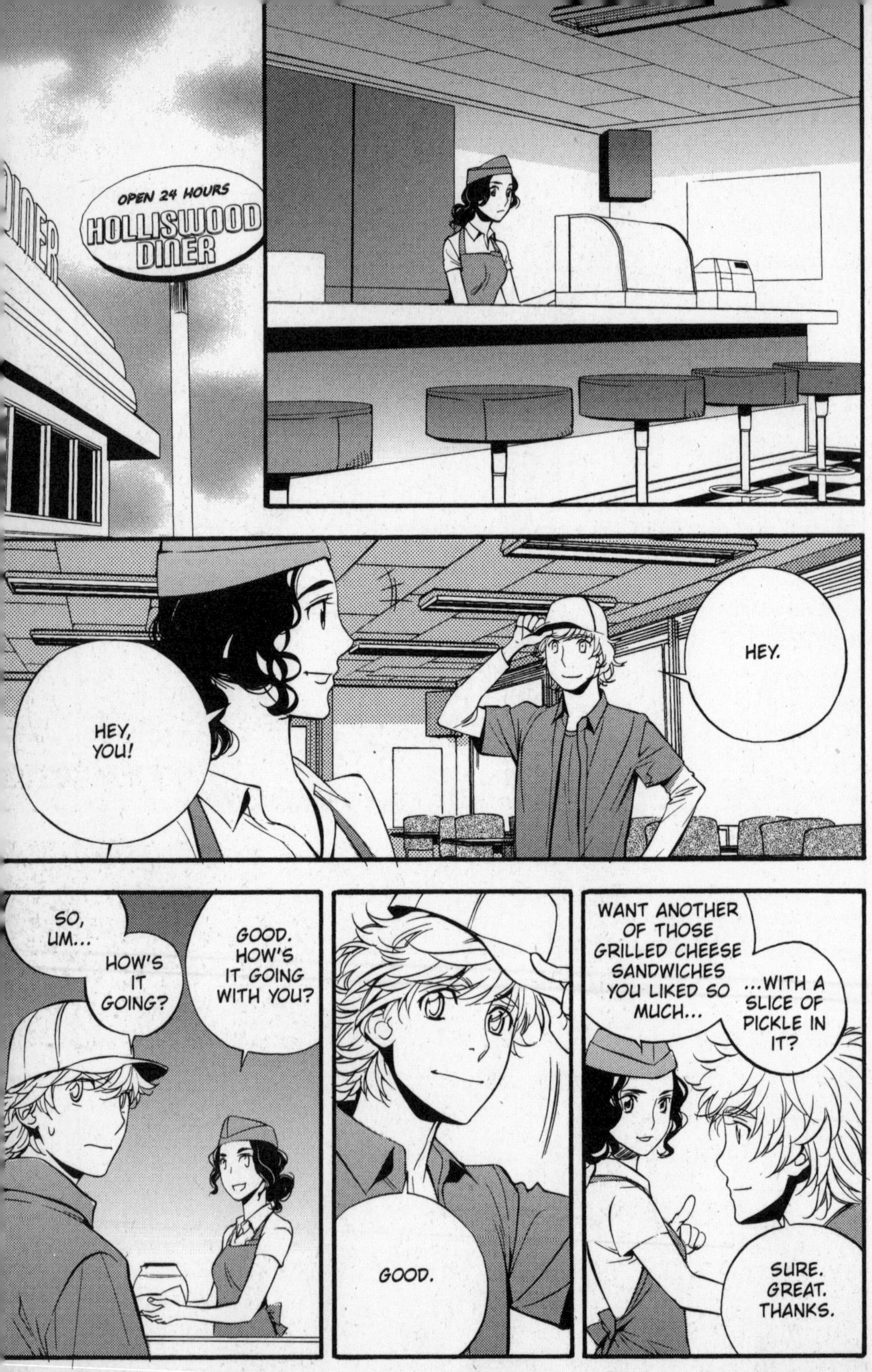
OPEN 24 HOURS
HOLLISWOOD DINER
DINER
HEY, YOU!
HEY.
SO, UM...
HOW'S IT GOING?
GOOD. HOW'S IT GOING WITH YOU?
GOOD.
WANT ANOTHER OF THOSE GRILLED CHEESE SANDWICHES YOU LIKED SO MUCH...
...WITH A SLICE OF PICKLE IN IT?
SURE. GREAT. THANKS.

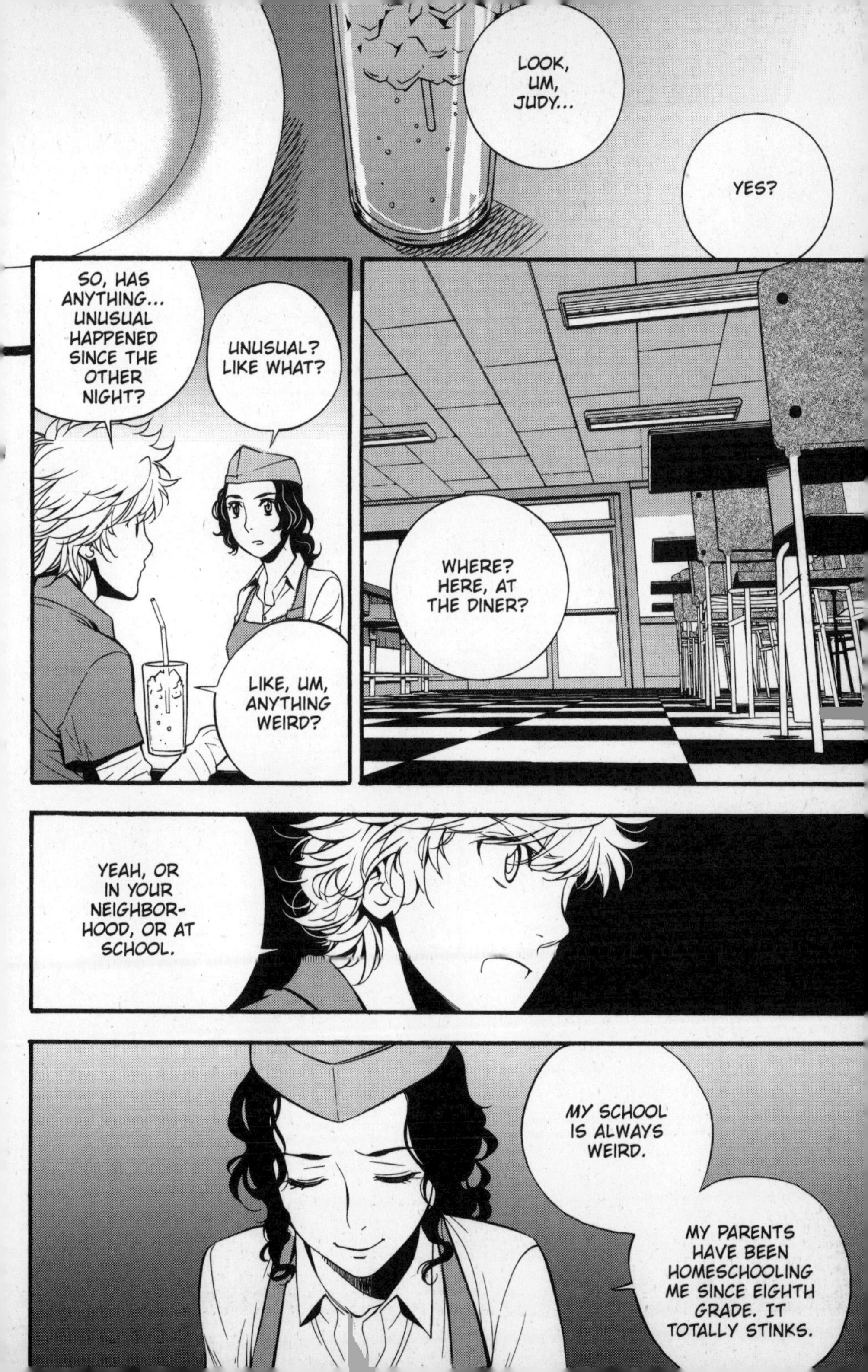
LOOK, UM, JUDY...
YES?
SO, HAS ANYTHING... UNUSUAL HAPPENED SINCE THE OTHER NIGHT?
UNUSUAL? LIKE WHAT?
LIKE, UM, ANYTHING WEIRD?
WHERE? HERE, AT THE DINER?
YEAH, OR IN YOUR NEIGHBOR-HOOD, OR AT SCHOOL.
MY SCHOOL IS ALWAYS WEIRD.
MY PARENTS HAVE BEEN HOMESCHOOLING ME SINCE EIGHTH GRADE. IT TOTALLY STINKS.

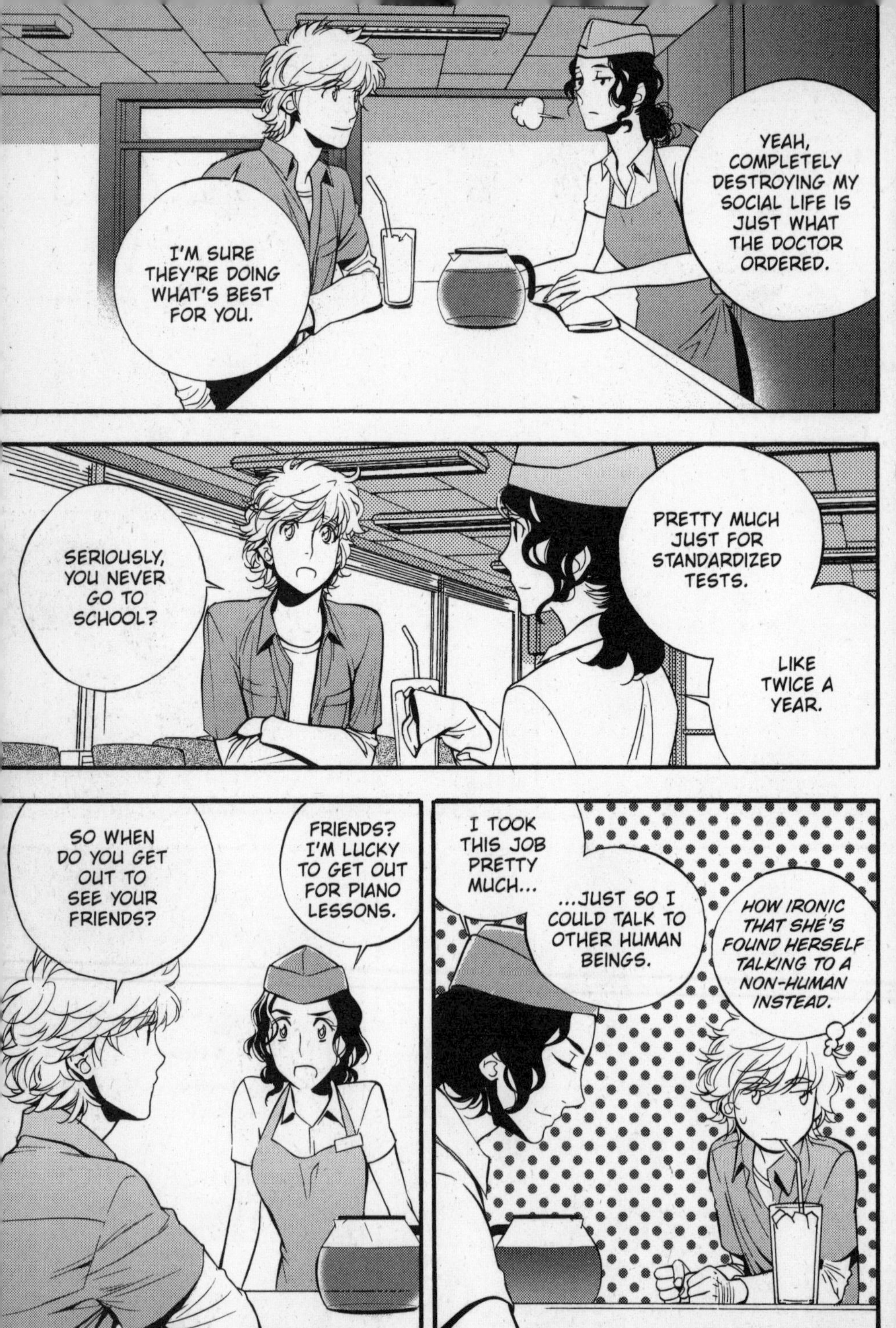
I'M SURE THEY'RE DOING WHAT'S BEST FOR YOU.
YEAH, COMPLETELY DESTROYING MY SOCIAL LIFE IS JUST WHAT THE DOCTOR ORDERED.
SERIOUSLY, YOU NEVER GO TO SCHOOL?
PRETTY MUCH JUST FOR STANDARDIZED TESTS.
LIKE TWICE A YEAR.
SO WHEN DO YOU GET OUT TO SEE YOUR FRIENDS?
FRIENDS? I'M LUCKY TO GET OUT FOR PIANO LESSONS.
I TOOK THIS JOB PRETTY MUCH...
...JUST SO I COULD TALK TO OTHER HUMAN BEINGS.
HOW IRONIC THAT SHE'S FOUND HERSELF TALKING TO A NON-HUMAN INSTEAD.

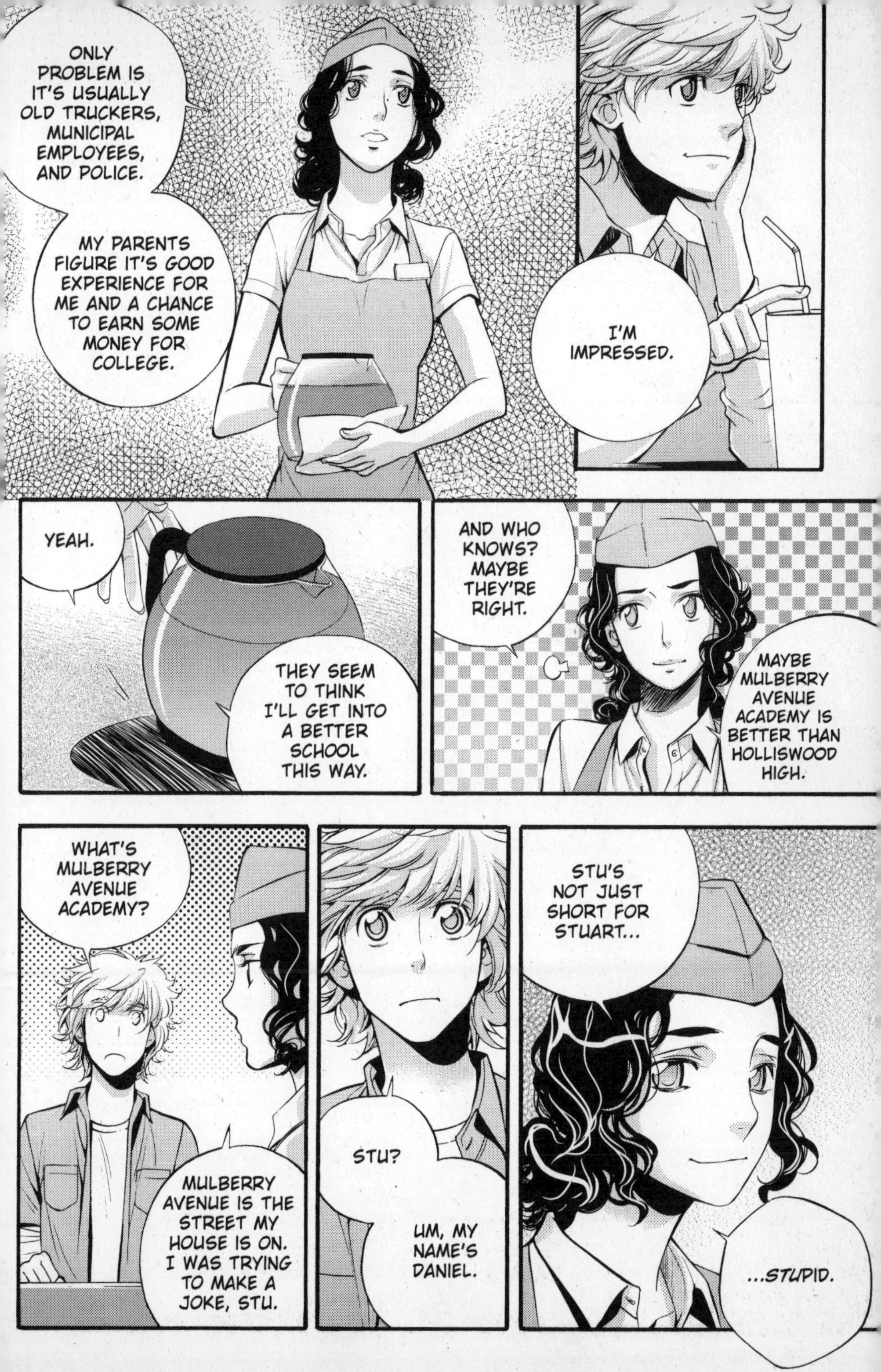
ONLY PROBLEM IS IT'S USUALLY OLD TRUCKERS, MUNICIPAL EMPLOYEES, AND POLICE.
MY PARENTS FIGURE IT'S GOOD EXPERIENCE FOR ME AND A CHANCE TO EARN SOME MONEY FOR COLLEGE.
I'M IMPRESSED.
YEAH.
THEY SEEM TO THINK I'LL GET INTO A BETTER SCHOOL THIS WAY.
AND WHO KNOWS? MAYBE THEY'RE RIGHT.
MAYBE MULBERRY AVENUE ACADEMY IS BETTER THAN HOLLISWOOD HIGH.
WHAT'S MULBERRY AVENUE ACADEMY?
MULBERRY AVENUE IS THE STREET MY HOUSE IS ON. I WAS TRYING TO MAKE A JOKE, STU.
STU?
UM, MY NAME'S DANIEL.
STU'S NOT JUST SHORT FOR STUART...
...STUPID.

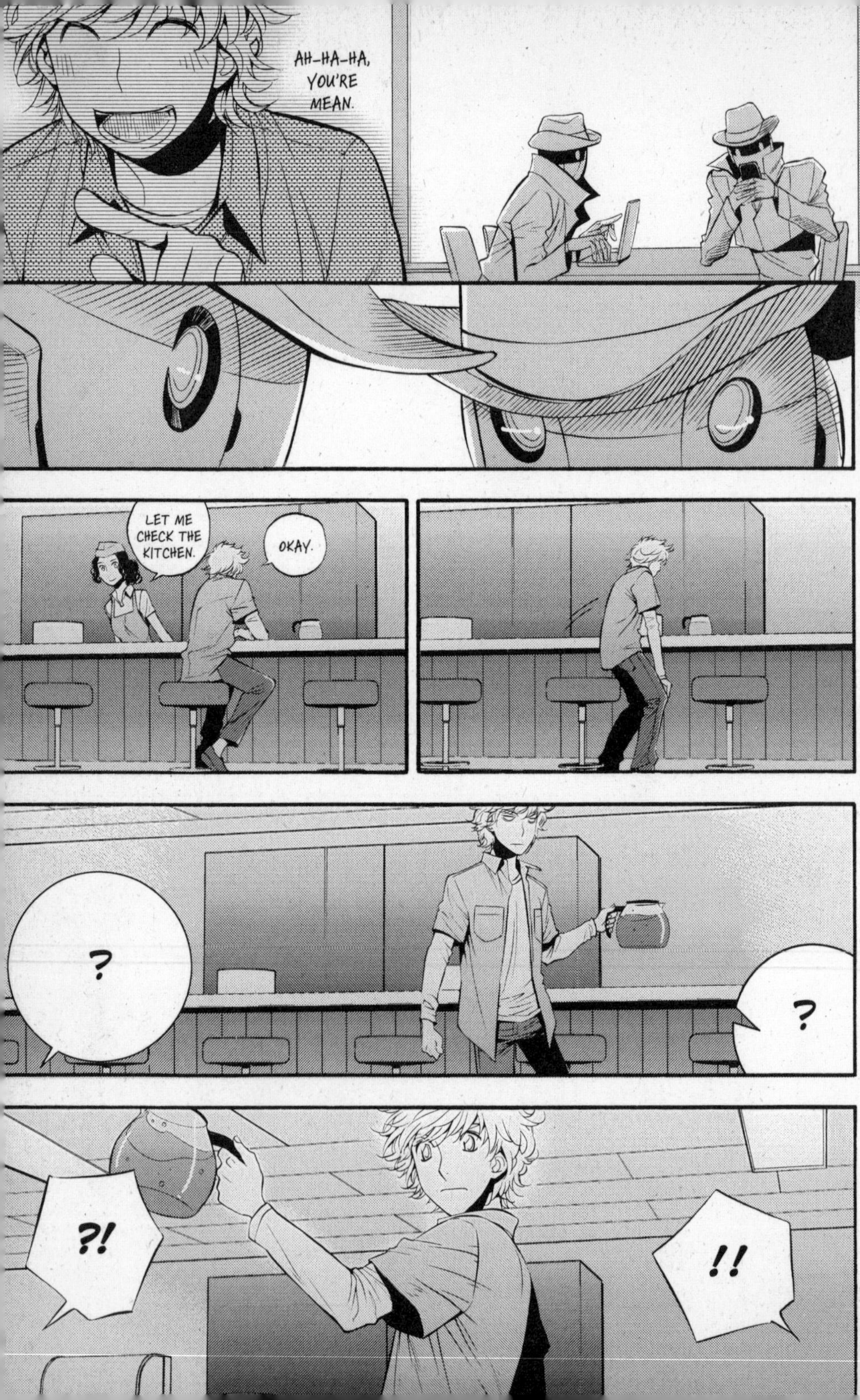
AH-HA-HA, YOU'RE MEAN.
LET ME CHECK THE KITCHEN.
OKAY.
?
?
?!
!!

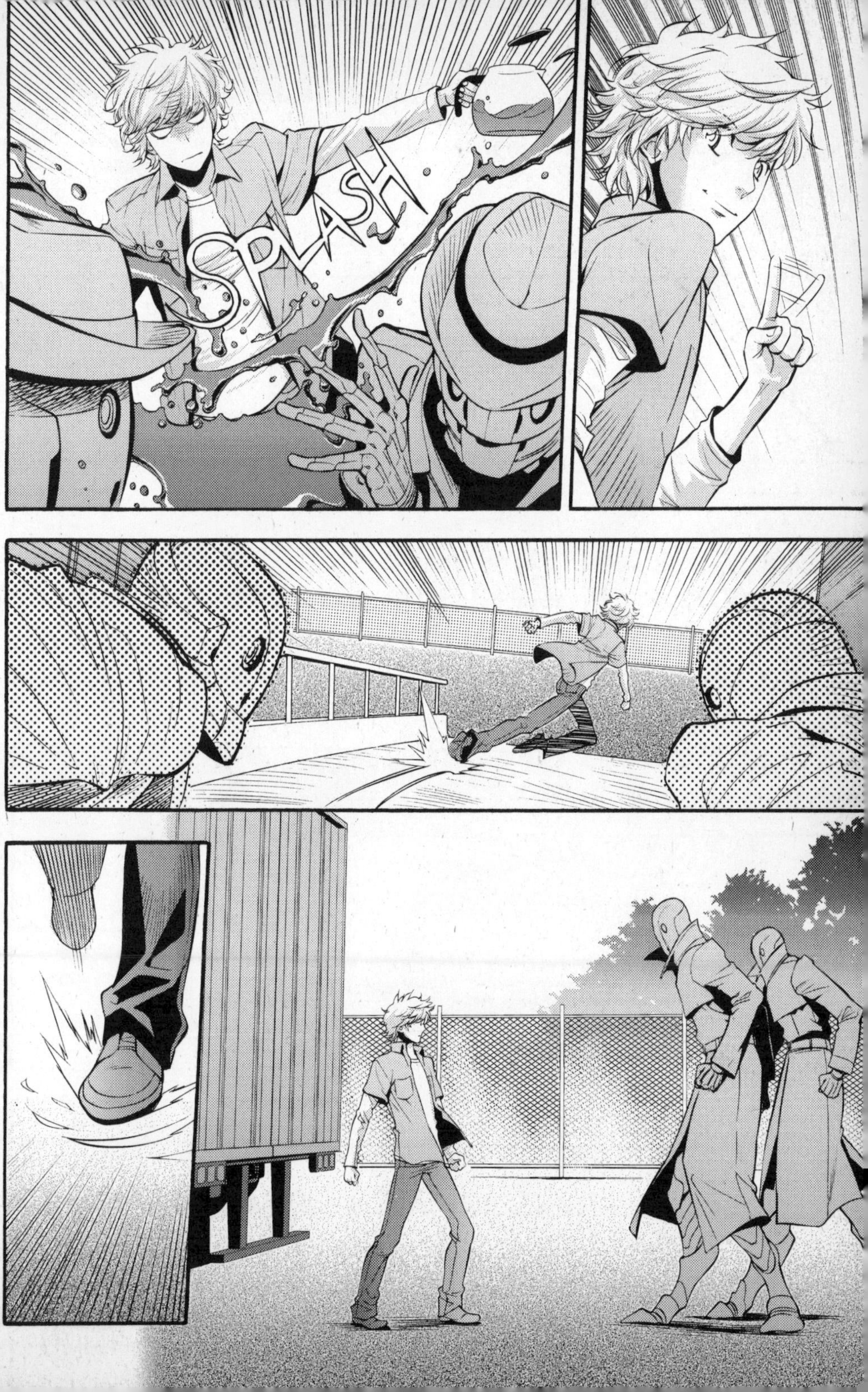
SPLASH

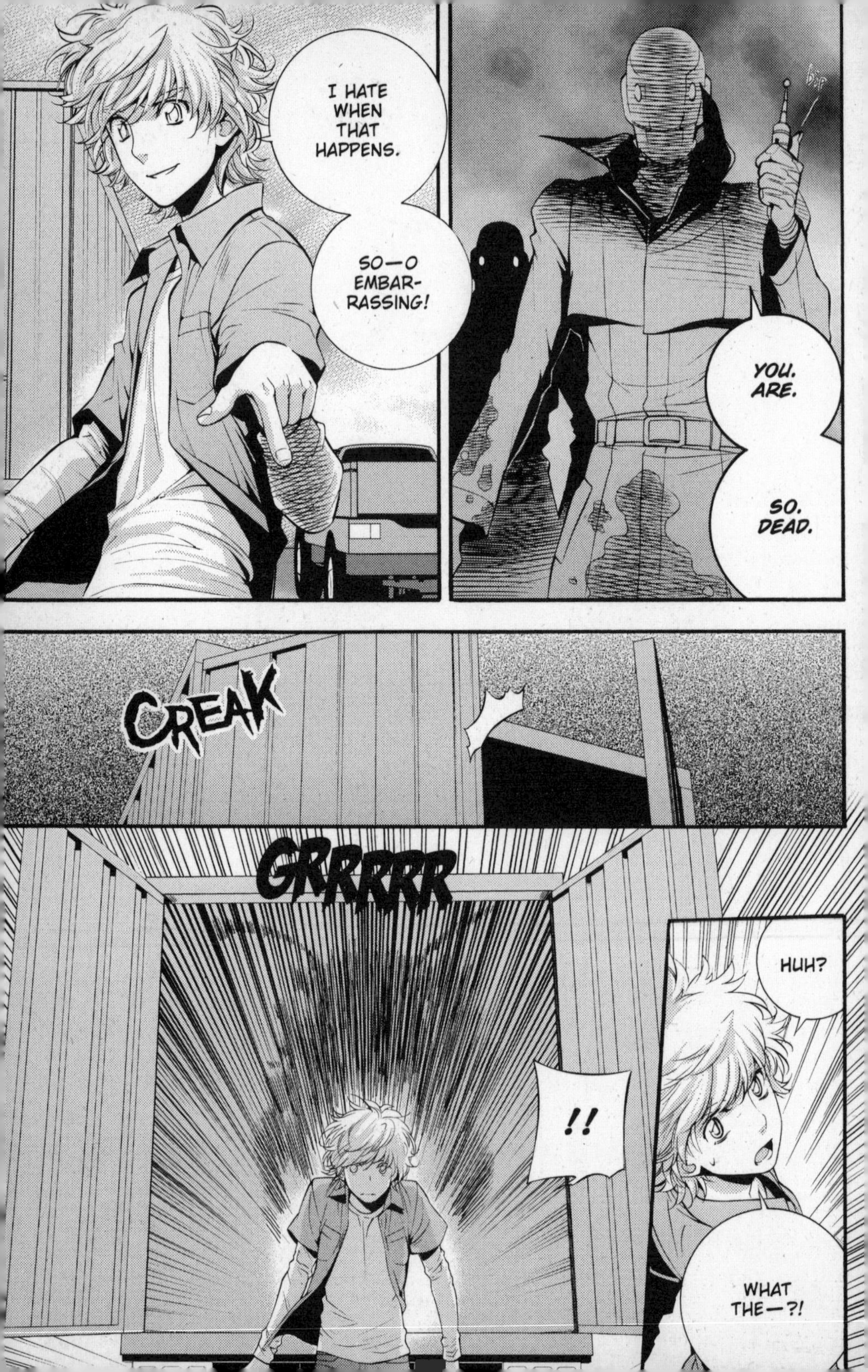
I HATE WHEN THAT HAPPENS.
SO—O EMBAR-RASSING!
YOU. ARE.
SO. DEAD.
CREAK
GRRRRR
!!
HUH?
WHAT THE—?!

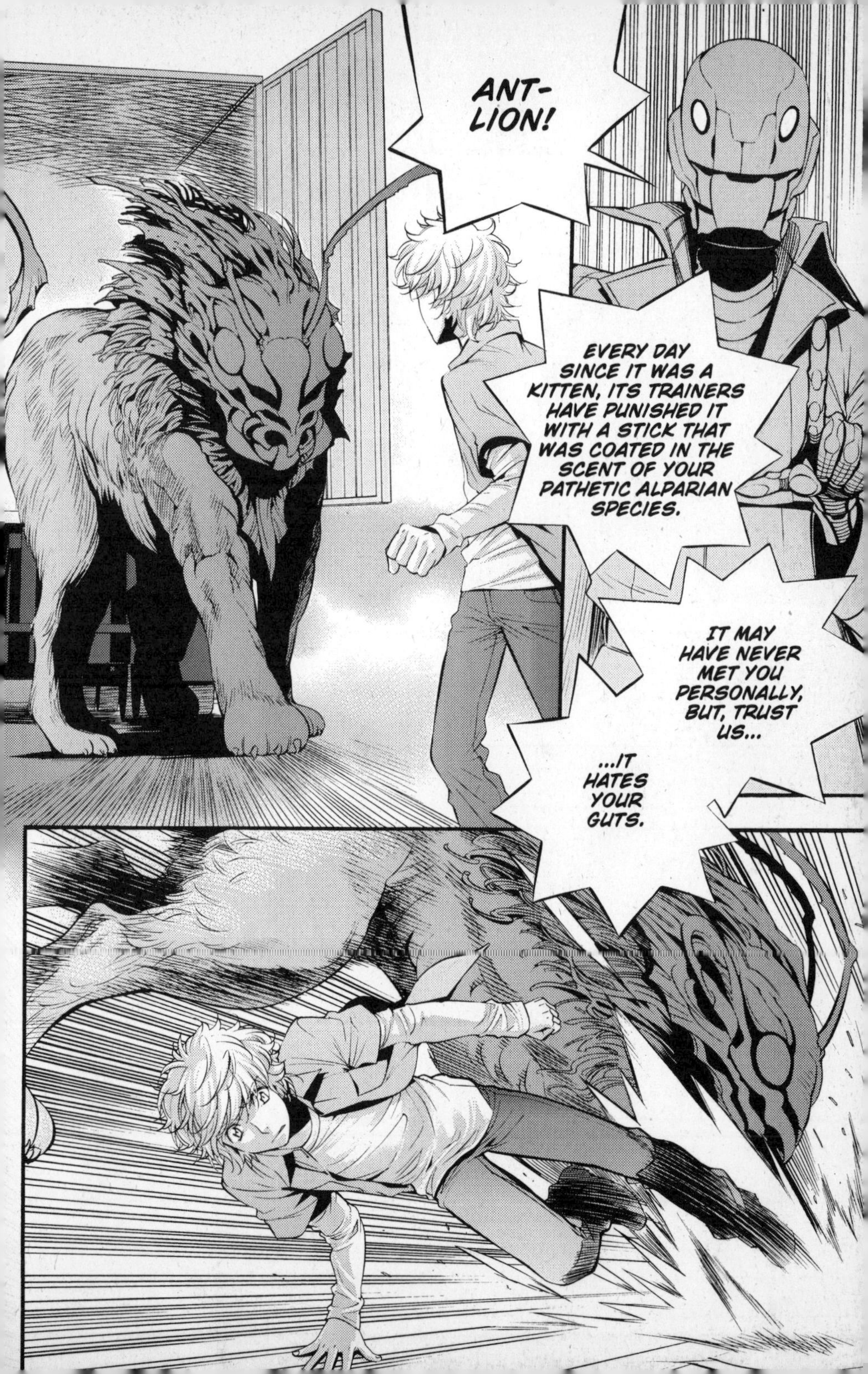
ANT-LION!
EVERY DAY SINCE IT WAS A KITTEN, ITS TRAINERS HAVE PUNISHED IT WITH A STICK THAT WAS COATED IN THE SCENT OF YOUR PATHETIC ALPARIAN SPECIES.
IT MAY HAVE NEVER MET YOU PERSONALLY, BUT, TRUST US...
...IT HATES YOUR GUTS.

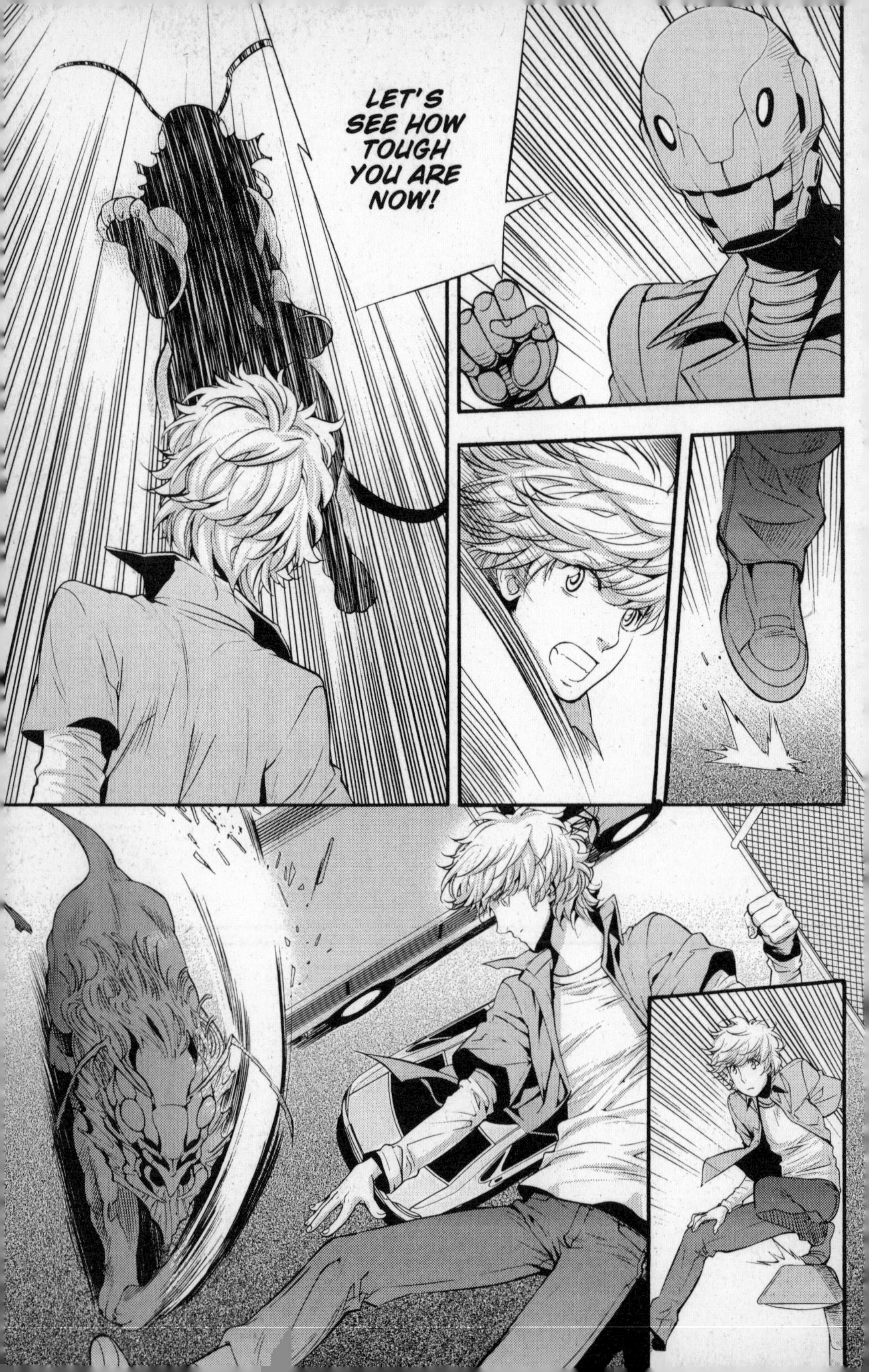
LET'S SEE HOW TOUGH YOU ARE NOW!

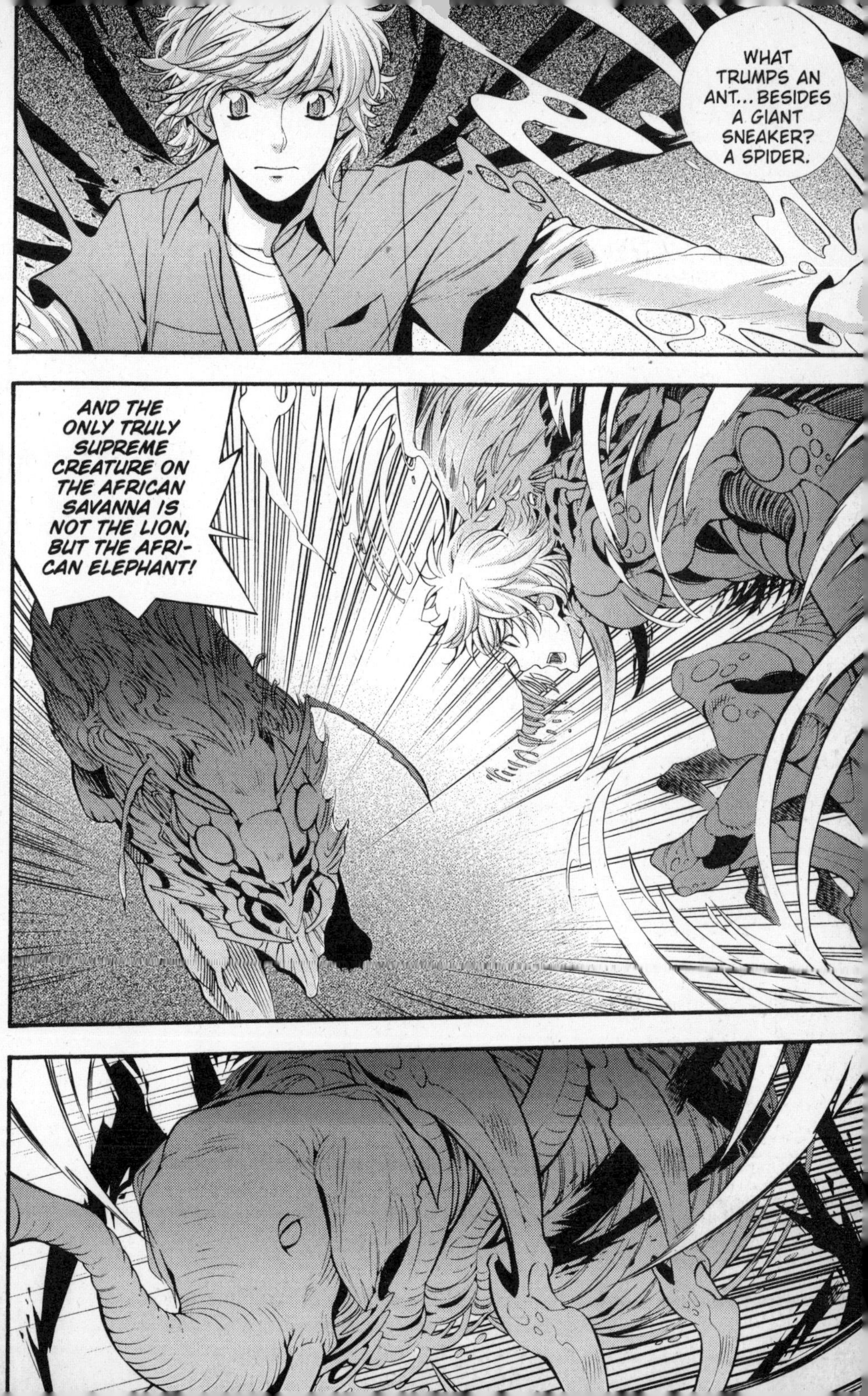
WHAT TRUMPS AN ANT... BESIDES A GIANT SNEAKER? A SPIDER.
AND THE ONLY TRULY SUPREME CREATURE ON THE AFRICAN SAVANNA IS NOT THE LION, BUT THE AFRI-CAN ELEPHANT!

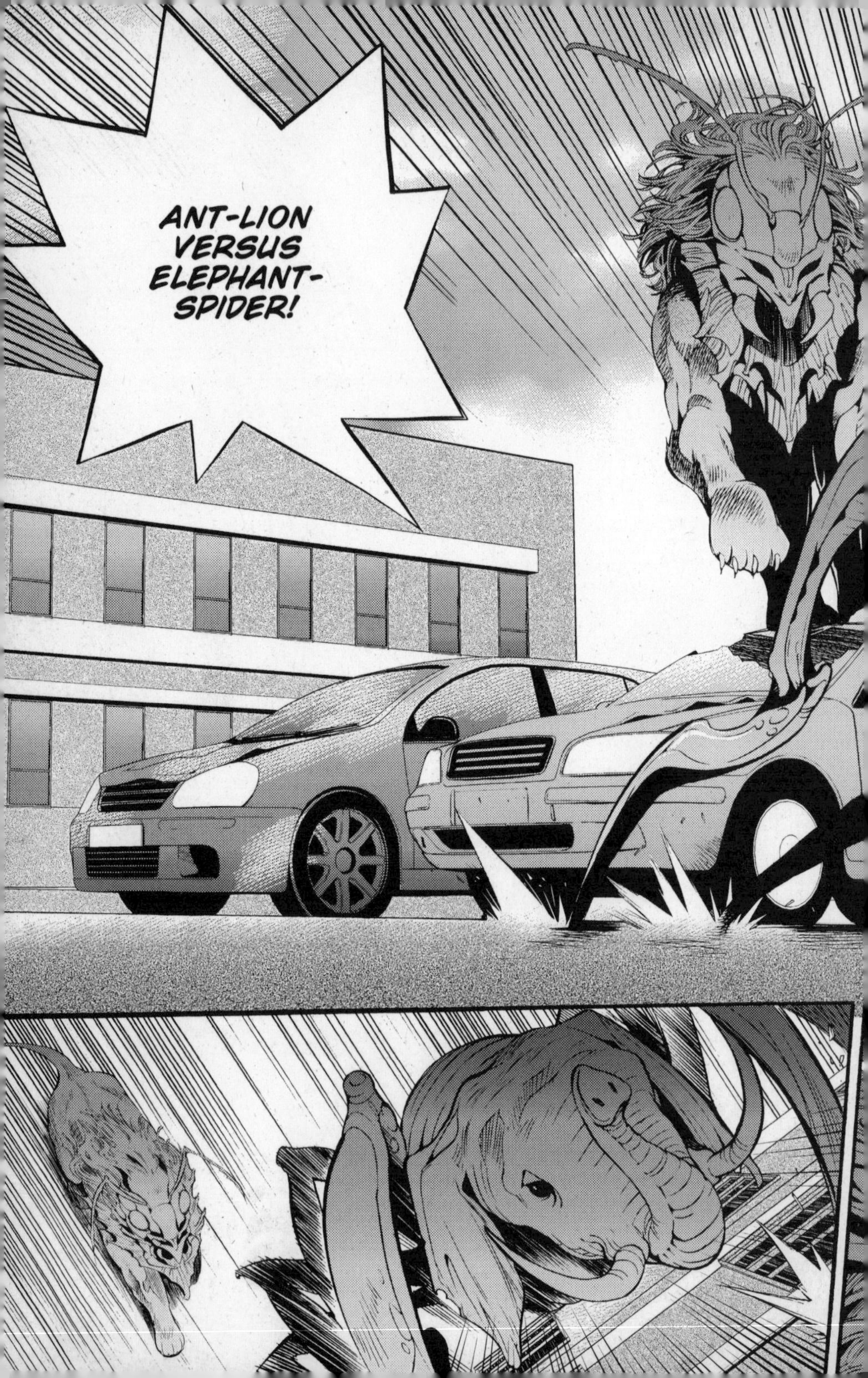
ANT-LION VERSUS ELEPHANT-SPIDER!

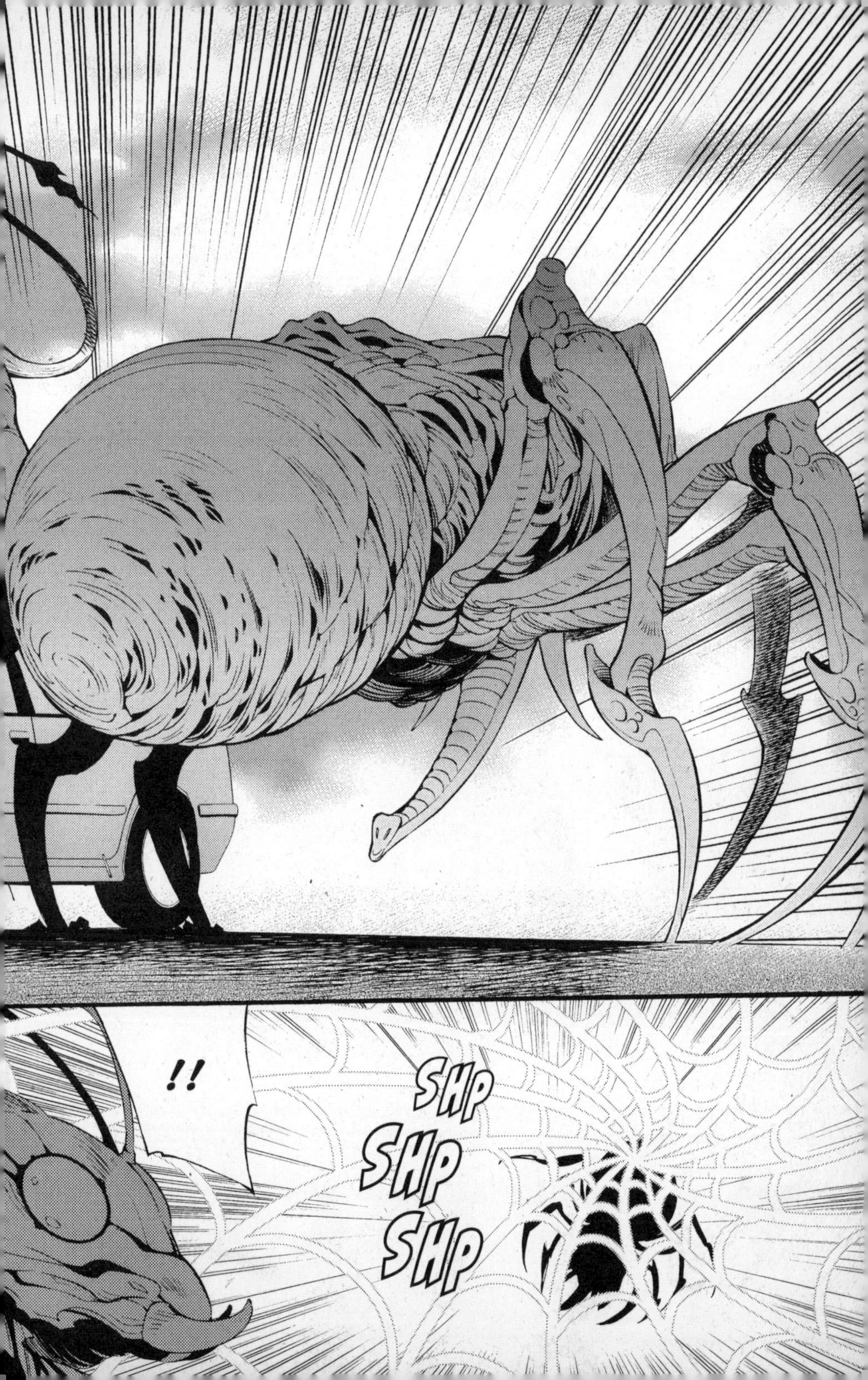
!!
SHP
SHP
SHP

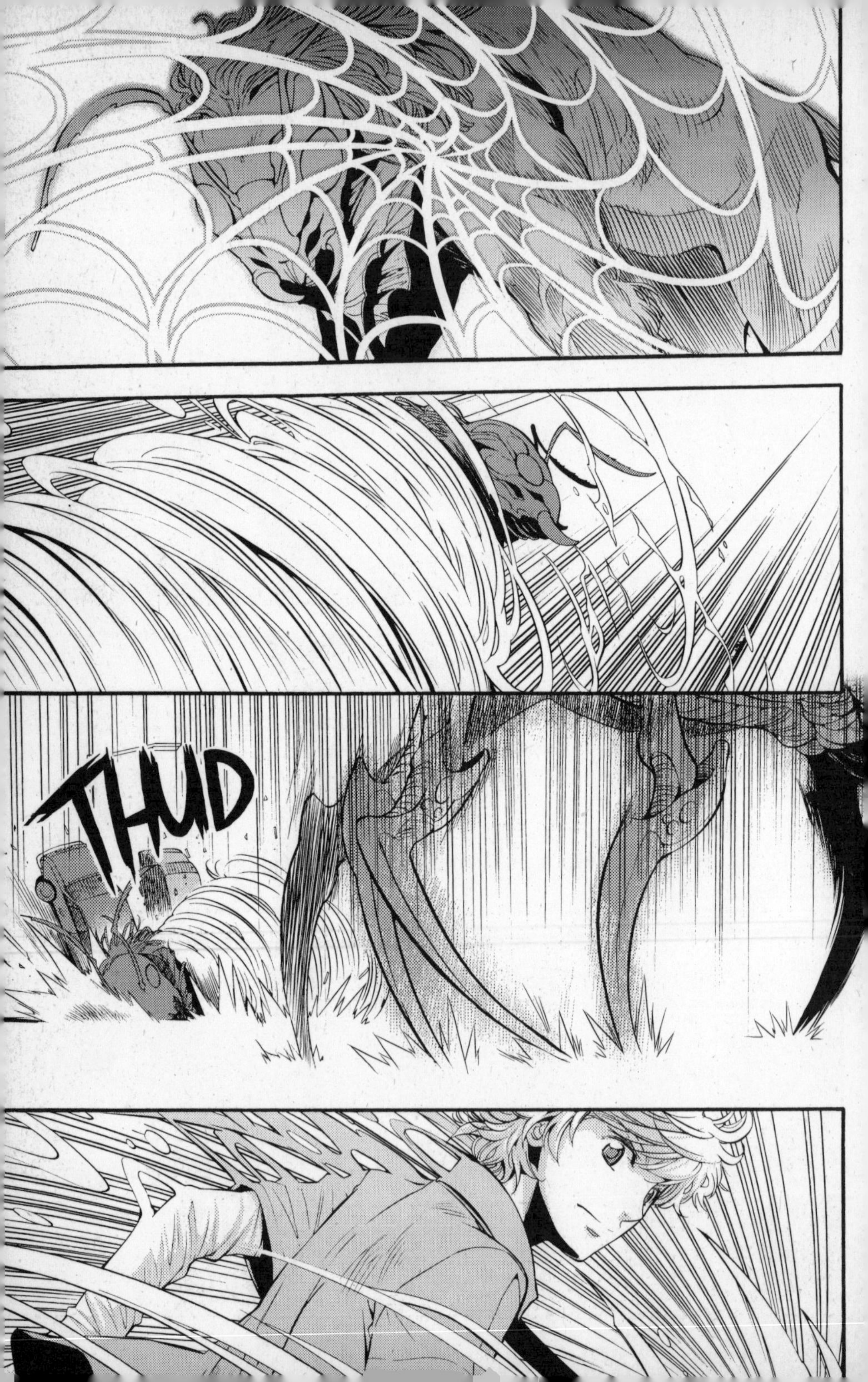
THUD

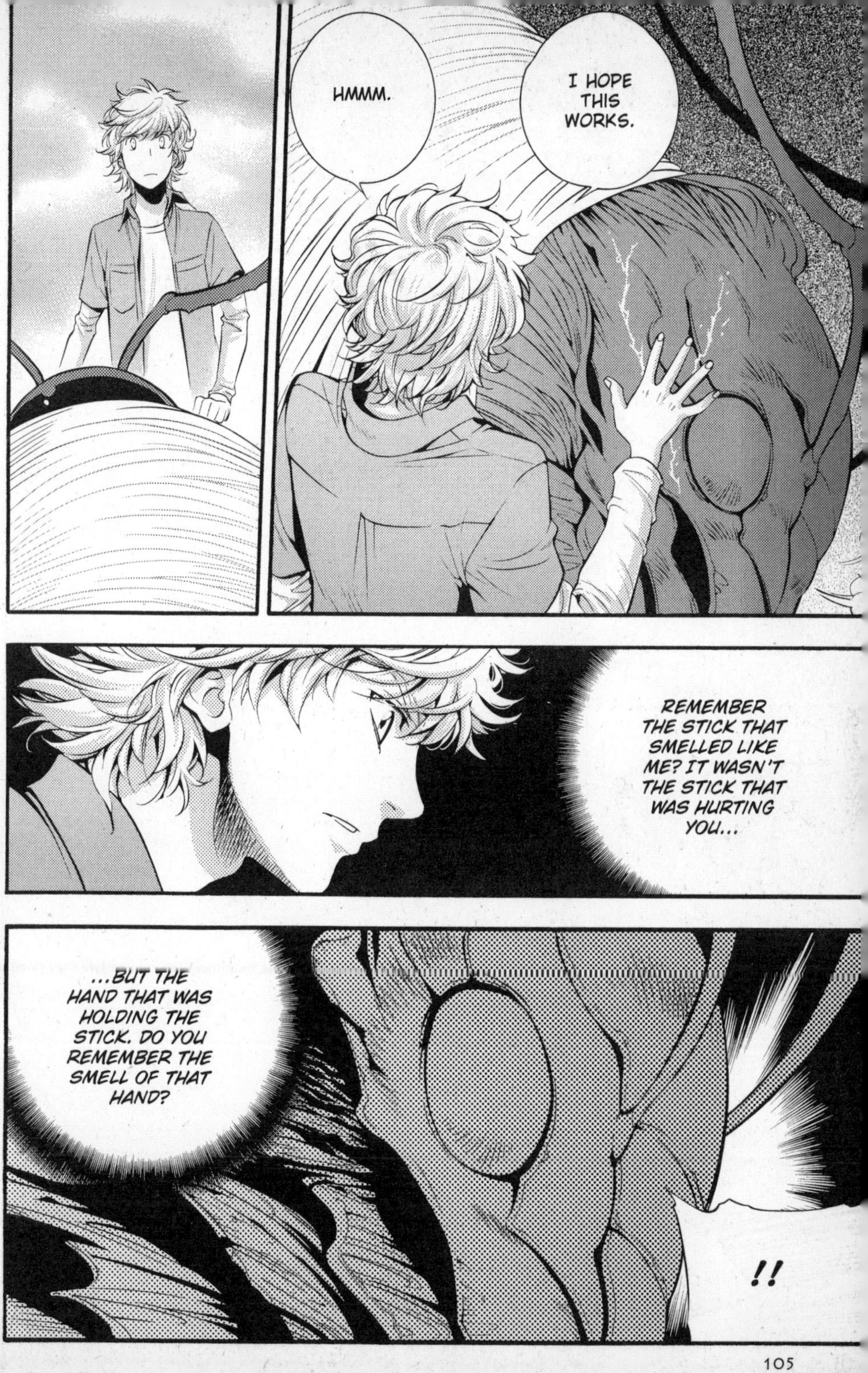
HMMM.
I HOPE THIS WORKS.
REMEMBER THE STICK THAT SMELLED LIKE ME? IT WASN'T THE STICK THAT WAS HURTING YOU...
...BUT THE HAND THAT WAS HOLDING THE STICK. DO YOU REMEMBER THE SMELL OF THAT HAND?
!!

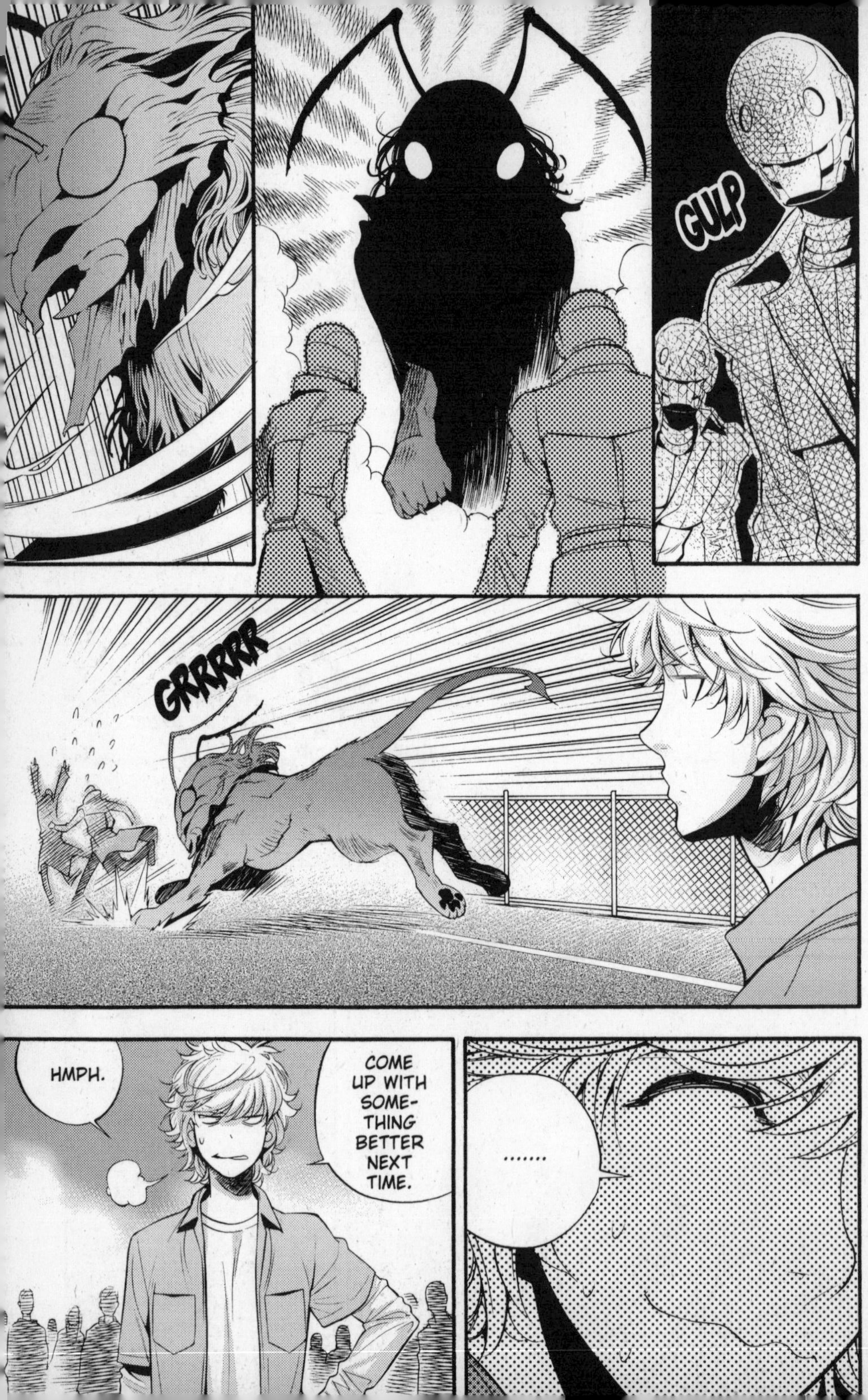
GULP
GRRRRR
HMPH.
COME UP WITH SOME-THING BETTER NEXT TIME.
....

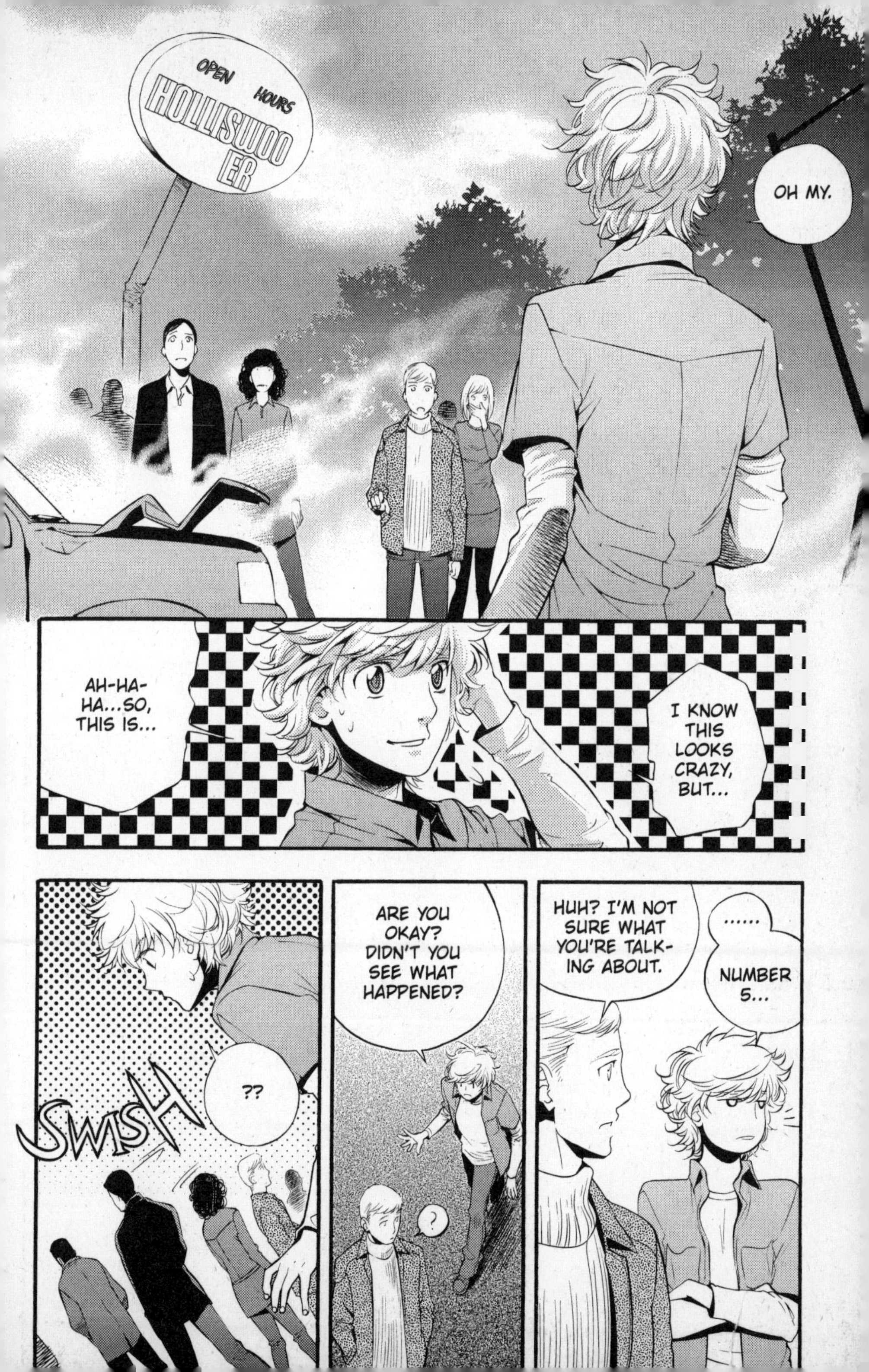
OPEN HOURS
HOLLISWOOER
OH MY.
AH-HA-HA...SO, THIS IS...
I KNOW THIS LOOKS CRAZY, BUT...
??
SWISH
ARE YOU OKAY? DIDN'T YOU SEE WHAT HAPPENED?
?
HUH? I'M NOT SURE WHAT YOU'RE TALKING ABOUT.
......
NUMBER 5...

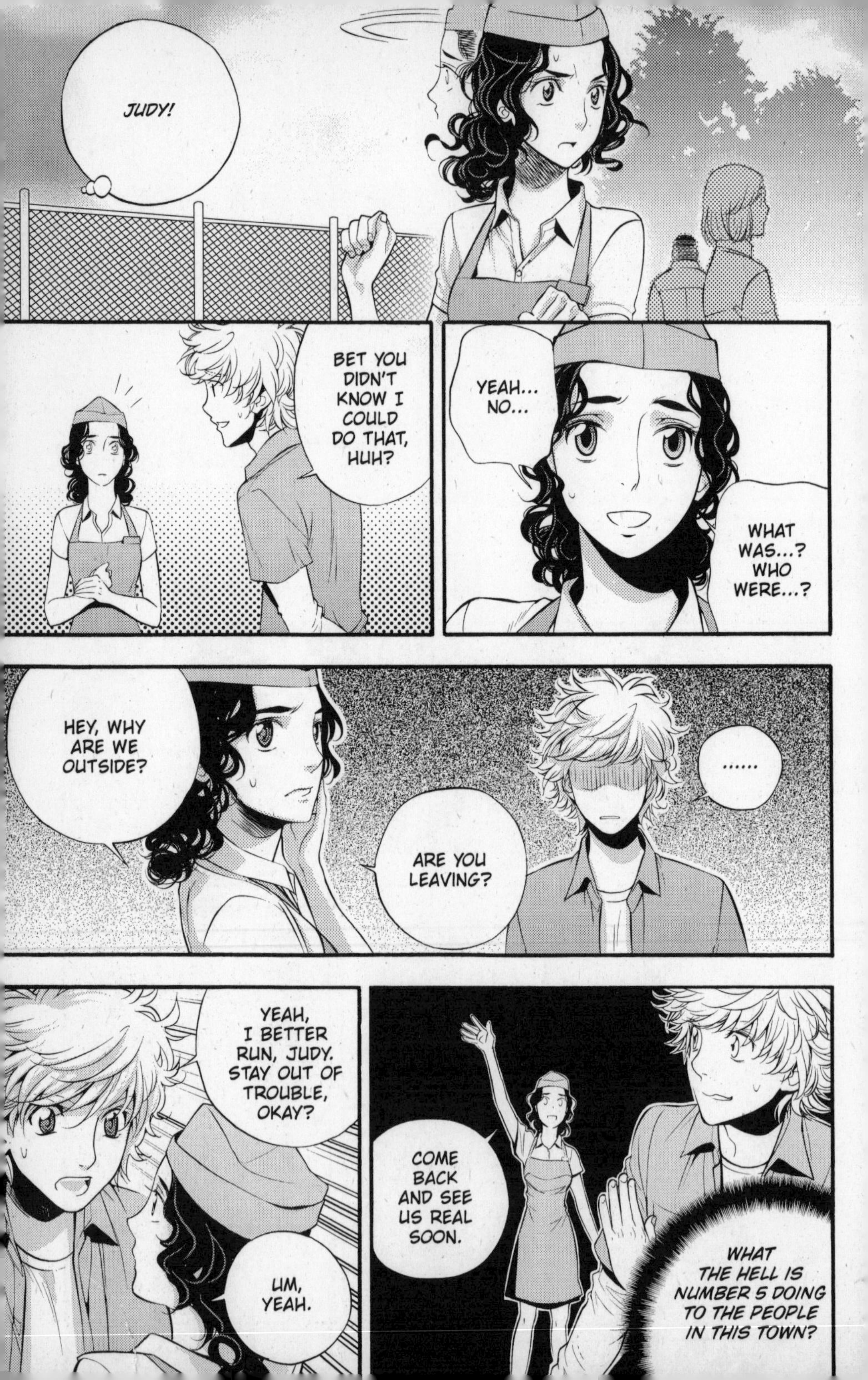
JUDY!
BET YOU DIDN'T KNOW I COULD DO THAT, HUH?
YEAH... NO...
WHAT WAS...? WHO WERE...?
HEY, WHY ARE WE OUTSIDE?
ARE YOU LEAVING?
......
YEAH, I BETTER RUN, JUDY. STAY OUT OF TROUBLE, OKAY?
UM, YEAH.
COME BACK AND SEE US REAL SOON.
WHAT THE HELL IS NUMBER 5 DOING TO THE PEOPLE IN THIS TOWN?

DANIEL X

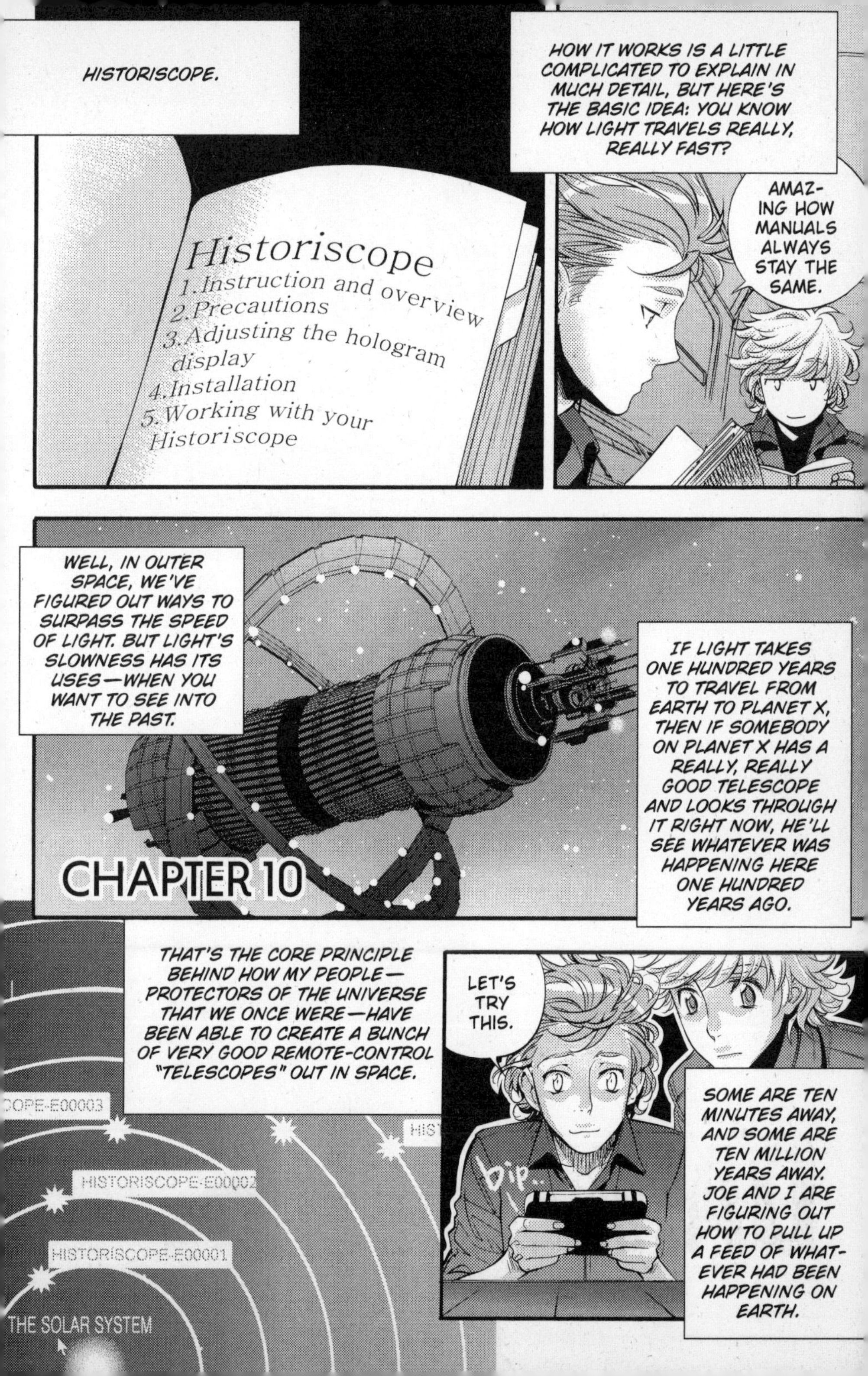
HISTORISCOPE.
Historiscope
1.Instruction and overview
2.Precautions
3.Adjusting the hologram display
4.Installation
5.Working with your Historiscope
HOW IT WORKS IS A LITTLE COMPLICATED TO EXPLAIN IN MUCH DETAIL, BUT HERE'S THE BASIC IDEA: YOU KNOW HOW LIGHT TRAVELS REALLY, REALLY FAST?
AMAZ-ING HOW MANUALS ALWAYS STAY THE SAME.
WELL, IN OUTER SPACE, WE'VE FIGURED OUT WAYS TO SURPASS THE SPEED OF LIGHT. BUT LIGHT'S SLOWNESS HAS ITS USES—WHEN YOU WANT TO SEE INTO THE PAST.
CHAPTER 10
IF LIGHT TAKES ONE HUNDRED YEARS TO TRAVEL FROM EARTH TO PLANET X, THEN IF SOMEBODY ON PLANET X HAS A REALLY, REALLY GOOD TELESCOPE AND LOOKS THROUGH IT RIGHT NOW, HE'LL SEE WHATEVER WAS HAPPENING HERE ONE HUNDRED YEARS AGO.
THAT'S THE CORE PRINCIPLE BEHIND HOW MY PEOPLE—PROTECTORS OF THE UNIVERSE THAT WE ONCE WERE—HAVE BEEN ABLE TO CREATE A BUNCH OF VERY GOOD REMOTE-CONTROL "TELESCOPES" OUT IN SPACE.
COPE-E00003
HIS
HISTORISCOPE-E0000
HISTORISCOPE-E00001
THE SOLAR SYSTEM
LET'S TRY THIS.
bip..
SOME ARE TEN MINUTES AWAY, AND SOME ARE TEN MILLION YEARS AWAY. JOE AND I ARE FIGURING OUT HOW TO PULL UP A FEED OF WHAT-EVER HAD BEEN HAPPENING ON EARTH.

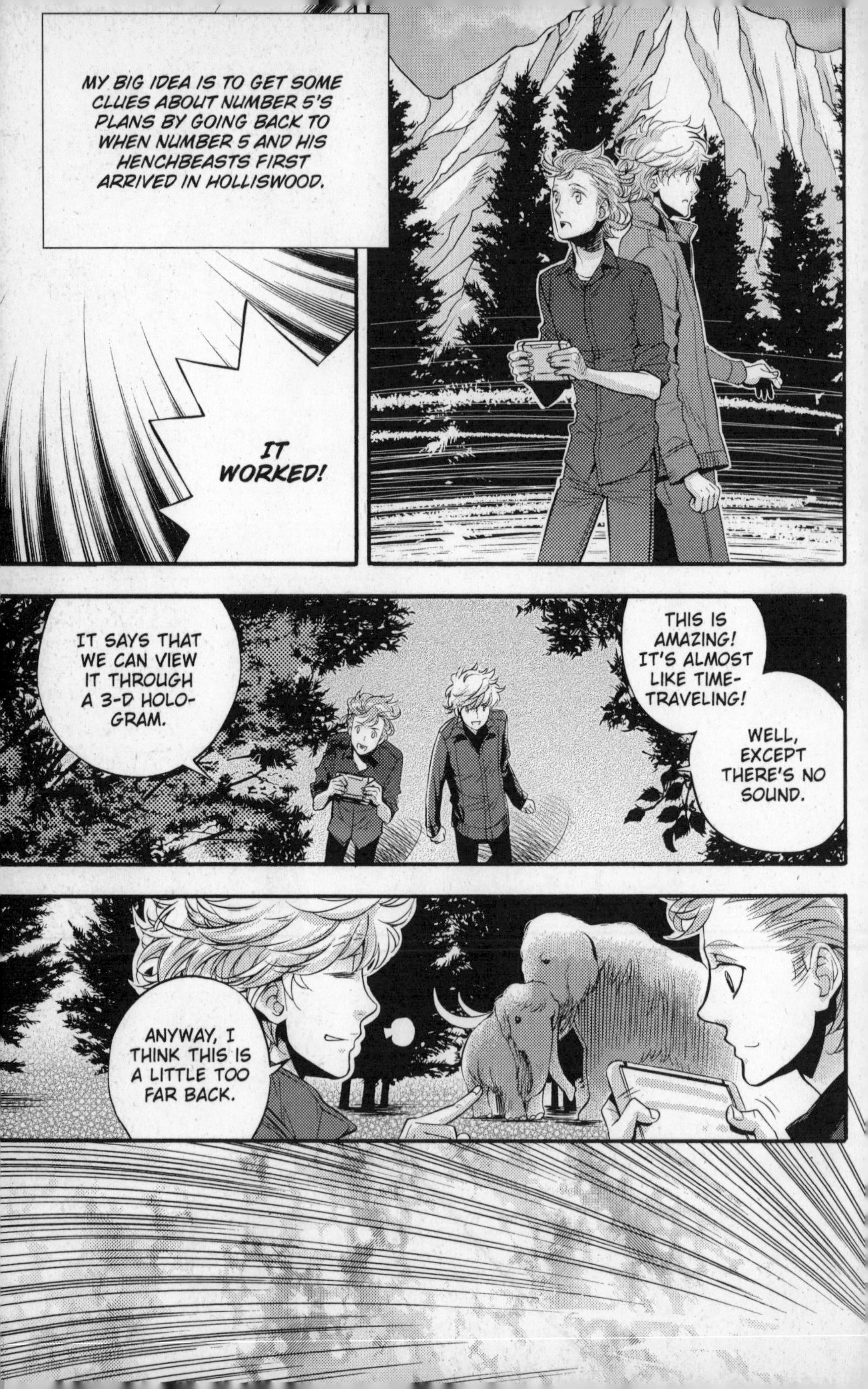

MY BIG IDEA IS TO GET SOME CLUES ABOUT NUMBER 5'S PLANS BY GOING BACK TO WHEN NUMBER 5 AND HIS HENCHBEASTS FIRST ARRIVED IN HOLLISWOOD.
IT WORKED!
IT SAYS THAT WE CAN VIEW IT THROUGH A 3-D HOLO-GRAM.
THIS IS AMAZING! IT'S ALMOST LIKE TIME-TRAVELING!
WELL, EXCEPT THERE'S NO SOUND.
ANYWAY, I THINK THIS IS A LITTLE TOO FAR BACK.

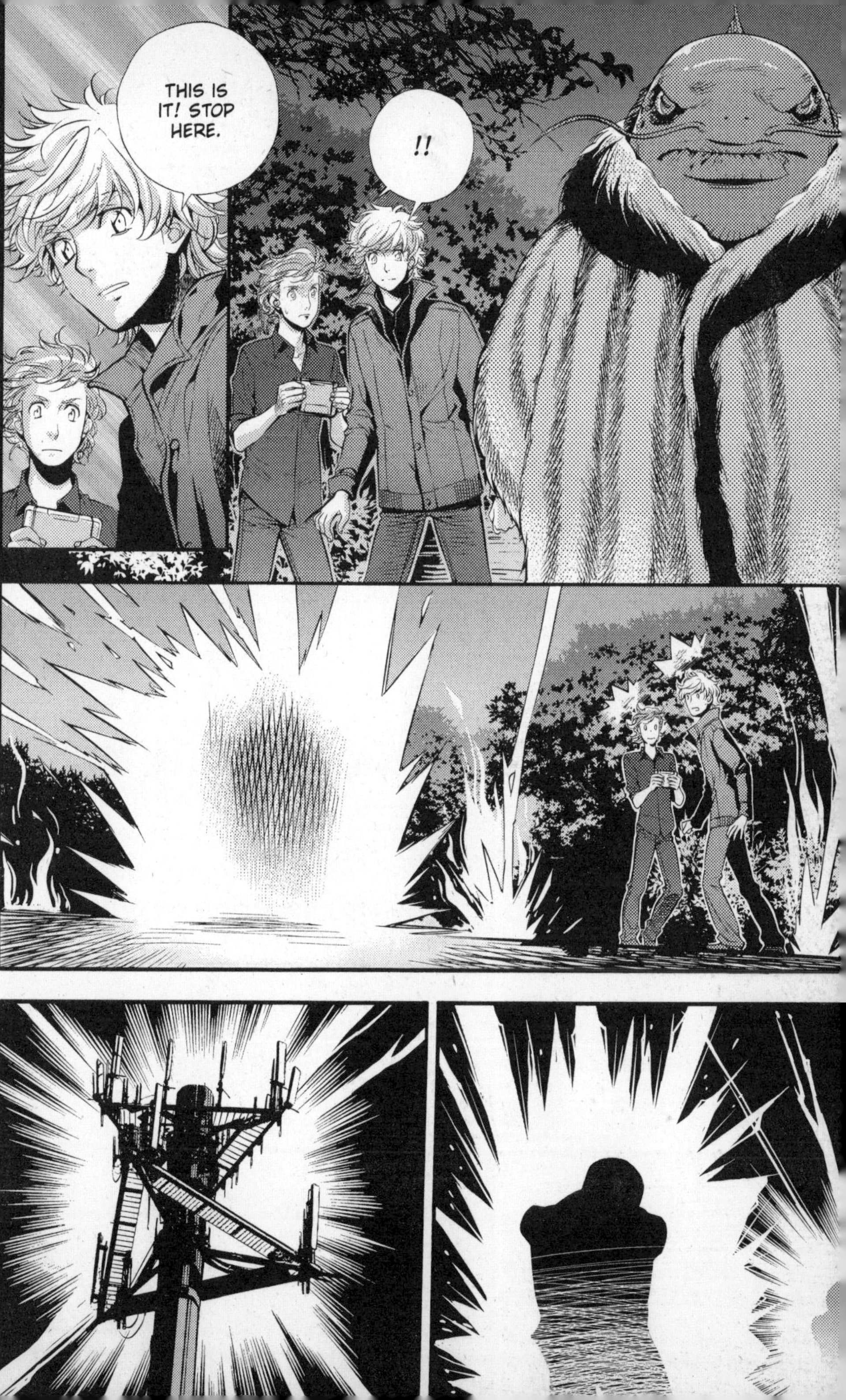
THIS IS IT! STOP HERE.
!!

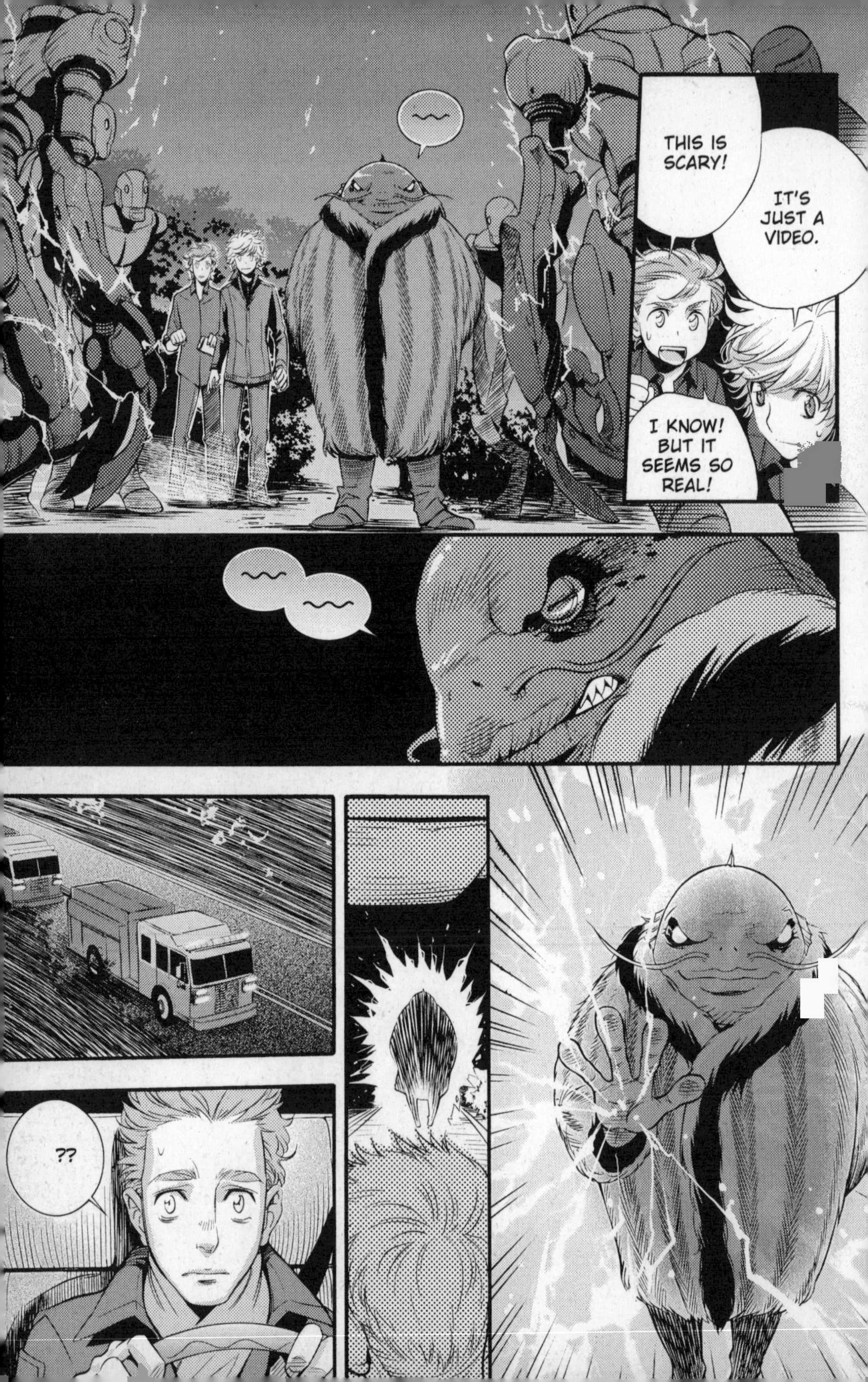

THIS IS SCARY!
IT'S JUST A VIDEO.
I KNOW! BUT IT SEEMS SO REAL!
??

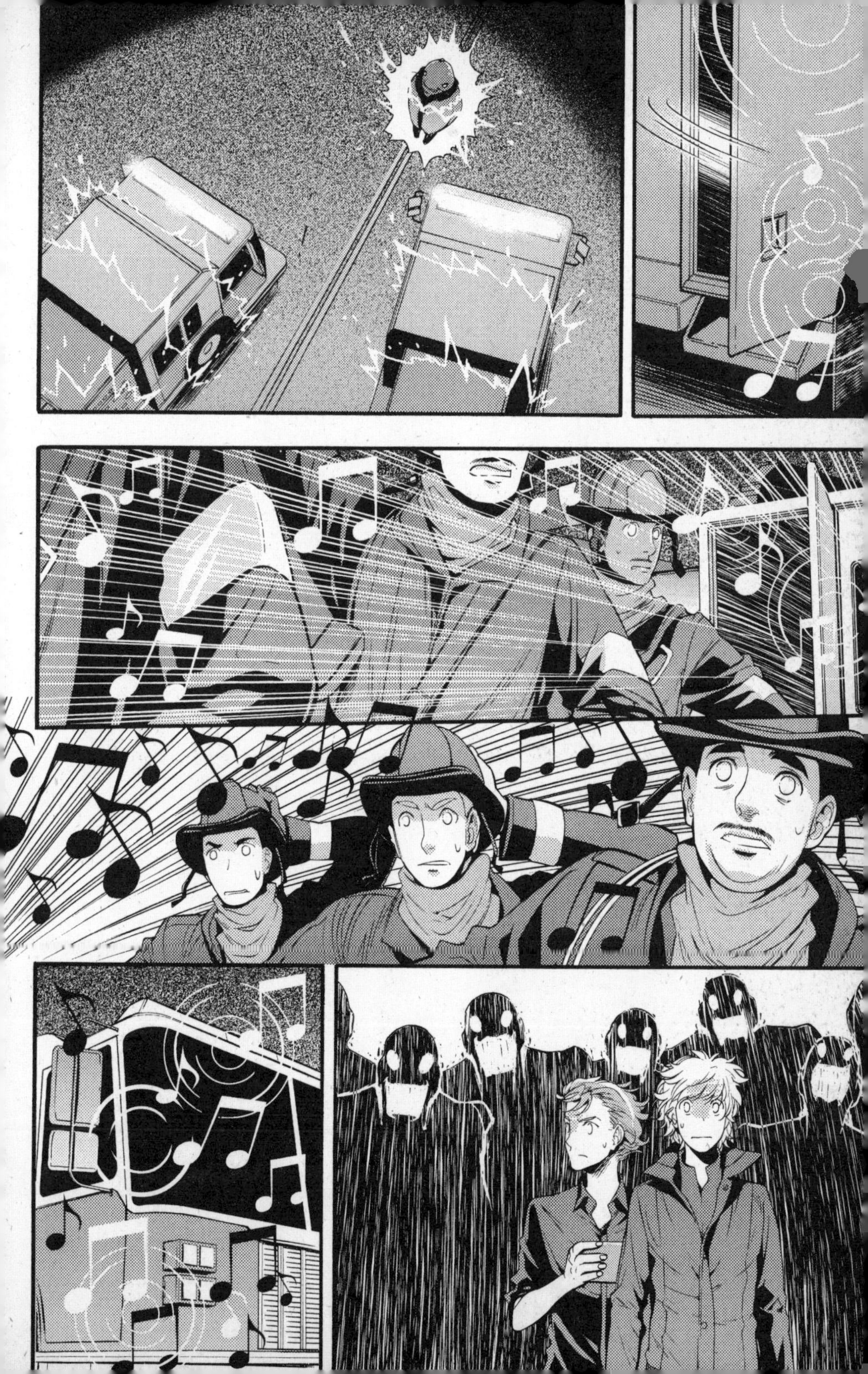

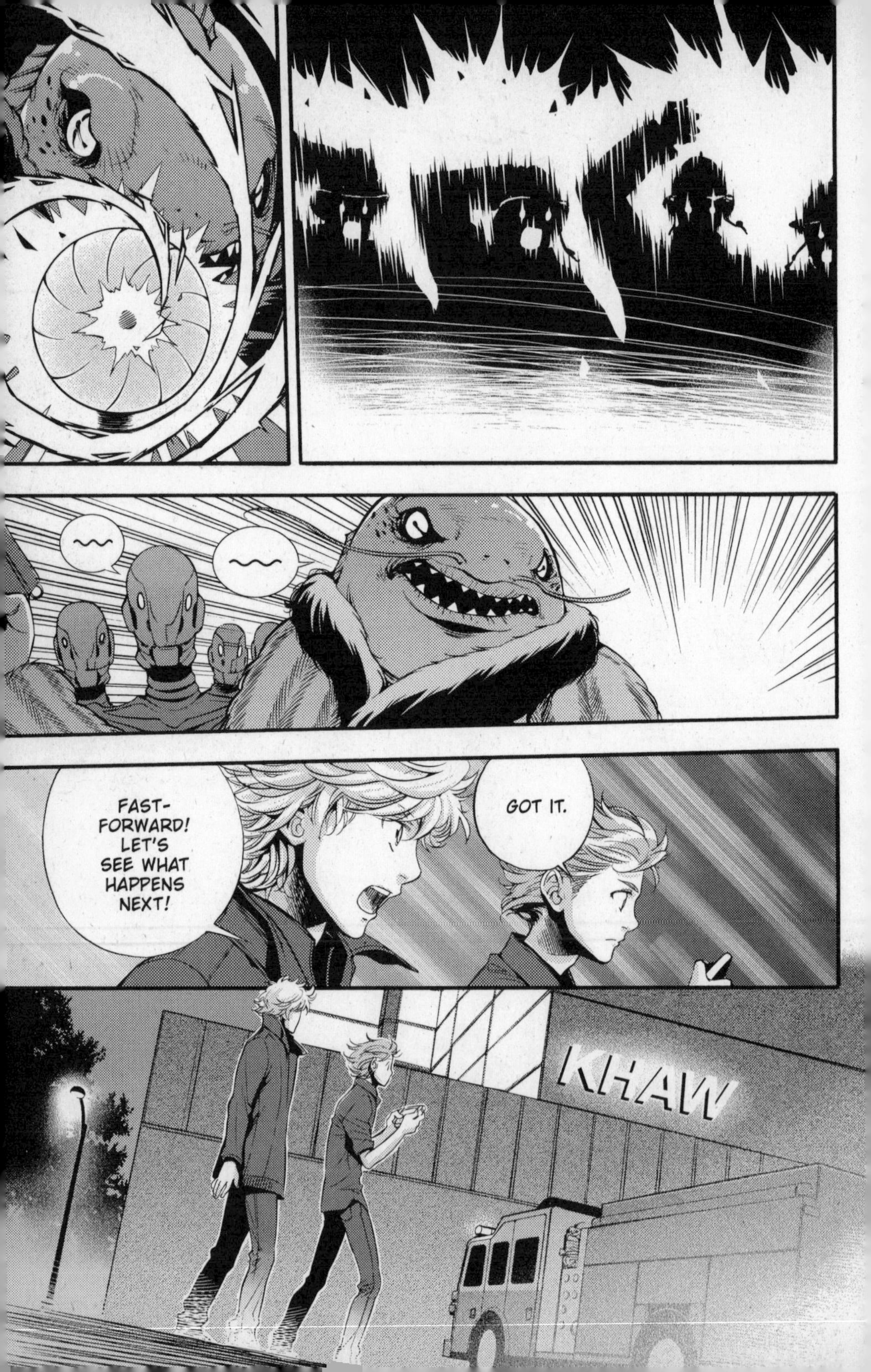
FAST-FORWARD! LET'S SEE WHAT HAPPENS NEXT!
GOT IT.
KHAW

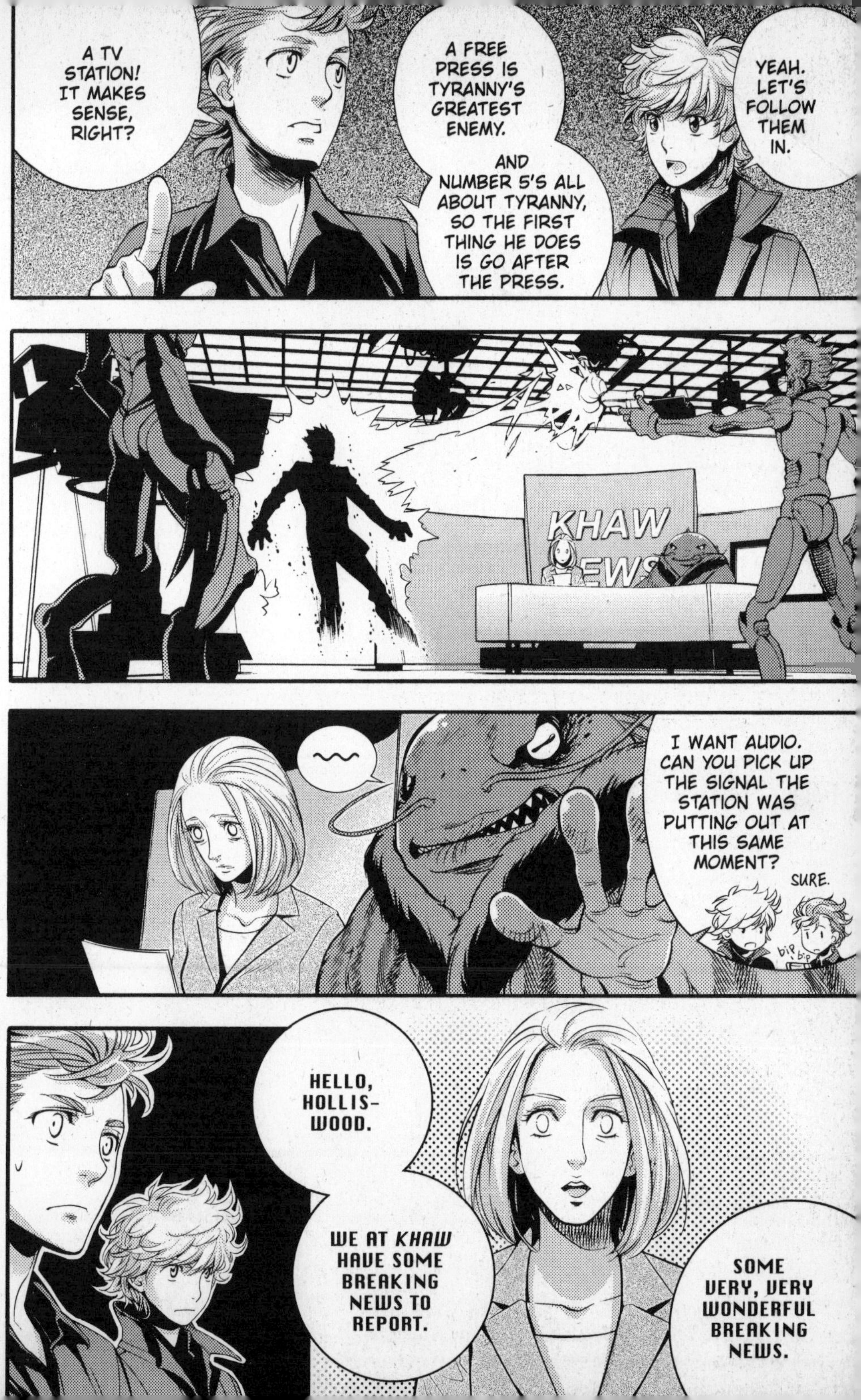
A TV STATION! IT MAKES SENSE, RIGHT?
A FREE PRESS IS TYRANNY'S GREATEST ENEMY.
AND NUMBER 5'S ALL ABOUT TYRANNY, SO THE FIRST THING HE DOES IS GO AFTER THE PRESS.
YEAH. LET'S FOLLOW THEM IN.
KHAW
I WANT AUDIO. CAN YOU PICK UP THE SIGNAL THE STATION WAS PUTTING OUT AT THIS SAME MOMENT?
SURE.
bip bip
HELLO, HOLLIS-WOOD.
WE AT *KHAW* HAVE SOME BREAKING NEWS TO REPORT.
SOME VERY, VERY WONDERFUL BREAKING NEWS.

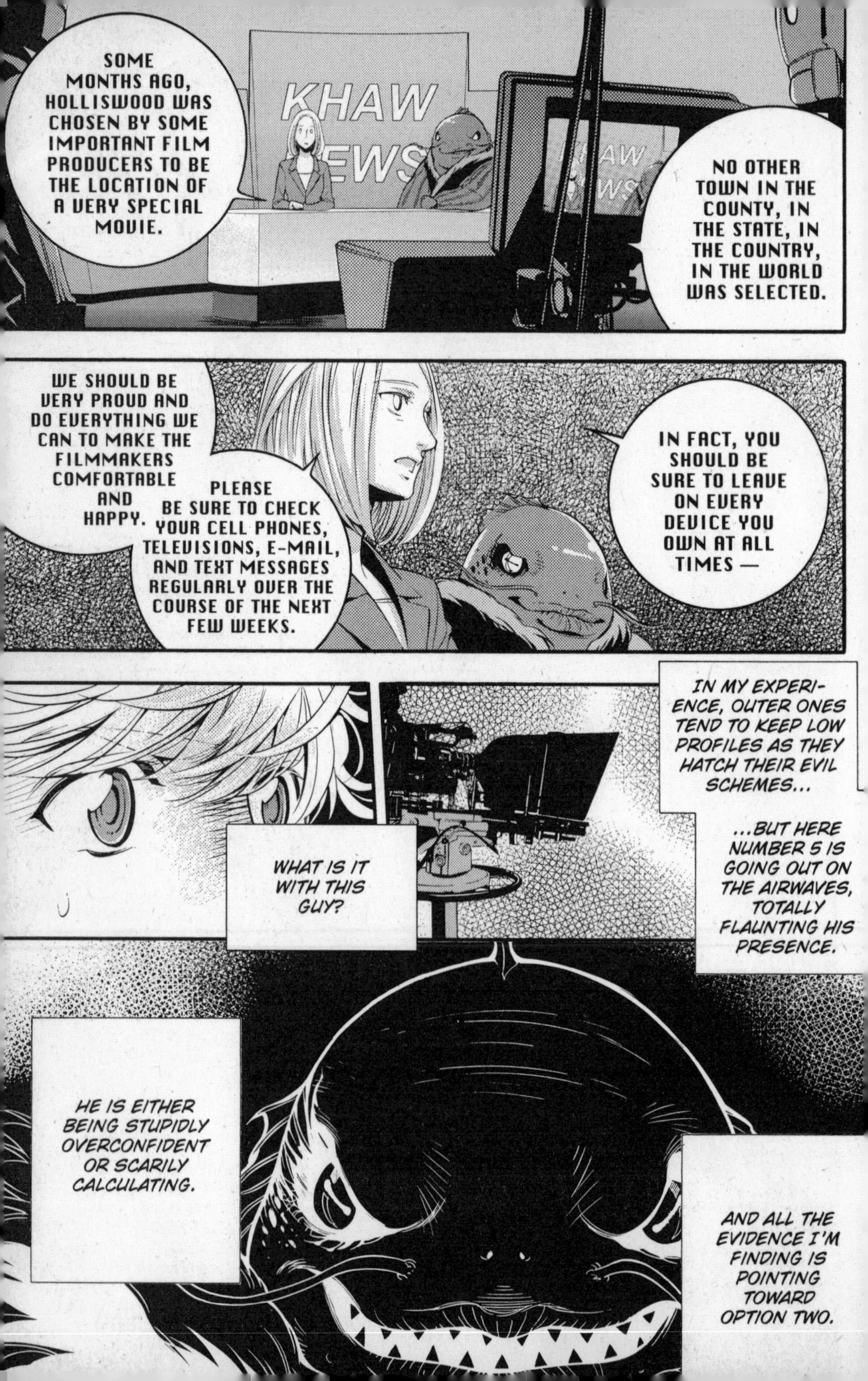
SOME MONTHS AGO, HOLLISWOOD WAS CHOSEN BY SOME IMPORTANT FILM PRODUCERS TO BE THE LOCATION OF A VERY SPECIAL MOVIE.
KHAW
NO OTHER TOWN IN THE COUNTY, IN THE STATE, IN THE COUNTRY, IN THE WORLD WAS SELECTED.
WE SHOULD BE VERY PROUD AND DO EVERYTHING WE CAN TO MAKE THE FILMMAKERS COMFORTABLE AND HAPPY.
PLEASE BE SURE TO CHECK YOUR CELL PHONES, TELEVISIONS, E-MAIL, AND TEXT MESSAGES REGULARLY OVER THE COURSE OF THE NEXT FEW WEEKS.
IN FACT, YOU SHOULD BE SURE TO LEAVE ON EVERY DEVICE YOU OWN AT ALL TIMES —
WHAT IS IT WITH THIS GUY?
IN MY EXPERIENCE, OUTER ONES TEND TO KEEP LOW PROFILES AS THEY HATCH THEIR EVIL SCHEMES...
...BUT HERE NUMBER 5 IS GOING OUT ON THE AIRWAVES, TOTALLY FLAUNTING HIS PRESENCE.
HE IS EITHER BEING STUPIDLY OVERCONFIDENT OR SCARILY CALCULATING.
AND ALL THE EVIDENCE I'M FINDING IS POINTING TOWARD OPTION TWO.

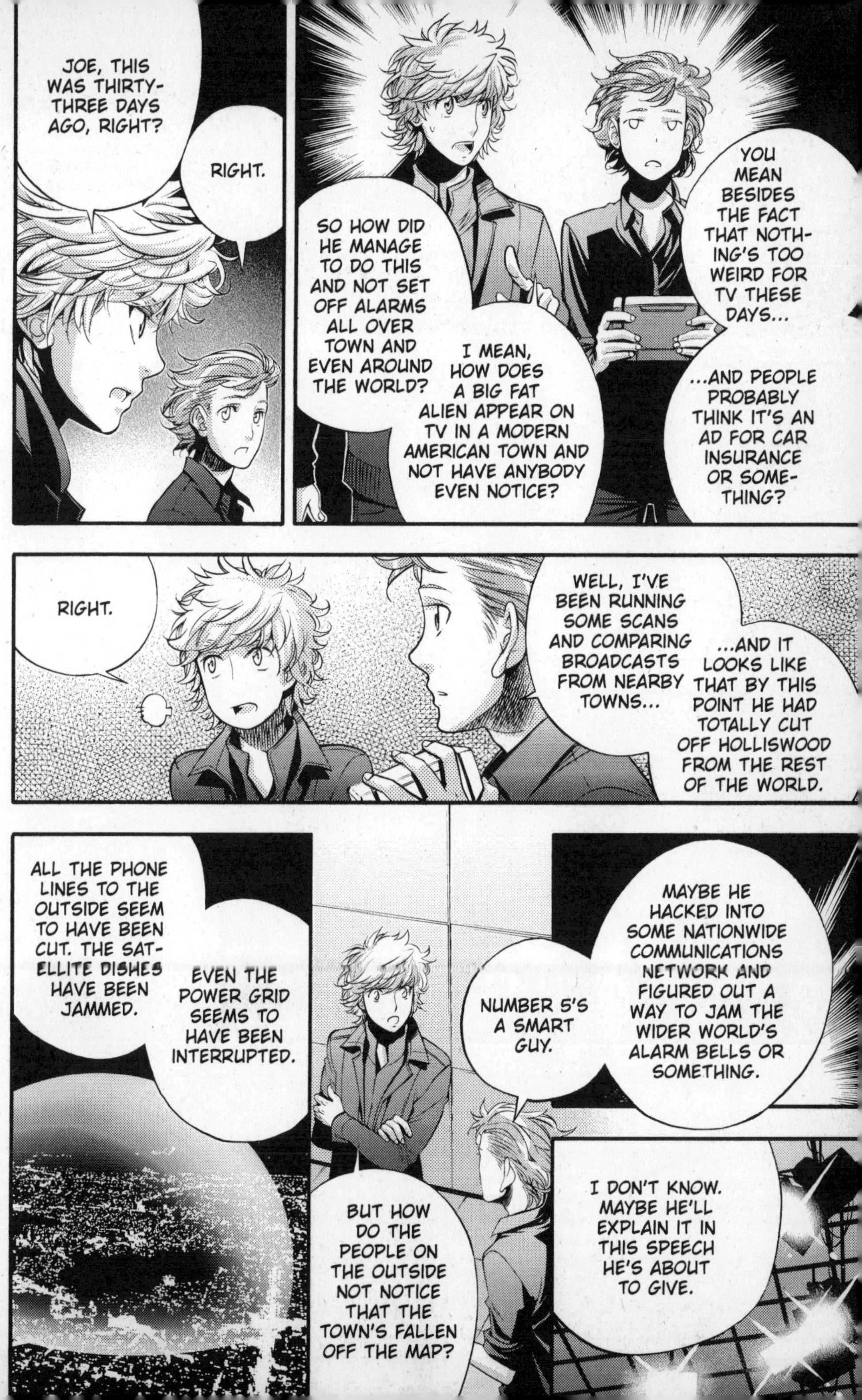
JOE, THIS WAS THIRTY-THREE DAYS AGO, RIGHT?
RIGHT.
SO HOW DID HE MANAGE TO DO THIS AND NOT SET OFF ALARMS ALL OVER TOWN AND EVEN AROUND THE WORLD?
I MEAN, HOW DOES A BIG FAT ALIEN APPEAR ON TV IN A MODERN AMERICAN TOWN AND NOT HAVE ANYBODY EVEN NOTICE?
YOU MEAN BESIDES THE FACT THAT NOTHING'S TOO WEIRD FOR TV THESE DAYS...
...AND PEOPLE PROBABLY THINK IT'S AN AD FOR CAR INSURANCE OR SOMETHING?
RIGHT.
WELL, I'VE BEEN RUNNING SOME SCANS AND COMPARING BROADCASTS FROM NEARBY TOWNS...
...AND IT LOOKS LIKE THAT BY THIS POINT HE HAD TOTALLY CUT OFF HOLLISWOOD FROM THE REST OF THE WORLD.
ALL THE PHONE LINES TO THE OUTSIDE SEEM TO HAVE BEEN CUT. THE SATELLITE DISHES HAVE BEEN JAMMED.
EVEN THE POWER GRID SEEMS TO HAVE BEEN INTERRUPTED.
NUMBER 5'S A SMART GUY.
MAYBE HE HACKED INTO SOME NATIONWIDE COMMUNICATIONS NETWORK AND FIGURED OUT A WAY TO JAM THE WIDER WORLD'S ALARM BELLS OR SOMETHING.
BUT HOW DO THE PEOPLE ON THE OUTSIDE NOT NOTICE THAT THE TOWN'S FALLEN OFF THE MAP?
I DON'T KNOW. MAYBE HE'LL EXPLAIN IT IN THIS SPEECH HE'S ABOUT TO GIVE.

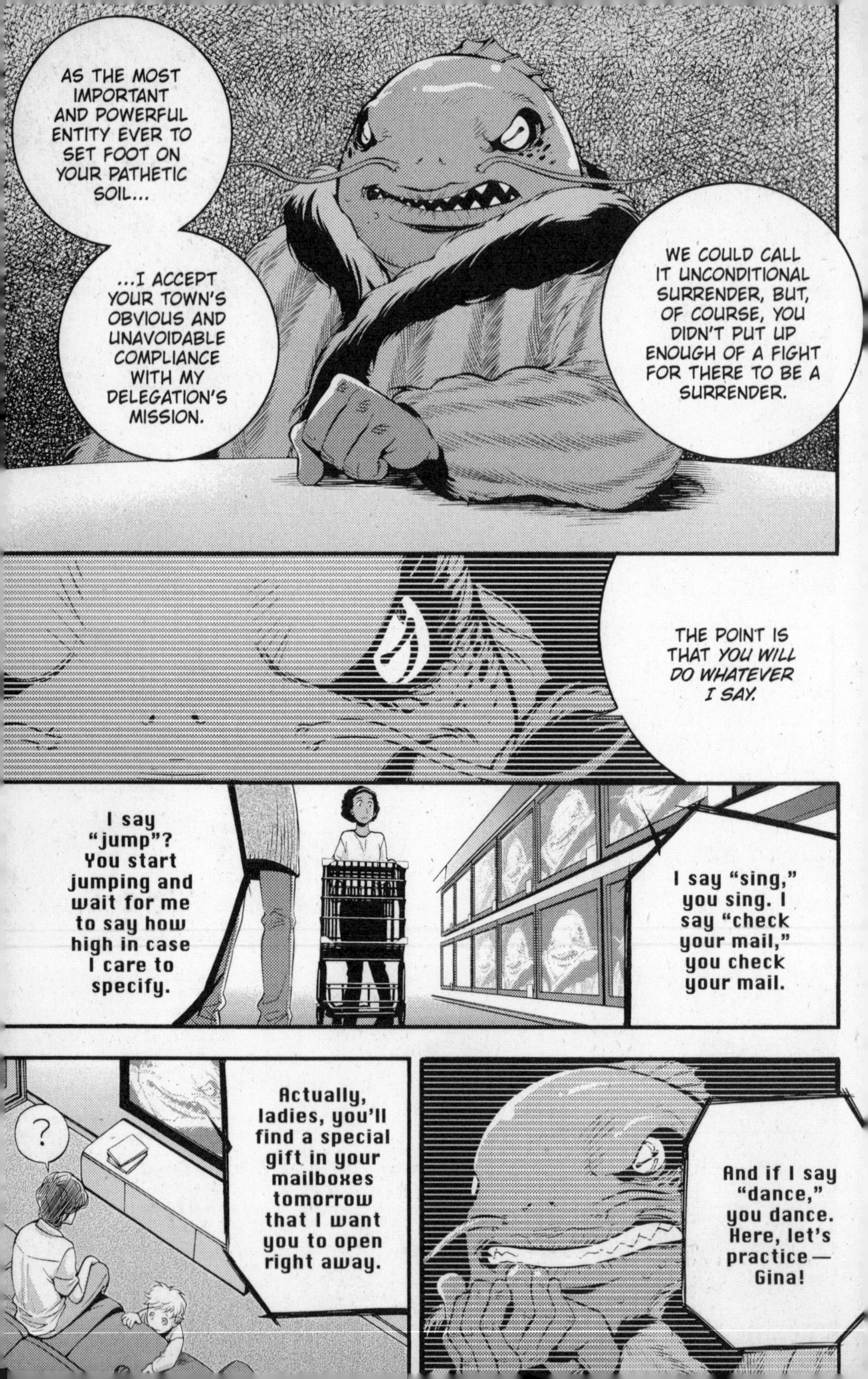
AS THE MOST IMPORTANT AND POWERFUL ENTITY EVER TO SET FOOT ON YOUR PATHETIC SOIL...
...I ACCEPT YOUR TOWN'S OBVIOUS AND UNAVOIDABLE COMPLIANCE WITH MY DELEGATION'S MISSION.
WE COULD CALL IT UNCONDITIONAL SURRENDER, BUT, OF COURSE, YOU DIDN'T PUT UP ENOUGH OF A FIGHT FOR THERE TO BE A SURRENDER.
THE POINT IS THAT *YOU WILL DO WHATEVER I SAY.*
I say "jump"? You start jumping and wait for me to say how high in case I care to specify.
I say "sing," you sing. I say "check your mail," you check your mail.
?
Actually, ladies, you'll find a special gift in your mailboxes tomorrow that I want you to open right away.
And if I say "dance," you dance. Here, let's practice — Gina!

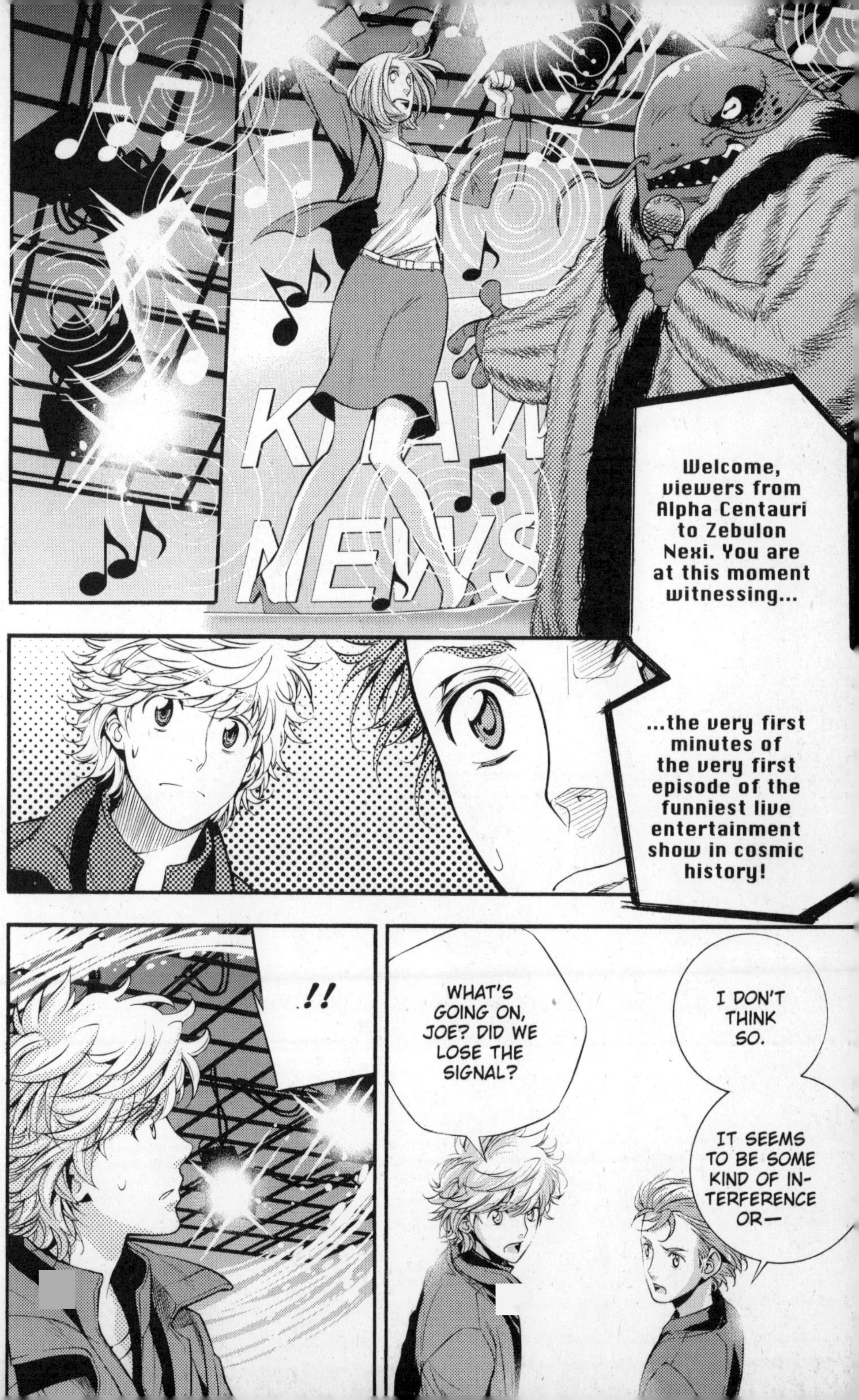
Welcome, viewers from Alpha Centauri to Zebulon Nexi. You are at this moment witnessing...
...the very first minutes of the very first episode of the funniest live entertainment show in cosmic history!
!!
WHAT'S GOING ON, JOE? DID WE LOSE THE SIGNAL?
I DON'T THINK SO.
IT SEEMS TO BE SOME KIND OF IN-TERFERENCE OR—

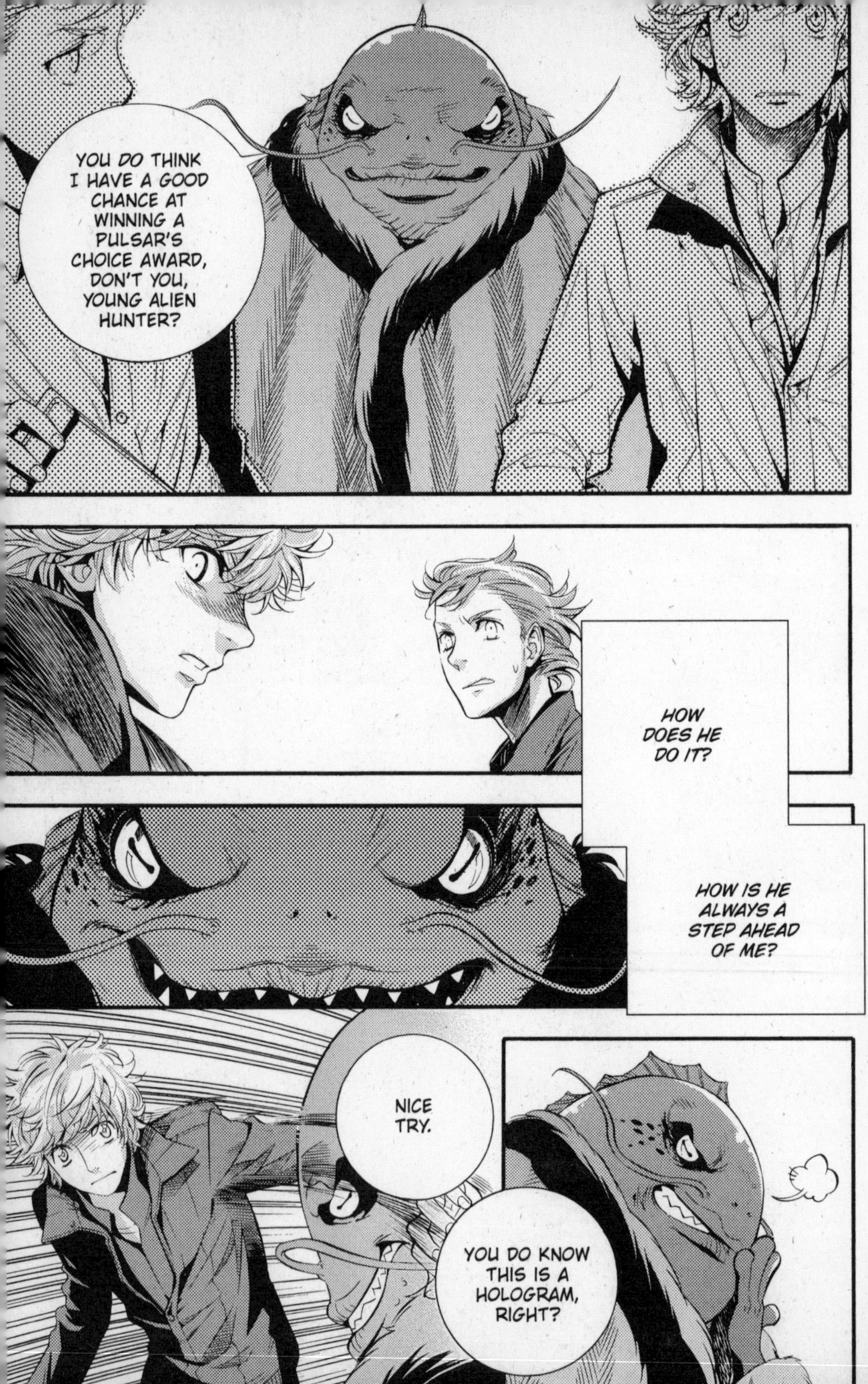
YOU DO THINK I HAVE A GOOD CHANCE AT WINNING A PULSAR'S CHOICE AWARD, DON'T YOU, YOUNG ALIEN HUNTER?
HOW DOES HE DO IT?
HOW IS HE ALWAYS A STEP AHEAD OF ME?
NICE TRY.
YOU DO KNOW THIS IS A HOLOGRAM, RIGHT?

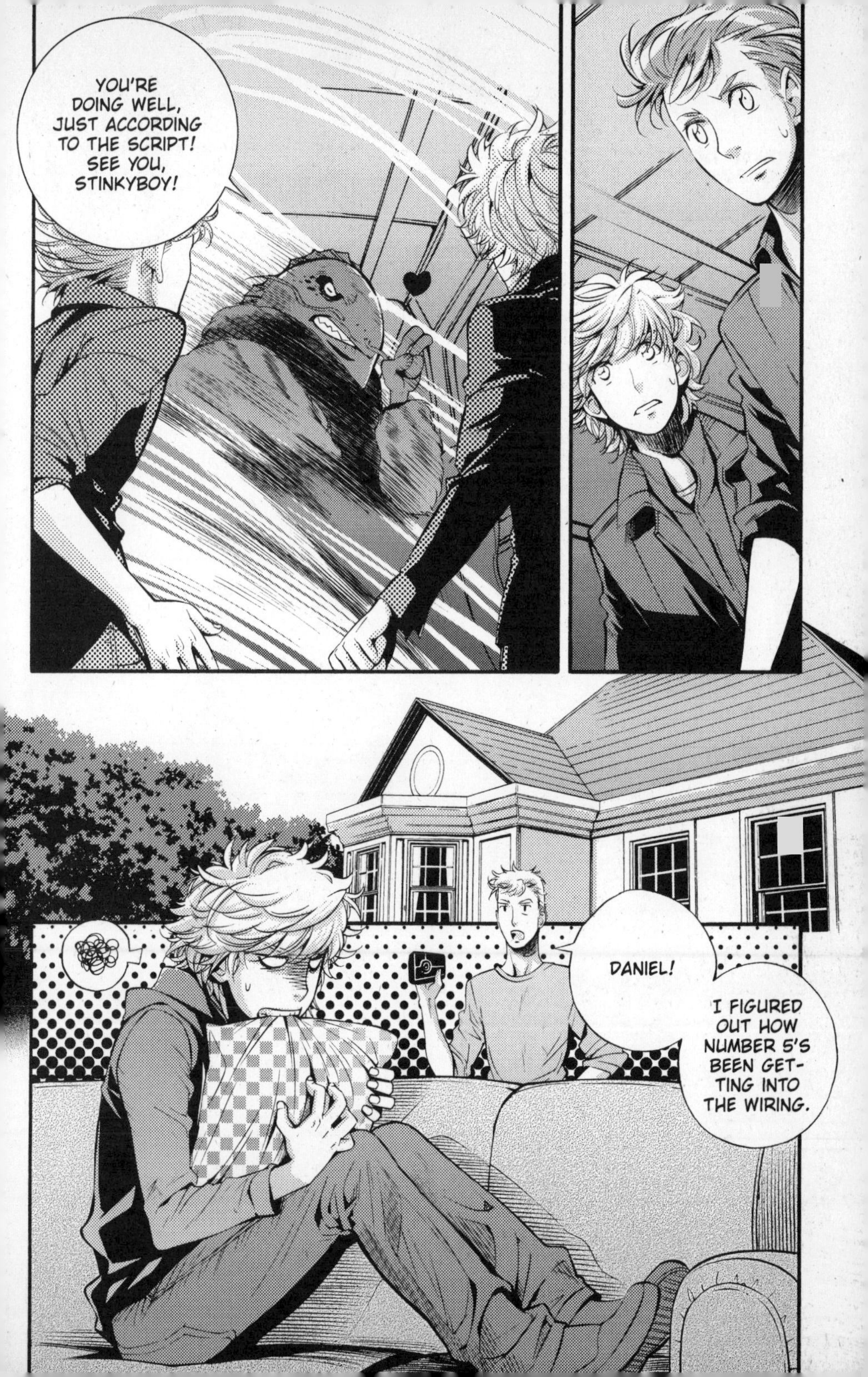
YOU'RE DOING WELL, JUST ACCORDING TO THE SCRIPT! SEE YOU, STINKYBOY!
DANIEL!
I FIGURED OUT HOW NUMBER 5'S BEEN GET-TING INTO THE WIRING.

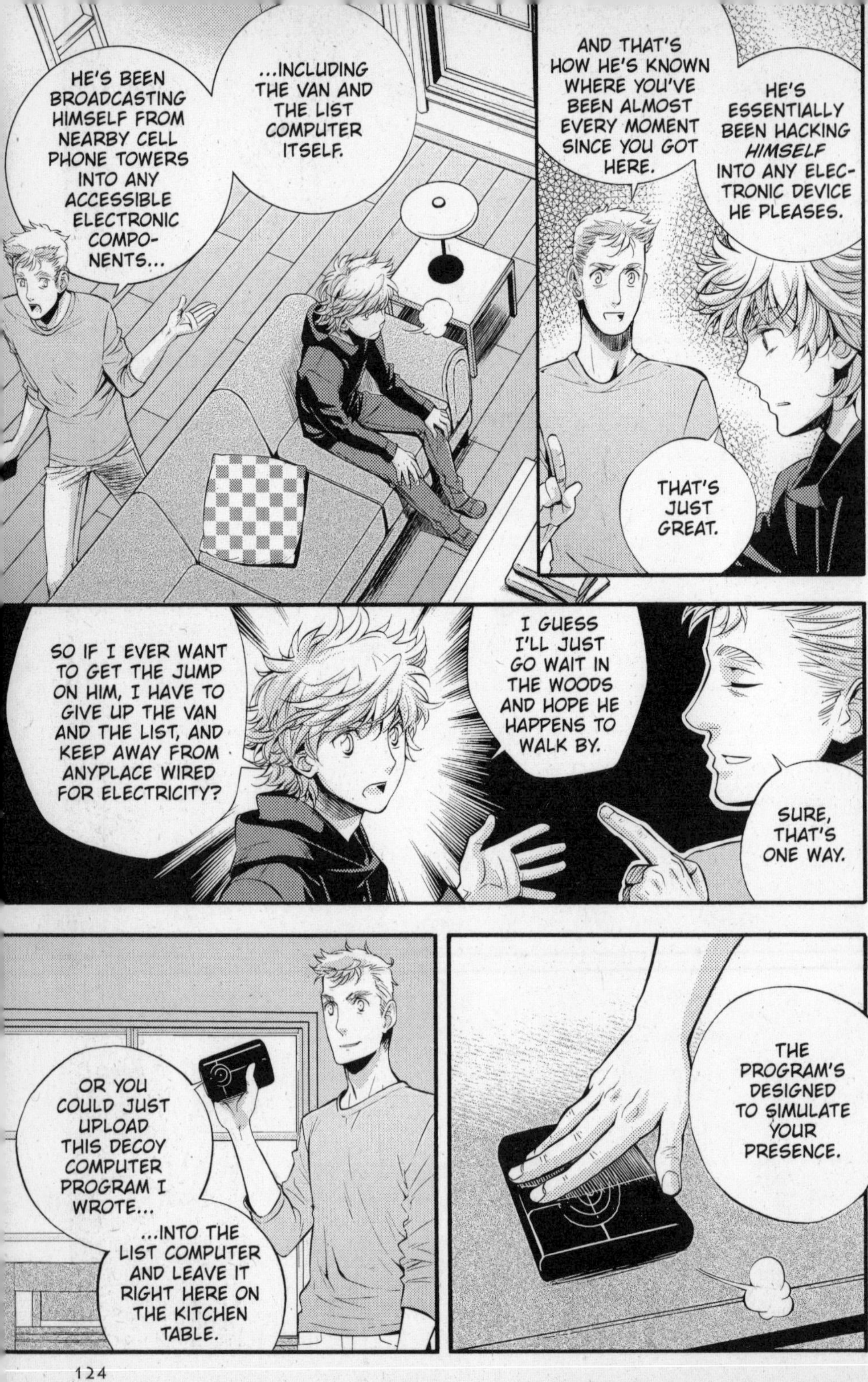
HE'S BEEN BROADCASTING HIMSELF FROM NEARBY CELL PHONE TOWERS INTO ANY ACCESSIBLE ELECTRONIC COMPONENTS...
...INCLUDING THE VAN AND THE LIST COMPUTER ITSELF.
AND THAT'S HOW HE'S KNOWN WHERE YOU'VE BEEN ALMOST EVERY MOMENT SINCE YOU GOT HERE.
HE'S ESSENTIALLY BEEN HACKING *HIMSELF* INTO ANY ELECTRONIC DEVICE HE PLEASES.
THAT'S JUST GREAT.
SO IF I EVER WANT TO GET THE JUMP ON HIM, I HAVE TO GIVE UP THE VAN AND THE LIST, AND KEEP AWAY FROM ANYPLACE WIRED FOR ELECTRICITY?
I GUESS I'LL JUST GO WAIT IN THE WOODS AND HOPE HE HAPPENS TO WALK BY.
SURE, THAT'S ONE WAY.
OR YOU COULD JUST UPLOAD THIS DECOY COMPUTER PROGRAM I WROTE...
...INTO THE LIST COMPUTER AND LEAVE IT RIGHT HERE ON THE KITCHEN TABLE.
THE PROGRAM'S DESIGNED TO SIMULATE YOUR PRESENCE.

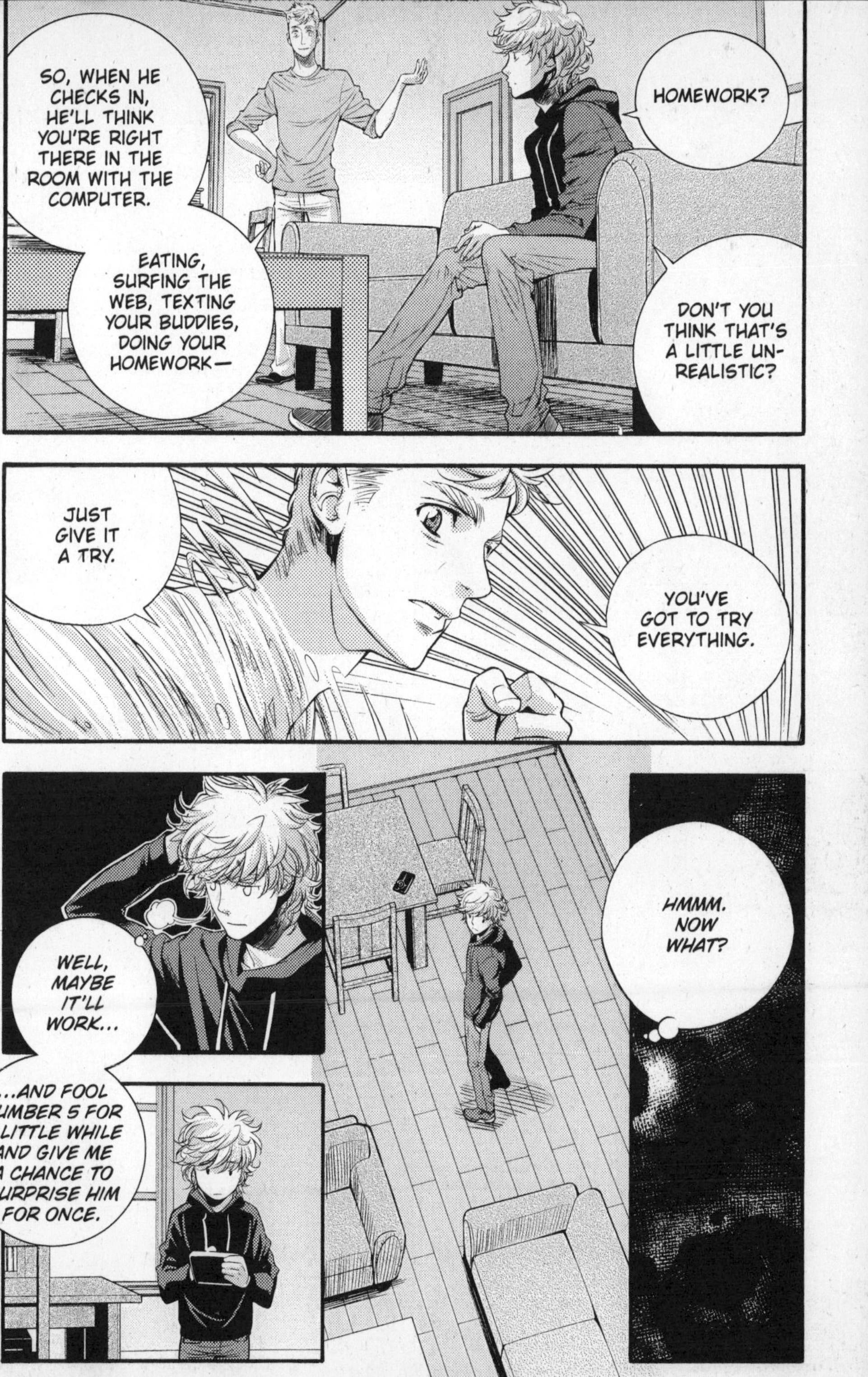

SO, WHEN HE CHECKS IN, HE'LL THINK YOU'RE RIGHT THERE IN THE ROOM WITH THE COMPUTER.
EATING, SURFING THE WEB, TEXTING YOUR BUDDIES, DOING YOUR HOMEWORK—
HOMEWORK?
DON'T YOU THINK THAT'S A LITTLE UN-REALISTIC?
JUST GIVE IT A TRY.
YOU'VE GOT TO TRY EVERYTHING.
WELL, MAYBE IT'LL WORK...
...AND FOOL NUMBER 5 FOR A LITTLE WHILE AND GIVE ME A CHANCE TO SURPRISE HIM FOR ONCE.
HMMM. NOW WHAT?

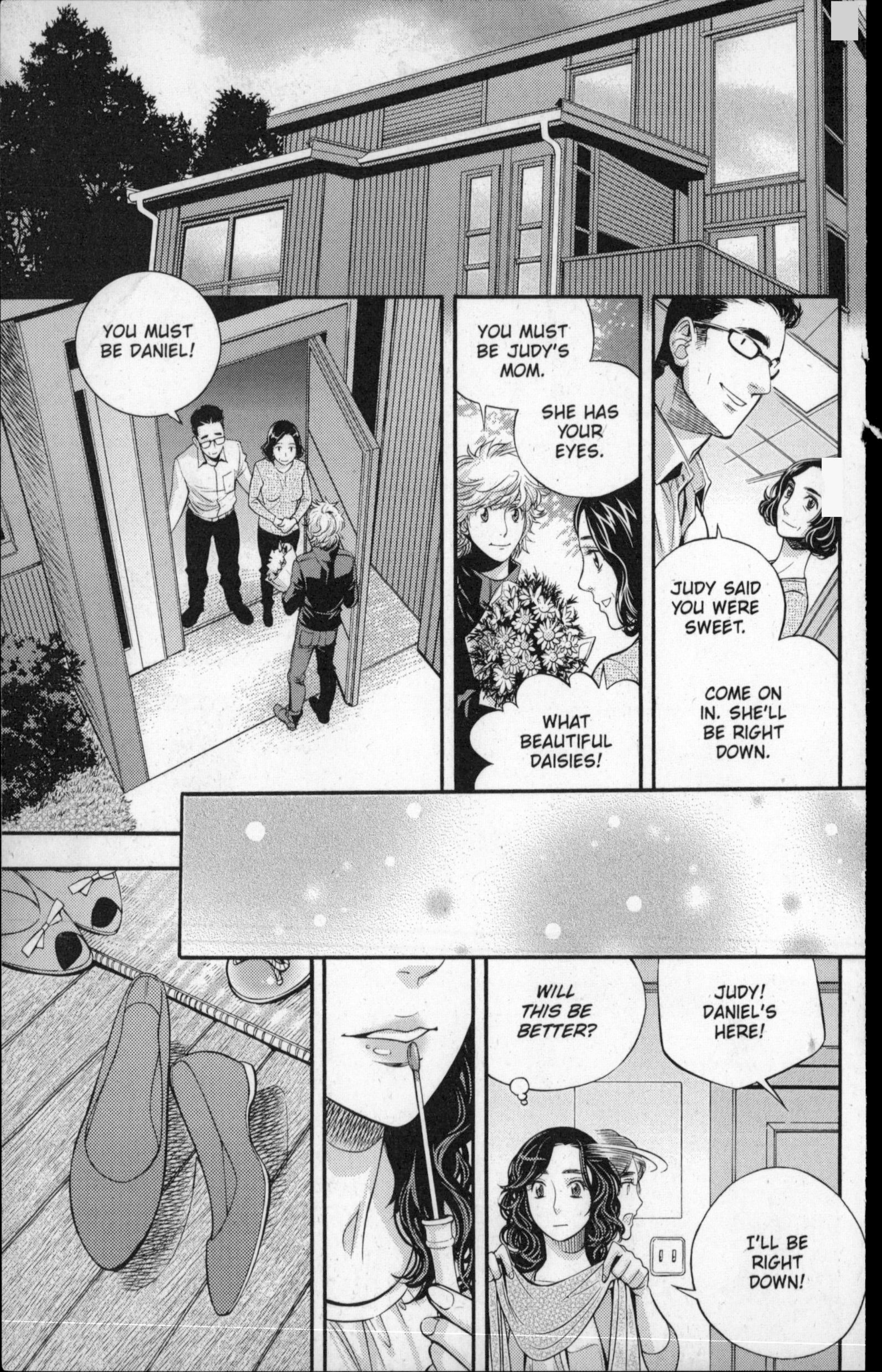
YOU MUST BE DANIEL!
YOU MUST BE JUDY'S MOM.
SHE HAS YOUR EYES.
WHAT BEAUTIFUL DAISIES!
JUDY SAID YOU WERE SWEET.
COME ON IN. SHE'LL BE RIGHT DOWN.
WILL THIS BE BETTER?
JUDY! DANIEL'S HERE!
I'LL BE RIGHT DOWN!

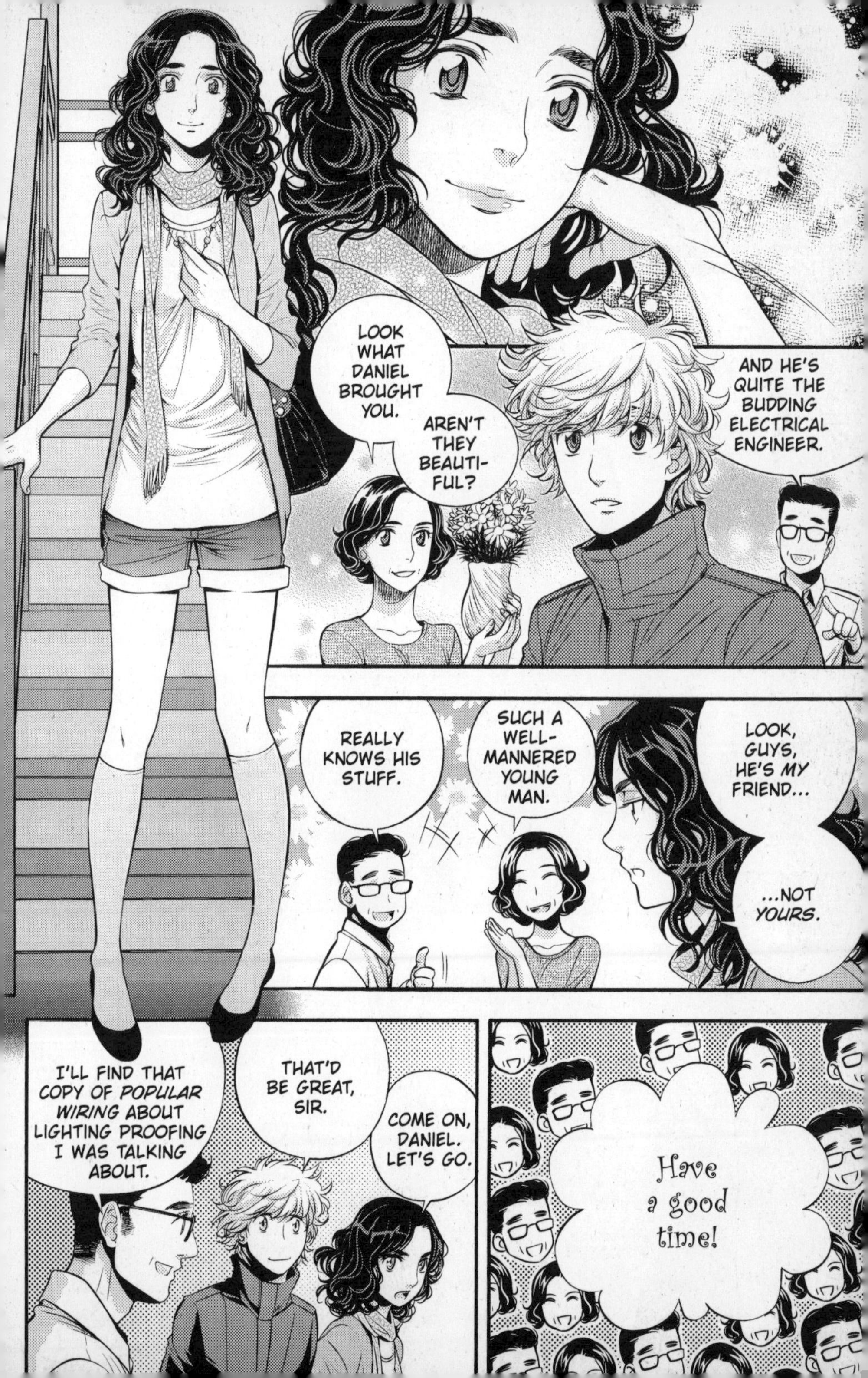
LOOK WHAT DANIEL BROUGHT YOU.
AREN'T THEY BEAUTI-FUL?
AND HE'S QUITE THE BUDDING ELECTRICAL ENGINEER.
REALLY KNOWS HIS STUFF.
SUCH A WELL-MANNERED YOUNG MAN.
LOOK, GUYS, HE'S *MY* FRIEND...
...NOT *YOURS*.
I'LL FIND THAT COPY OF *POPULAR WIRING* ABOUT LIGHTING PROOFING I WAS TALKING ABOUT.
THAT'D BE GREAT, SIR.
COME ON, DANIEL. LET'S GO.
Have a good time!

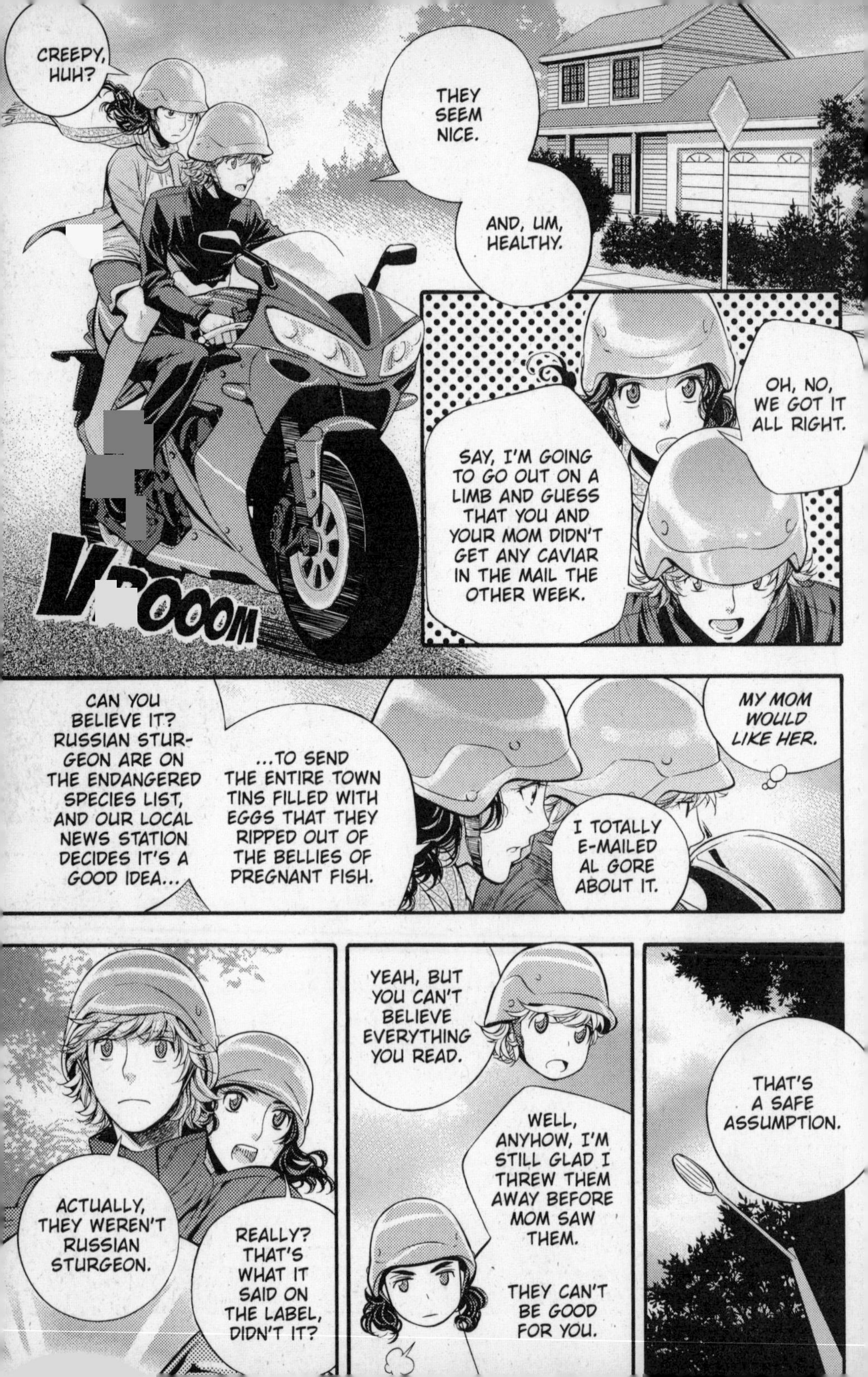
CREEPY, HUH?
THEY SEEM NICE.
AND, UM, HEALTHY.
SAY, I'M GOING TO GO OUT ON A LIMB AND GUESS THAT YOU AND YOUR MOM DIDN'T GET ANY CAVIAR IN THE MAIL THE OTHER WEEK.
OH, NO, WE GOT IT ALL RIGHT.
CAN YOU BELIEVE IT? RUSSIAN STURGEON ARE ON THE ENDANGERED SPECIES LIST, AND OUR LOCAL NEWS STATION DECIDES IT'S A GOOD IDEA...
...TO SEND THE ENTIRE TOWN TINS FILLED WITH EGGS THAT THEY RIPPED OUT OF THE BELLIES OF PREGNANT FISH.
I TOTALLY E-MAILED AL GORE ABOUT IT.
MY MOM WOULD LIKE HER.
ACTUALLY, THEY WEREN'T RUSSIAN STURGEON.
REALLY? THAT'S WHAT IT SAID ON THE LABEL, DIDN'T IT?
YEAH, BUT YOU CAN'T BELIEVE EVERYTHING YOU READ.
WELL, ANYHOW, I'M STILL GLAD I THREW THEM AWAY BEFORE MOM SAW THEM.
THEY CAN'T BE GOOD FOR YOU.
THAT'S A SAFE ASSUMPTION.

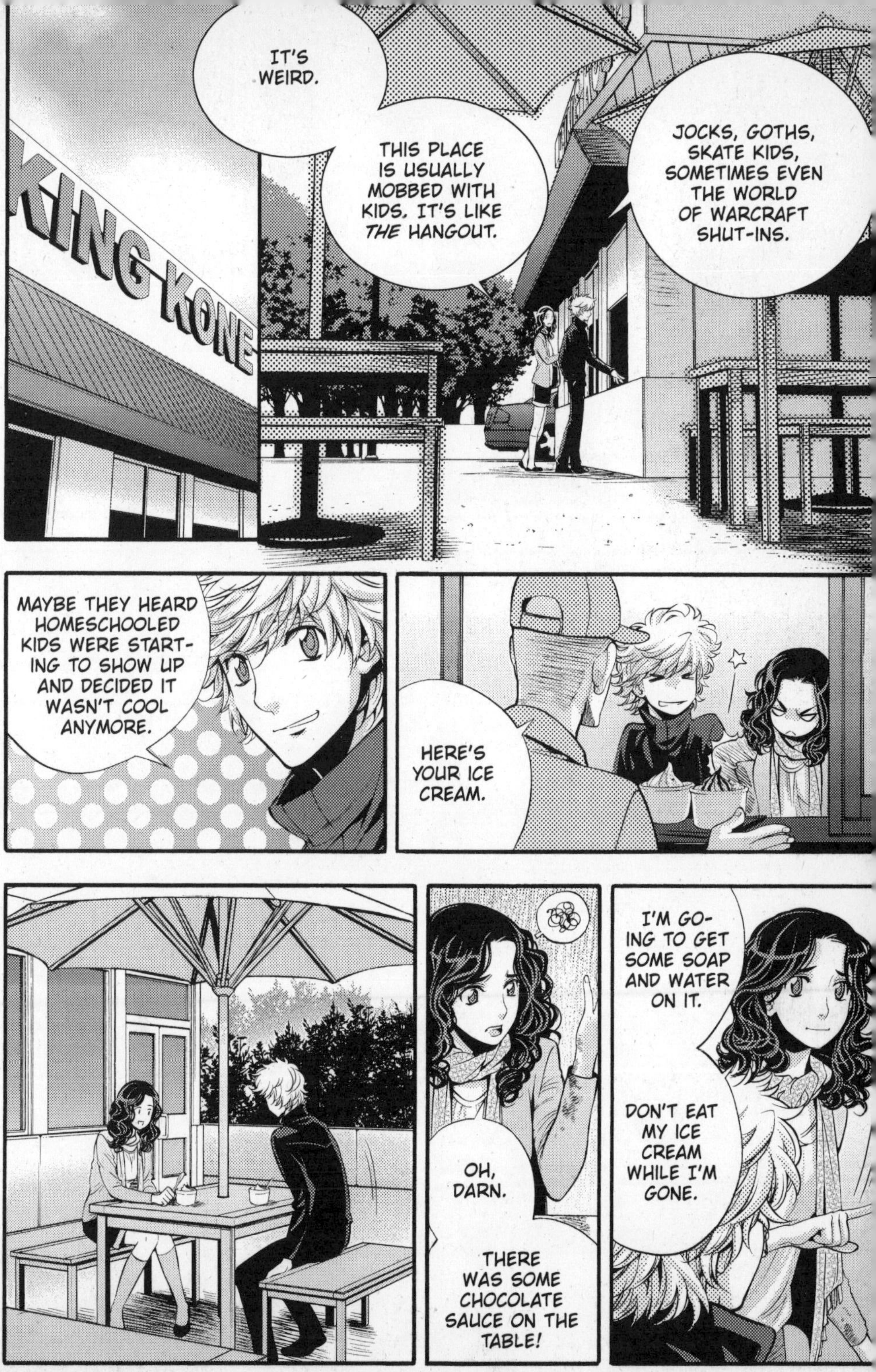
KING KONE
IT'S WEIRD.
THIS PLACE IS USUALLY MOBBED WITH KIDS. IT'S LIKE *THE* HANGOUT.
JOCKS, GOTHS, SKATE KIDS, SOMETIMES EVEN THE WORLD OF WARCRAFT SHUT-INS.
MAYBE THEY HEARD HOMESCHOOLED KIDS WERE STARTING TO SHOW UP AND DECIDED IT WASN'T COOL ANYMORE.
HERE'S YOUR ICE CREAM.
OH, DARN.
THERE WAS SOME CHOCOLATE SAUCE ON THE TABLE!
I'M GOING TO GET SOME SOAP AND WATER ON IT.
DON'T EAT MY ICE CREAM WHILE I'M GONE.

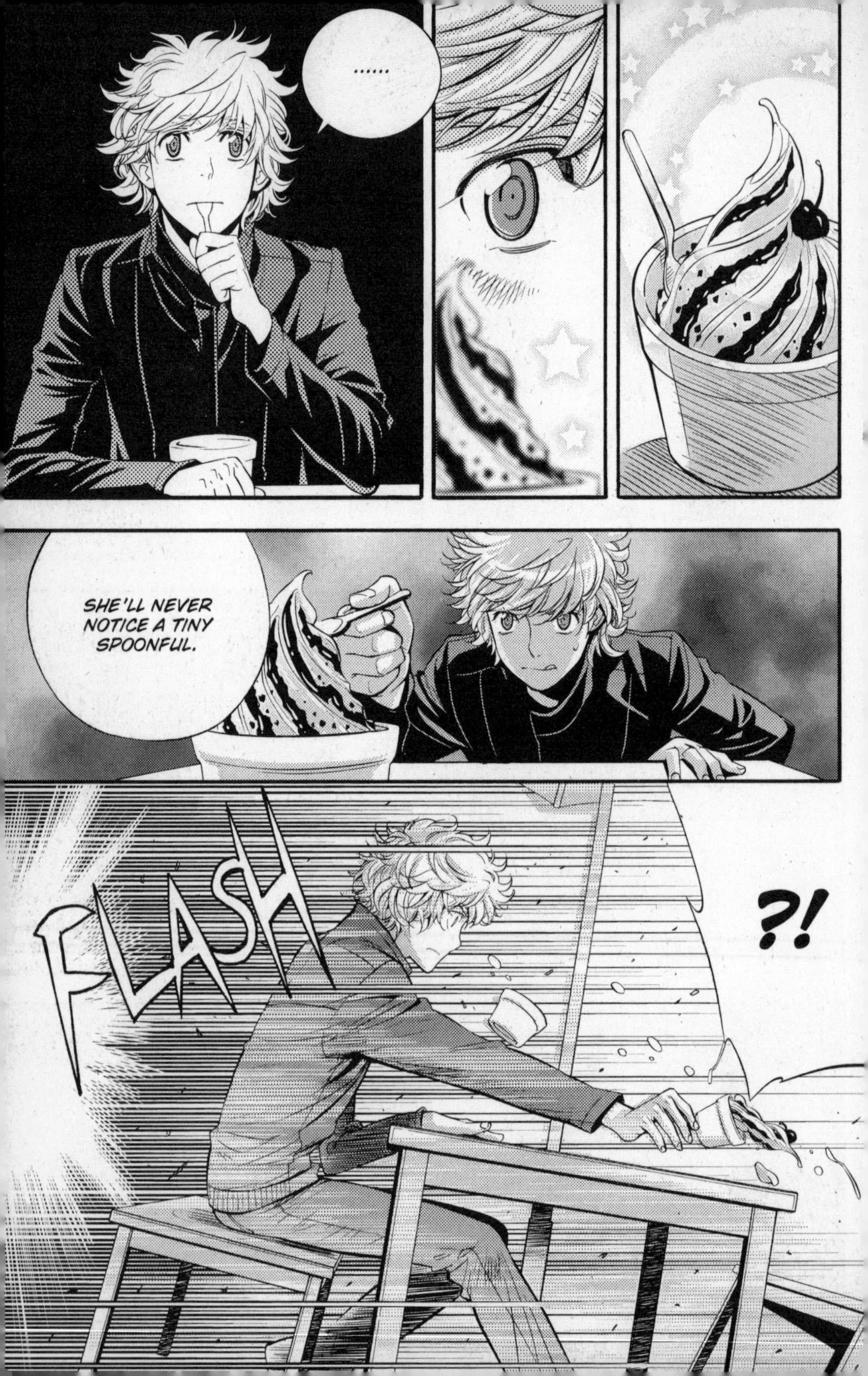
......
SHE'LL NEVER NOTICE A TINY SPOONFUL.
FLASH
?!

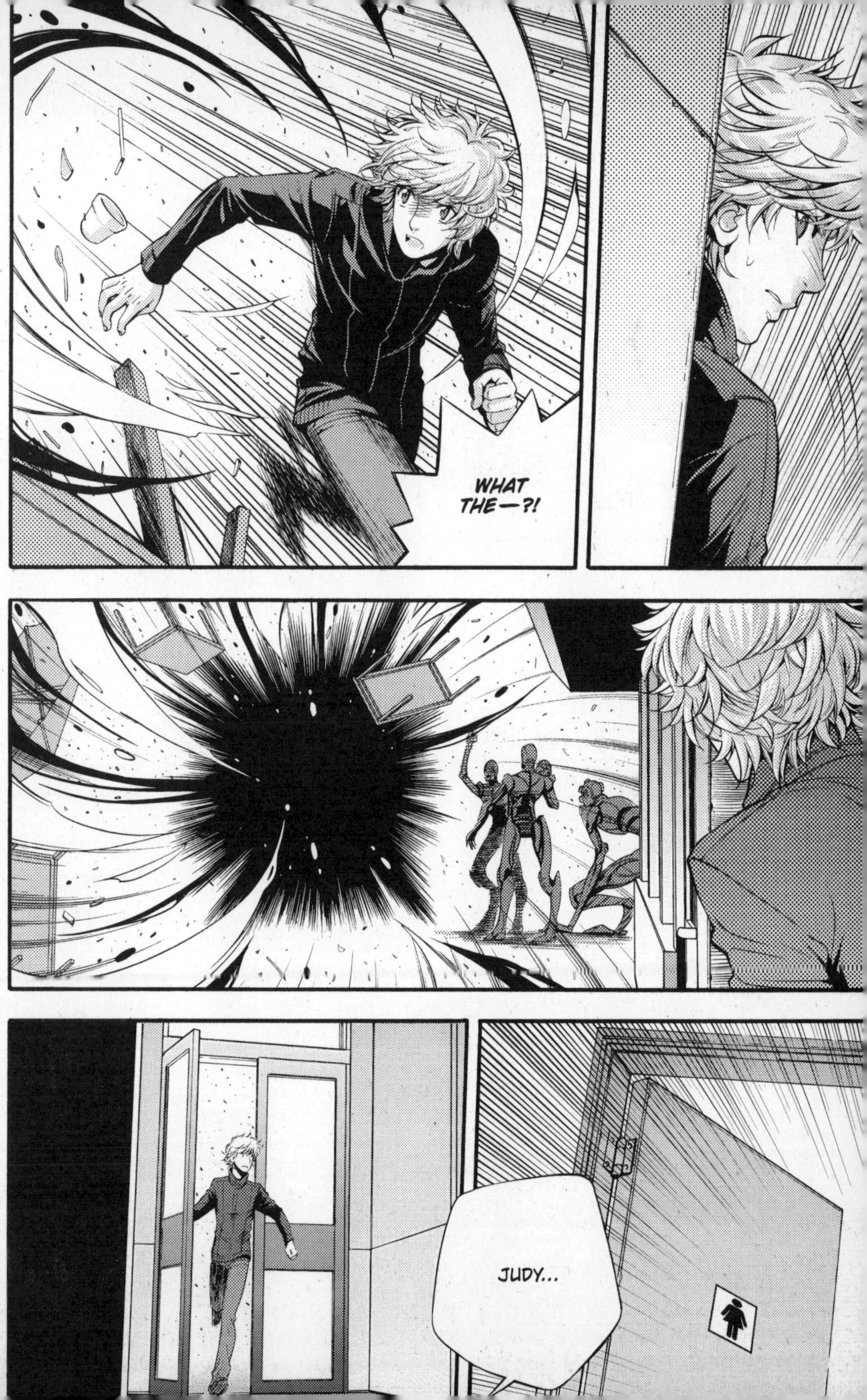
WHAT THE—?!
JUDY...

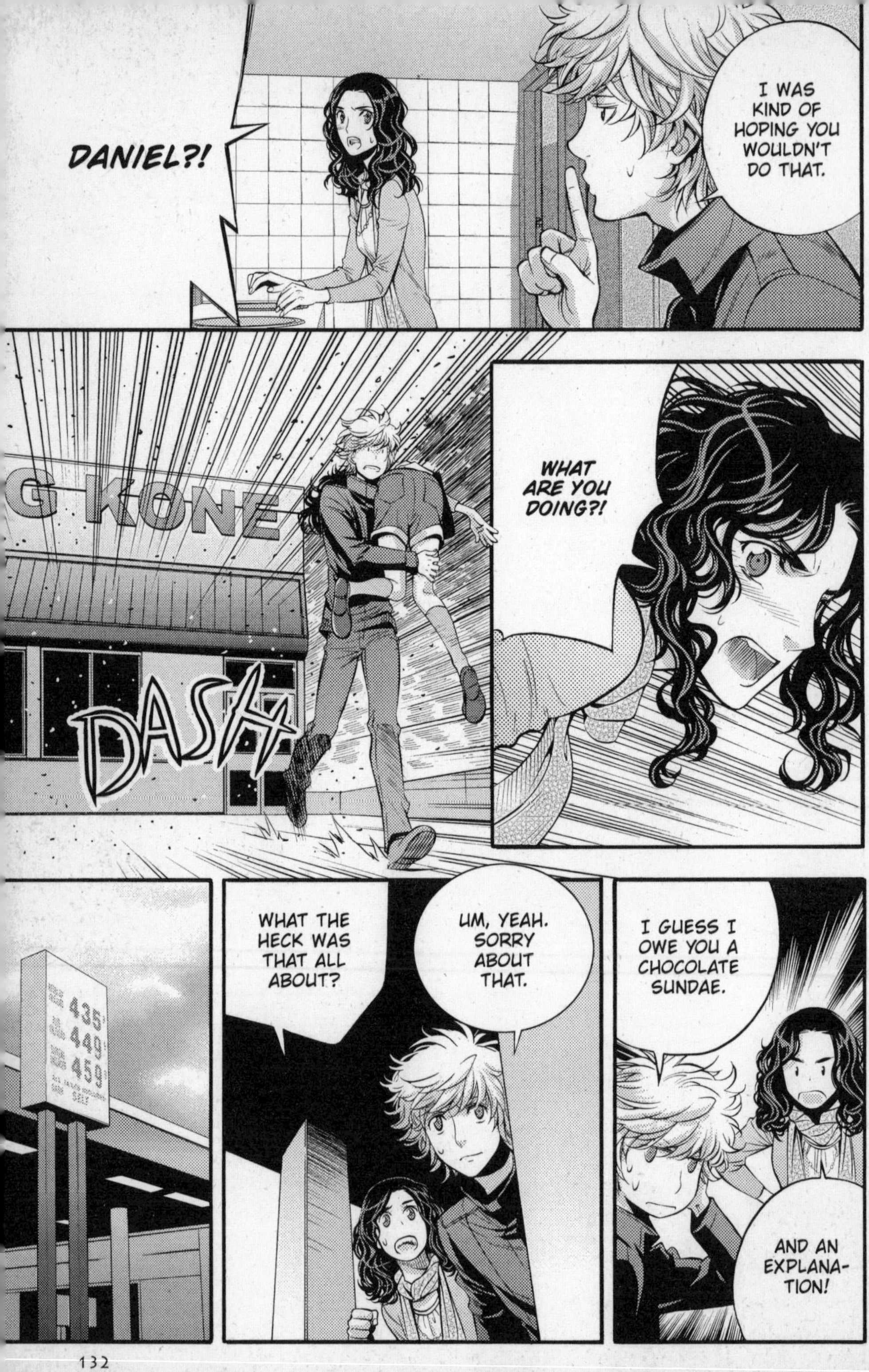
DANIEL?!
I WAS KIND OF HOPING YOU WOULDN'T DO THAT.
G KONE
DASH
WHAT ARE YOU DOING?!
435
449
459
WHAT THE HECK WAS THAT ALL ABOUT?
UM, YEAH. SORRY ABOUT THAT.
I GUESS I OWE YOU A CHOCOLATE SUNDAE.
AND AN EXPLANA-TION!

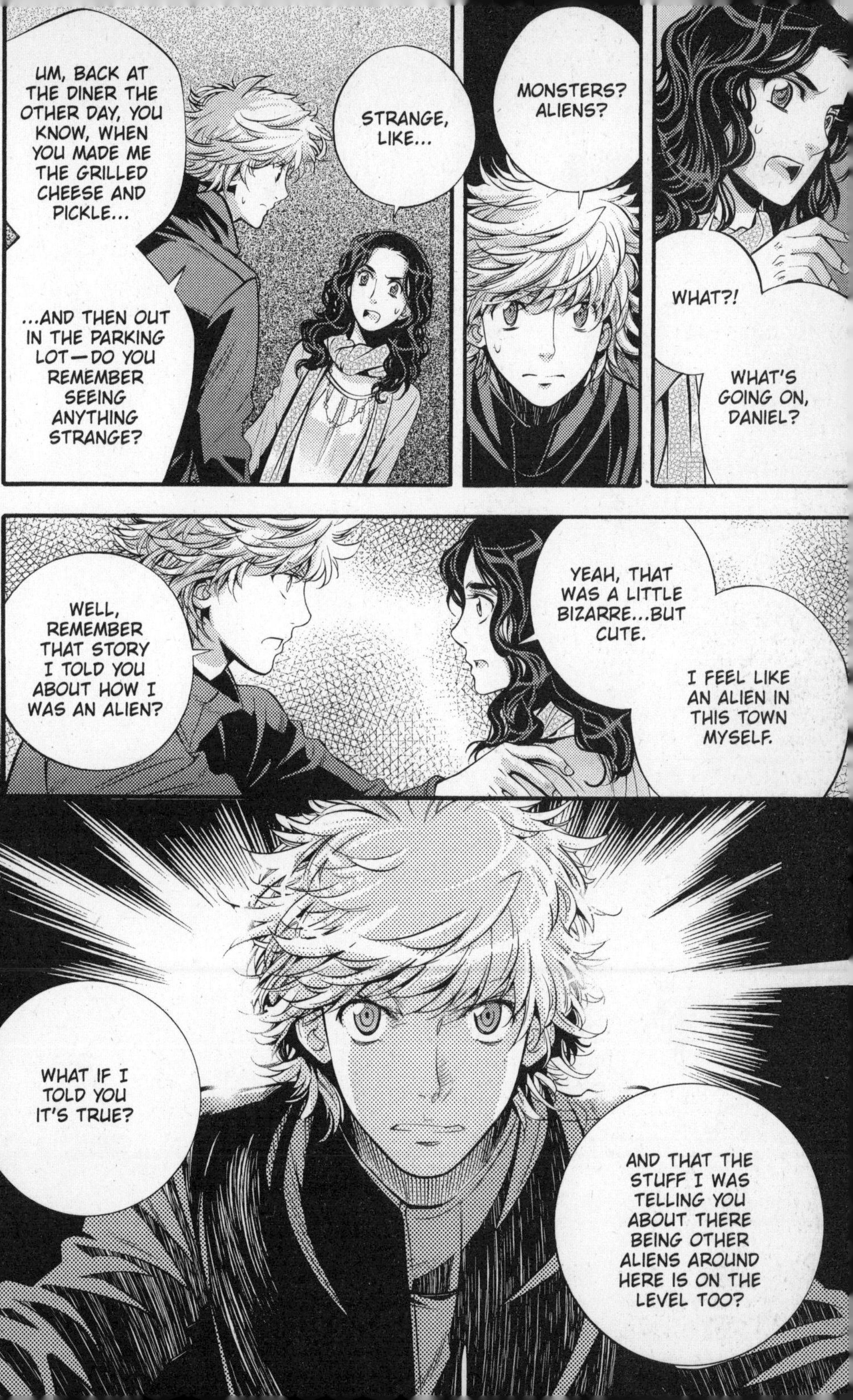
UM, BACK AT THE DINER THE OTHER DAY, YOU KNOW, WHEN YOU MADE ME THE GRILLED CHEESE AND PICKLE...
...AND THEN OUT IN THE PARKING LOT—DO YOU REMEMBER SEEING ANYTHING STRANGE?
STRANGE, LIKE...
MONSTERS? ALIENS?
WHAT?!
WHAT'S GOING ON, DANIEL?
WELL, REMEMBER THAT STORY I TOLD YOU ABOUT HOW I WAS AN ALIEN?
YEAH, THAT WAS A LITTLE BIZARRE...BUT CUTE.
I FEEL LIKE AN ALIEN IN THIS TOWN MYSELF.
WHAT IF I TOLD YOU IT'S TRUE?
AND THAT THE STUFF I WAS TELLING YOU ABOUT THERE BEING OTHER ALIENS AROUND HERE IS ON THE LEVEL TOO?

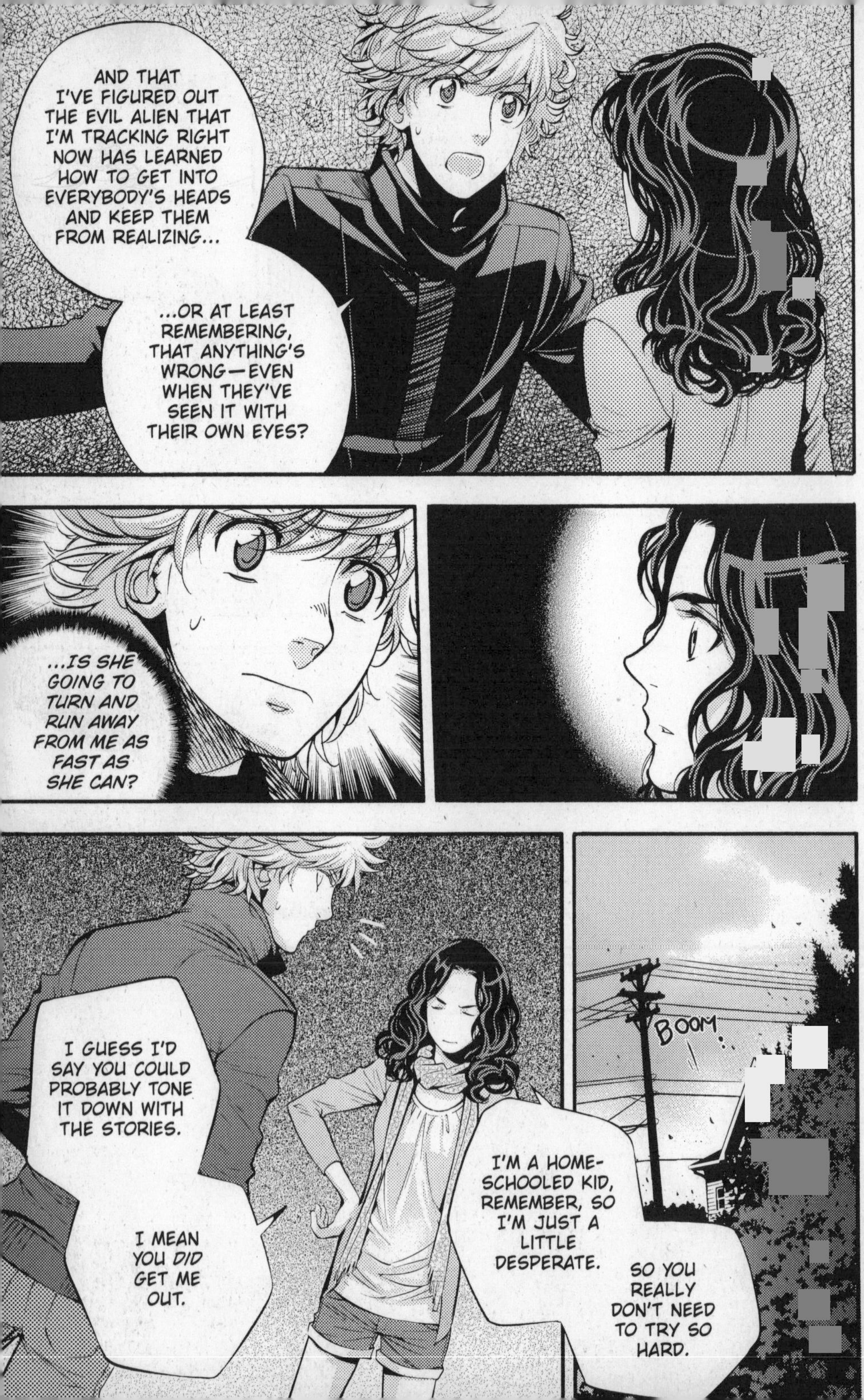
AND THAT I'VE FIGURED OUT THE EVIL ALIEN THAT I'M TRACKING RIGHT NOW HAS LEARNED HOW TO GET INTO EVERYBODY'S HEADS AND KEEP THEM FROM REALIZING...
...OR AT LEAST REMEMBERING, THAT ANYTHING'S WRONG—EVEN WHEN THEY'VE SEEN IT WITH THEIR OWN EYES?
...IS SHE GOING TO TURN AND RUN AWAY FROM ME AS FAST AS SHE CAN?
I GUESS I'D SAY YOU COULD PROBABLY TONE IT DOWN WITH THE STORIES.
I MEAN YOU *DID* GET ME OUT.
I'M A HOME-SCHOOLED KID, REMEMBER, SO I'M JUST A LITTLE DESPERATE.
SO YOU REALLY DON'T NEED TO TRY SO HARD.
BOOM...

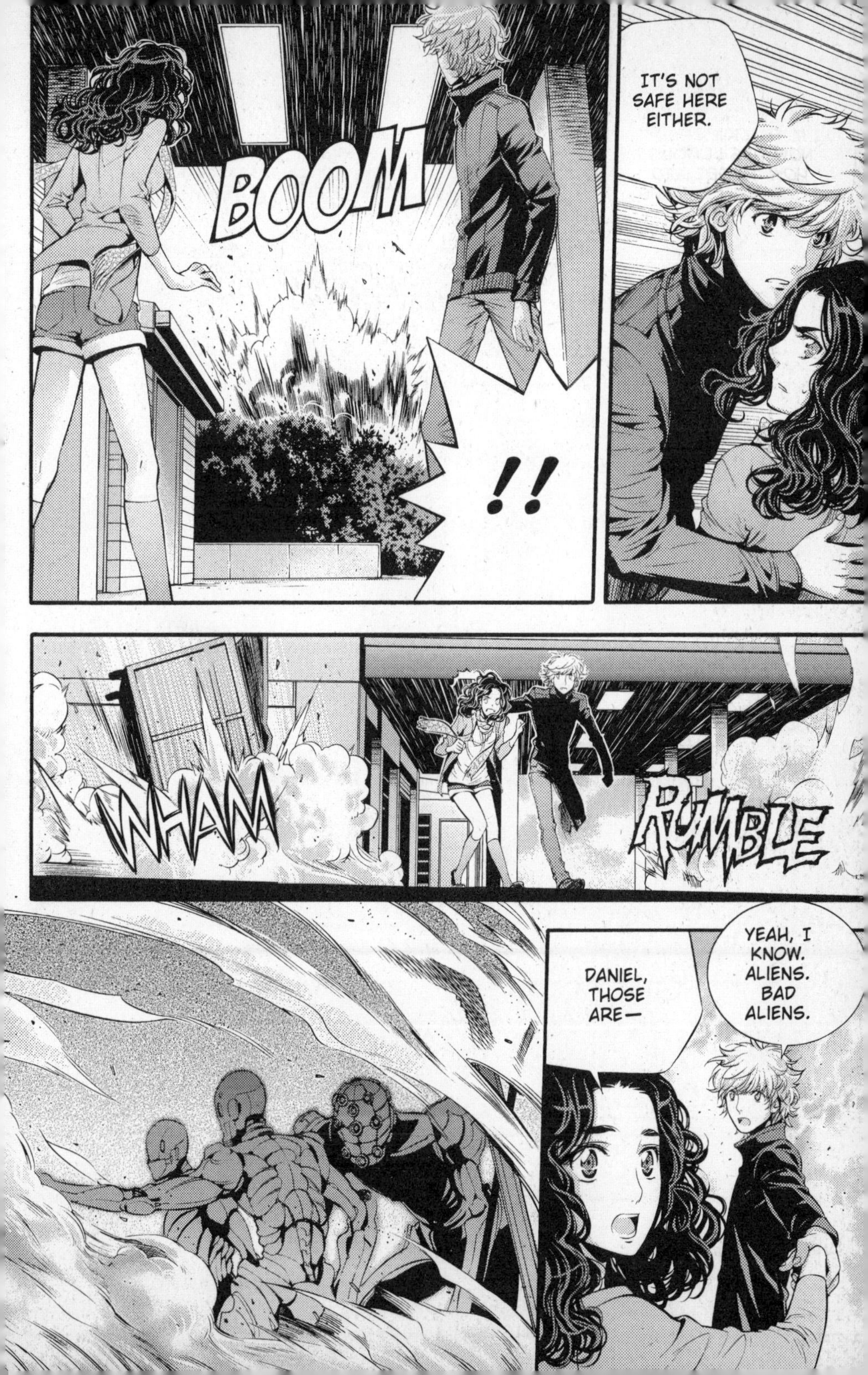
BOOM
!!
IT'S NOT SAFE HERE EITHER.
WHAM
RUMBLE
DANIEL, THOSE ARE—
YEAH, I KNOW. ALIENS. BAD ALIENS.

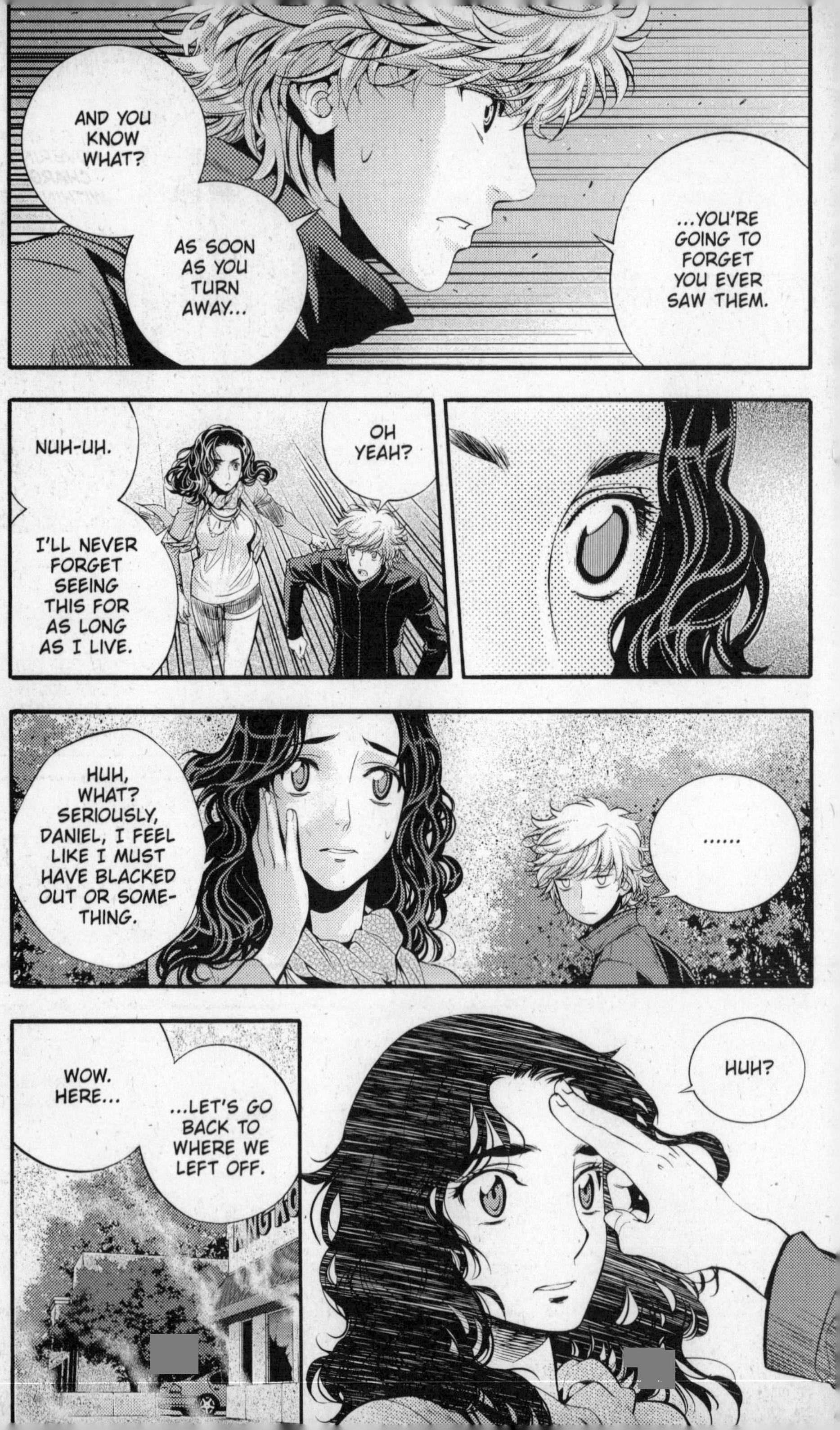
AND YOU KNOW WHAT?
AS SOON AS YOU TURN AWAY...
...YOU'RE GOING TO FORGET YOU EVER SAW THEM.
NUH-UH.
OH YEAH?
I'LL NEVER FORGET SEEING THIS FOR AS LONG AS I LIVE.
HUH, WHAT? SERIOUSLY, DANIEL, I FEEL LIKE I MUST HAVE BLACKED OUT OR SOME-THING.
......
WOW. HERE...
...LET'S GO BACK TO WHERE WE LEFT OFF.
HUH?

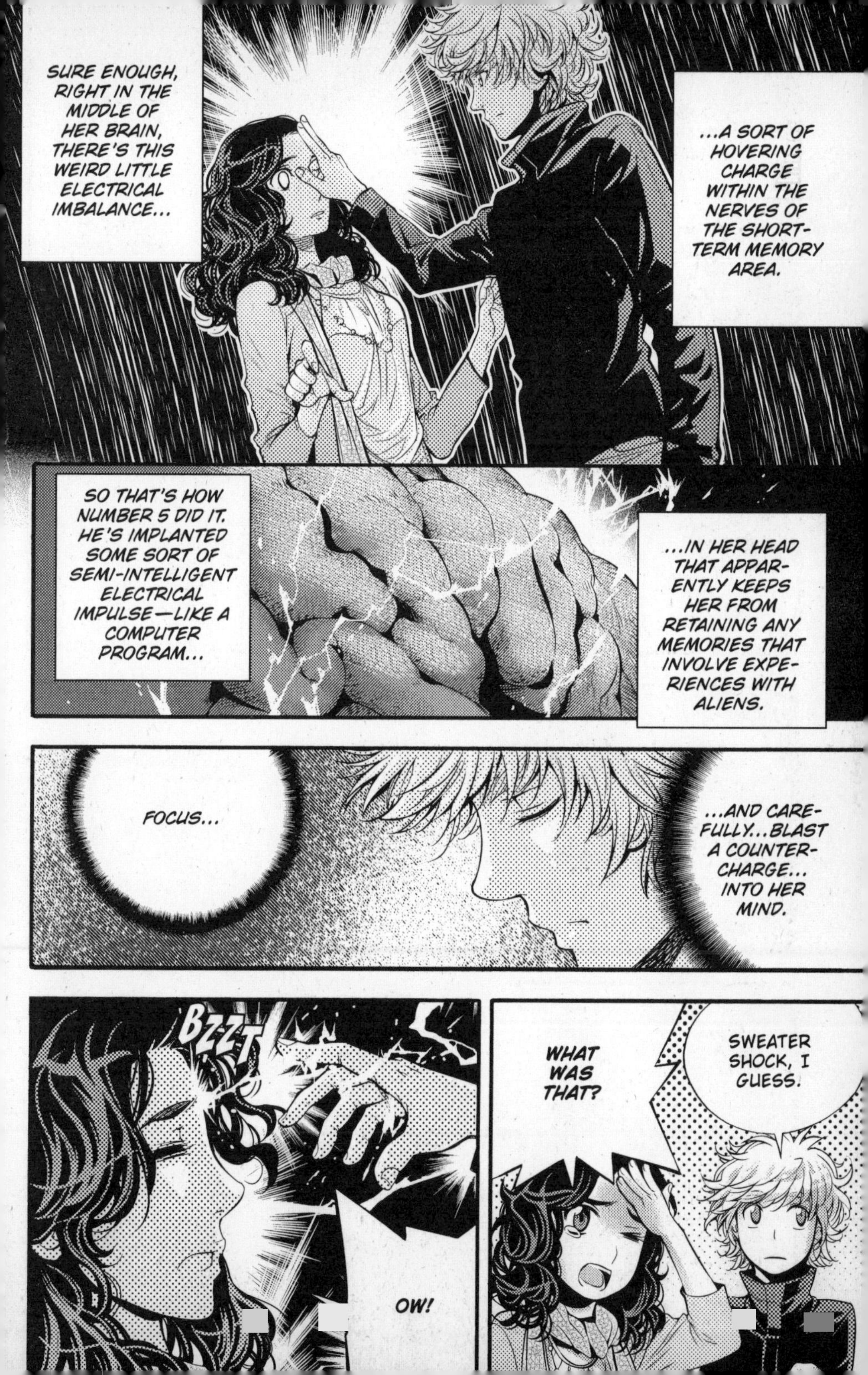
SURE ENOUGH, RIGHT IN THE MIDDLE OF HER BRAIN, THERE'S THIS WEIRD LITTLE ELECTRICAL IMBALANCE...
...A SORT OF HOVERING CHARGE WITHIN THE NERVES OF THE SHORT-TERM MEMORY AREA.
SO THAT'S HOW NUMBER 5 DID IT. HE'S IMPLANTED SOME SORT OF SEMI-INTELLIGENT ELECTRICAL IMPULSE—LIKE A COMPUTER PROGRAM...
...IN HER HEAD THAT APPARENTLY KEEPS HER FROM RETAINING ANY MEMORIES THAT INVOLVE EXPERIENCES WITH ALIENS.
FOCUS...
...AND CAREFULLY...BLAST A COUNTER-CHARGE... INTO HER MIND.
BZZT
OW!
WHAT WAS THAT?
SWEATER SHOCK, I GUESS.

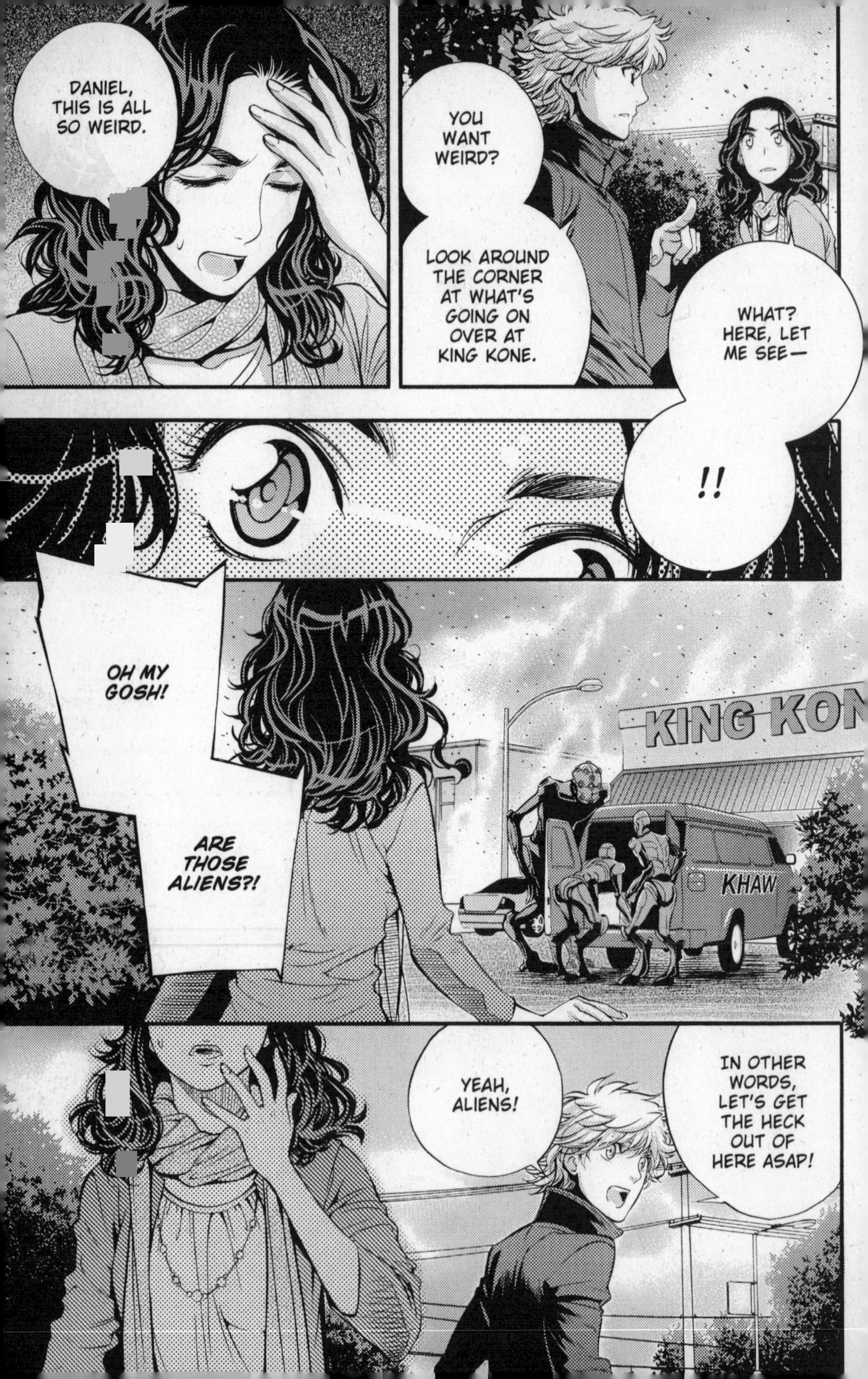
DANIEL, THIS IS ALL SO WEIRD.
YOU WANT WEIRD?
LOOK AROUND THE CORNER AT WHAT'S GOING ON OVER AT KING KONE.
WHAT? HERE, LET ME SEE—
!!
OH MY GOSH!
ARE THOSE ALIENS?!
KING KON
KHAW
YEAH, ALIENS!
IN OTHER WORDS, LET'S GET THE HECK OUT OF HERE ASAP!

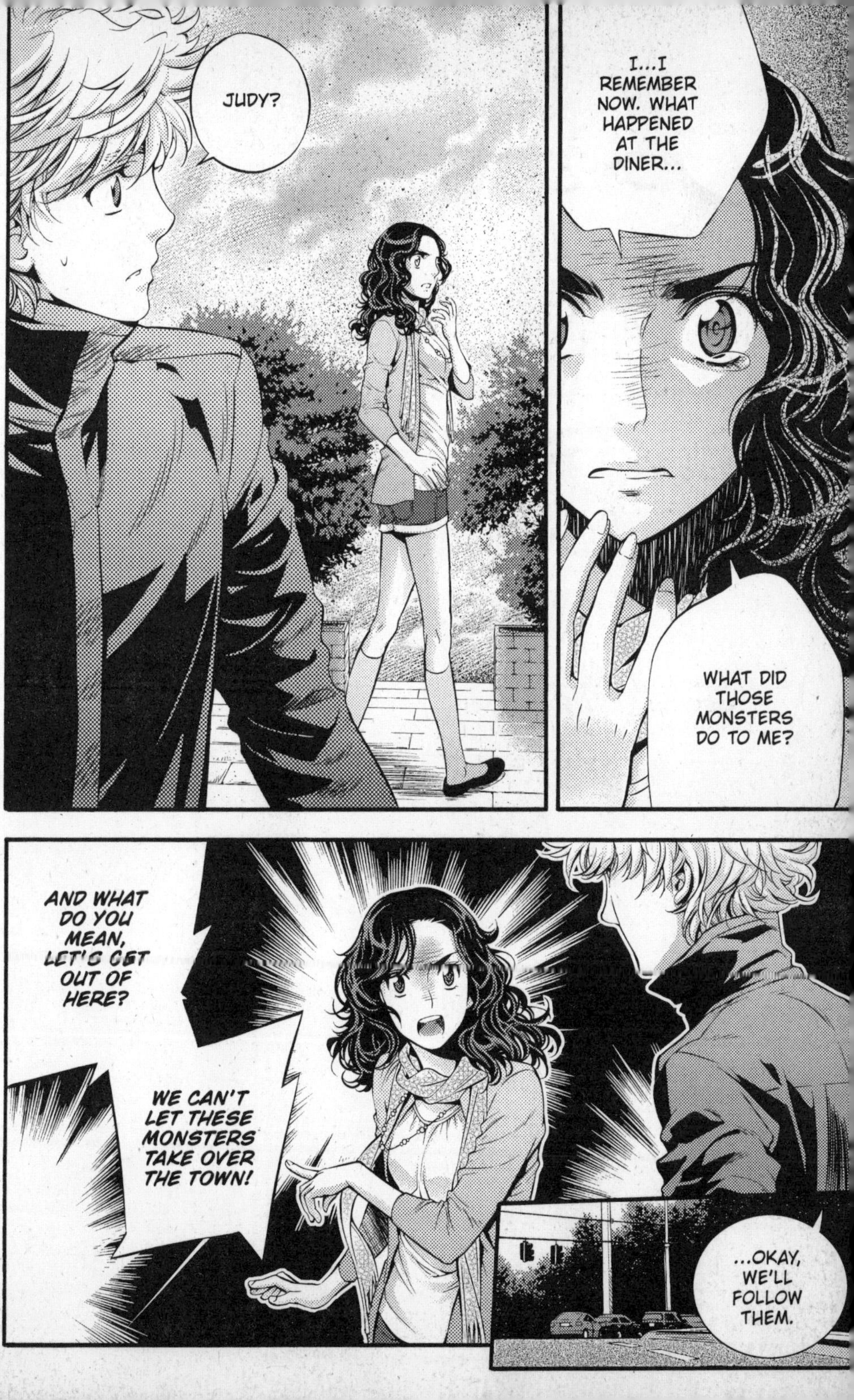
JUDY?
I...I REMEMBER NOW. WHAT HAPPENED AT THE DINER...
WHAT DID THOSE MONSTERS DO TO ME?
AND WHAT DO YOU MEAN, LET'S GET OUT OF HERE?
WE CAN'T LET THESE MONSTERS TAKE OVER THE TOWN!
...OKAY, WE'LL FOLLOW THEM.

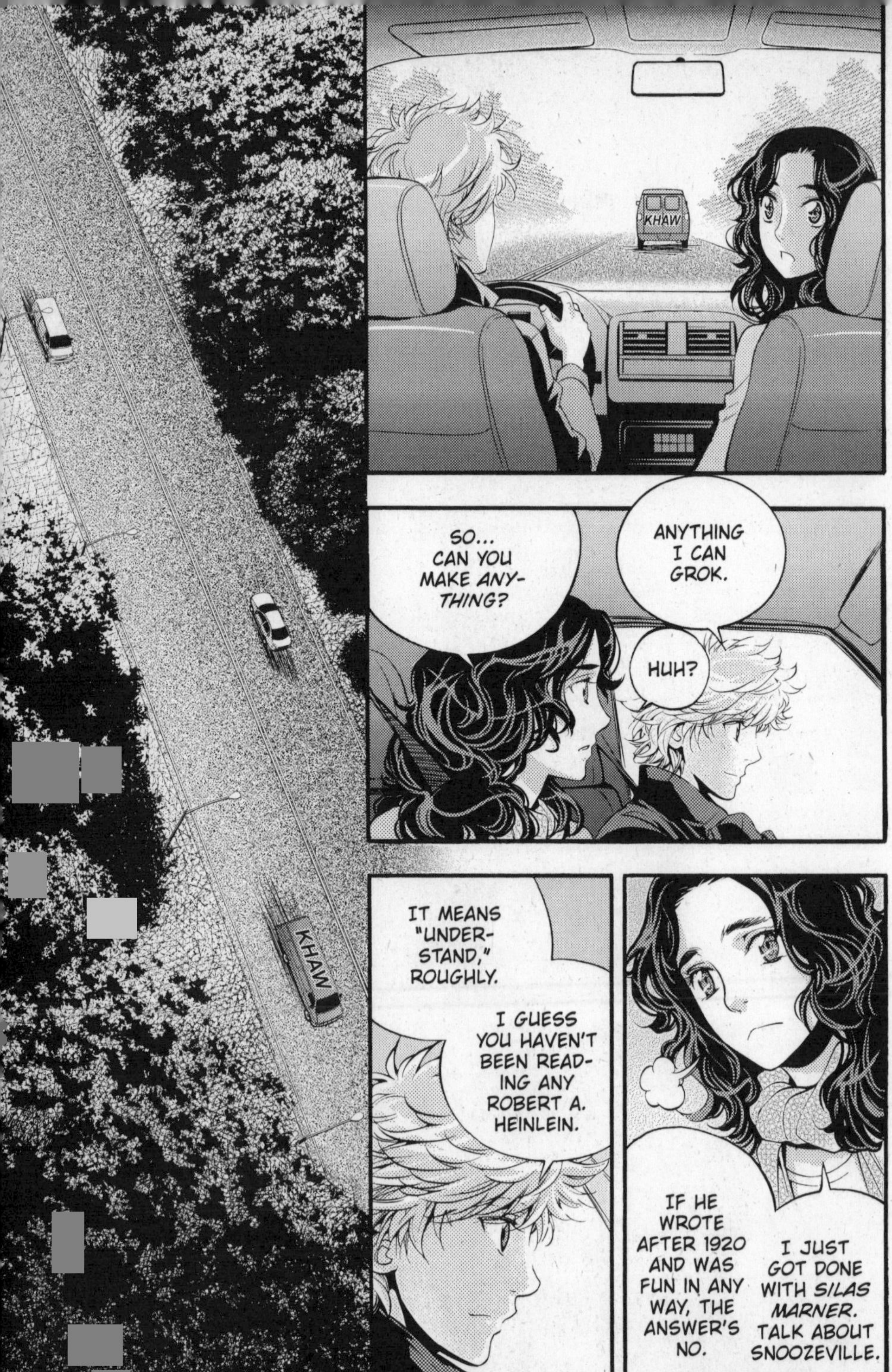
KHAW
KHAW
SO... CAN YOU MAKE *ANY-THING?*
ANYTHING I CAN GROK.
HUH?
IT MEANS "UNDER-STAND," ROUGHLY.
I GUESS YOU HAVEN'T BEEN READ-ING ANY ROBERT A. HEINLEIN.
IF HE WROTE AFTER 1920 AND WAS FUN IN ANY WAY, THE ANSWER'S NO.
I JUST GOT DONE WITH *SILAS MARNER.* TALK ABOUT SNOOZEVILLE.

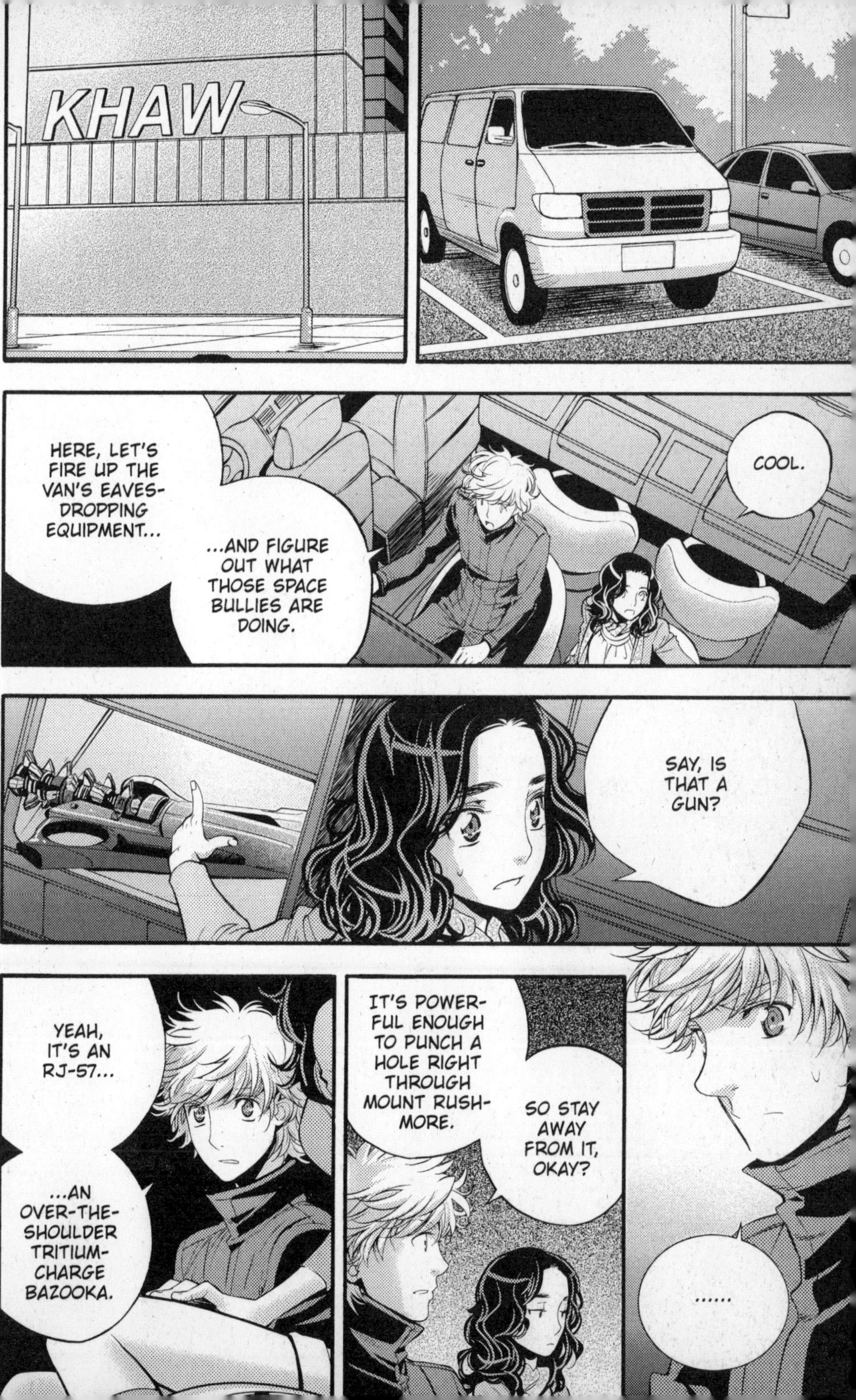
KHAW
HERE, LET'S FIRE UP THE VAN'S EAVES-DROPPING EQUIPMENT...
...AND FIGURE OUT WHAT THOSE SPACE BULLIES ARE DOING.
COOL.
SAY, IS THAT A GUN?
YEAH, IT'S AN RJ-57...
...AN OVER-THE-SHOULDER TRITIUM-CHARGE BAZOOKA.
IT'S POWER-FUL ENOUGH TO PUNCH A HOLE RIGHT THROUGH MOUNT RUSH-MORE.
SO STAY AWAY FROM IT, OKAY?
......

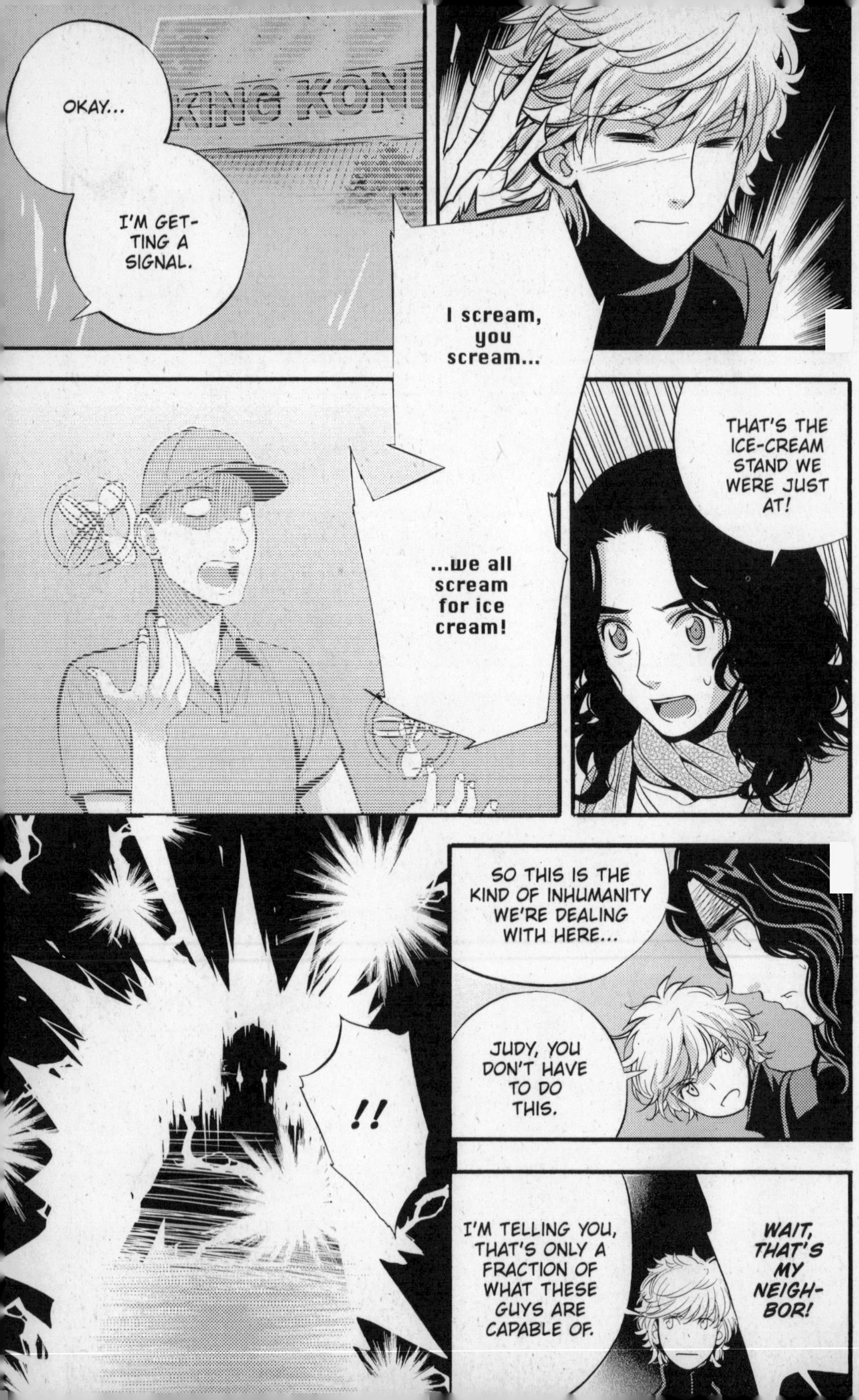
KING KON
OKAY...
I'M GET-TING A SIGNAL.
I scream, you scream...
...we all scream for ice cream!
THAT'S THE ICE-CREAM STAND WE WERE JUST AT!
!!
SO THIS IS THE KIND OF INHUMANITY WE'RE DEALING WITH HERE...
JUDY, YOU DON'T HAVE TO DO THIS.
I'M TELLING YOU, THAT'S ONLY A FRACTION OF WHAT THESE GUYS ARE CAPABLE OF.
WAIT, THAT'S MY NEIGH-BOR!

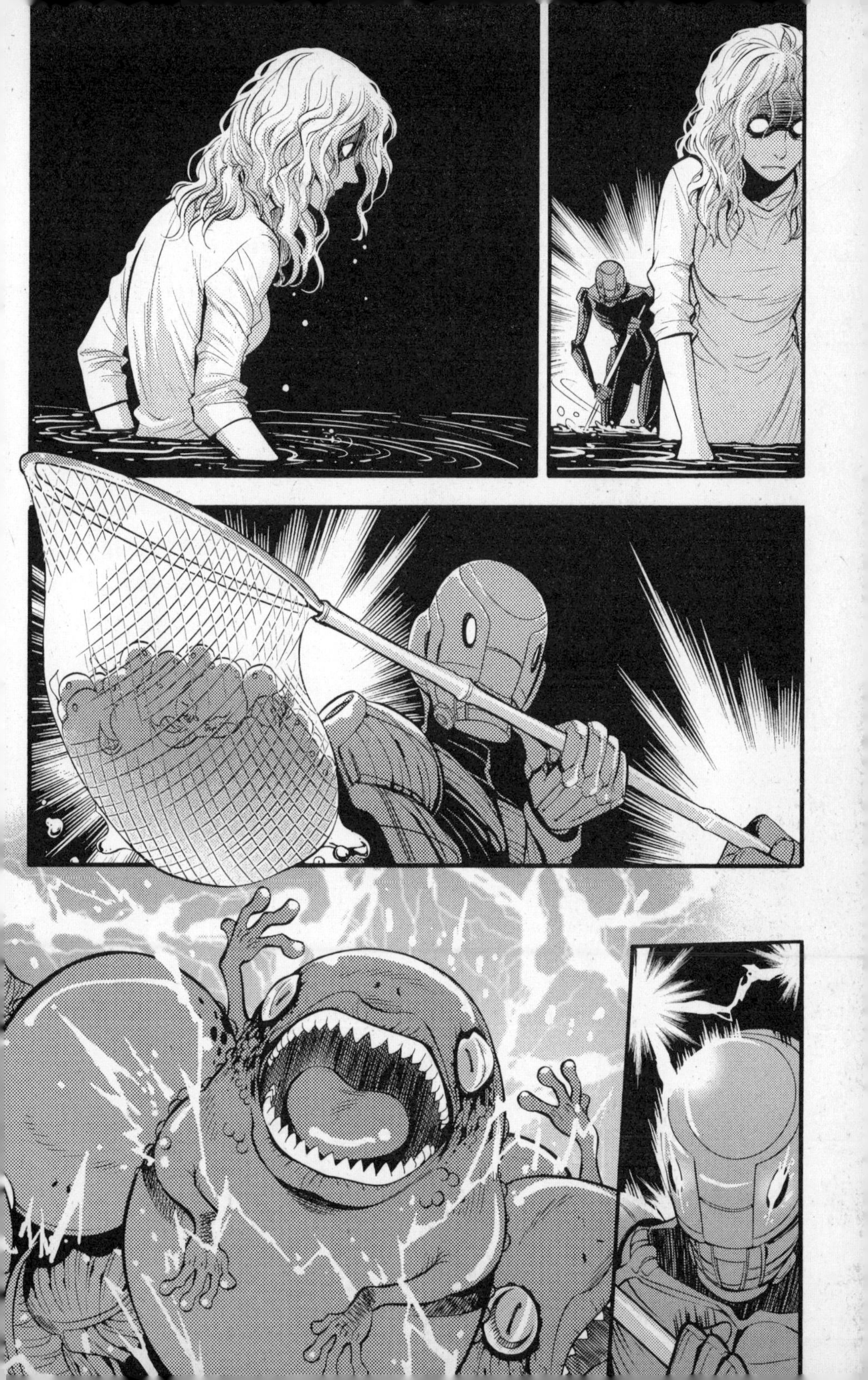

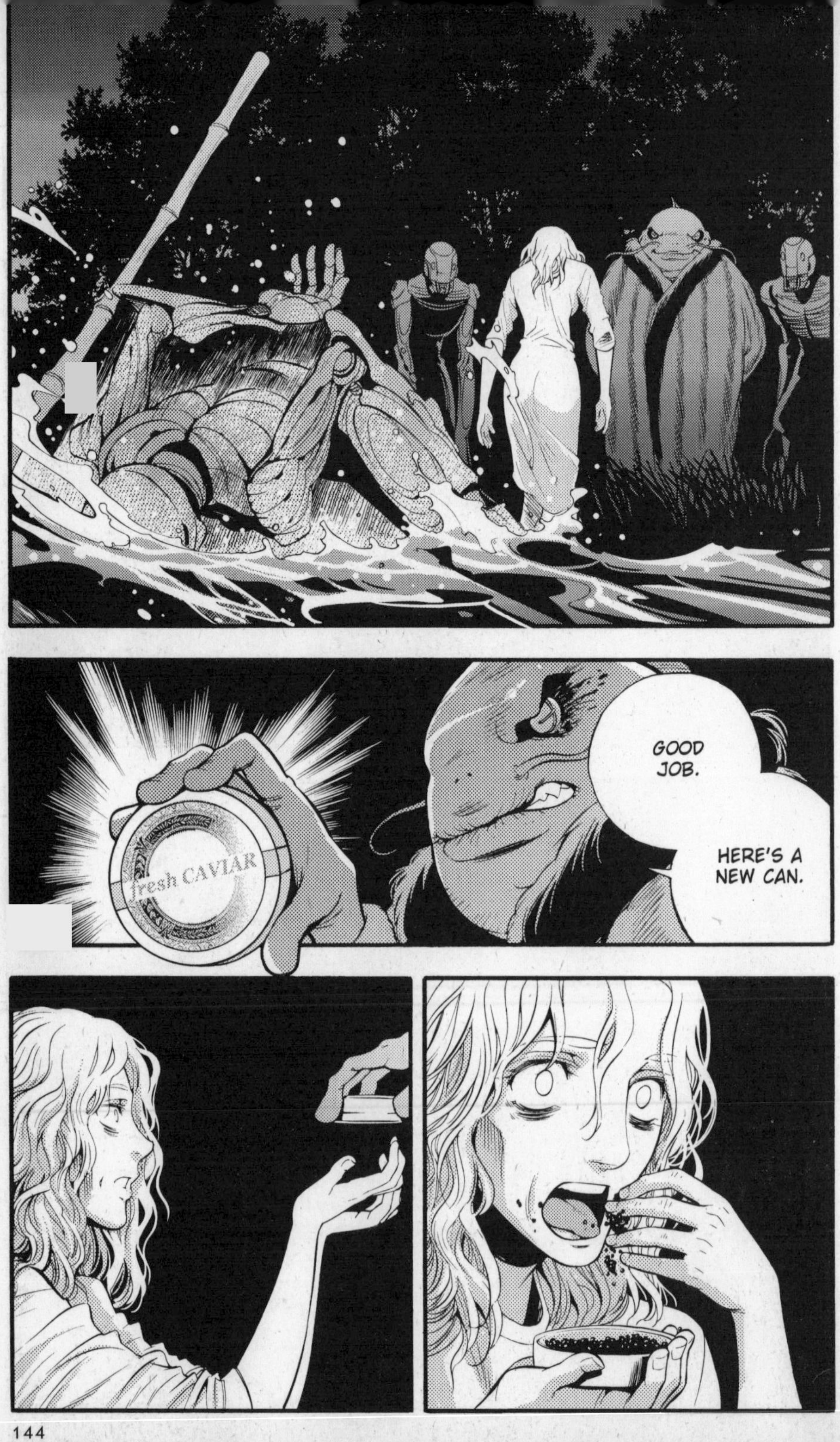
fresh CAVIAR
GOOD JOB.
HERE'S A NEW CAN.

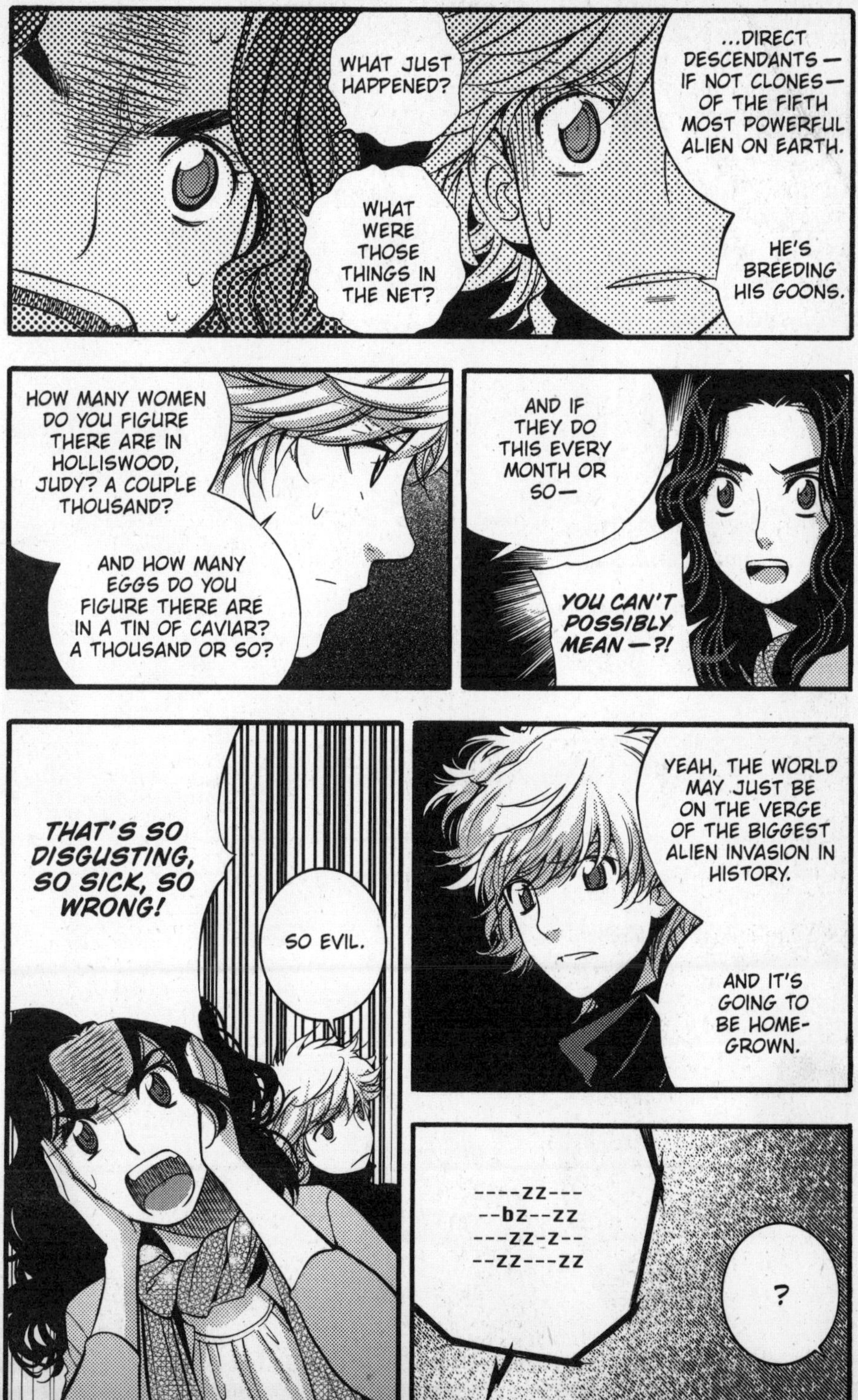
WHAT JUST HAPPENED?
WHAT WERE THOSE THINGS IN THE NET?
...DIRECT DESCENDANTS— IF NOT CLONES— OF THE FIFTH MOST POWERFUL ALIEN ON EARTH.
HE'S BREEDING HIS GOONS.
HOW MANY WOMEN DO YOU FIGURE THERE ARE IN HOLLISWOOD, JUDY? A COUPLE THOUSAND?
AND HOW MANY EGGS DO YOU FIGURE THERE ARE IN A TIN OF CAVIAR? A THOUSAND OR SO?
AND IF THEY DO THIS EVERY MONTH OR SO—
YOU CAN'T POSSIBLY MEAN—?!
THAT'S SO DISGUSTING, SO SICK, SO WRONG!
SO EVIL.
YEAH, THE WORLD MAY JUST BE ON THE VERGE OF THE BIGGEST ALIEN INVASION IN HISTORY.
AND IT'S GOING TO BE HOME-GROWN.
----zz---
--bz--zz
---zz-z--
--zz---zz
?

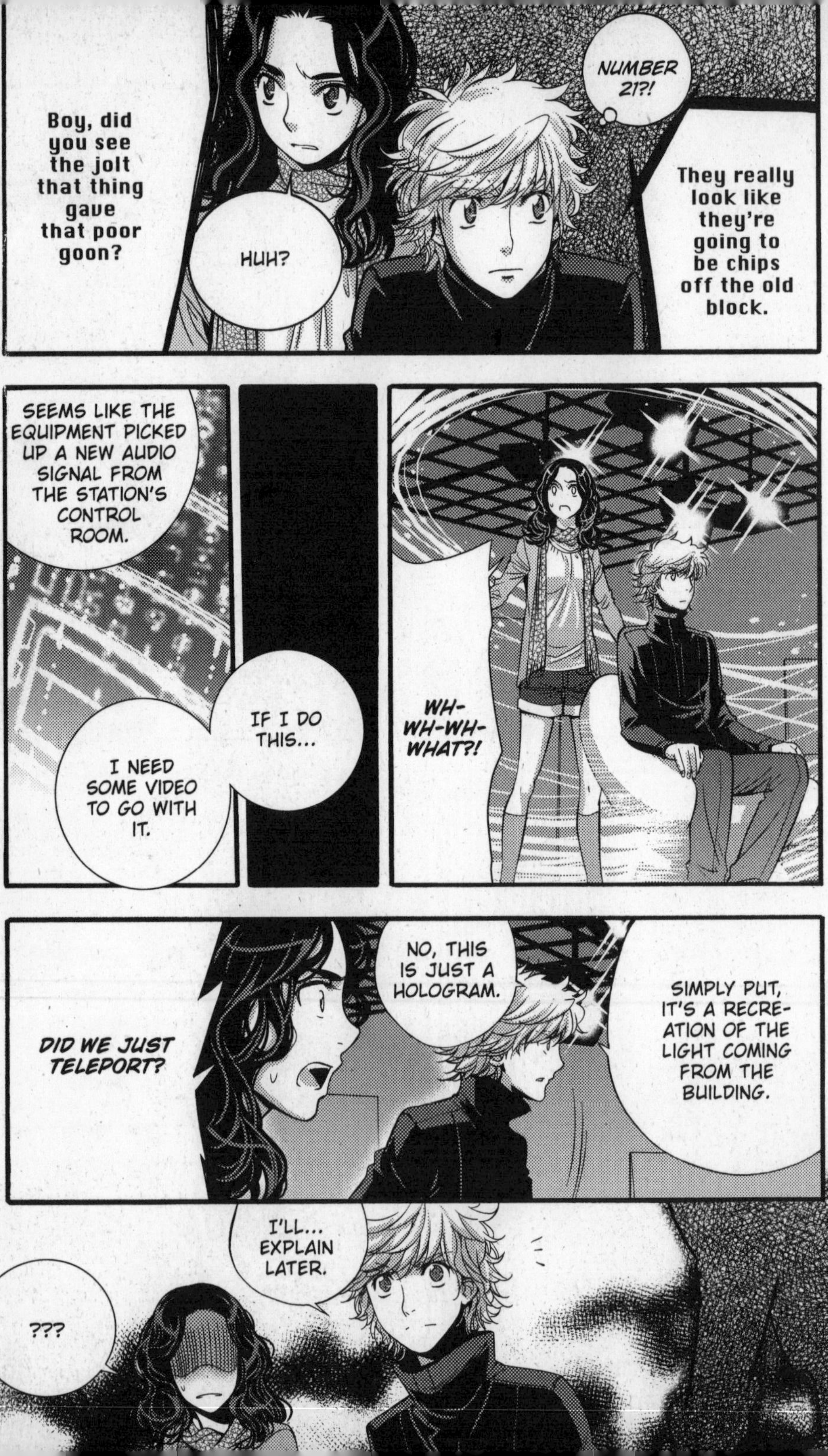
Boy, did you see the jolt that thing gave that poor goon?
HUH?
NUMBER 21?!
They really look like they're going to be chips off the old block.
SEEMS LIKE THE EQUIPMENT PICKED UP A NEW AUDIO SIGNAL FROM THE STATION'S CONTROL ROOM.
I NEED SOME VIDEO TO GO WITH IT.
IF I DO THIS...
WH-WH-WH-WHAT?!
DID WE JUST TELEPORT?
NO, THIS IS JUST A HOLOGRAM.
SIMPLY PUT, IT'S A RECRE-ATION OF THE LIGHT COMING FROM THE BUILDING.
I'LL... EXPLAIN LATER.
???

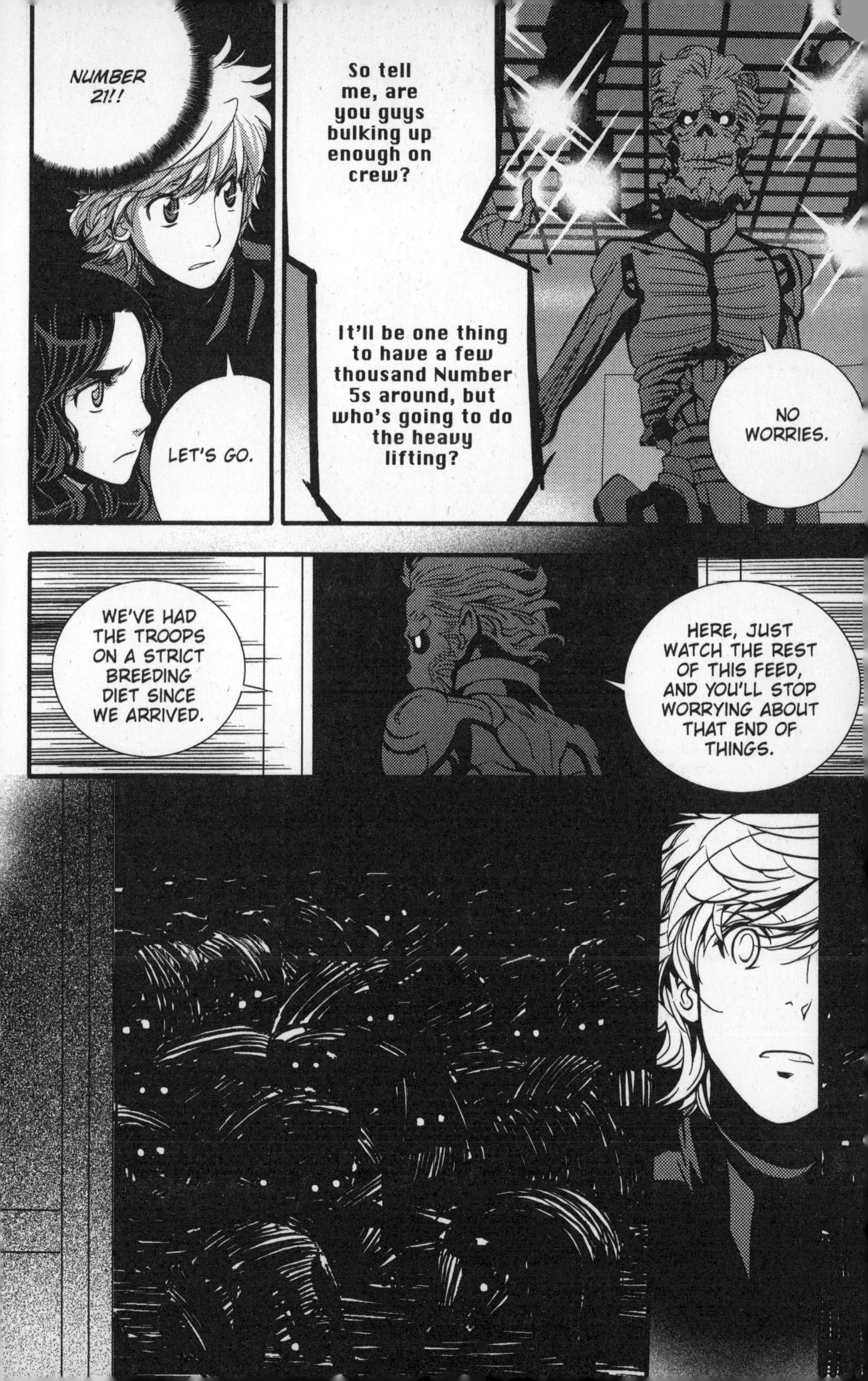
NUMBER 21!!
LET'S GO.
So tell me, are you guys bulking up enough on crew?
It'll be one thing to have a few thousand Number 5s around, but who's going to do the heavy lifting?
NO WORRIES.
WE'VE HAD THE TROOPS ON A STRICT BREEDING DIET SINCE WE ARRIVED.
HERE, JUST WATCH THE REST OF THIS FEED, AND YOU'LL STOP WORRYING ABOUT THAT END OF THINGS.

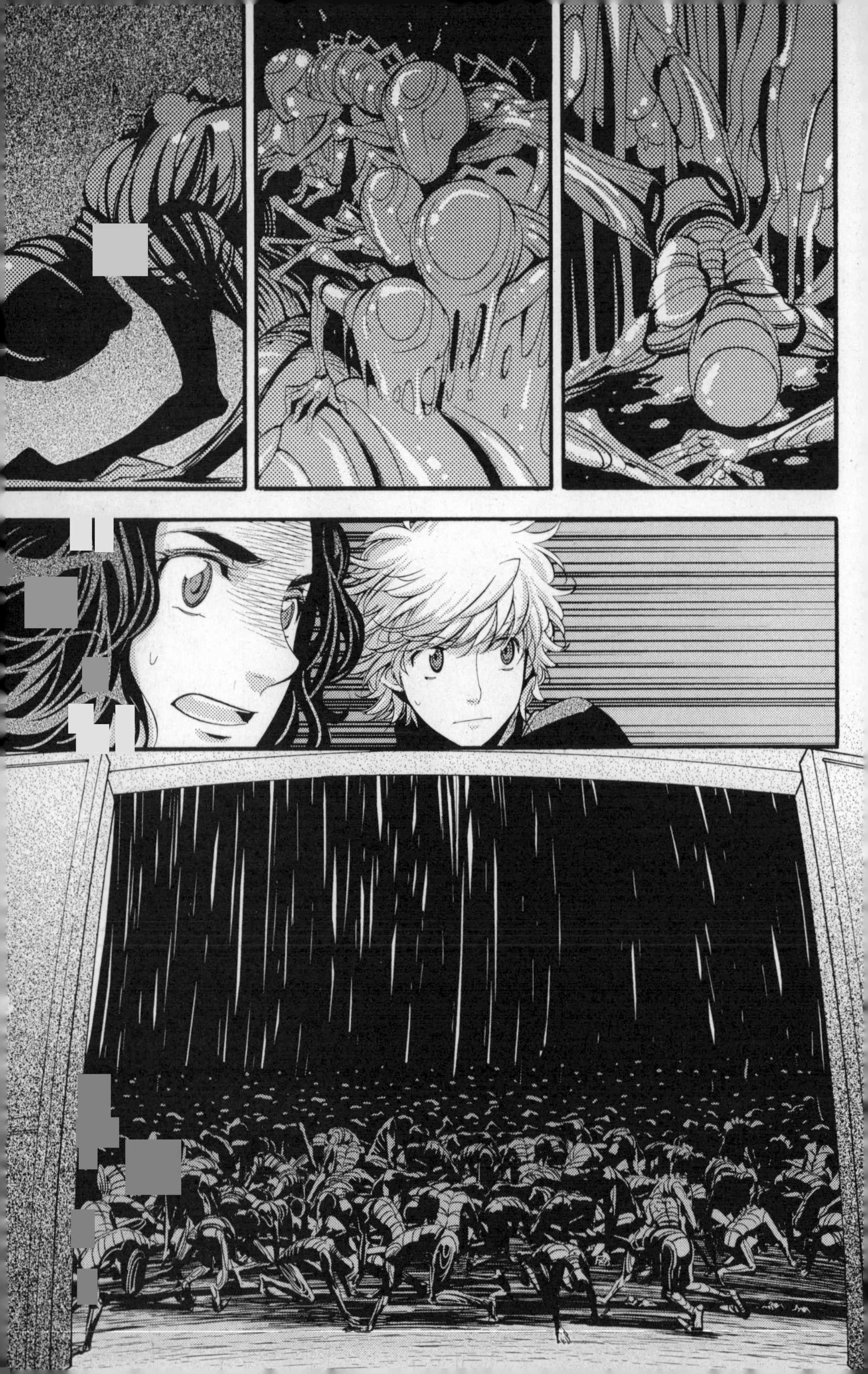

DANIEL X

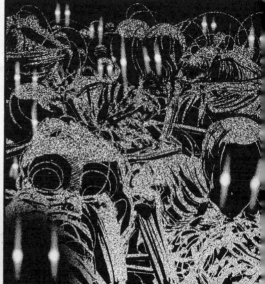

CHAPTER 11

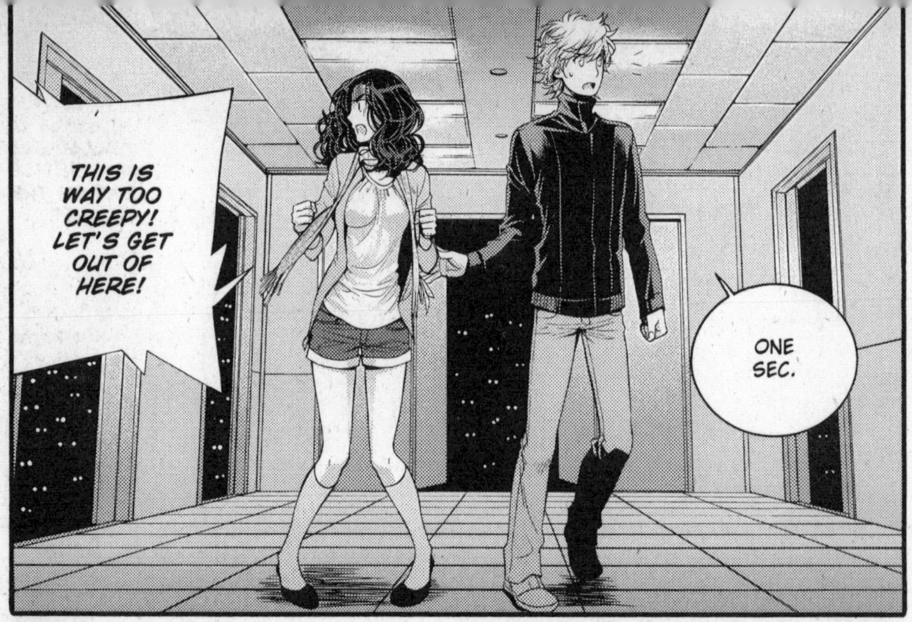
THIS IS WAY TOO CREEPY! LET'S GET OUT OF HERE!
ONE SEC.

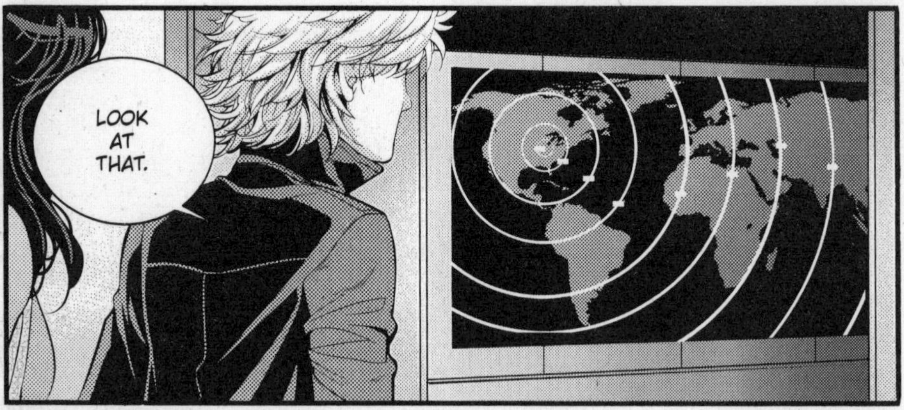
LOOK AT THAT.

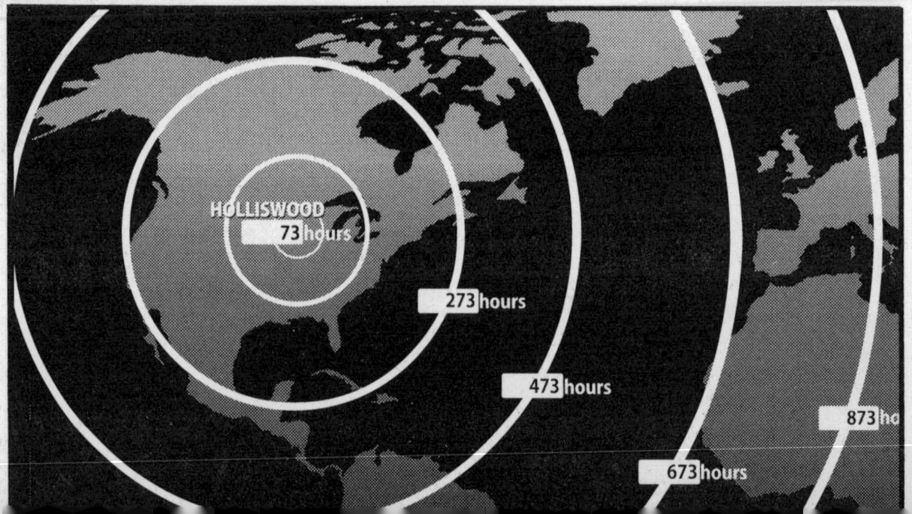
HOLLISWOOD
73 hours
273 hours
473 hours
873 ho
673 hours

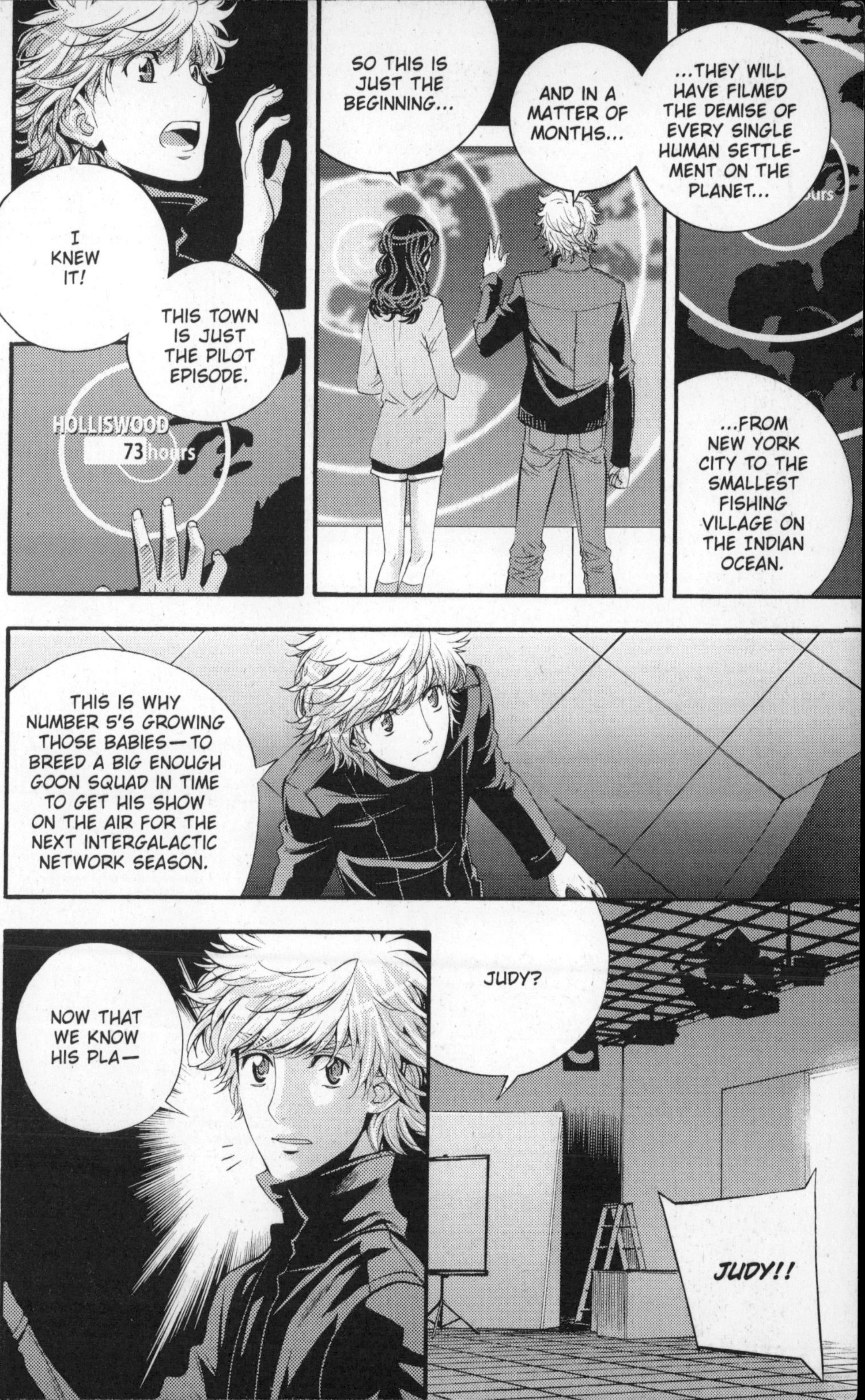
I KNEW IT!
THIS TOWN IS JUST THE PILOT EPISODE.
HOLLISWOOD
73 hours
SO THIS IS JUST THE BEGINNING...
AND IN A MATTER OF MONTHS...
...THEY WILL HAVE FILMED THE DEMISE OF EVERY SINGLE HUMAN SETTLE-MENT ON THE PLANET...
...FROM NEW YORK CITY TO THE SMALLEST FISHING VILLAGE ON THE INDIAN OCEAN.
THIS IS WHY NUMBER 5'S GROWING THOSE BABIES—TO BREED A BIG ENOUGH GOON SQUAD IN TIME TO GET HIS SHOW ON THE AIR FOR THE NEXT INTERGALACTIC NETWORK SEASON.
NOW THAT WE KNOW HIS PLA—
JUDY?
JUDY!!

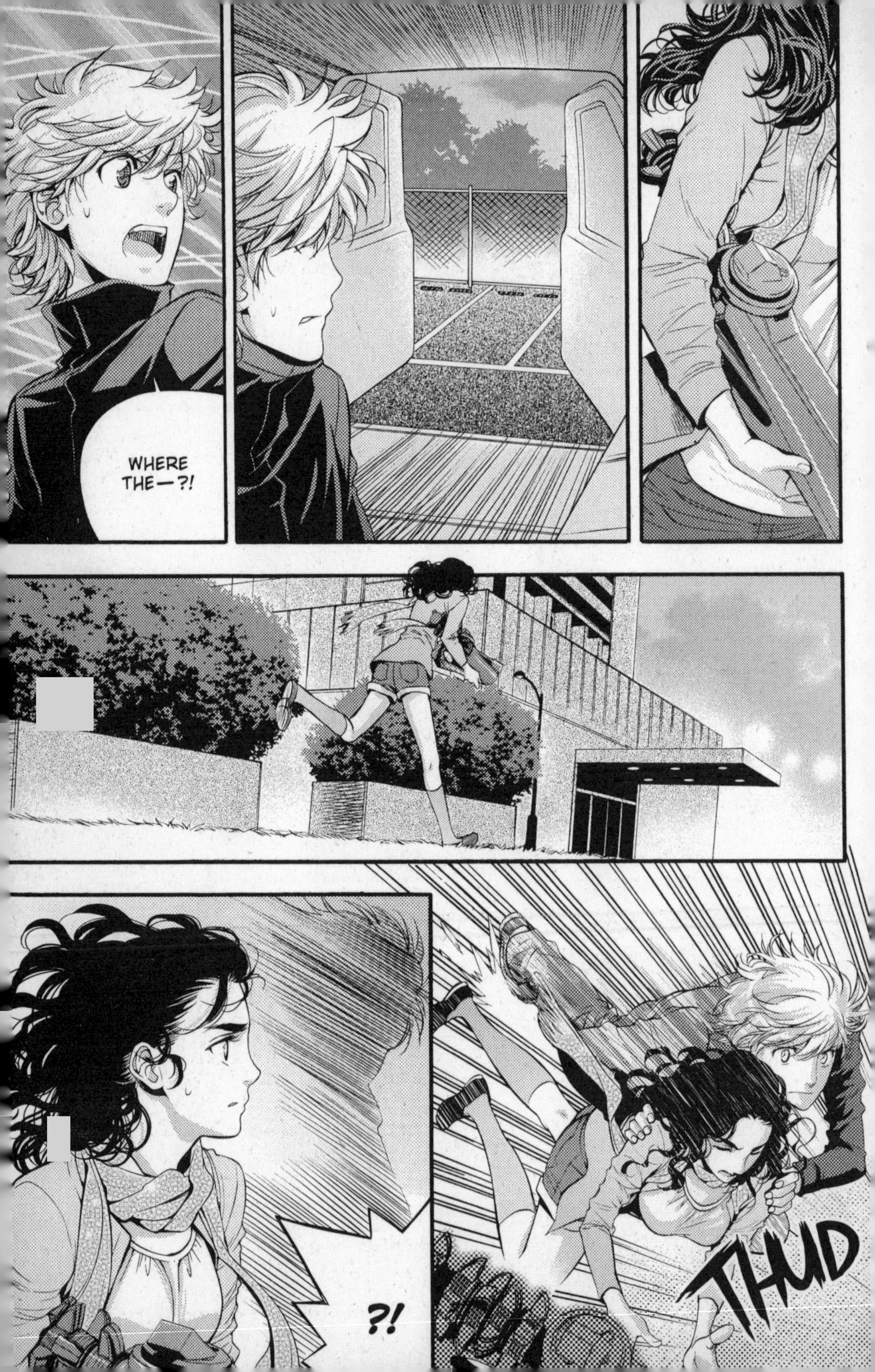
WHERE THE—?!
?!
THUD

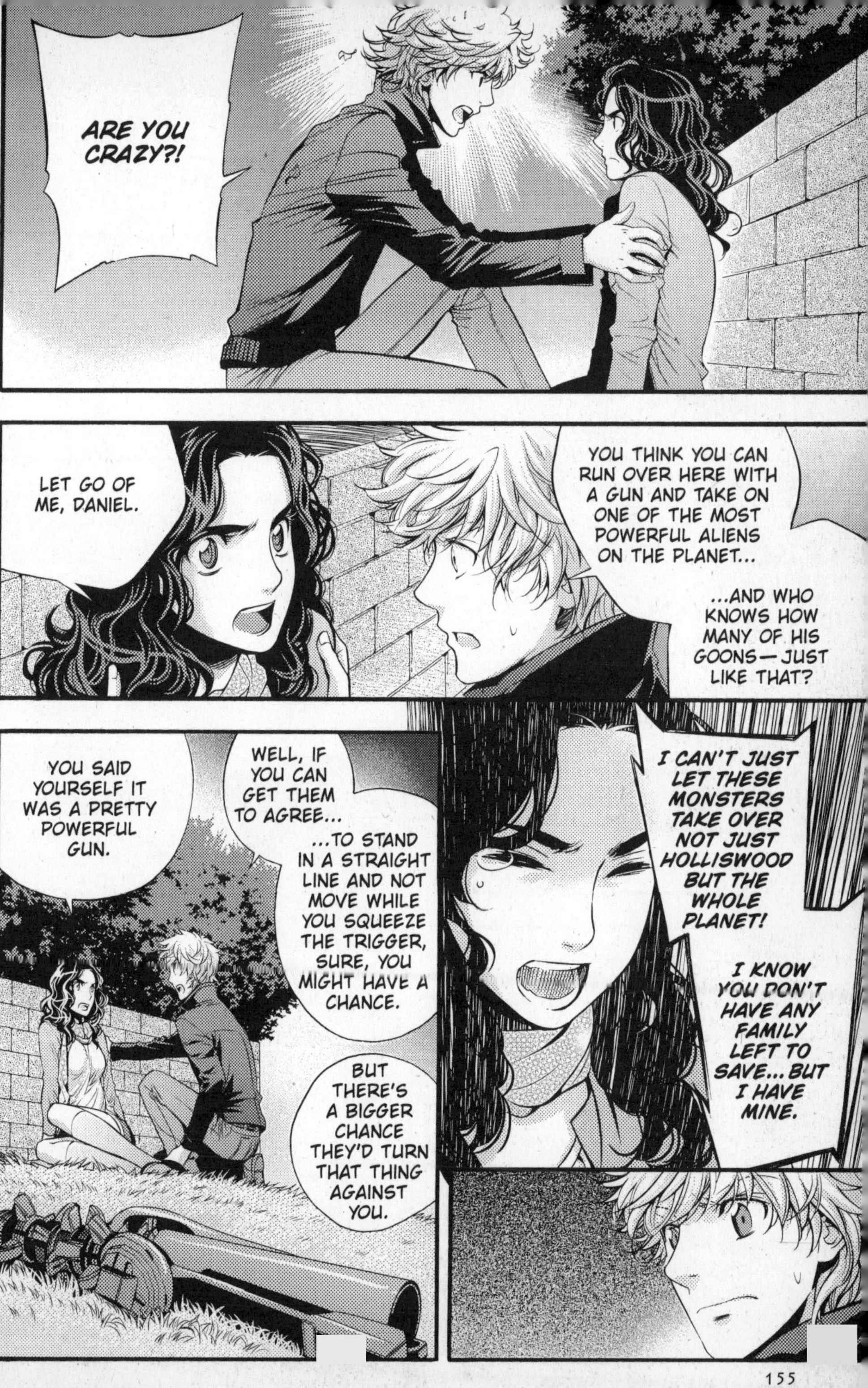
ARE YOU CRAZY?!
LET GO OF ME, DANIEL.
YOU THINK YOU CAN RUN OVER HERE WITH A GUN AND TAKE ON ONE OF THE MOST POWERFUL ALIENS ON THE PLANET...
...AND WHO KNOWS HOW MANY OF HIS GOONS—JUST LIKE THAT?
YOU SAID YOURSELF IT WAS A PRETTY POWERFUL GUN.
WELL, IF YOU CAN GET THEM TO AGREE...
...TO STAND IN A STRAIGHT LINE AND NOT MOVE WHILE YOU SQUEEZE THE TRIGGER, SURE, YOU MIGHT HAVE A CHANCE.
BUT THERE'S A BIGGER CHANCE THEY'D TURN THAT THING AGAINST YOU.
I CAN'T JUST LET THESE MONSTERS TAKE OVER NOT JUST HOLLISWOOD BUT THE WHOLE PLANET!
I KNOW YOU DON'T HAVE ANY FAMILY LEFT TO SAVE... BUT I HAVE MINE.

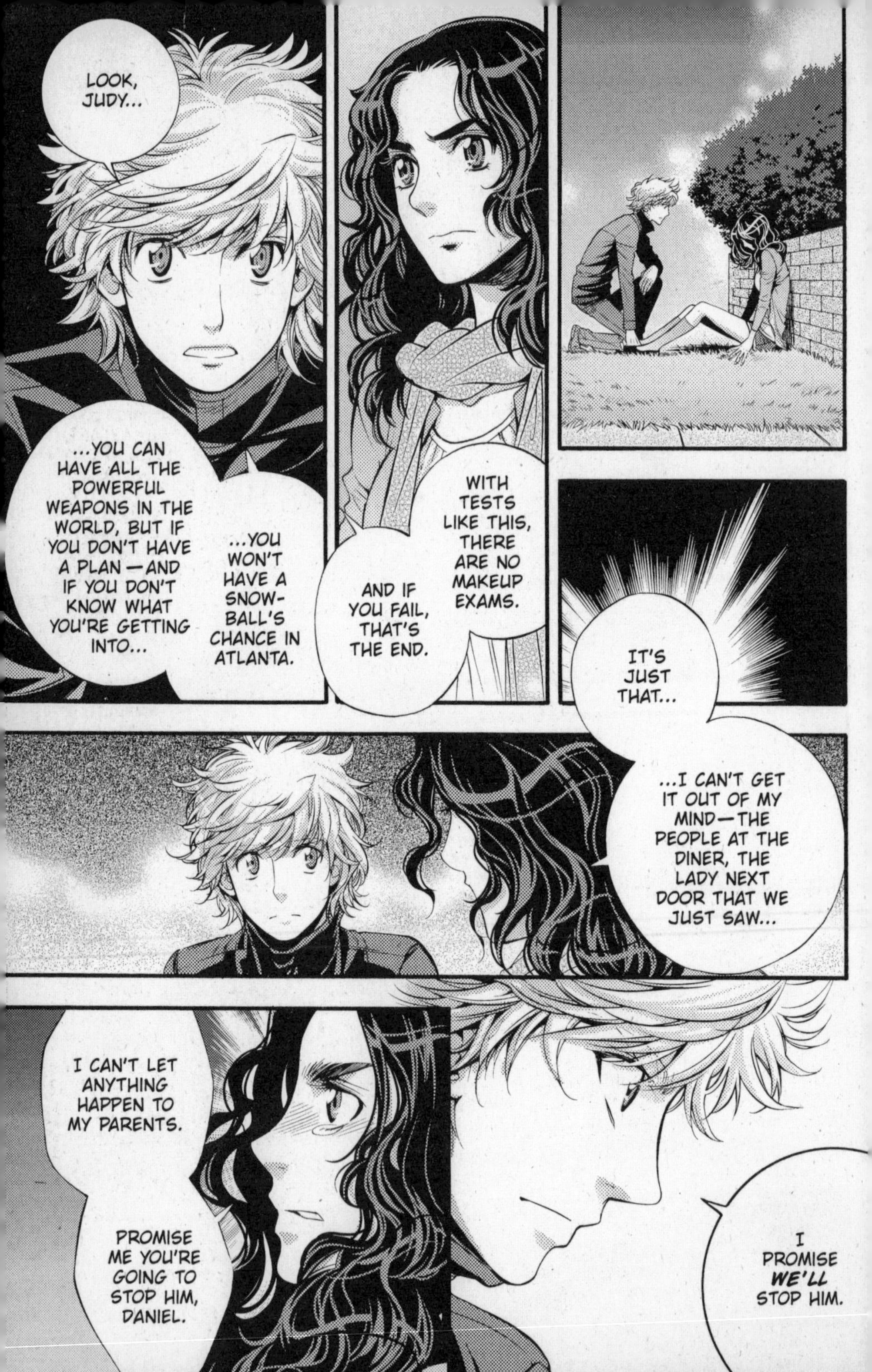
LOOK, JUDY...
...YOU CAN HAVE ALL THE POWERFUL WEAPONS IN THE WORLD, BUT IF YOU DON'T HAVE A PLAN—AND IF YOU DON'T KNOW WHAT YOU'RE GETTING INTO...
...YOU WON'T HAVE A SNOW-BALL'S CHANCE IN ATLANTA.
WITH TESTS LIKE THIS, THERE ARE NO MAKEUP EXAMS.
AND IF YOU FAIL, THAT'S THE END.
IT'S JUST THAT...
...I CAN'T GET IT OUT OF MY MIND—THE PEOPLE AT THE DINER, THE LADY NEXT DOOR THAT WE JUST SAW...
I CAN'T LET ANYTHING HAPPEN TO MY PARENTS.
PROMISE ME YOU'RE GOING TO STOP HIM, DANIEL.
I PROMISE ***WE'LL*** STOP HIM.

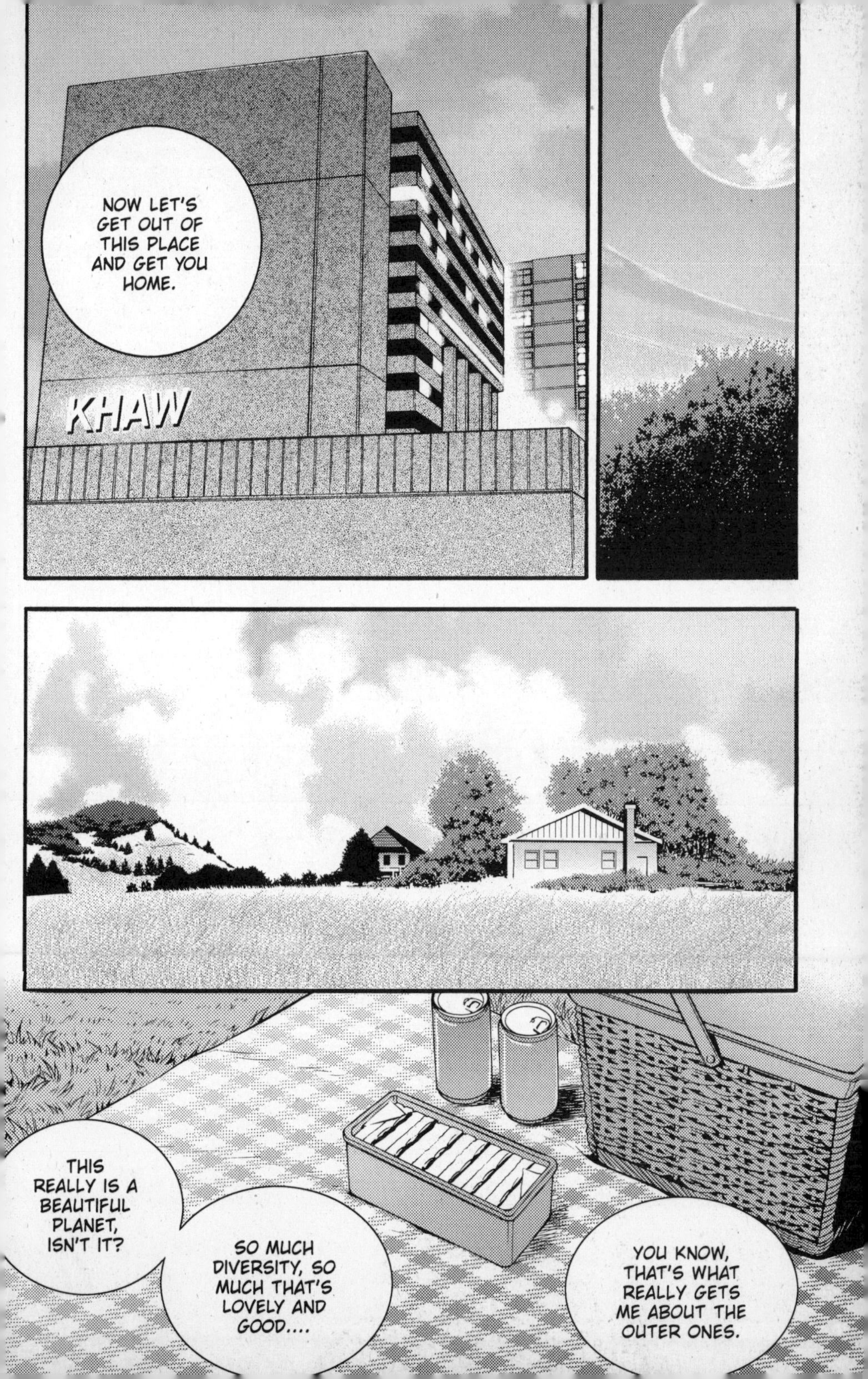
NOW LET'S GET OUT OF THIS PLACE AND GET YOU HOME.
KHAW
THIS REALLY IS A BEAUTIFUL PLANET, ISN'T IT?
SO MUCH DIVERSITY, SO MUCH THAT'S LOVELY AND GOOD....
YOU KNOW, THAT'S WHAT REALLY GETS ME ABOUT THE OUTER ONES.

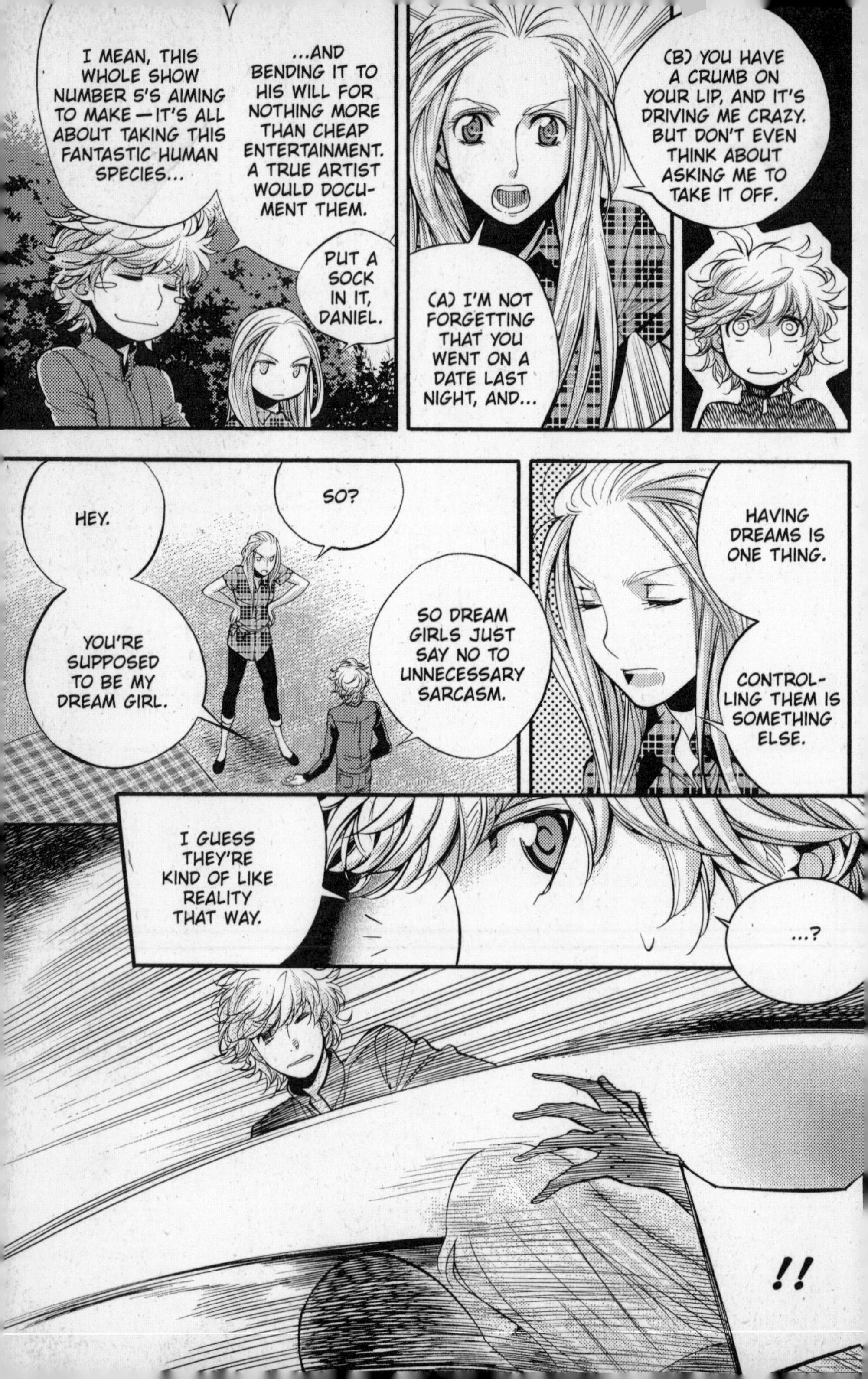
I MEAN, THIS WHOLE SHOW NUMBER 5'S AIMING TO MAKE—IT'S ALL ABOUT TAKING THIS FANTASTIC HUMAN SPECIES...
...AND BENDING IT TO HIS WILL FOR NOTHING MORE THAN CHEAP ENTERTAINMENT. A TRUE ARTIST WOULD DOCUMENT THEM.
PUT A SOCK IN IT, DANIEL.
(A) I'M NOT FORGETTING THAT YOU WENT ON A DATE LAST NIGHT, AND...
(B) YOU HAVE A CRUMB ON YOUR LIP, AND IT'S DRIVING ME CRAZY. BUT DON'T EVEN THINK ABOUT ASKING ME TO TAKE IT OFF.
HEY.
YOU'RE SUPPOSED TO BE MY DREAM GIRL.
SO?
SO DREAM GIRLS JUST SAY NO TO UNNECESSARY SARCASM.
HAVING DREAMS IS ONE THING.
CONTROLLING THEM IS SOMETHING ELSE.
I GUESS THEY'RE KIND OF LIKE REALITY THAT WAY.
...?
!!

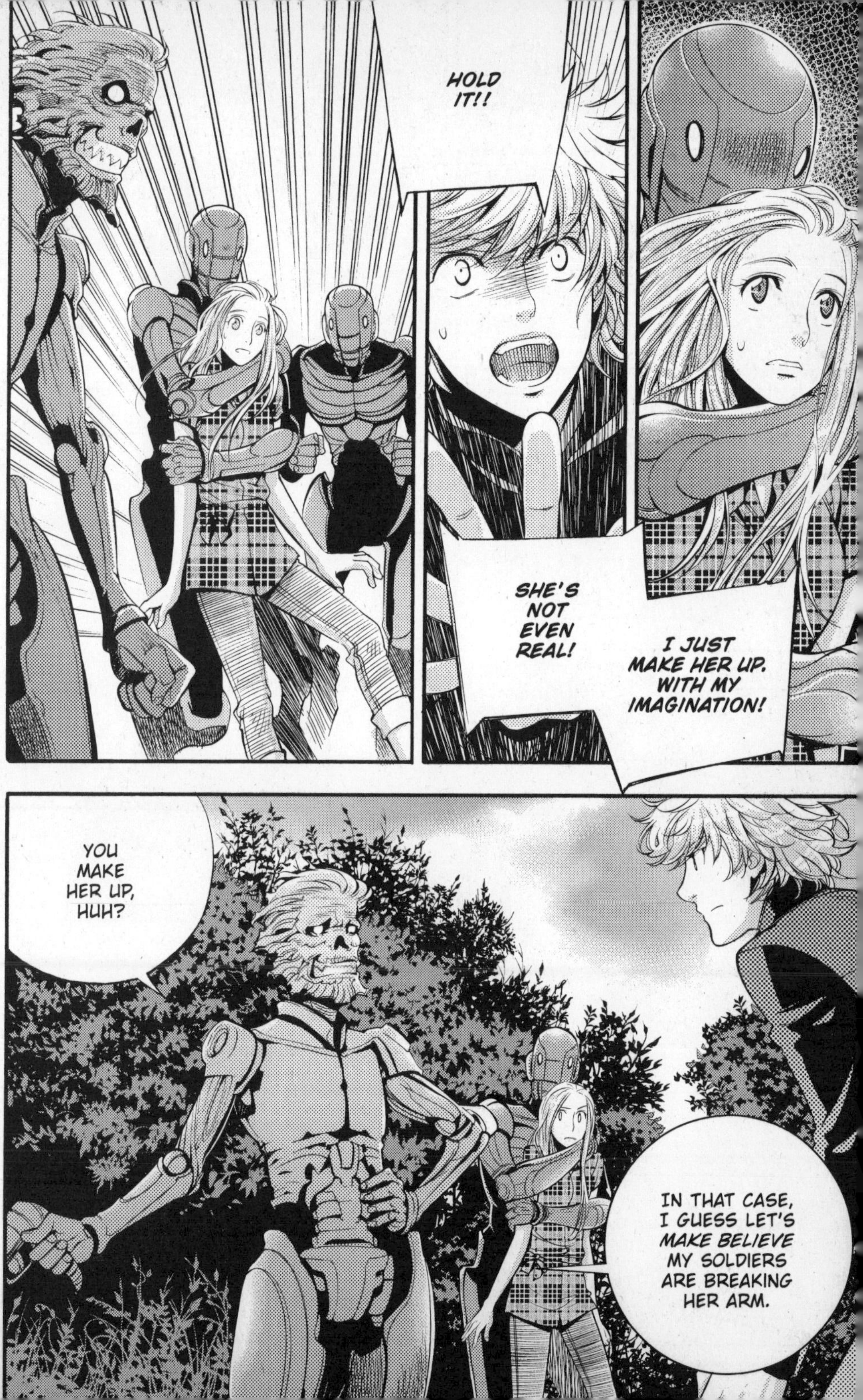
HOLD IT!!
SHE'S NOT EVEN REAL!
I JUST MAKE HER UP. WITH MY IMAGINATION!
YOU MAKE HER UP, HUH?
IN THAT CASE, I GUESS LET'S *MAKE BELIEVE* MY SOLDIERS ARE BREAKING HER ARM.

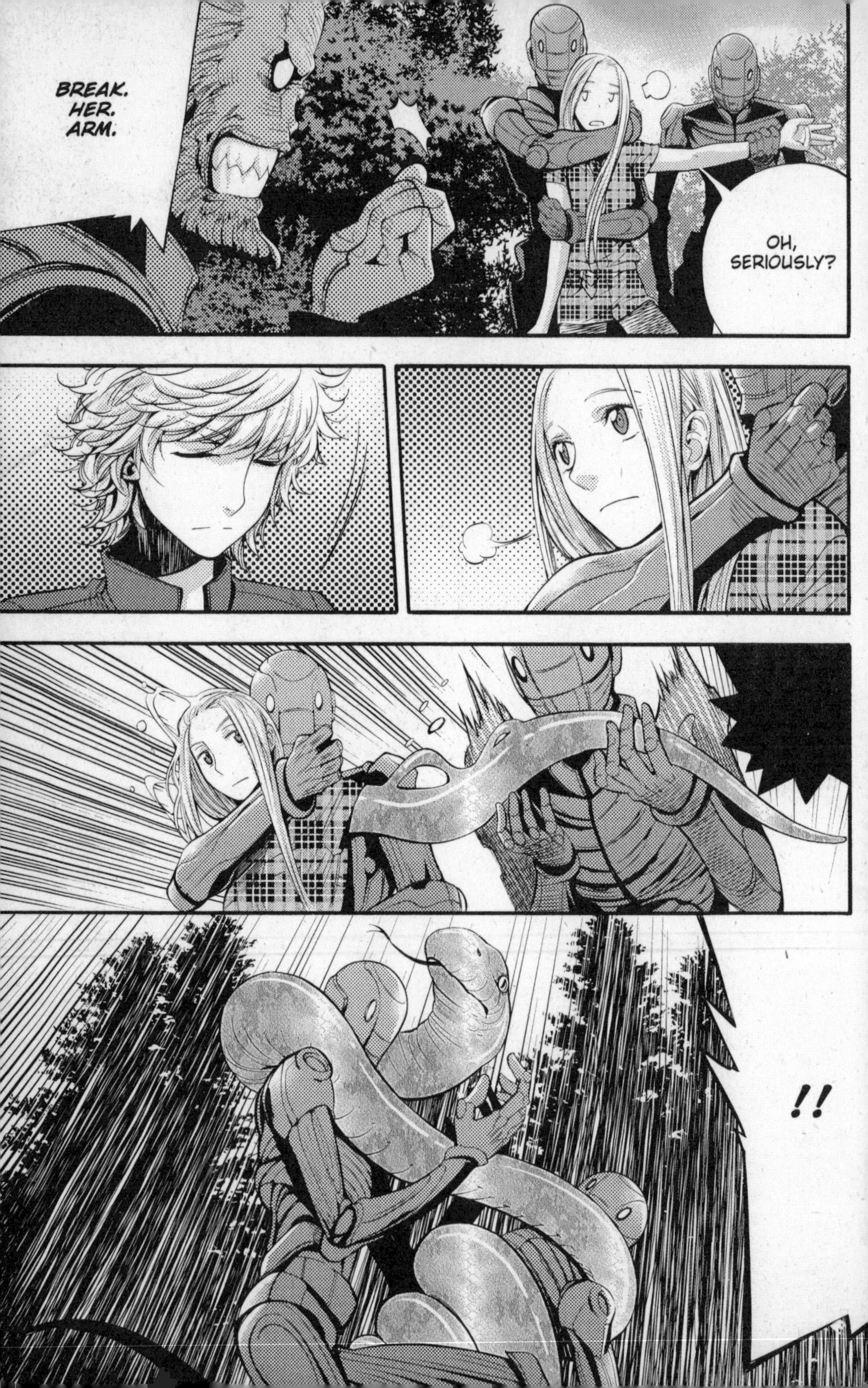
BREAK. HER. ARM.
OH, SERIOUSLY?
!!

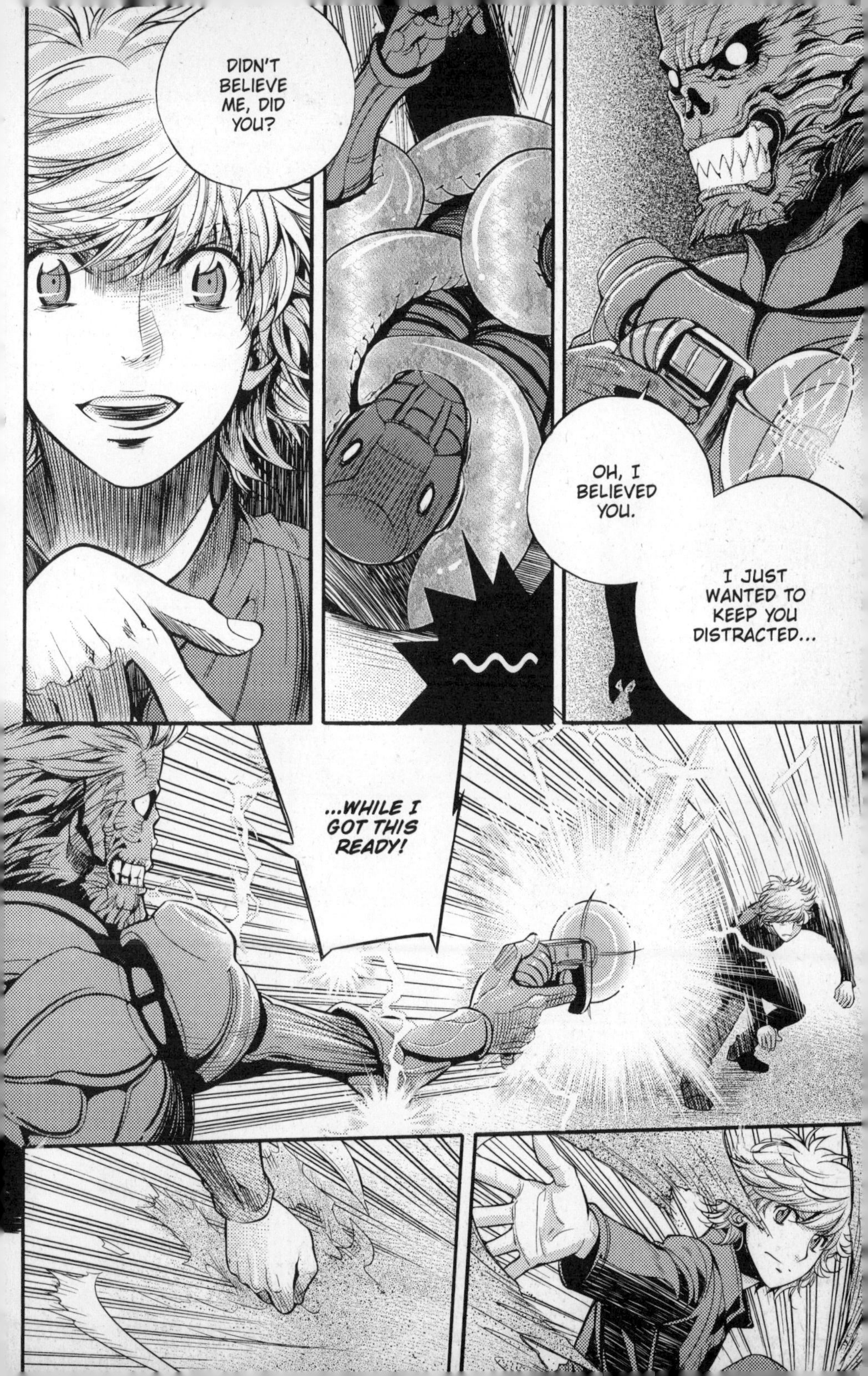
DIDN'T BELIEVE ME, DID YOU?
OH, I BELIEVED YOU.
I JUST WANTED TO KEEP YOU DISTRACTED...
...WHILE I GOT THIS READY!

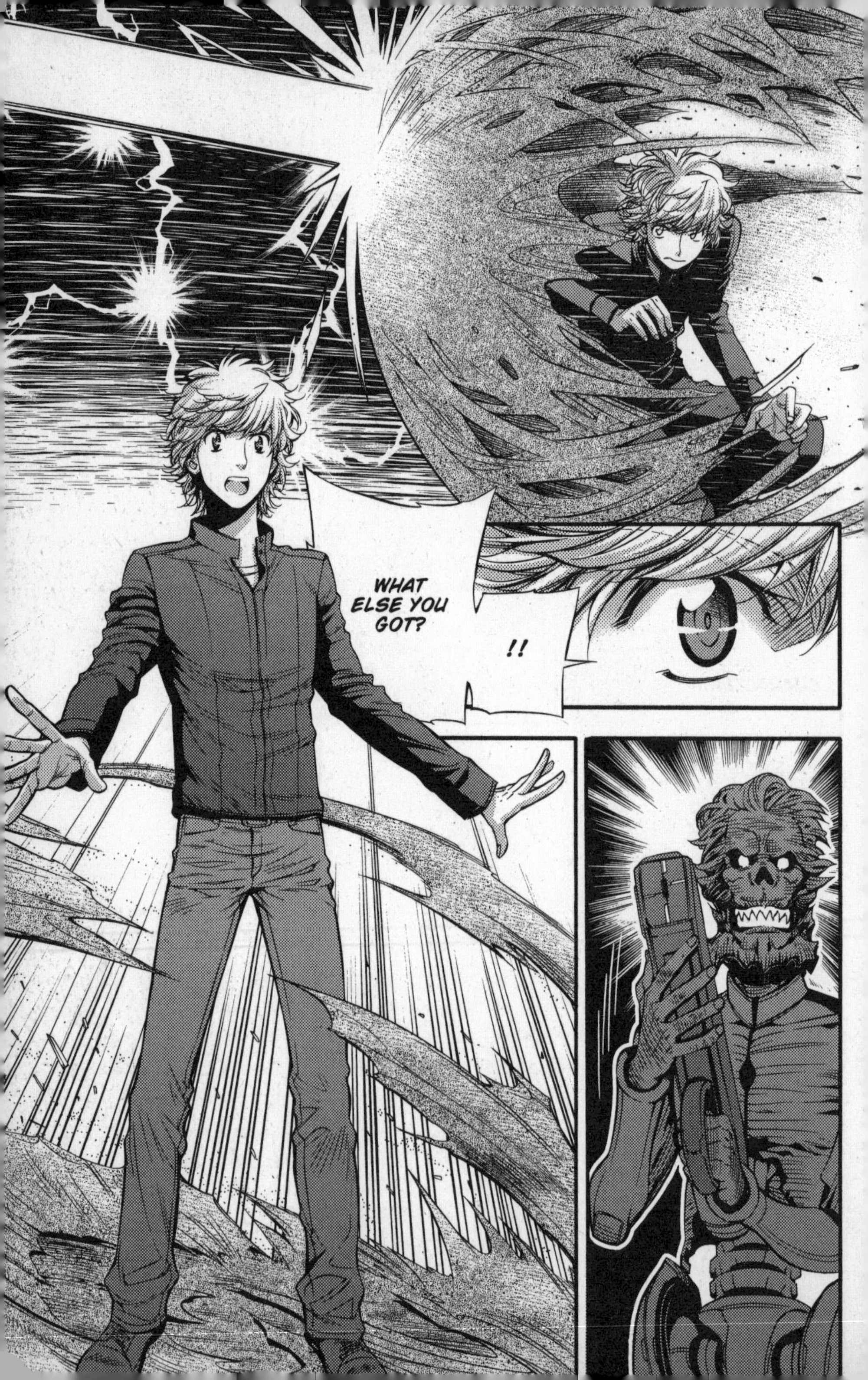
WHAT ELSE YOU GOT?
!!

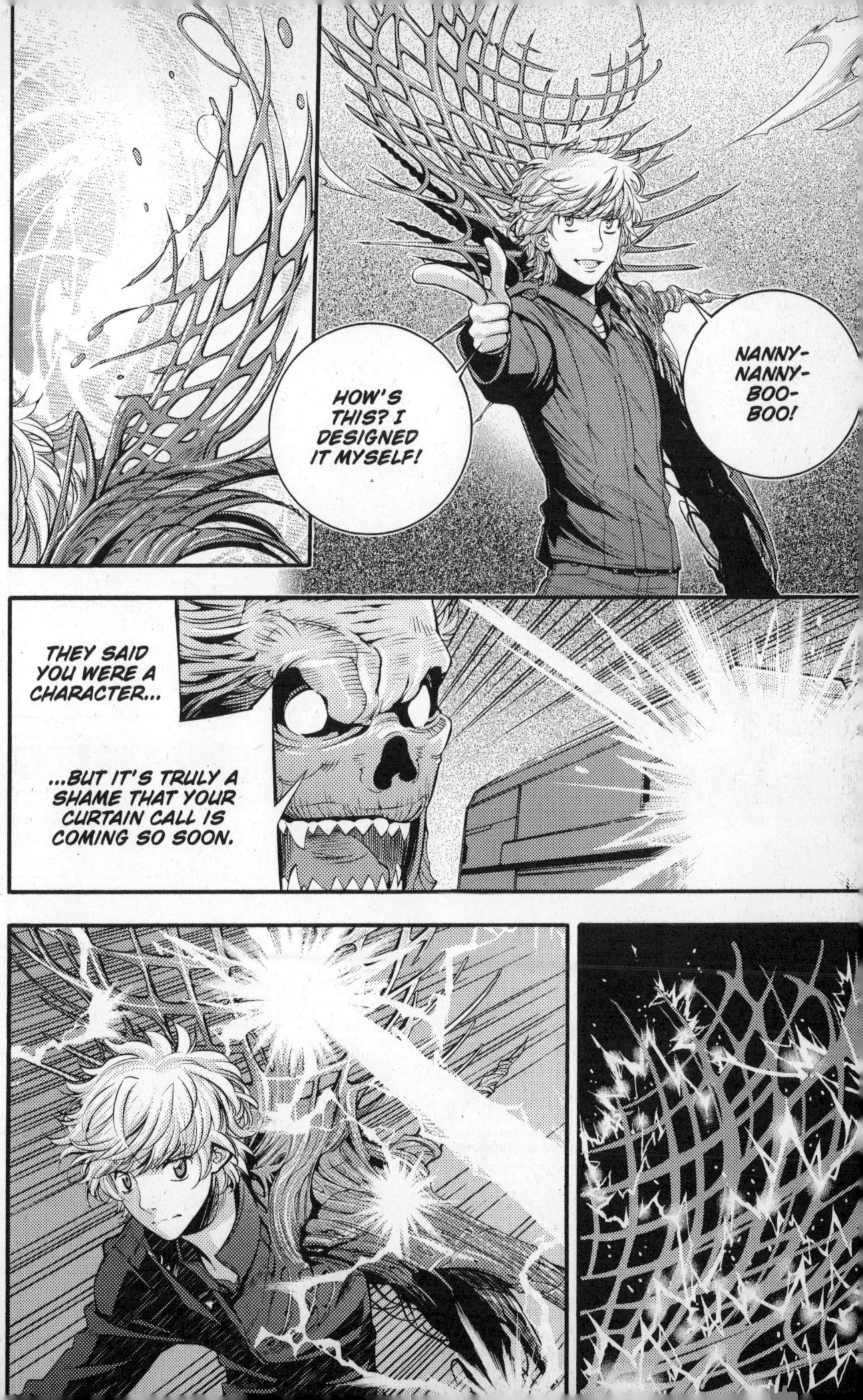
HOW'S THIS? I DESIGNED IT MYSELF!
NANNY-NANNY-BOO-BOO!
THEY SAID YOU WERE A CHARACTER...
...BUT IT'S TRULY A SHAME THAT YOUR CURTAIN CALL IS COMING SO SOON.

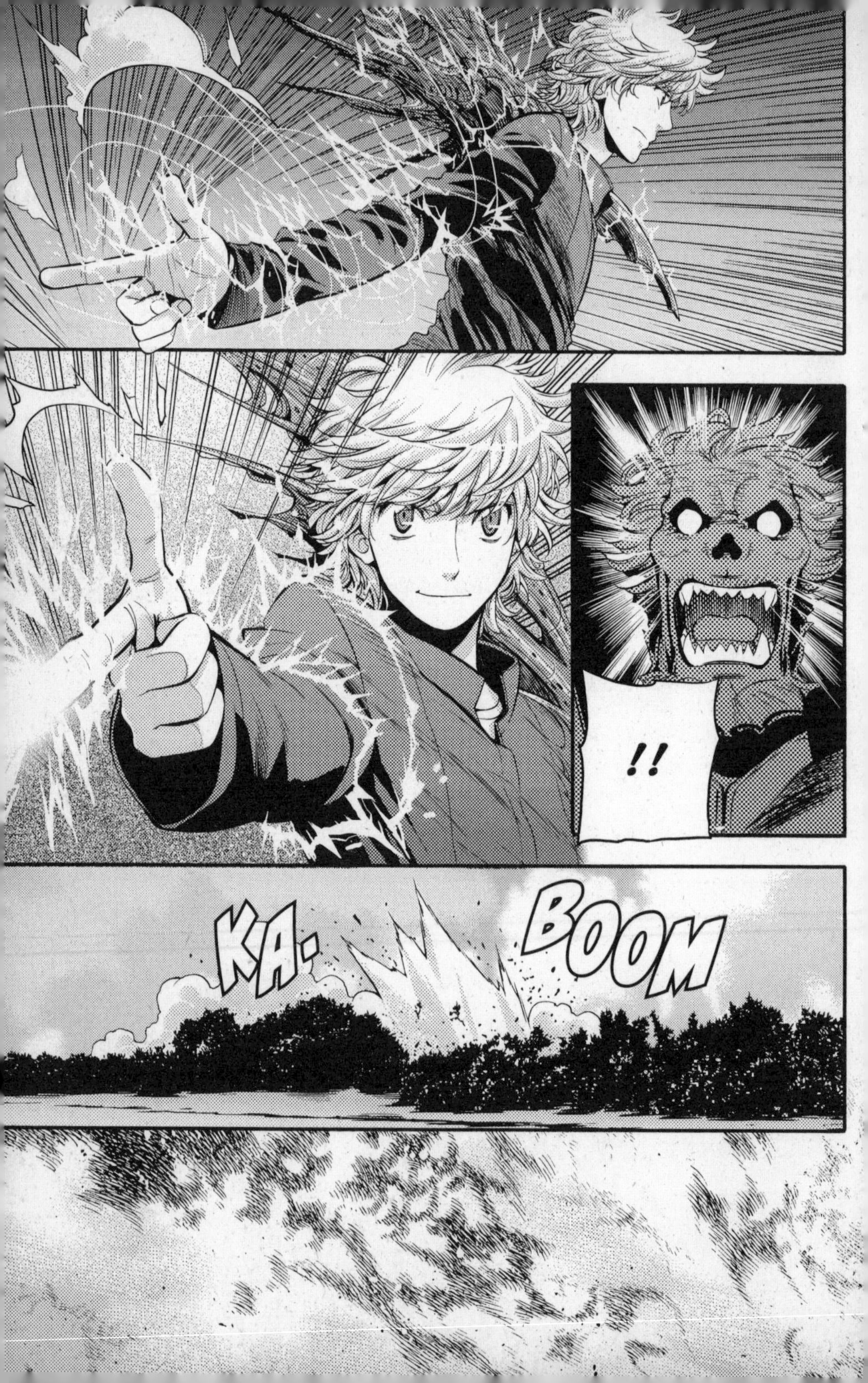
!!
KA-
BOOM

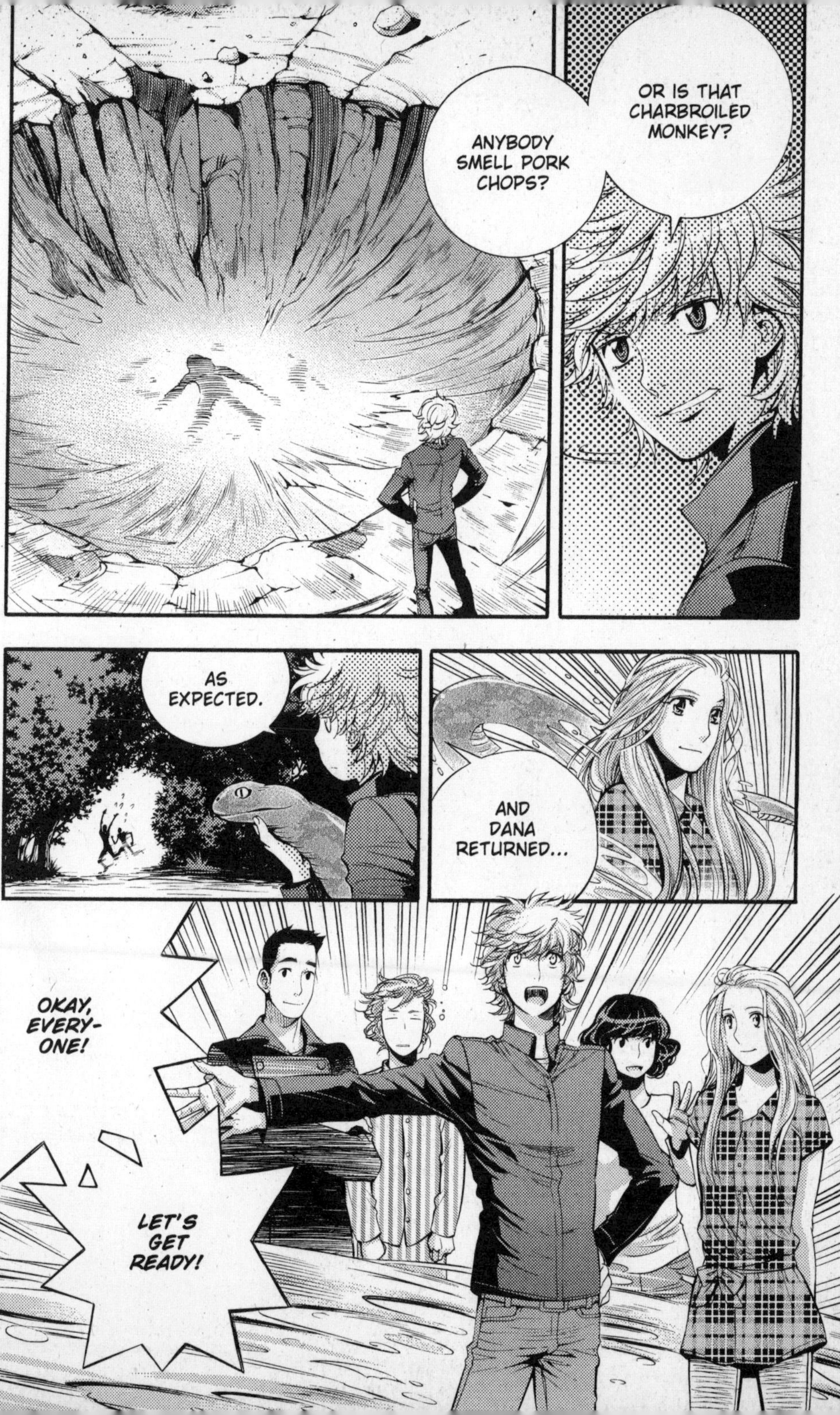
ANYBODY SMELL PORK CHOPS?
OR IS THAT CHARBROILED MONKEY?
AS EXPECTED.
AND DANA RETURNED...
OKAY, EVERY-ONE!
LET'S GET READY!

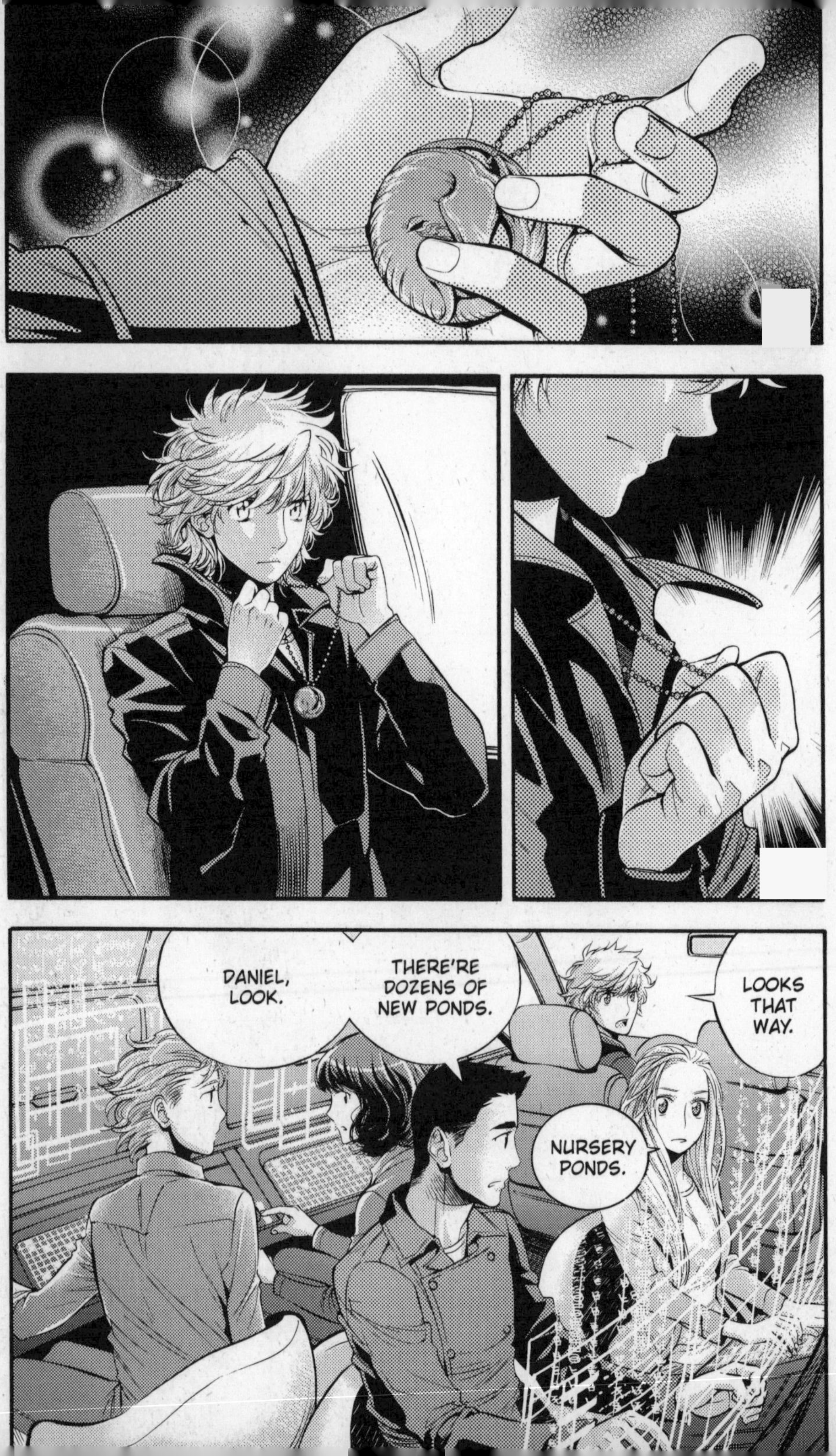

DANIEL, LOOK.
THERE'RE DOZENS OF NEW PONDS.
LOOKS THAT WAY.
NURSERY PONDS.

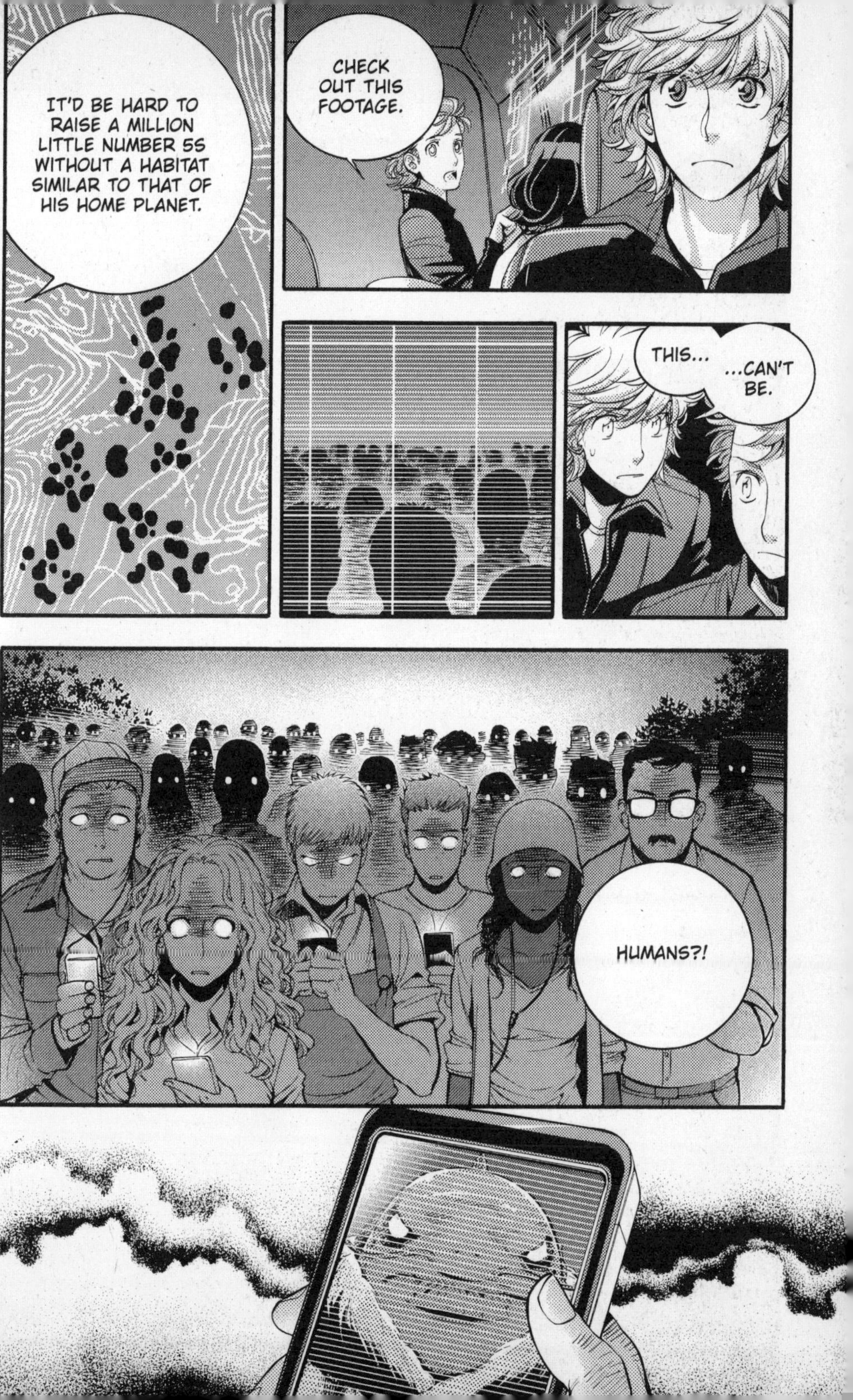
IT'D BE HARD TO RAISE A MILLION LITTLE NUMBER 5S WITHOUT A HABITAT SIMILAR TO THAT OF HIS HOME PLANET.
CHECK OUT THIS FOOTAGE.
THIS...
...CAN'T BE.
HUMANS?!

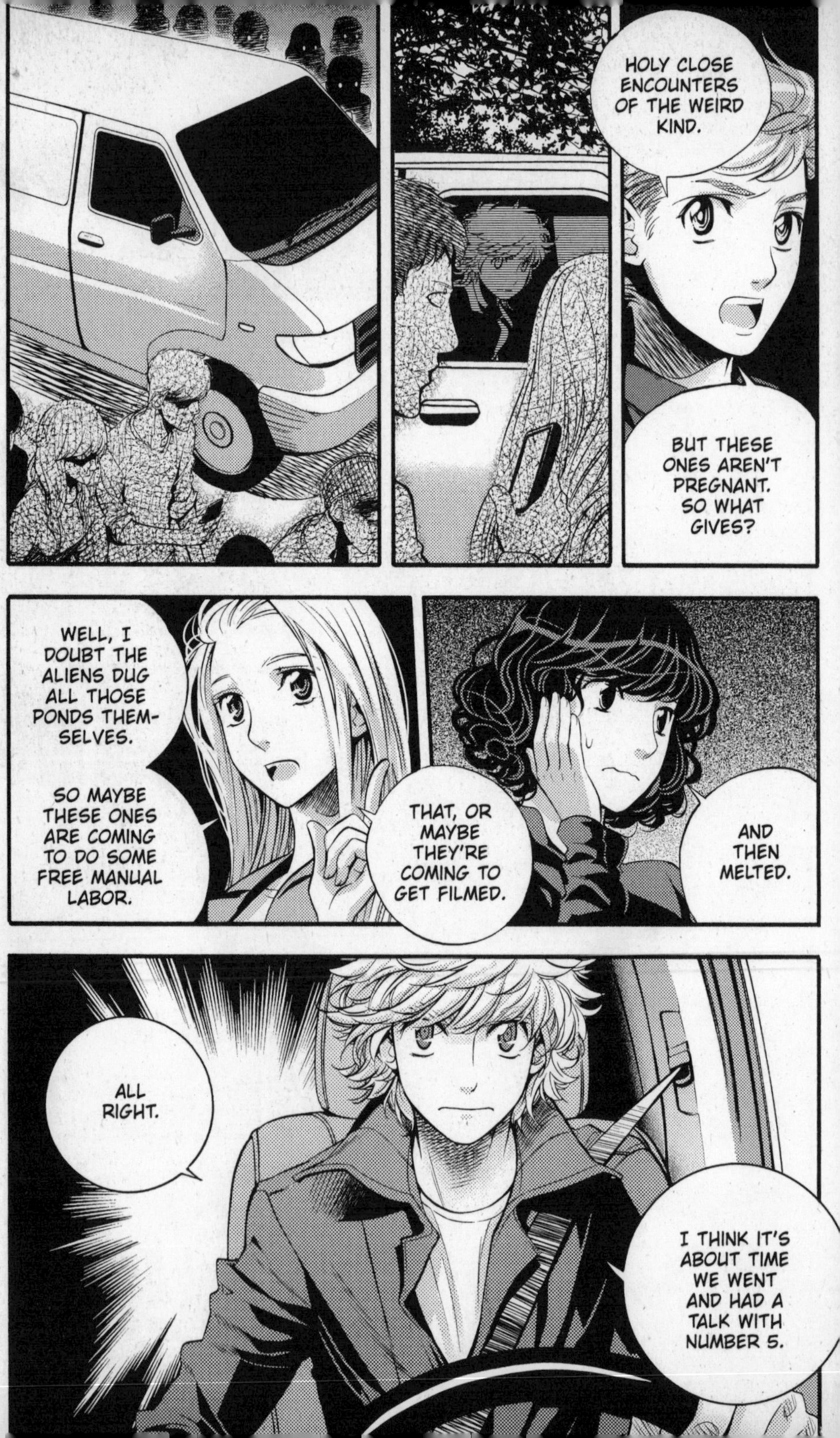
HOLY CLOSE ENCOUNTERS OF THE WEIRD KIND.
BUT THESE ONES AREN'T PREGNANT. SO WHAT GIVES?
WELL, I DOUBT THE ALIENS DUG ALL THOSE PONDS THEM-SELVES.
SO MAYBE THESE ONES ARE COMING TO DO SOME FREE MANUAL LABOR.
THAT, OR MAYBE THEY'RE COMING TO GET FILMED.
AND THEN MELTED.
ALL RIGHT.
I THINK IT'S ABOUT TIME WE WENT AND HAD A TALK WITH NUMBER 5.

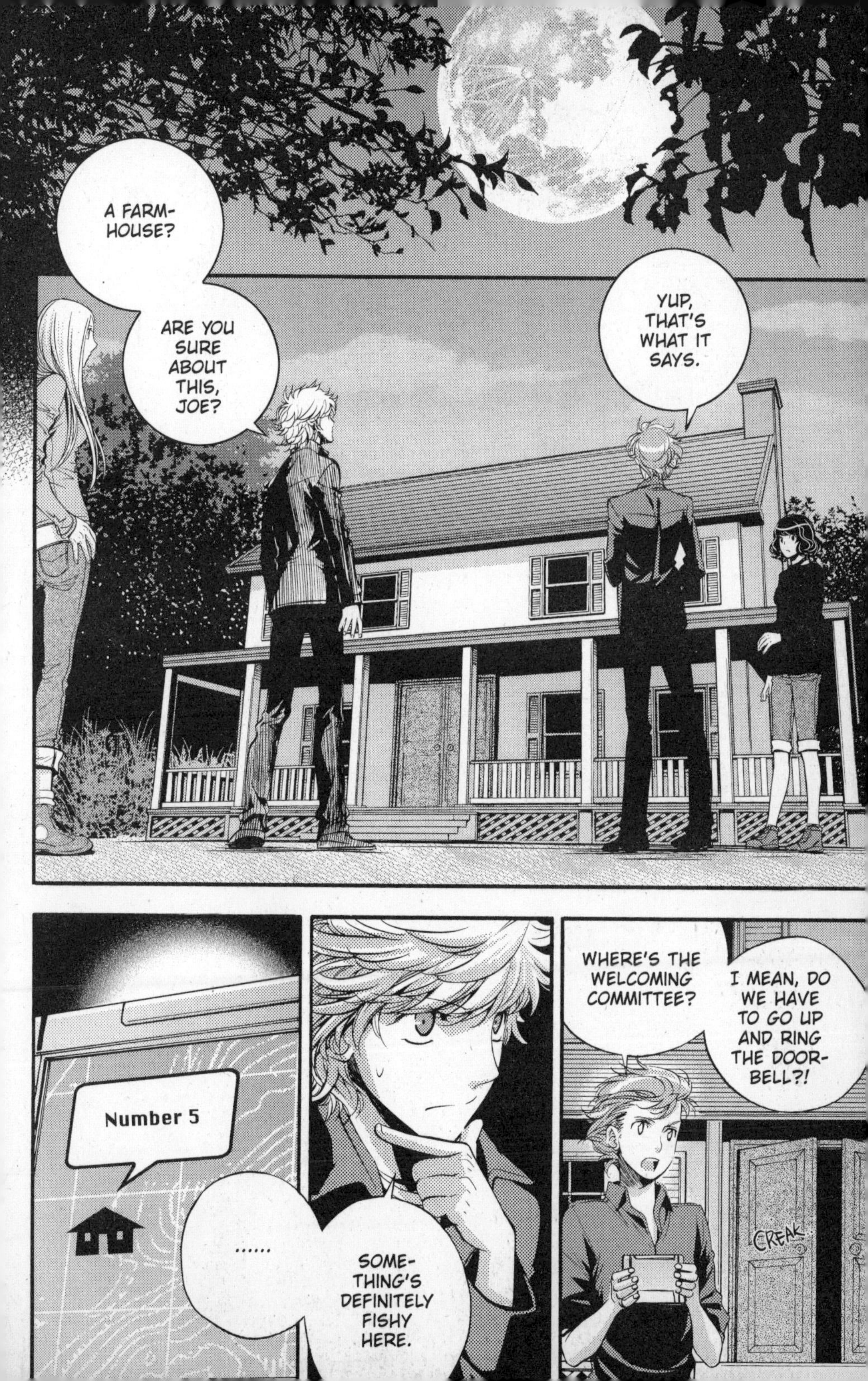
A FARM-HOUSE?
ARE YOU SURE ABOUT THIS, JOE?
YUP, THAT'S WHAT IT SAYS.
Number 5
......
SOME-THING'S DEFINITELY FISHY HERE.
WHERE'S THE WELCOMING COMMITTEE?
I MEAN, DO WE HAVE TO GO UP AND RING THE DOOR-BELL?!
CREAK

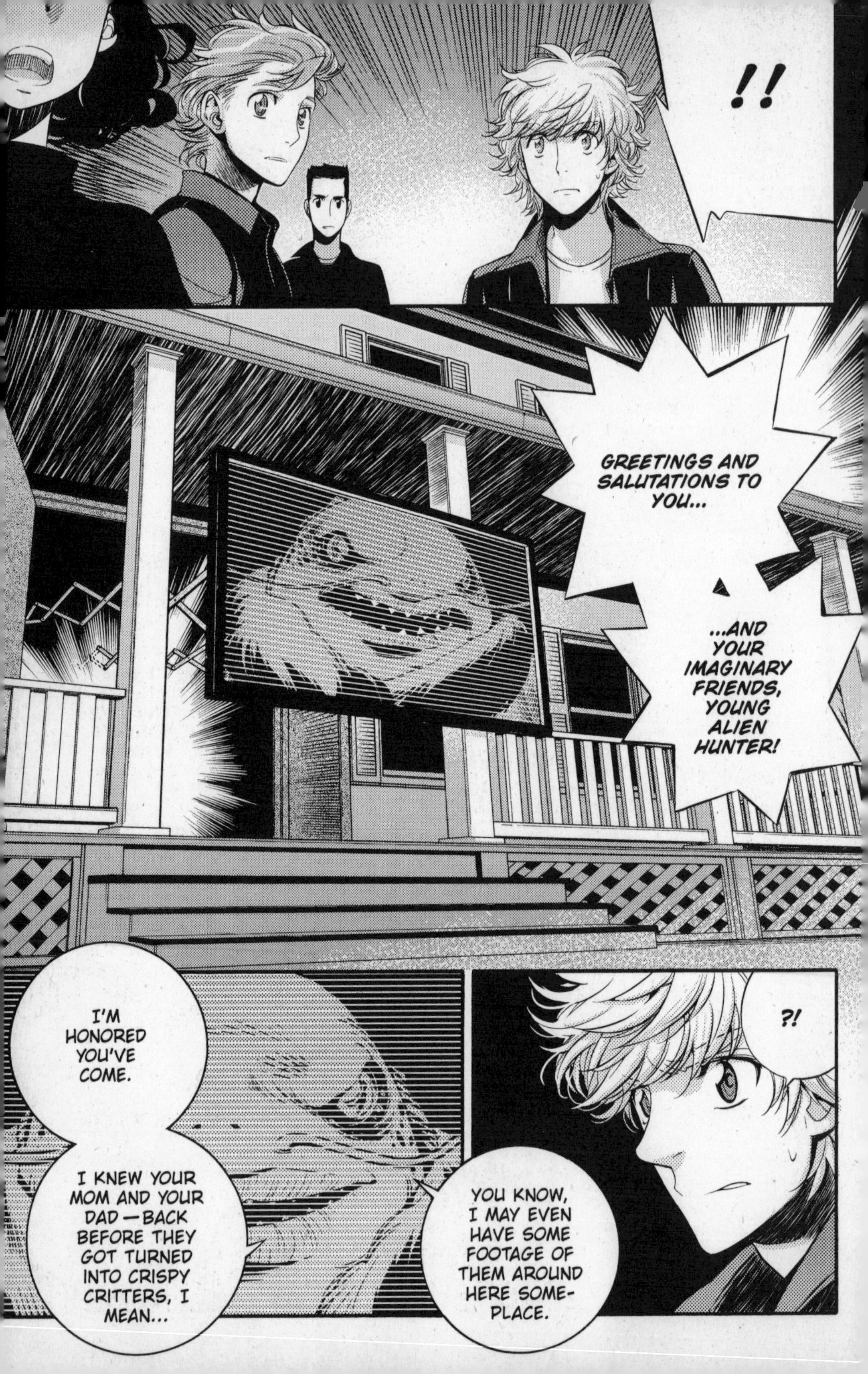
!!
GREETINGS AND SALUTATIONS TO YOU...
...AND YOUR IMAGINARY FRIENDS, YOUNG ALIEN HUNTER!
I'M HONORED YOU'VE COME.
I KNEW YOUR MOM AND YOUR DAD—BACK BEFORE THEY GOT TURNED INTO CRISPY CRITTERS, I MEAN...
YOU KNOW, I MAY EVEN HAVE SOME FOOTAGE OF THEM AROUND HERE SOME-PLACE.
?!

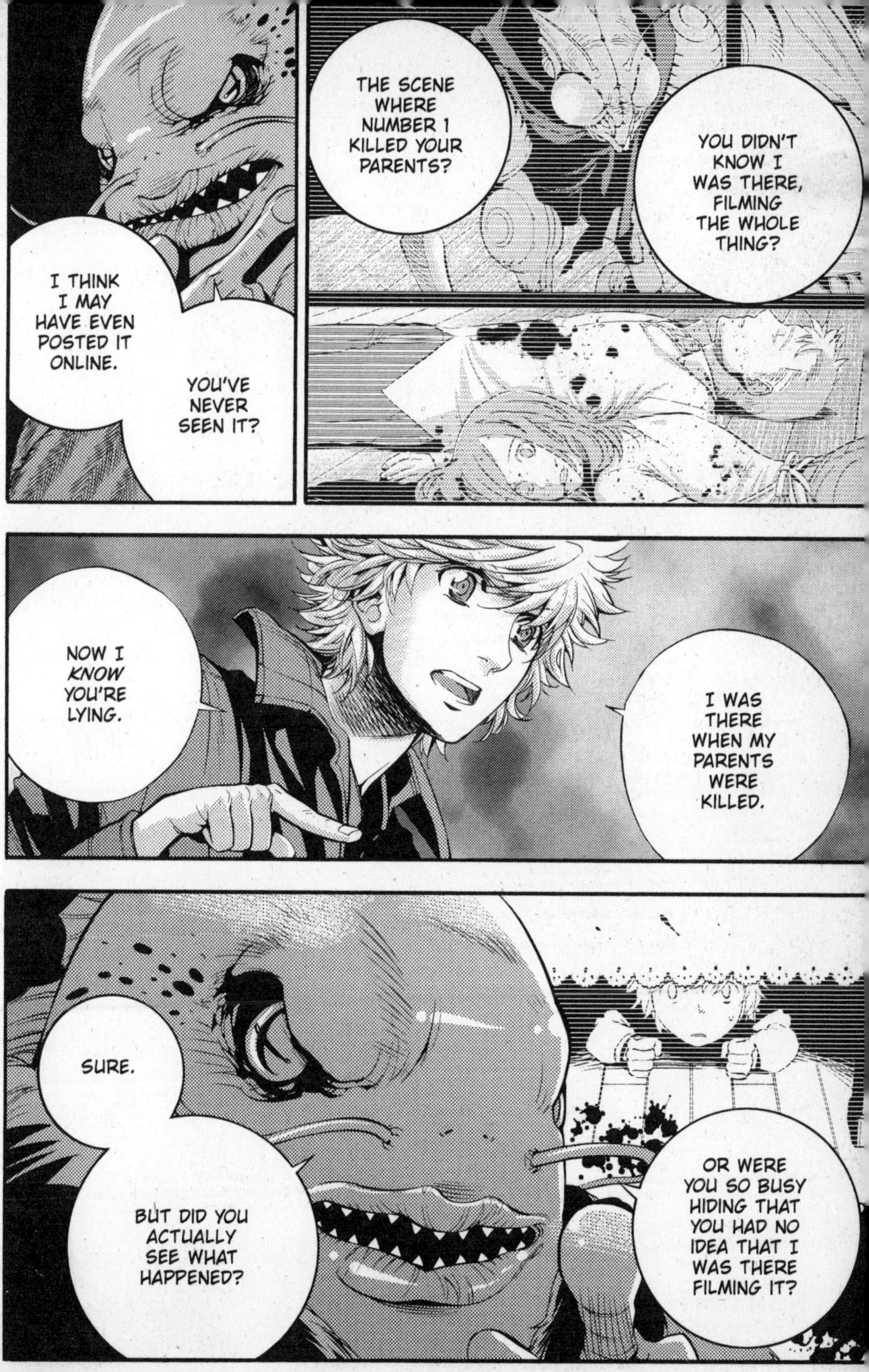
I THINK I MAY HAVE EVEN POSTED IT ONLINE.
YOU'VE NEVER SEEN IT?
THE SCENE WHERE NUMBER 1 KILLED YOUR PARENTS?
YOU DIDN'T KNOW I WAS THERE, FILMING THE WHOLE THING?
NOW I *KNOW* YOU'RE LYING.
I WAS THERE WHEN MY PARENTS WERE KILLED.
SURE.
BUT DID YOU ACTUALLY SEE WHAT HAPPENED?
OR WERE YOU SO BUSY HIDING THAT YOU HAD NO IDEA THAT I WAS THERE FILMING IT?

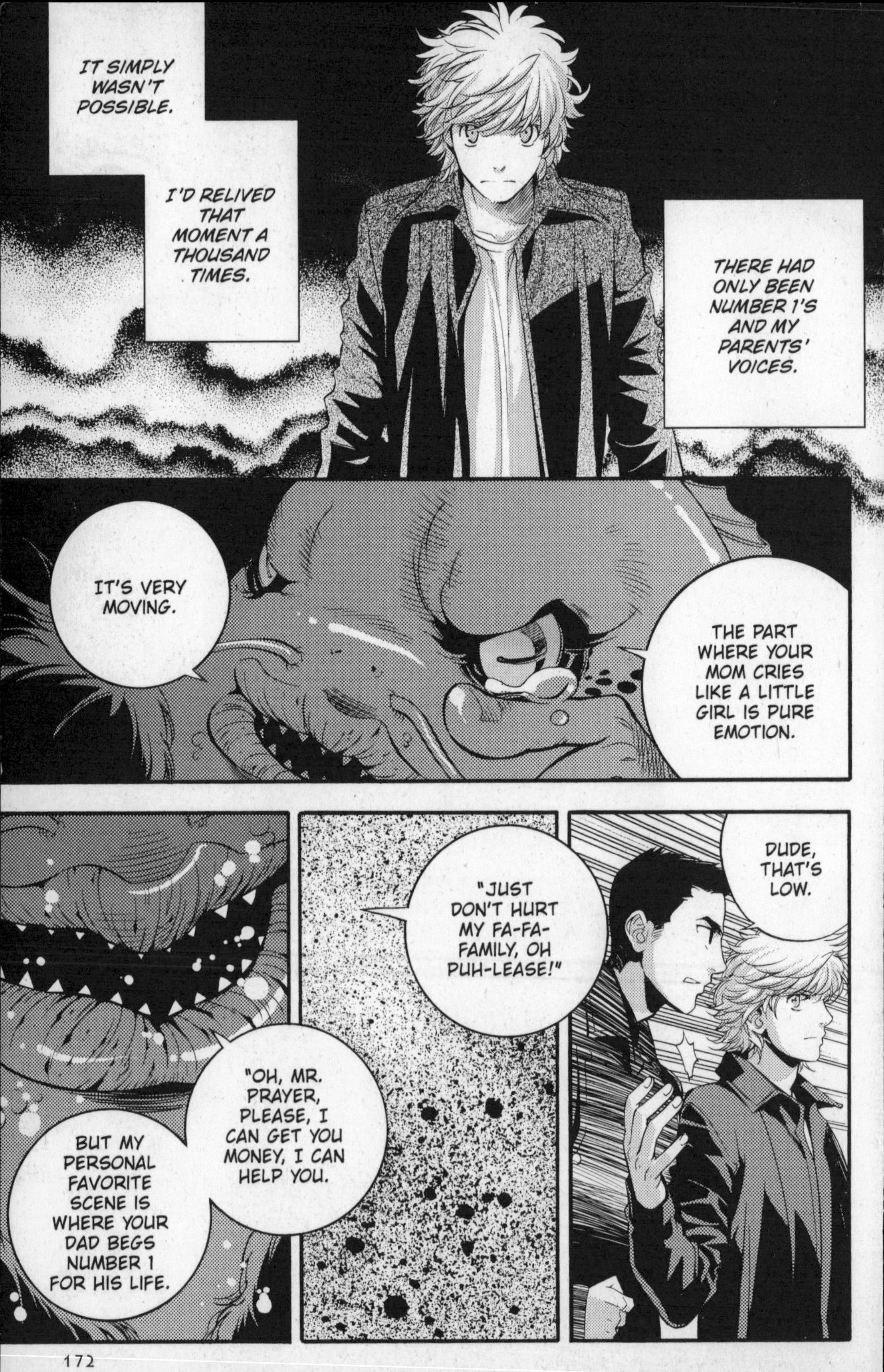
IT SIMPLY WASN'T POSSIBLE.
I'D RELIVED THAT MOMENT A THOUSAND TIMES.
THERE HAD ONLY BEEN NUMBER 1'S AND MY PARENTS' VOICES.
IT'S VERY MOVING.
THE PART WHERE YOUR MOM CRIES LIKE A LITTLE GIRL IS PURE EMOTION.
BUT MY PERSONAL FAVORITE SCENE IS WHERE YOUR DAD BEGS NUMBER 1 FOR HIS LIFE.
"OH, MR. PRAYER, PLEASE, I CAN GET YOU MONEY, I CAN HELP YOU.
"JUST DON'T HURT MY FA-FA-FAMILY, OH PUH-LEASE!"
DUDE, THAT'S LOW.

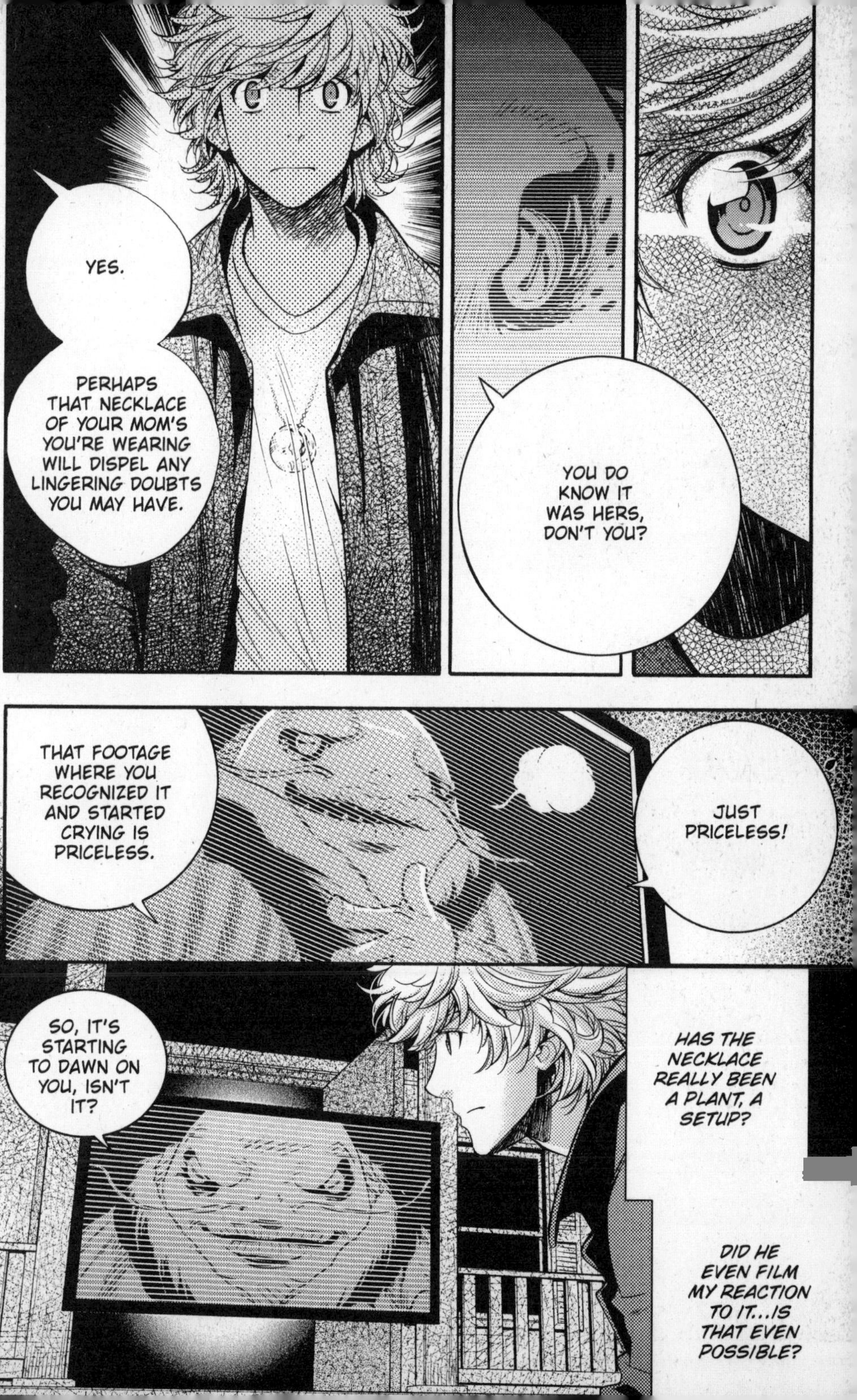
YES.
PERHAPS THAT NECKLACE OF YOUR MOM'S YOU'RE WEARING WILL DISPEL ANY LINGERING DOUBTS YOU MAY HAVE.
YOU DO KNOW IT WAS HERS, DON'T YOU?
THAT FOOTAGE WHERE YOU RECOGNIZED IT AND STARTED CRYING IS PRICELESS.
JUST PRICELESS!
SO, IT'S STARTING TO DAWN ON YOU, ISN'T IT?
HAS THE NECKLACE REALLY BEEN A PLANT, A SETUP?
DID HE EVEN FILM MY REACTION TO IT...IS THAT EVEN POSSIBLE?

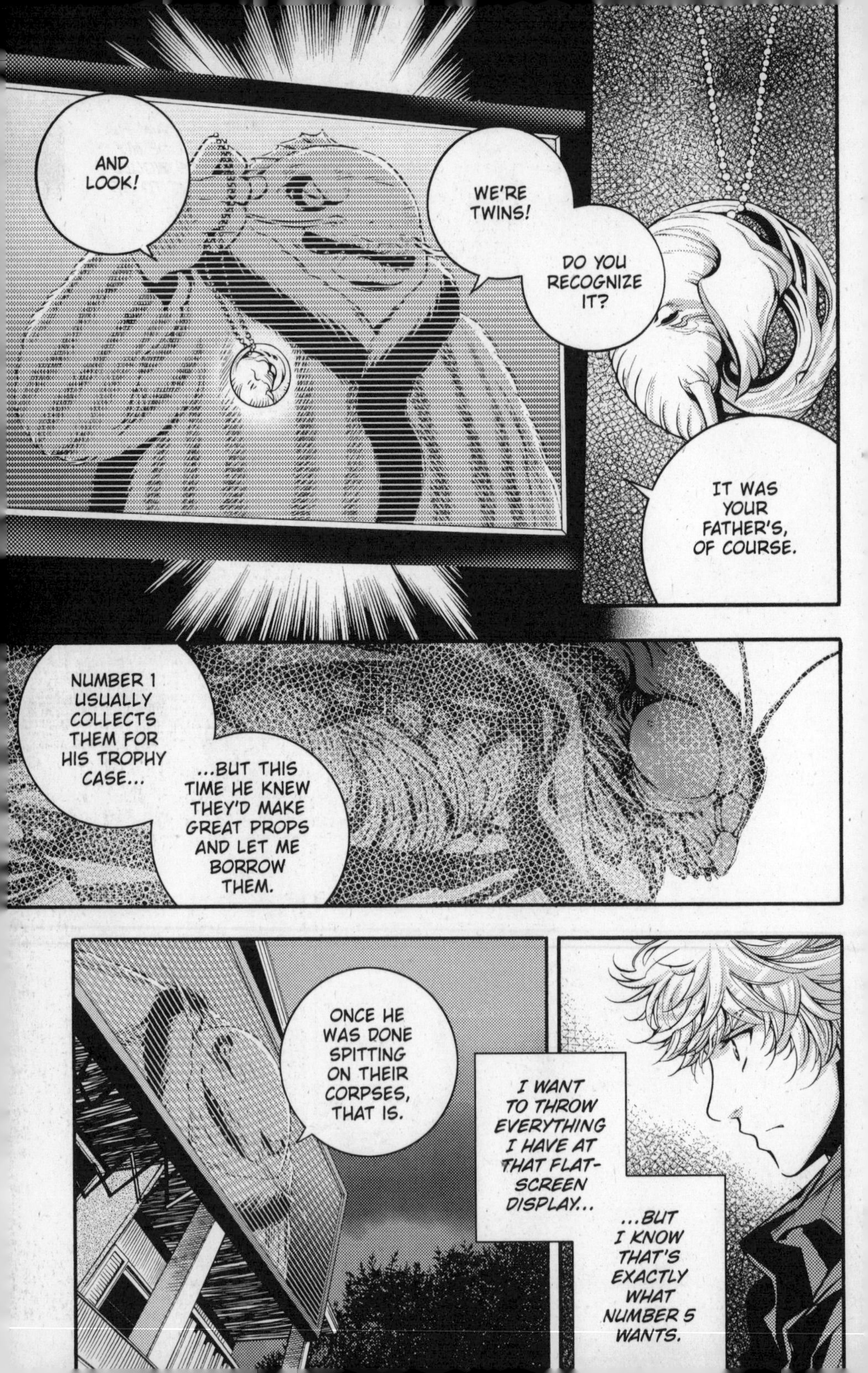
AND LOOK!
WE'RE TWINS!
DO YOU RECOGNIZE IT?
IT WAS YOUR FATHER'S, OF COURSE.
NUMBER 1 USUALLY COLLECTS THEM FOR HIS TROPHY CASE...
...BUT THIS TIME HE KNEW THEY'D MAKE GREAT PROPS AND LET ME BORROW THEM.
ONCE HE WAS DONE SPITTING ON THEIR CORPSES, THAT IS.
I WANT TO THROW EVERYTHING I HAVE AT THAT FLAT-SCREEN DISPLAY...
...BUT I KNOW THAT'S EXACTLY WHAT NUMBER 5 WANTS.

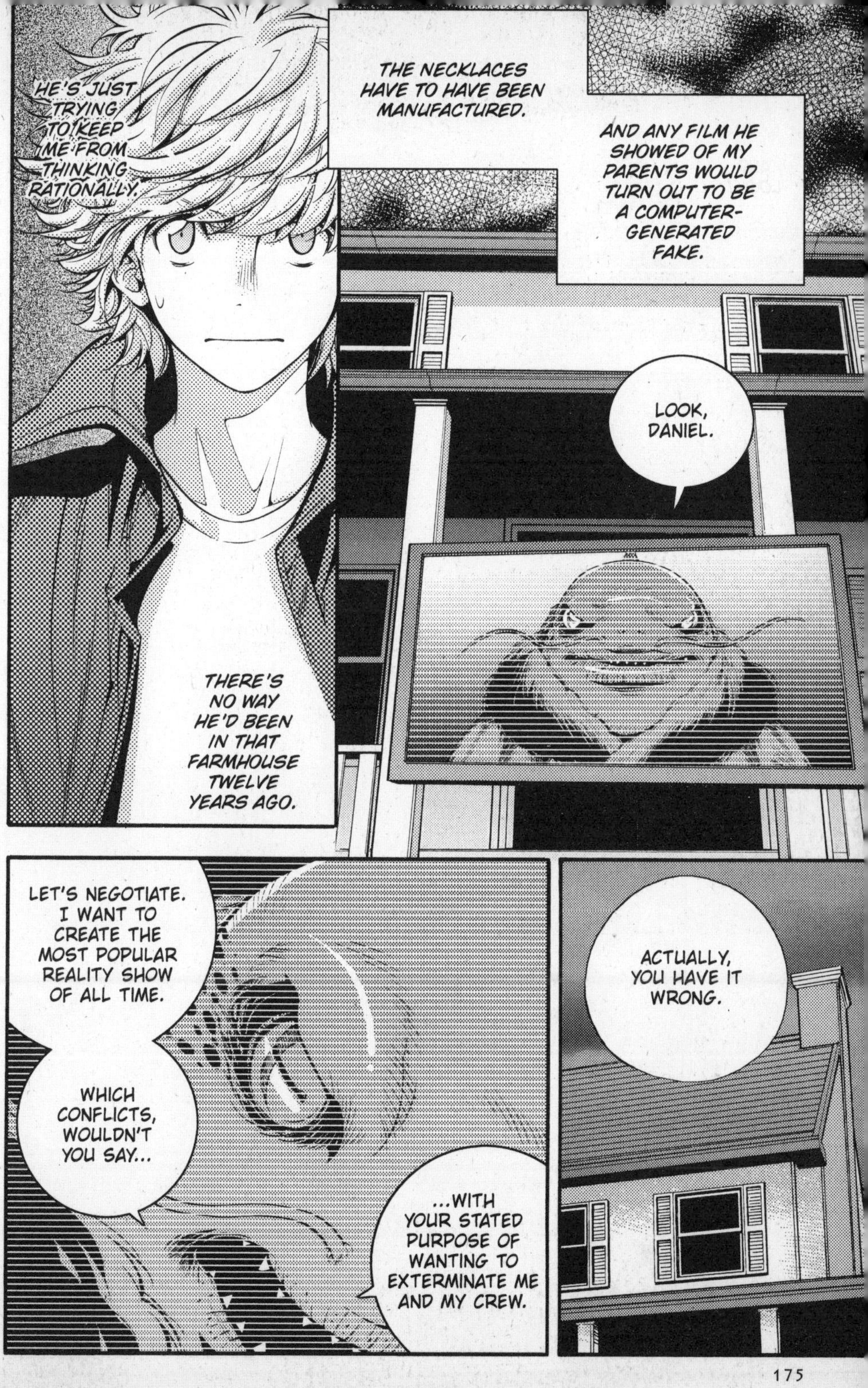
HE'S JUST TRYING TO KEEP ME FROM THINKING RATIONALLY.
THERE'S NO WAY HE'D BEEN IN THAT FARMHOUSE TWELVE YEARS AGO.
THE NECKLACES HAVE TO HAVE BEEN MANUFACTURED.
AND ANY FILM HE SHOWED OF MY PARENTS WOULD TURN OUT TO BE A COMPUTER-GENERATED FAKE.
LOOK, DANIEL.
LET'S NEGOTIATE. I WANT TO CREATE THE MOST POPULAR REALITY SHOW OF ALL TIME.
WHICH CONFLICTS, WOULDN'T YOU SAY...
...WITH YOUR STATED PURPOSE OF WANTING TO EXTERMINATE ME AND MY CREW.
ACTUALLY, YOU HAVE IT WRONG.

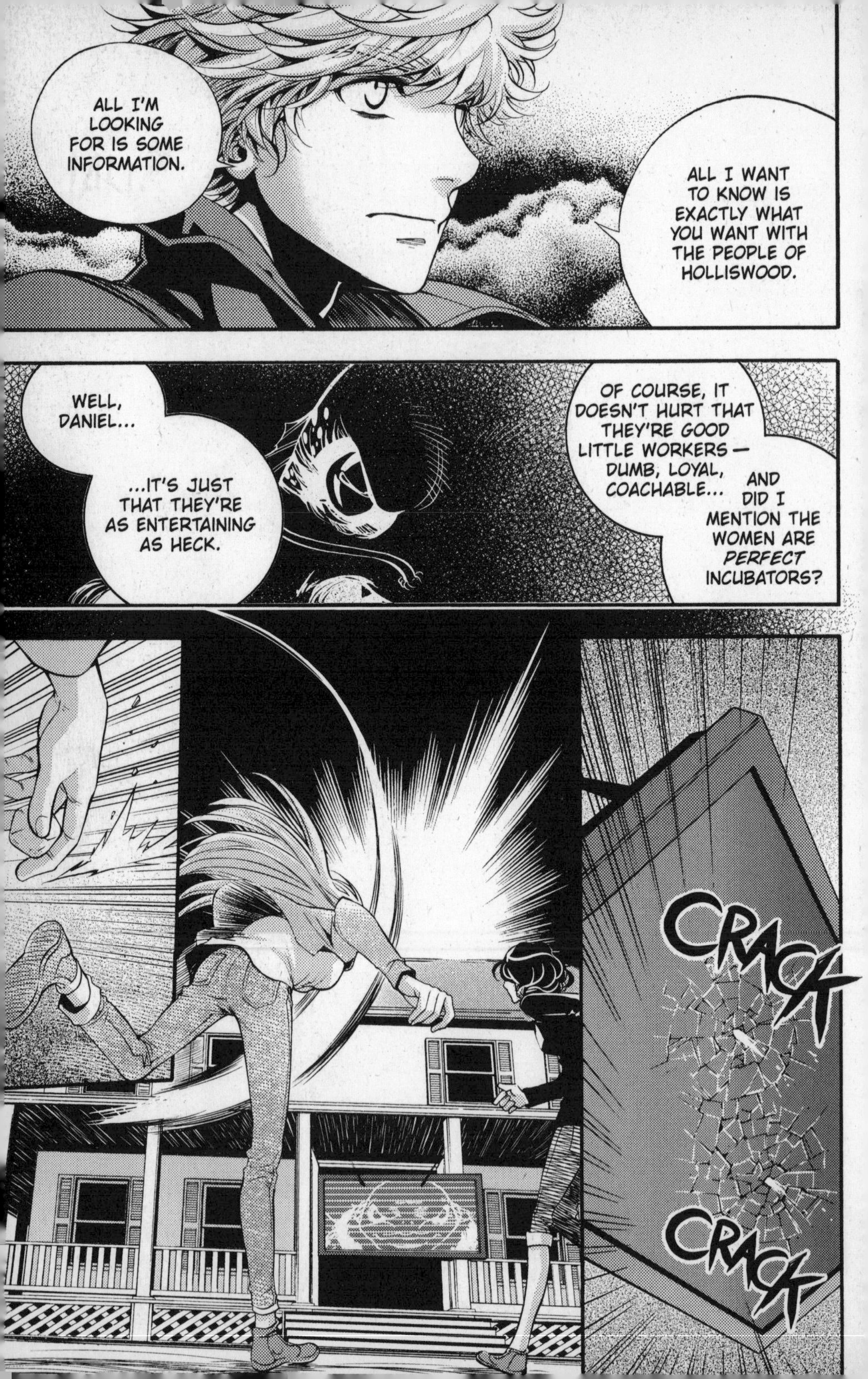
ALL I'M LOOKING FOR IS SOME INFORMATION.
ALL I WANT TO KNOW IS EXACTLY WHAT YOU WANT WITH THE PEOPLE OF HOLLISWOOD.
WELL, DANIEL...
...IT'S JUST THAT THEY'RE AS ENTERTAINING AS HECK.
OF COURSE, IT DOESN'T HURT THAT THEY'RE GOOD LITTLE WORKERS— DUMB, LOYAL, COACHABLE...
AND DID I MENTION THE WOMEN ARE *PERFECT* INCUBATORS?
CRACK
CRACK

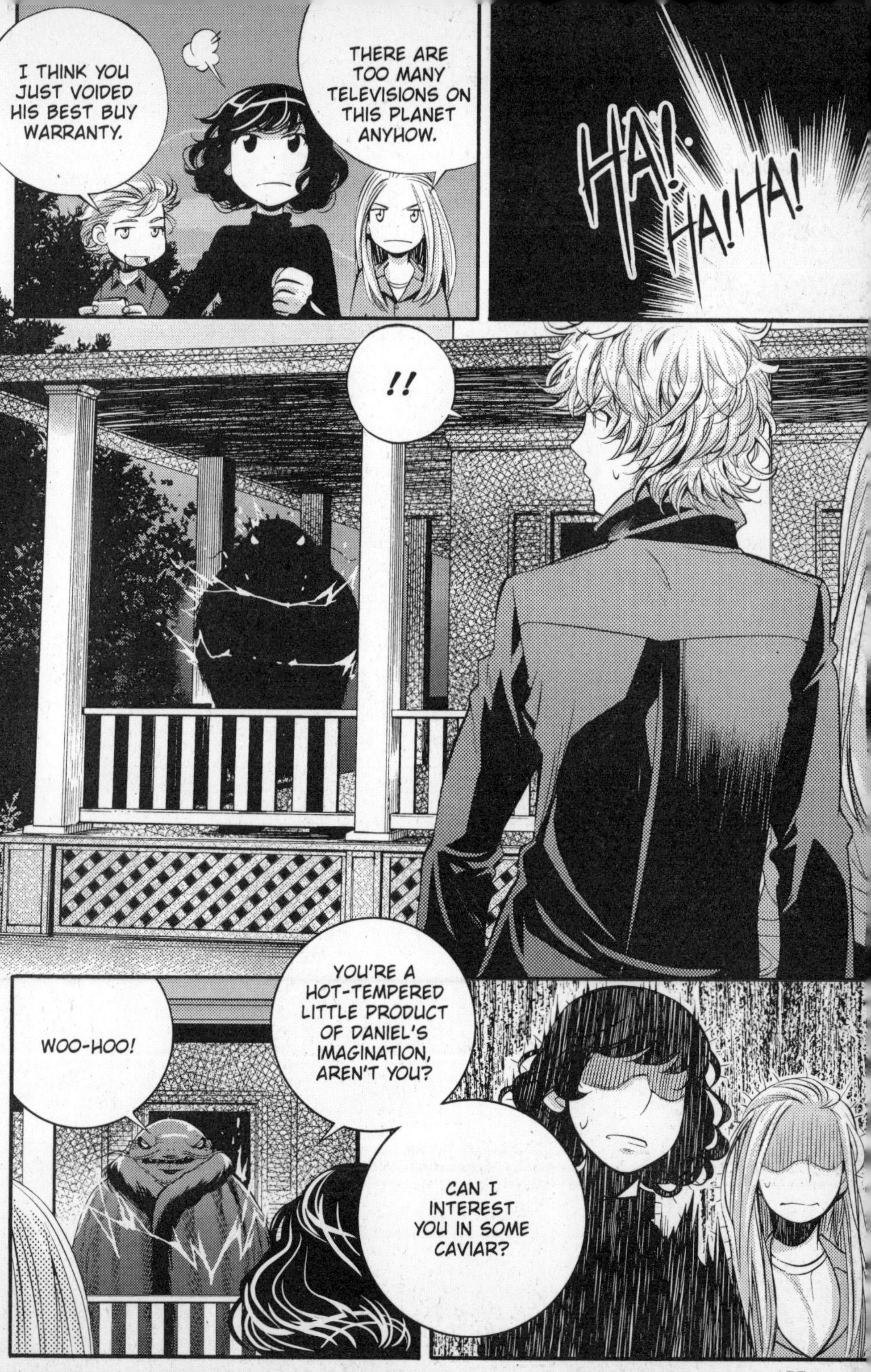
I THINK YOU JUST VOIDED HIS BEST BUY WARRANTY.
THERE ARE TOO MANY TELEVISIONS ON THIS PLANET ANYHOW.
HA! HA!HA!
!!
WOO-HOO!
YOU'RE A HOT-TEMPERED LITTLE PRODUCT OF DANIEL'S IMAGINATION, AREN'T YOU?
CAN I INTEREST YOU IN SOME CAVIAR?

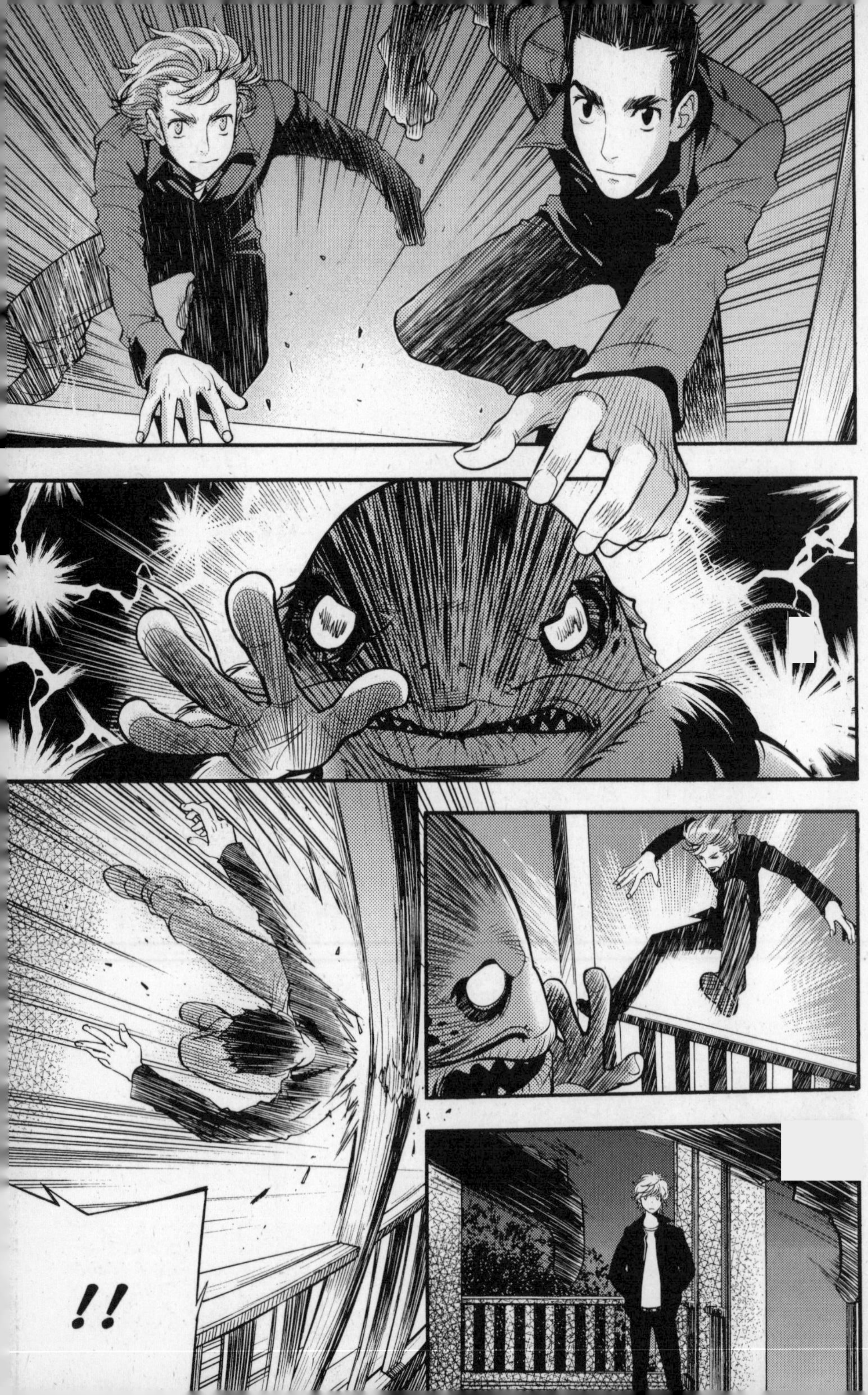
!!

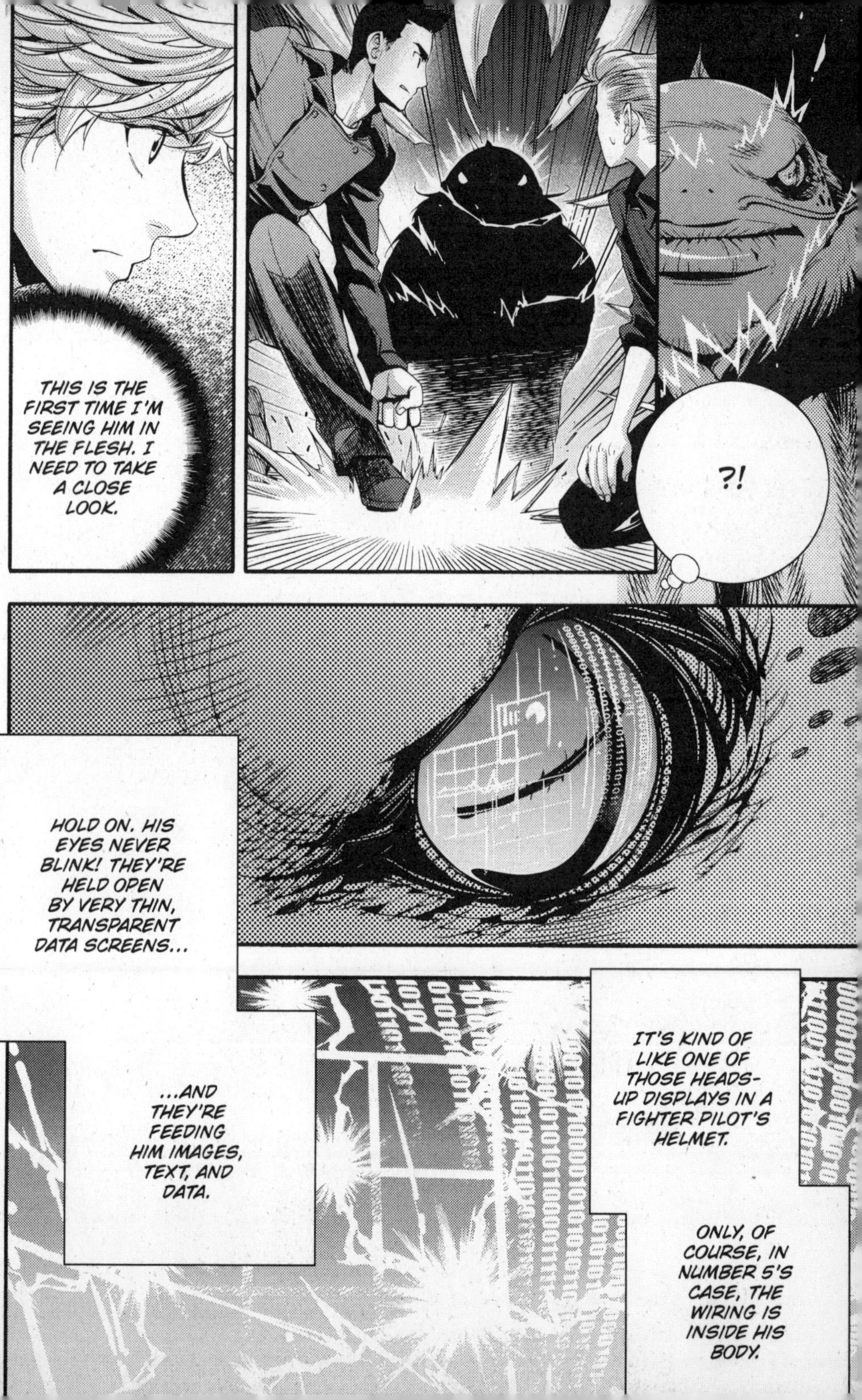
THIS IS THE FIRST TIME I'M SEEING HIM IN THE FLESH. I NEED TO TAKE A CLOSE LOOK.
?!
HOLD ON. HIS EYES NEVER BLINK! THEY'RE HELD OPEN BY VERY THIN, TRANSPARENT DATA SCREENS...
...AND THEY'RE FEEDING HIM IMAGES, TEXT, AND DATA.
IT'S KIND OF LIKE ONE OF THOSE HEADS-UP DISPLAYS IN A FIGHTER PILOT'S HELMET.
ONLY, OF COURSE, IN NUMBER 5'S CASE, THE WIRING IS INSIDE HIS BODY.

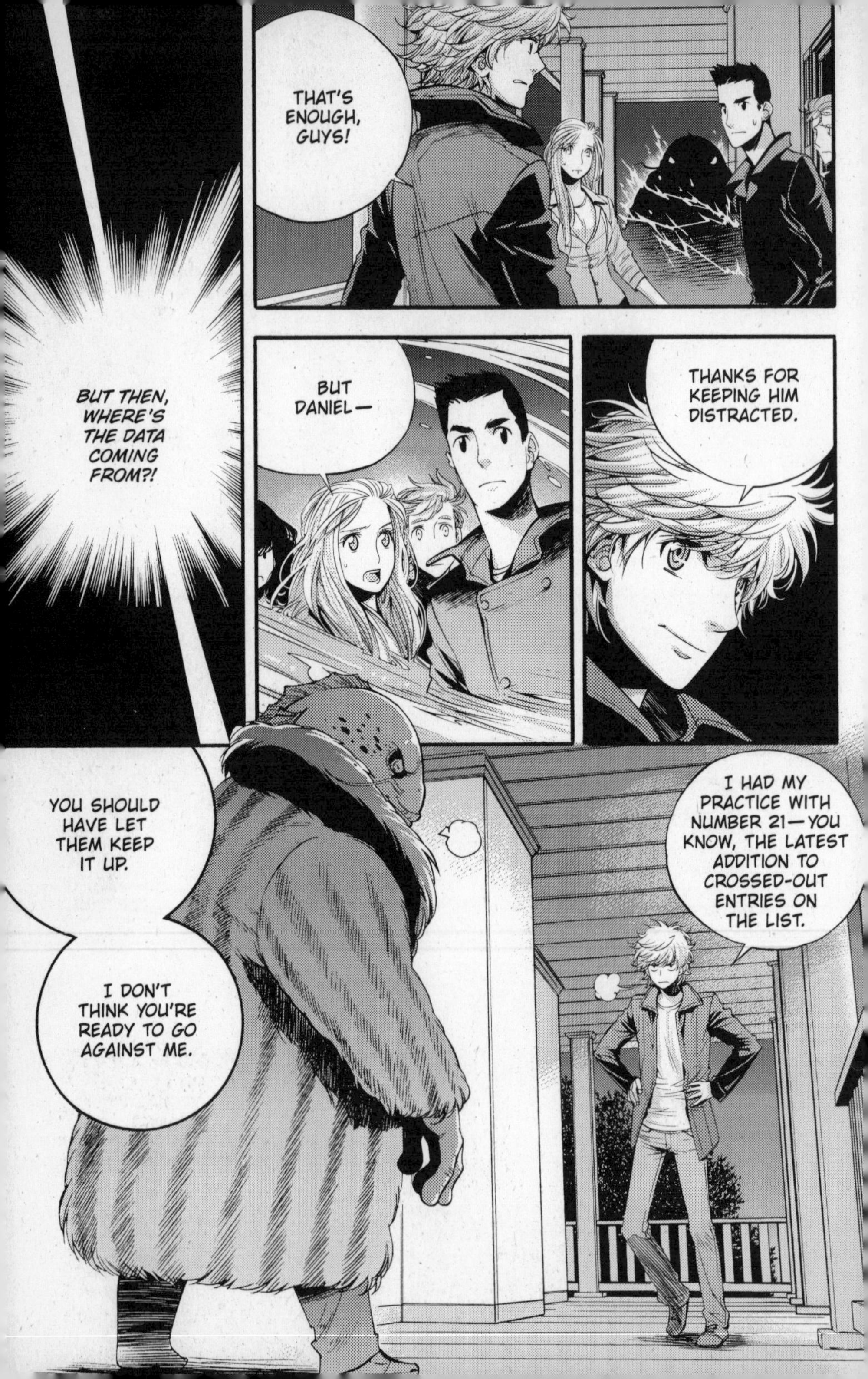
BUT THEN, WHERE'S THE DATA COMING FROM?!
THAT'S ENOUGH, GUYS!
BUT DANIEL—
THANKS FOR KEEPING HIM DISTRACTED.
YOU SHOULD HAVE LET THEM KEEP IT UP.
I DON'T THINK YOU'RE READY TO GO AGAINST ME.
I HAD MY PRACTICE WITH NUMBER 21—YOU KNOW, THE LATEST ADDITION TO CROSSED-OUT ENTRIES ON THE LIST.

DANIEL X

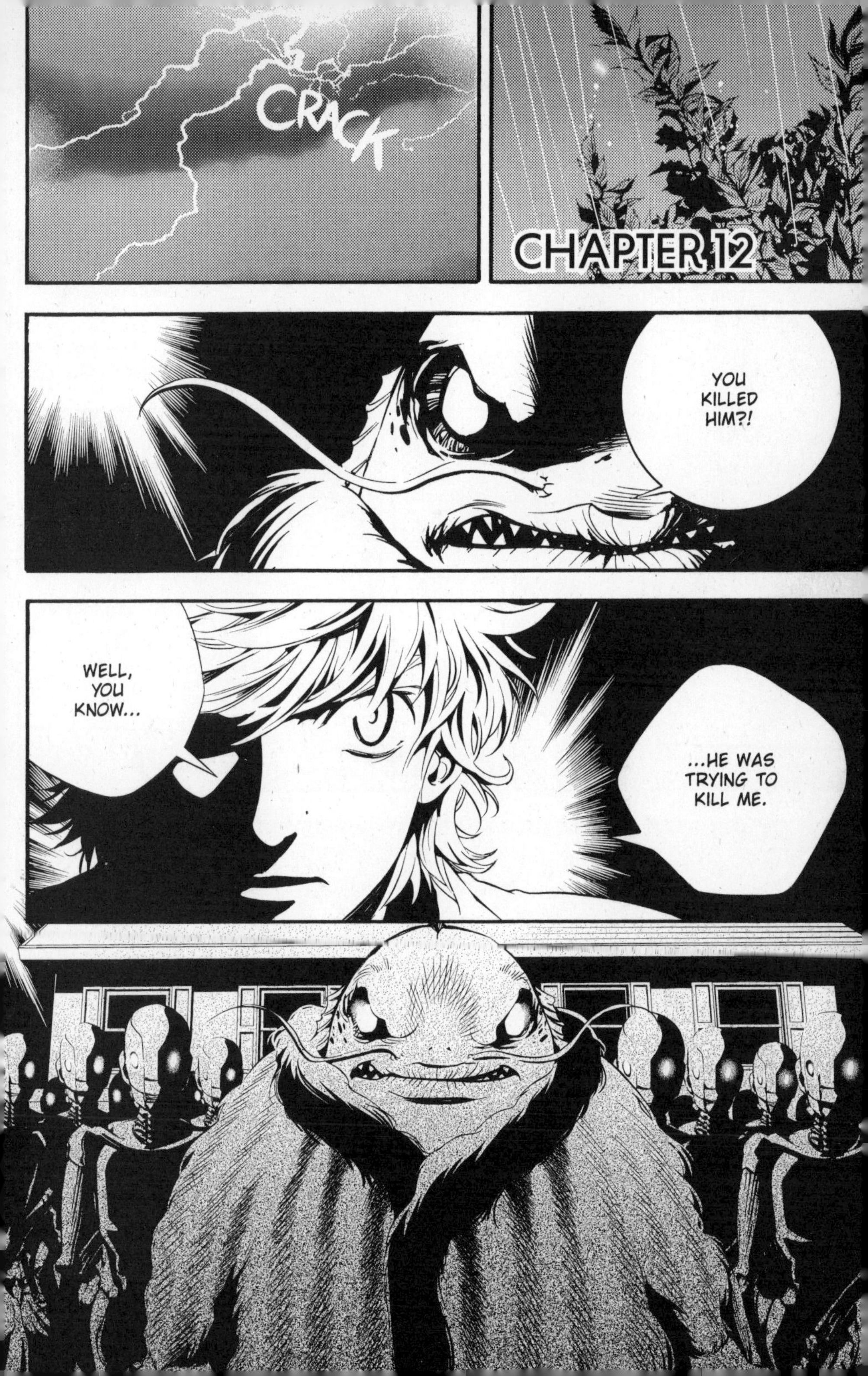
CRACK
CHAPTER 12
YOU KILLED HIM?!
WELL, YOU KNOW...
...HE WAS TRYING TO KILL ME.

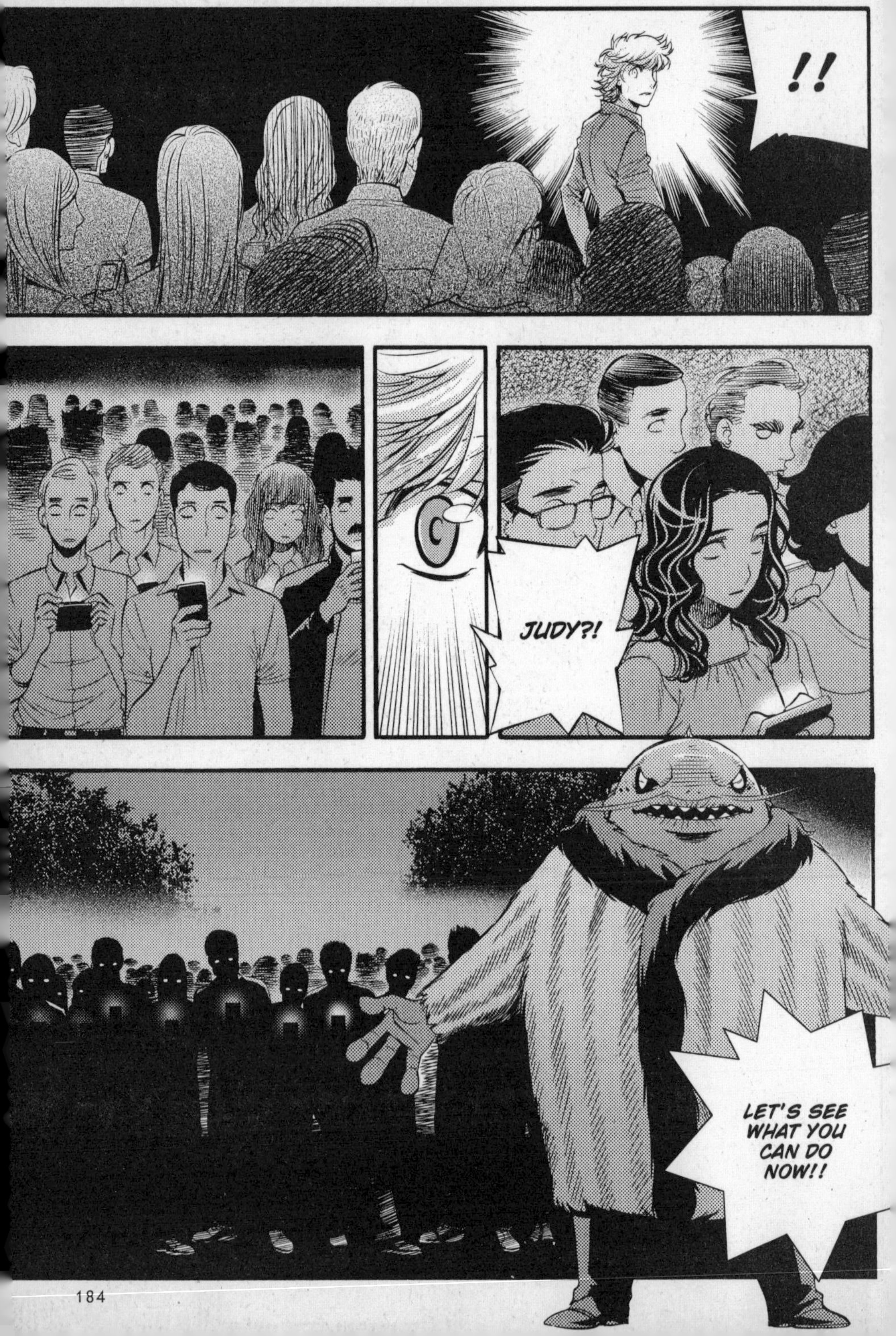
!!
JUDY?!
LET'S SEE WHAT YOU CAN DO NOW!!

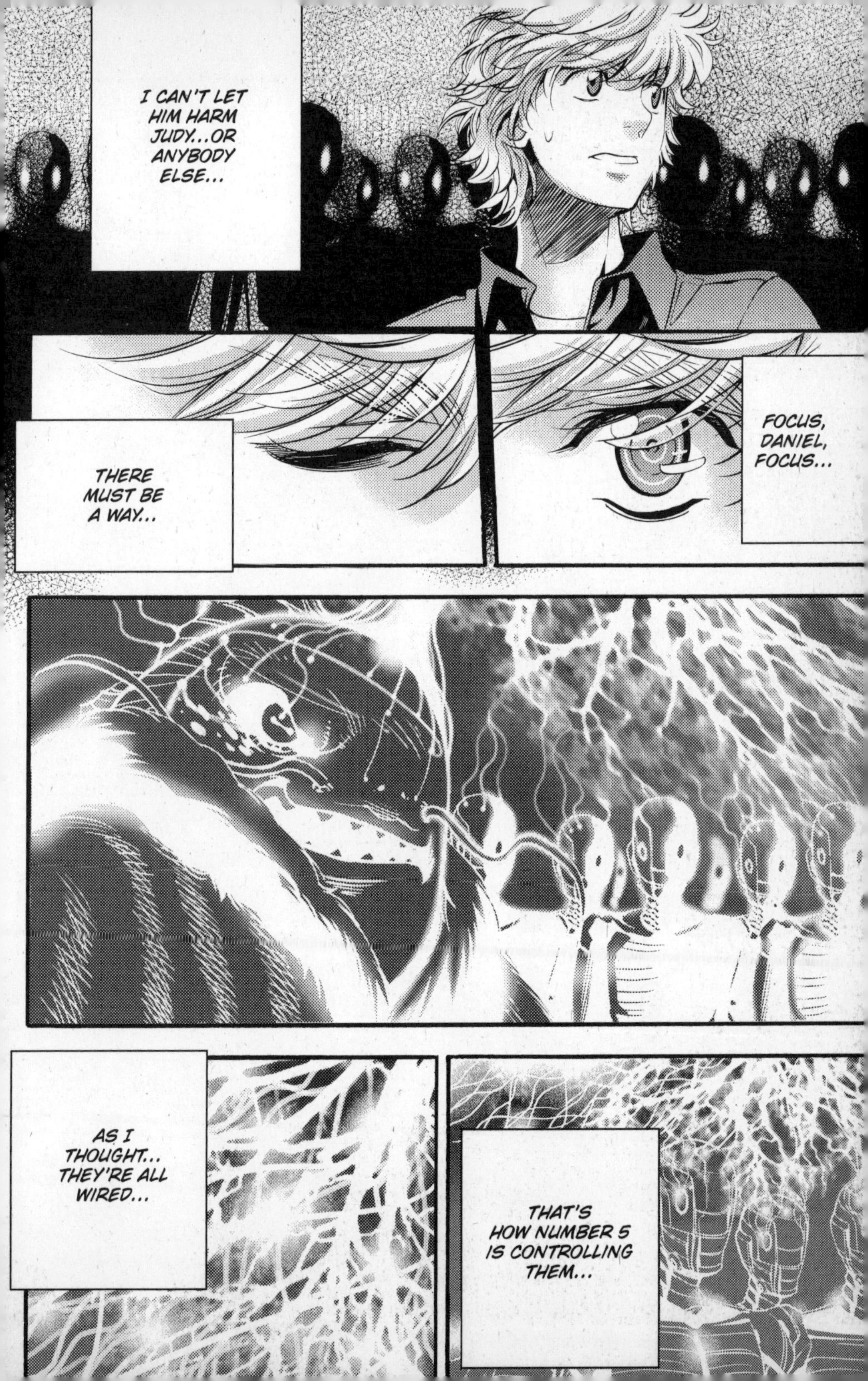
I CAN'T LET HIM HARM JUDY...OR ANYBODY ELSE...
THERE MUST BE A WAY...
FOCUS, DANIEL, FOCUS...
AS I THOUGHT... THEY'RE ALL WIRED...
THAT'S HOW NUMBER 5 IS CONTROLLING THEM...

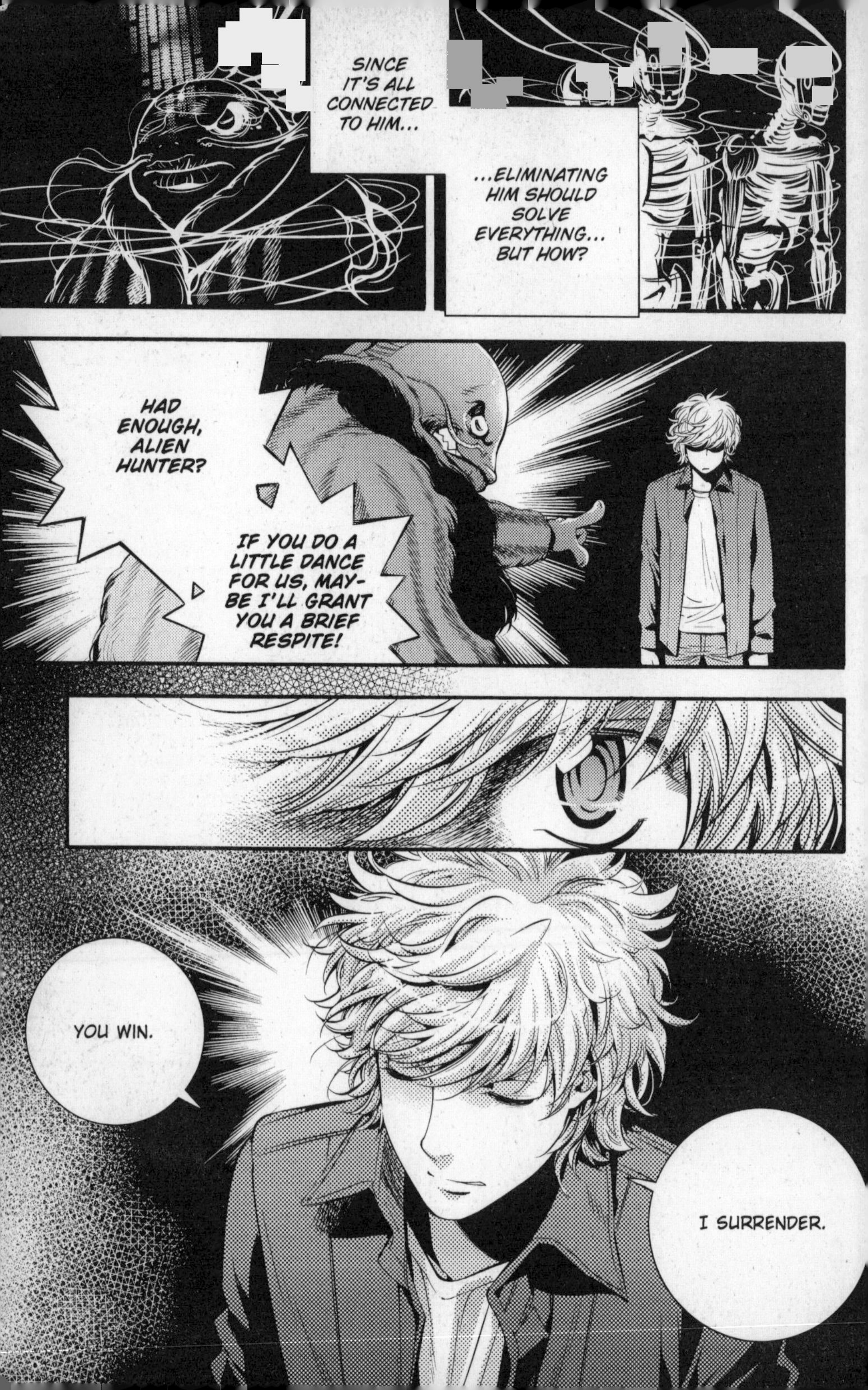
SINCE IT'S ALL CONNECTED TO HIM...
...ELIMINATING HIM SHOULD SOLVE EVERYTHING... BUT HOW?
HAD ENOUGH, ALIEN HUNTER?
IF YOU DO A LITTLE DANCE FOR US, MAY-BE I'LL GRANT YOU A BRIEF RESPITE!
YOU WIN.
I SURRENDER.

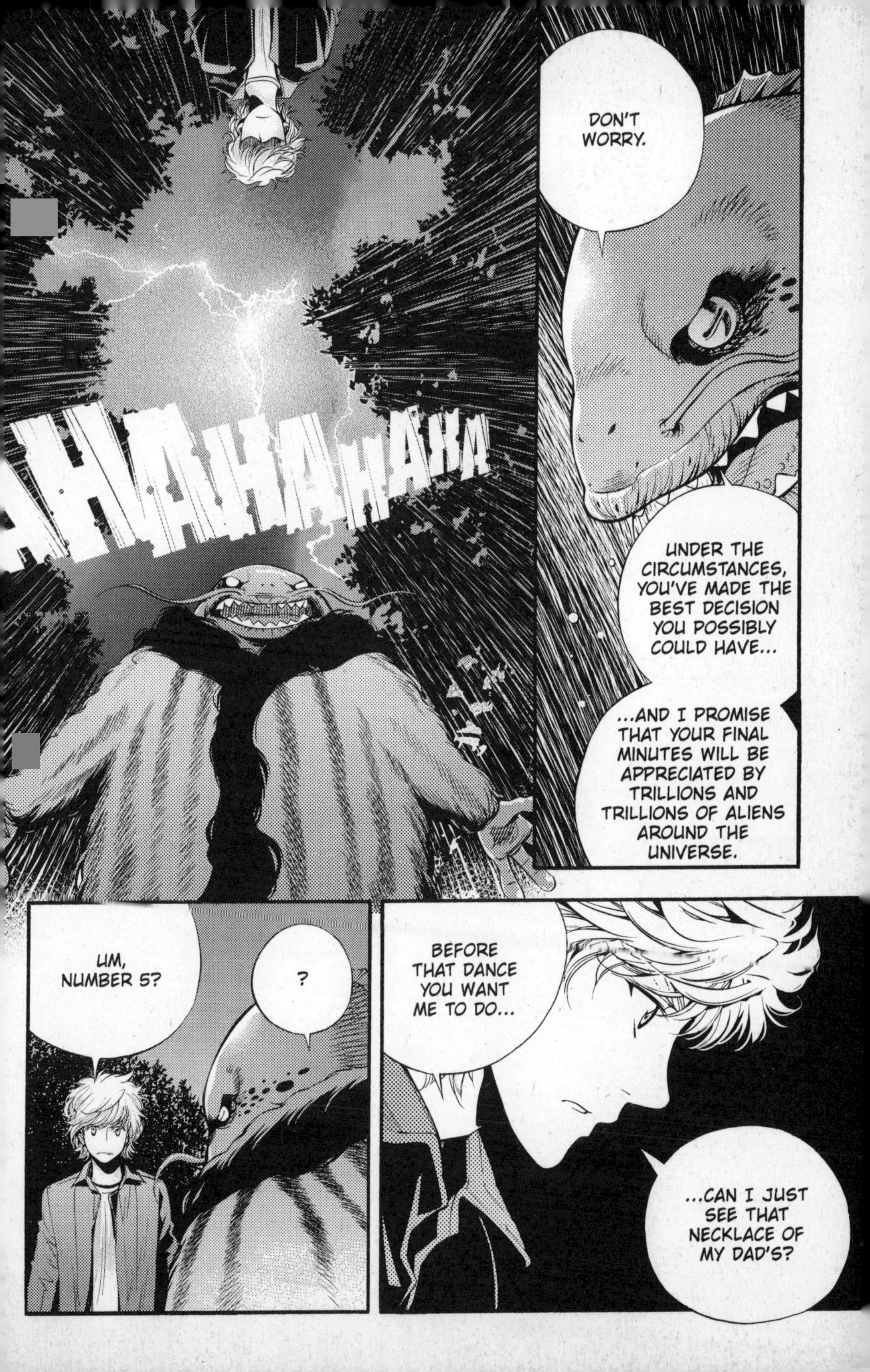
HAHAHAHAHA
DON'T WORRY.
UNDER THE CIRCUMSTANCES, YOU'VE MADE THE BEST DECISION YOU POSSIBLY COULD HAVE...
...AND I PROMISE THAT YOUR FINAL MINUTES WILL BE APPRECIATED BY TRILLIONS AND TRILLIONS OF ALIENS AROUND THE UNIVERSE.
UM, NUMBER 5?
?
BEFORE THAT DANCE YOU WANT ME TO DO...
...CAN I JUST SEE THAT NECKLACE OF MY DAD'S?

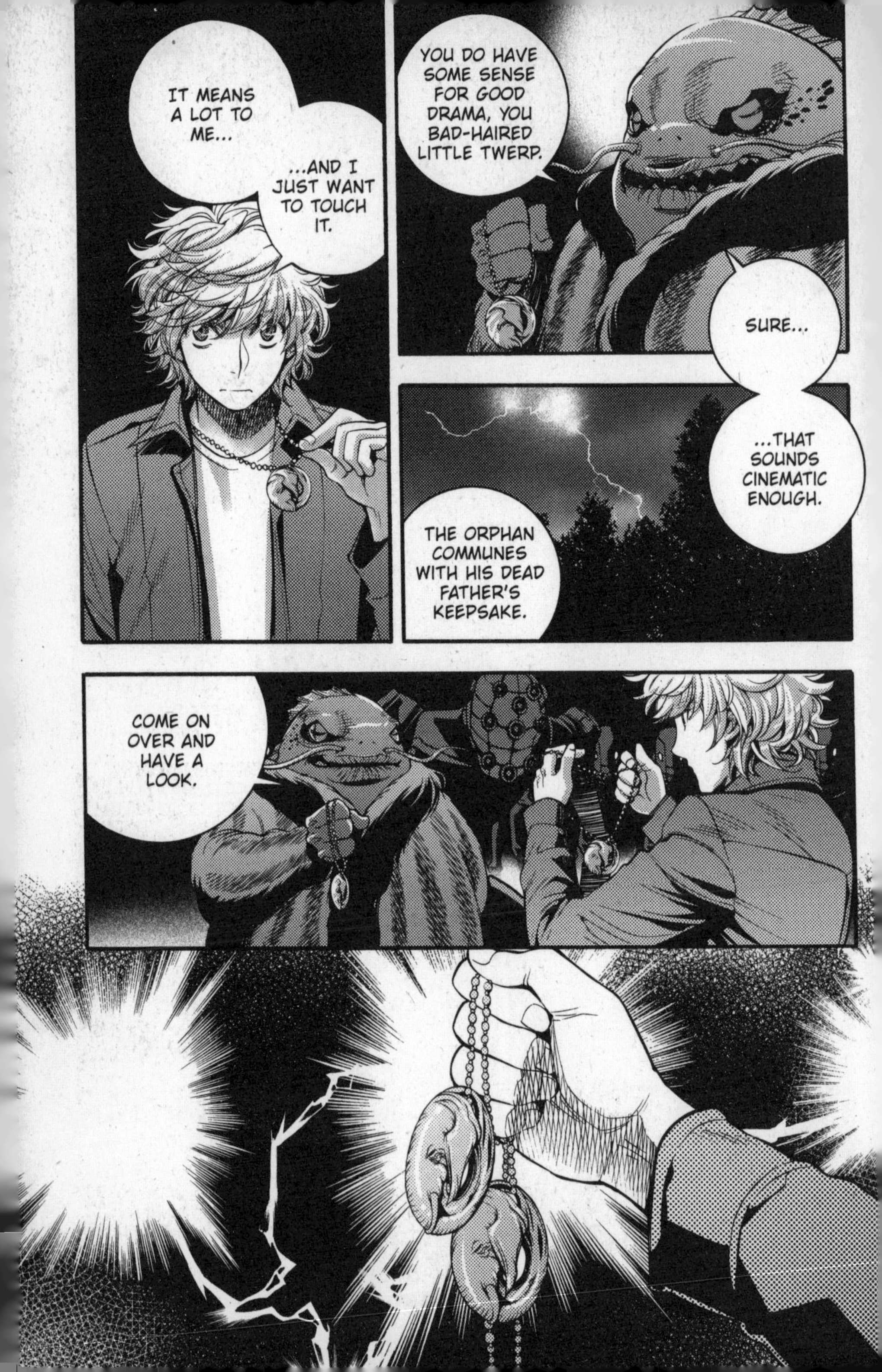
IT MEANS A LOT TO ME...
...AND I JUST WANT TO TOUCH IT.
YOU DO HAVE SOME SENSE FOR GOOD DRAMA, YOU BAD-HAIRED LITTLE TWERP.
SURE...
THE ORPHAN COMMUNES WITH HIS DEAD FATHER'S KEEPSAKE.
...THAT SOUNDS CINEMATIC ENOUGH.
COME ON OVER AND HAVE A LOOK.

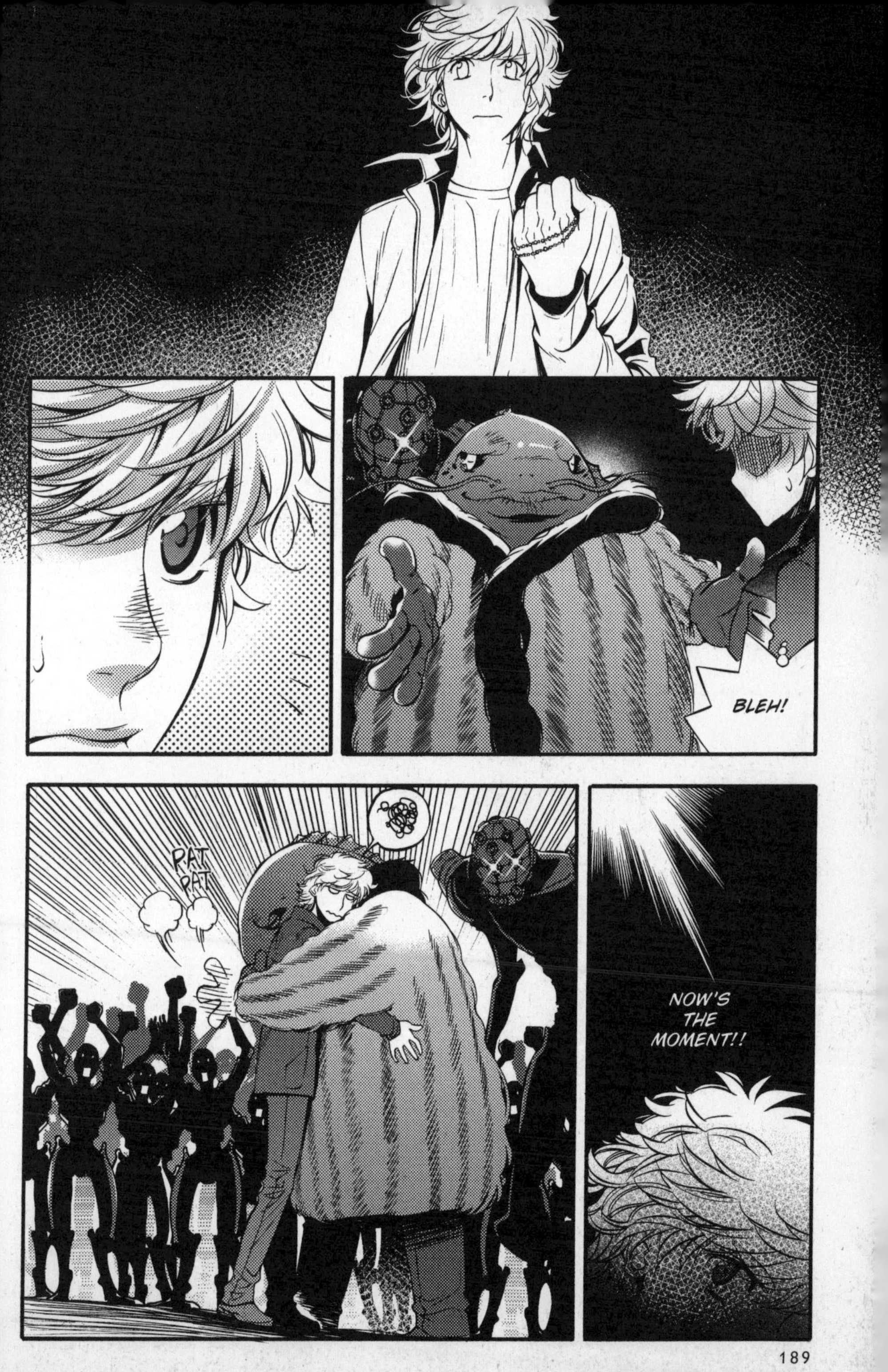
BLEH!
PAT PAT
NOW'S THE MOMENT!!

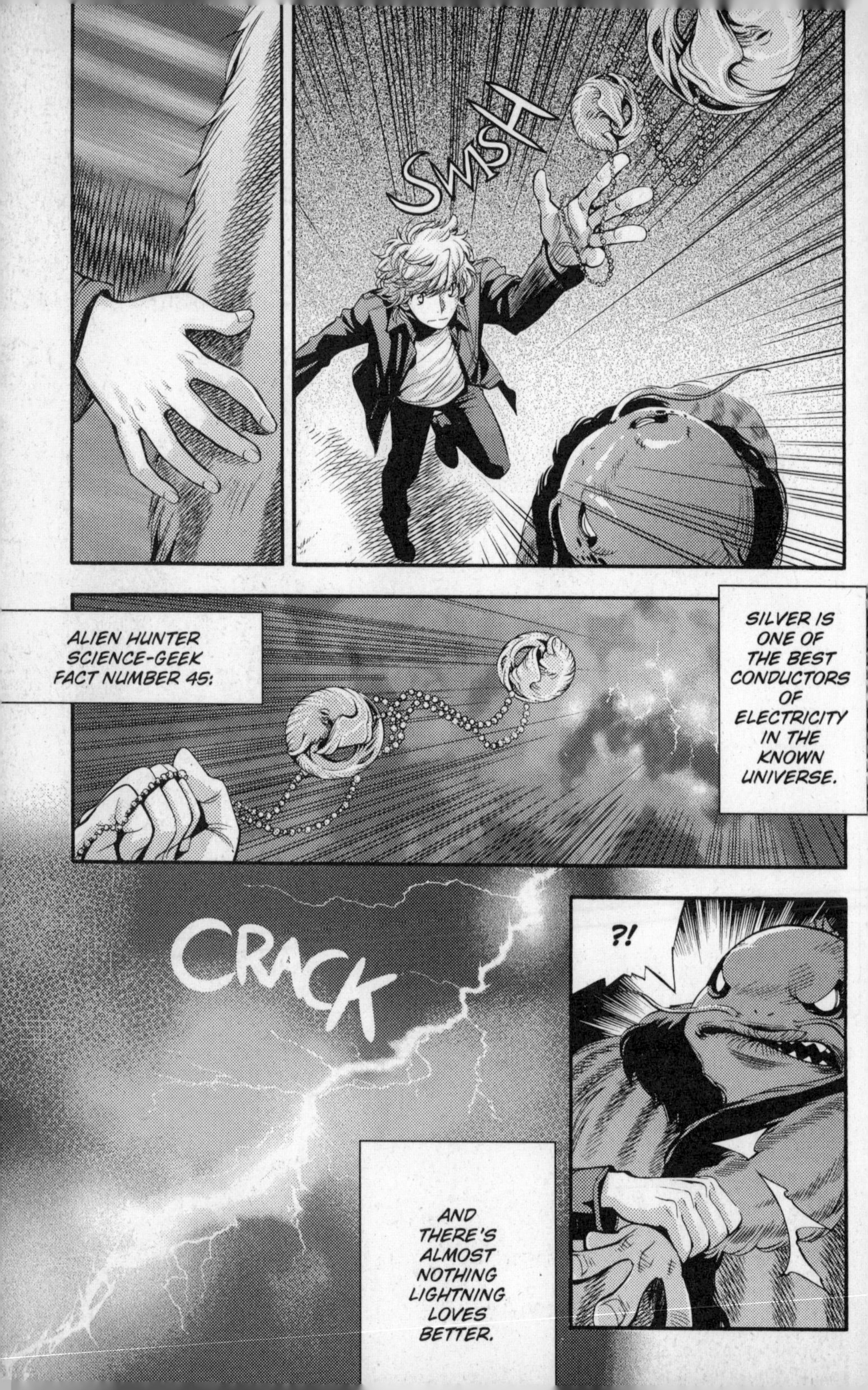
SWISH
ALIEN HUNTER SCIENCE-GEEK FACT NUMBER 45:
SILVER IS ONE OF THE BEST CONDUCTORS OF ELECTRICITY IN THE KNOWN UNIVERSE.
CRACK
AND THERE'S ALMOST NOTHING LIGHTNING LOVES BETTER.
?!

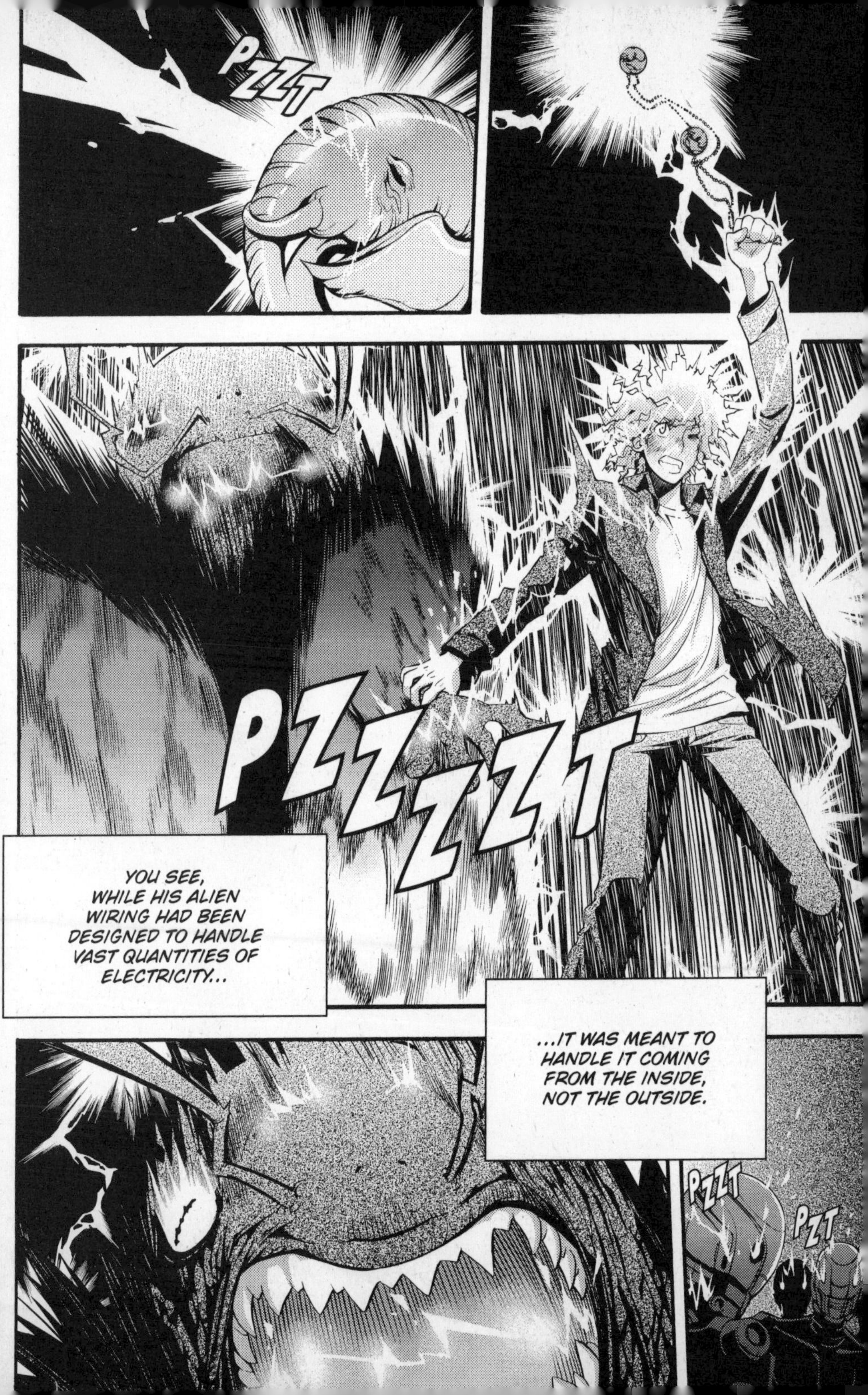
PZZT
PZZZZZT
YOU SEE, WHILE HIS ALIEN WIRING HAD BEEN DESIGNED TO HANDLE VAST QUANTITIES OF ELECTRICITY...
...IT WAS MEANT TO HANDLE IT COMING FROM THE INSIDE, NOT THE OUTSIDE.
PZZT
PZT

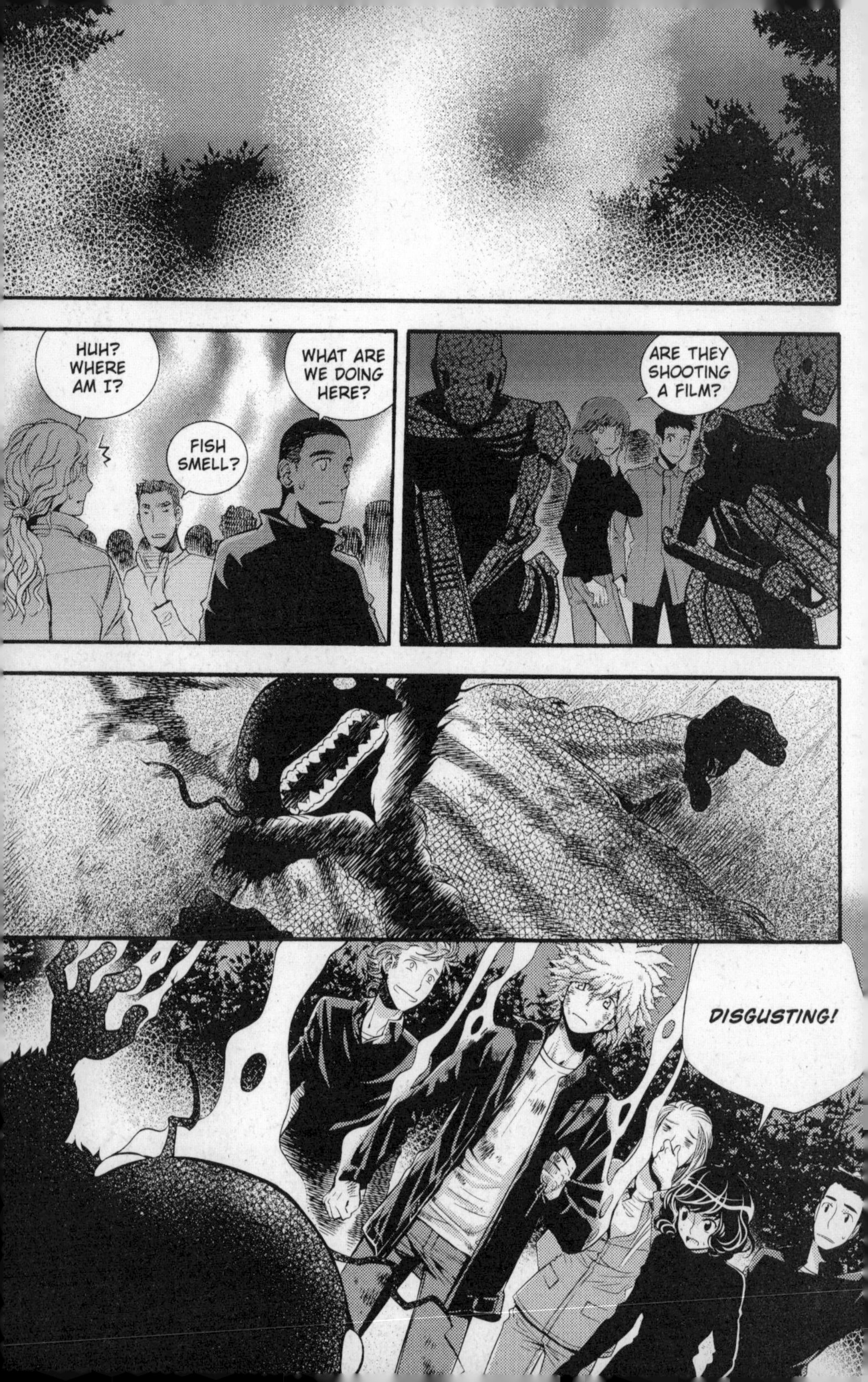
HUH? WHERE AM I?
FISH SMELL?
WHAT ARE WE DOING HERE?
ARE THEY SHOOTING A FILM?
DISGUSTING!

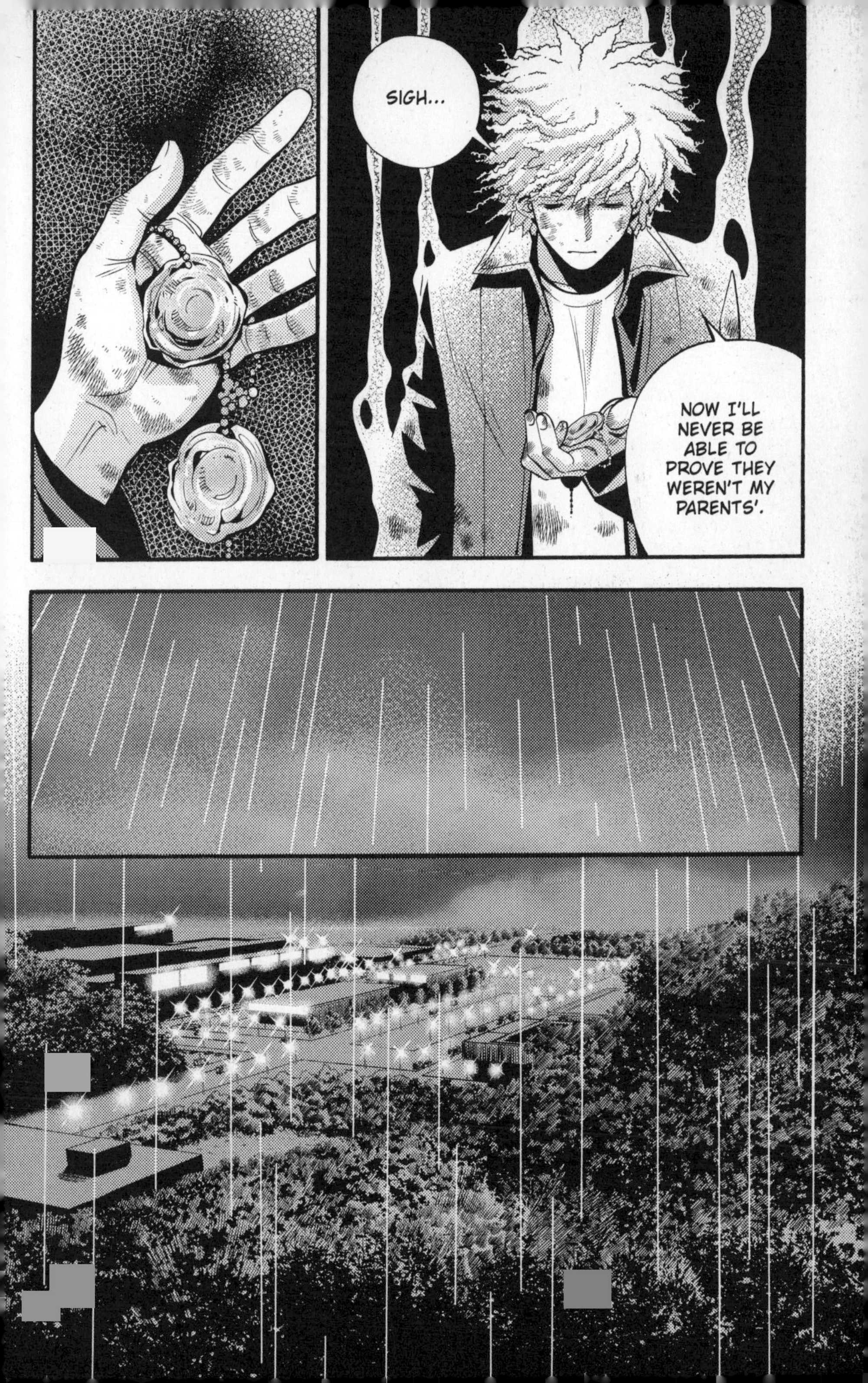
SIGH...
NOW I'LL NEVER BE ABLE TO PROVE THEY WEREN'T MY PARENTS'.

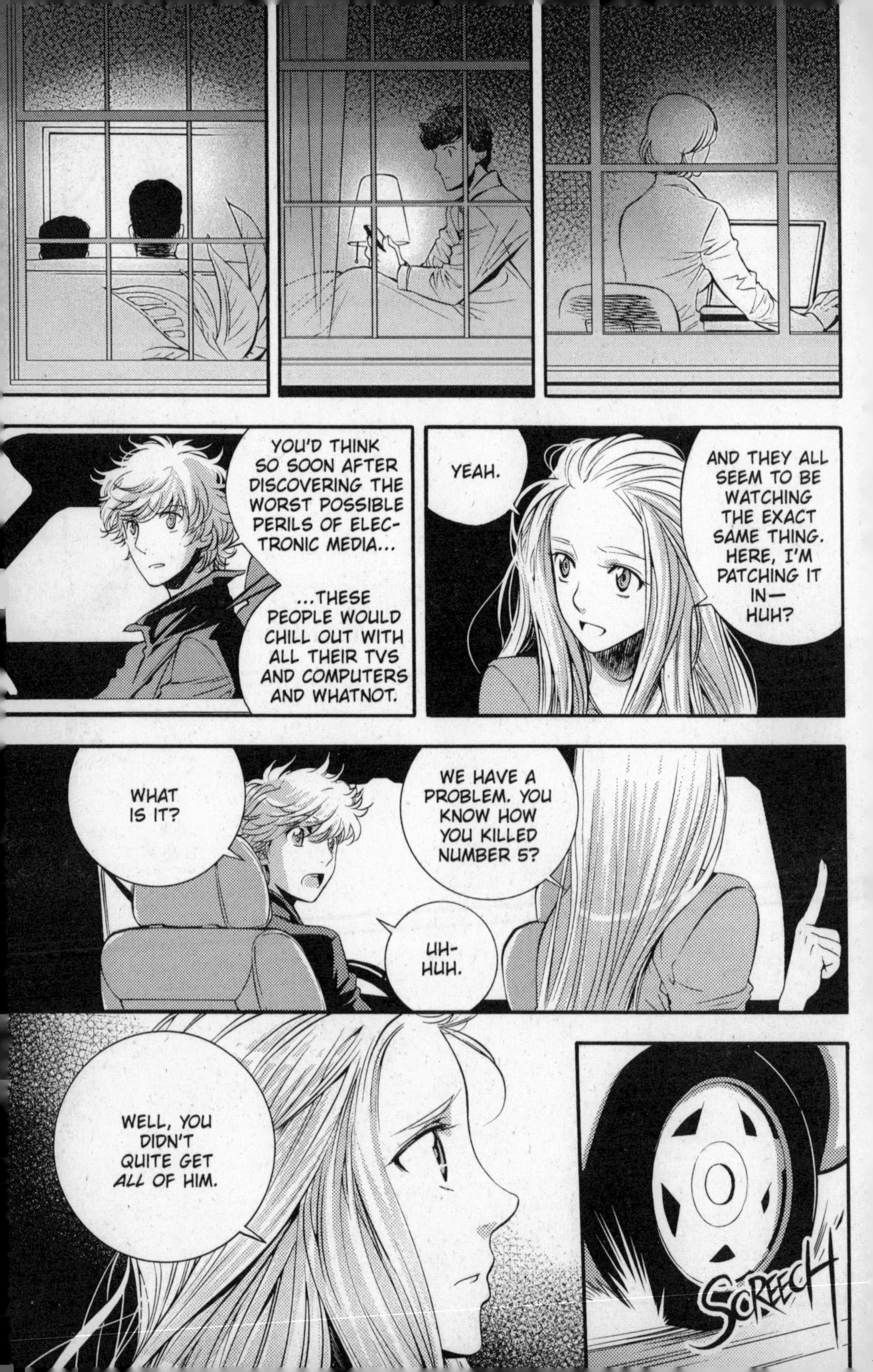
YOU'D THINK SO SOON AFTER DISCOVERING THE WORST POSSIBLE PERILS OF ELECTRONIC MEDIA...
...THESE PEOPLE WOULD CHILL OUT WITH ALL THEIR TVS AND COMPUTERS AND WHATNOT.
YEAH.
AND THEY ALL SEEM TO BE WATCHING THE EXACT SAME THING. HERE, I'M PATCHING IT IN—
HUH?
WHAT IS IT?
WE HAVE A PROBLEM. YOU KNOW HOW YOU KILLED NUMBER 5?
UH-HUH.
WELL, YOU DIDN'T QUITE GET ALL OF HIM.
SCREECH

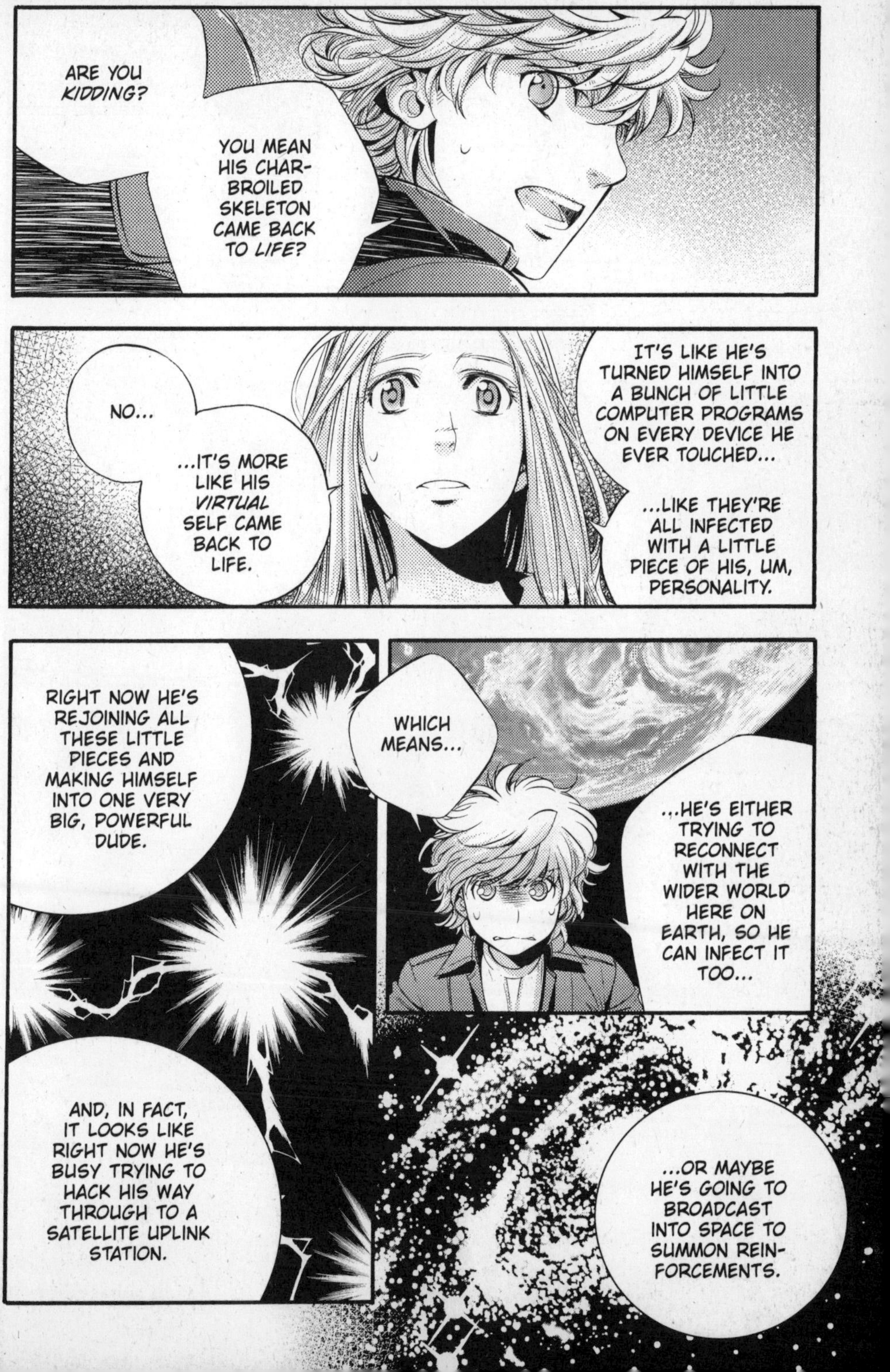
ARE YOU *KIDDING?*
YOU MEAN HIS CHAR-BROILED SKELETON CAME BACK TO *LIFE?*
NO...
...IT'S MORE LIKE HIS *VIRTUAL* SELF CAME BACK TO LIFE.
IT'S LIKE HE'S TURNED HIMSELF INTO A BUNCH OF LITTLE COMPUTER PROGRAMS ON EVERY DEVICE HE EVER TOUCHED...
...LIKE THEY'RE ALL INFECTED WITH A LITTLE PIECE OF HIS, UM, PERSONALITY.
RIGHT NOW HE'S REJOINING ALL THESE LITTLE PIECES AND MAKING HIMSELF INTO ONE VERY BIG, POWERFUL DUDE.
AND, IN FACT, IT LOOKS LIKE RIGHT NOW HE'S BUSY TRYING TO HACK HIS WAY THROUGH TO A SATELLITE UPLINK STATION.
WHICH MEANS...
...HE'S EITHER TRYING TO RECONNECT WITH THE WIDER WORLD HERE ON EARTH, SO HE CAN INFECT IT TOO...
...OR MAYBE HE'S GOING TO BROADCAST INTO SPACE TO SUMMON REIN-FORCEMENTS.

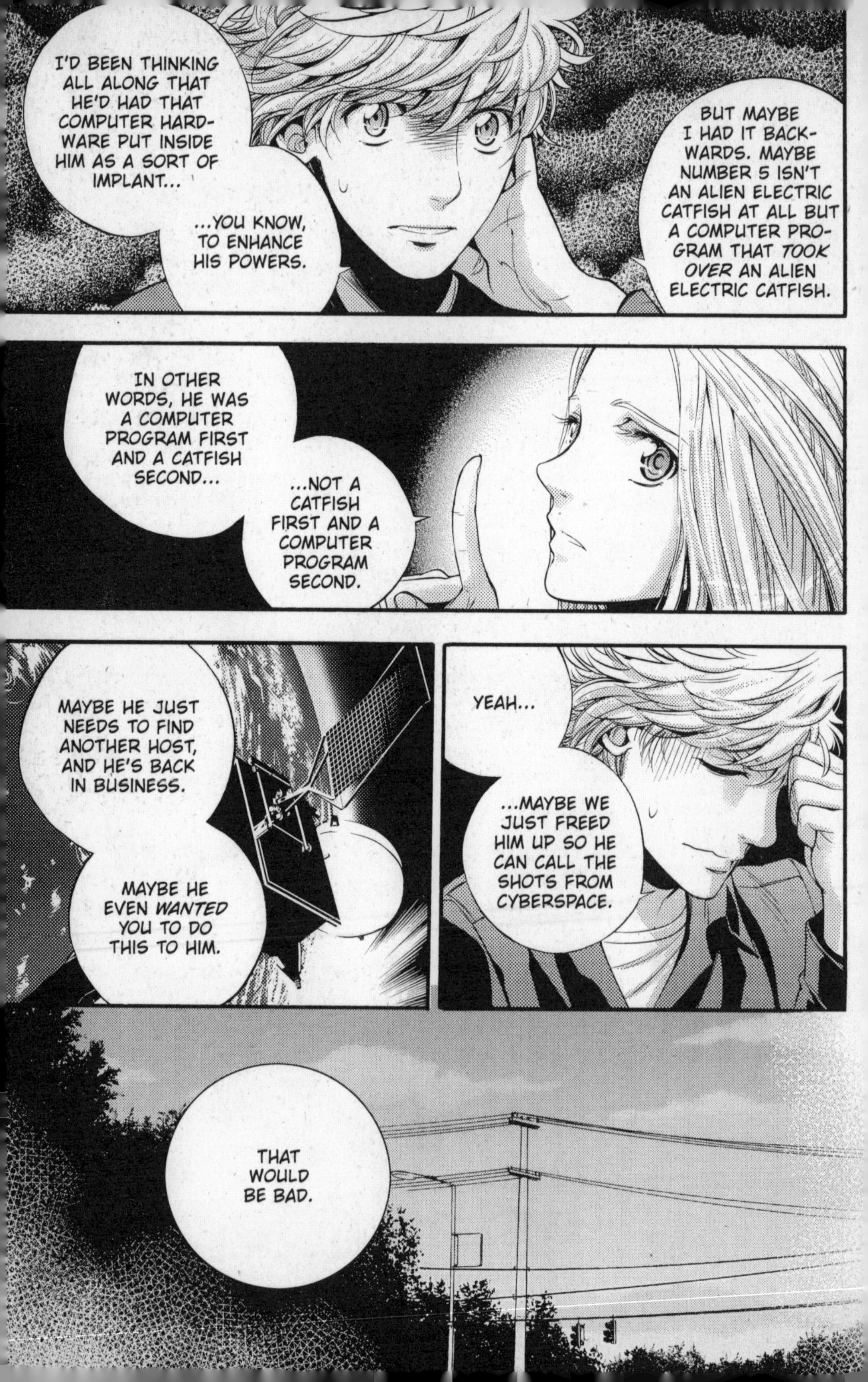
I'D BEEN THINKING ALL ALONG THAT HE'D HAD THAT COMPUTER HARDWARE PUT INSIDE HIM AS A SORT OF IMPLANT...
...YOU KNOW, TO ENHANCE HIS POWERS.
BUT MAYBE I HAD IT BACKWARDS. MAYBE NUMBER 5 ISN'T AN ALIEN ELECTRIC CATFISH AT ALL BUT A COMPUTER PROGRAM THAT *TOOK OVER* AN ALIEN ELECTRIC CATFISH.
IN OTHER WORDS, HE WAS A COMPUTER PROGRAM FIRST AND A CATFISH SECOND...
...NOT A CATFISH FIRST AND A COMPUTER PROGRAM SECOND.
MAYBE HE JUST NEEDS TO FIND ANOTHER HOST, AND HE'S BACK IN BUSINESS.
MAYBE HE EVEN *WANTED* YOU TO DO THIS TO HIM.
YEAH...
...MAYBE WE JUST FREED HIM UP SO HE CAN CALL THE SHOTS FROM CYBERSPACE.
THAT WOULD BE BAD.

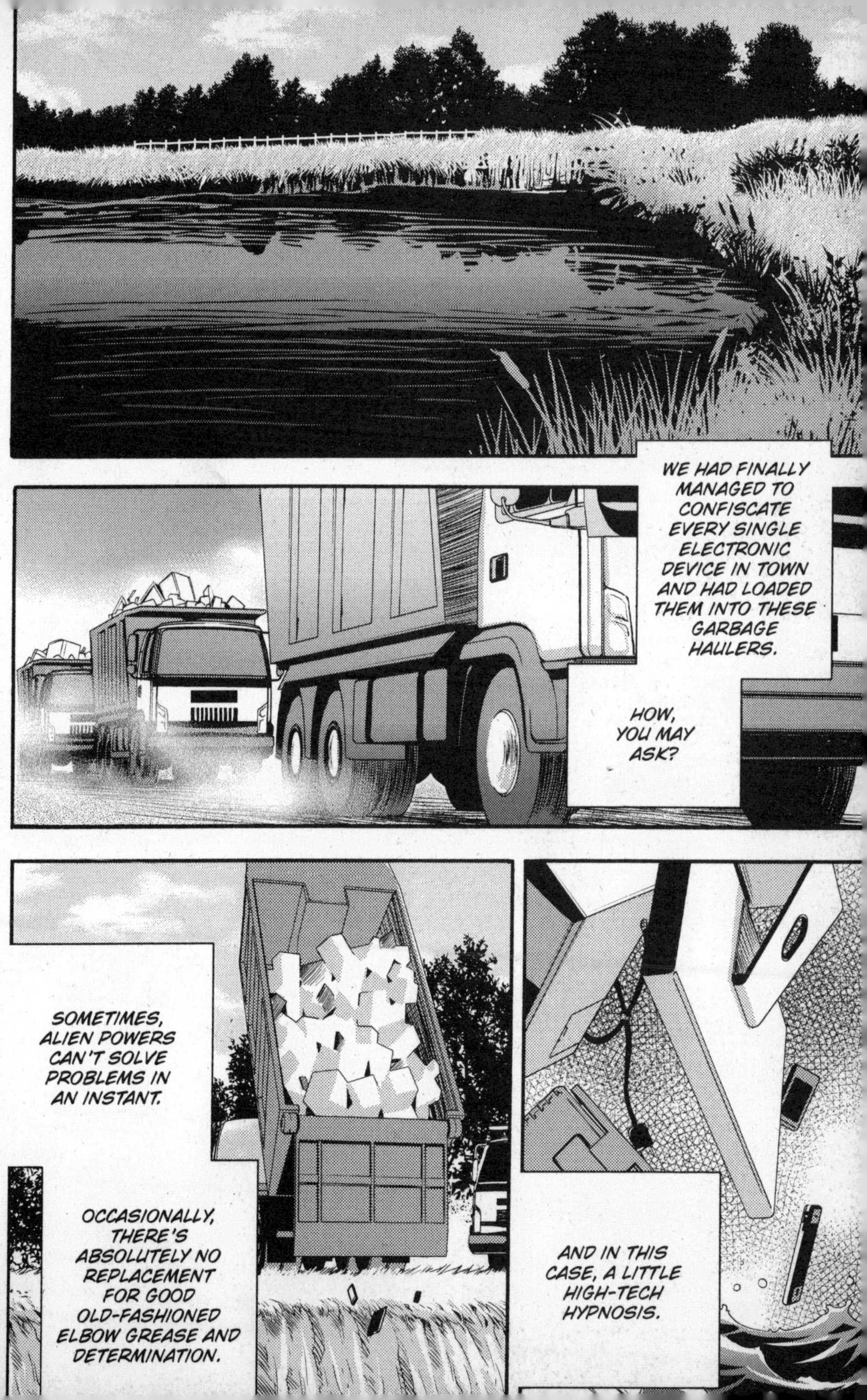
WE HAD FINALLY MANAGED TO CONFISCATE EVERY SINGLE ELECTRONIC DEVICE IN TOWN AND HAD LOADED THEM INTO THESE GARBAGE HAULERS.
HOW, YOU MAY ASK?
SOMETIMES, ALIEN POWERS CAN'T SOLVE PROBLEMS IN AN INSTANT.
OCCASIONALLY, THERE'S ABSOLUTELY NO REPLACEMENT FOR GOOD OLD-FASHIONED ELBOW GREASE AND DETERMINATION.
AND IN THIS CASE, A LITTLE HIGH-TECH HYPNOSIS.

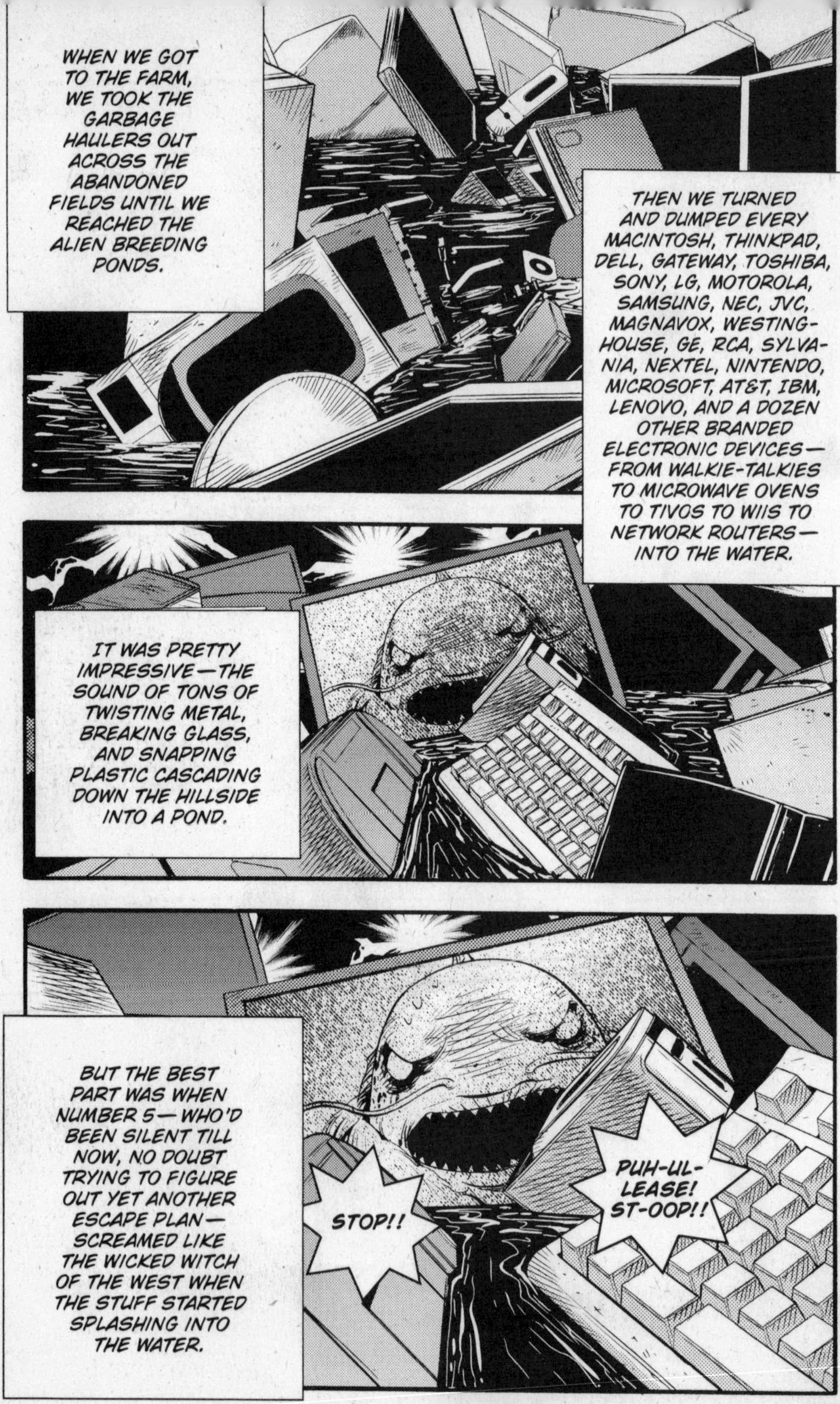
WHEN WE GOT TO THE FARM, WE TOOK THE GARBAGE HAULERS OUT ACROSS THE ABANDONED FIELDS UNTIL WE REACHED THE ALIEN BREEDING PONDS.
THEN WE TURNED AND DUMPED EVERY MACINTOSH, THINKPAD, DELL, GATEWAY, TOSHIBA, SONY, LG, MOTOROLA, SAMSUNG, NEC, JVC, MAGNAVOX, WESTING-HOUSE, GE, RCA, SYLVANIA, NEXTEL, NINTENDO, MICROSOFT, AT&T, IBM, LENOVO, AND A DOZEN OTHER BRANDED ELECTRONIC DEVICES—FROM WALKIE-TALKIES TO MICROWAVE OVENS TO TIVOS TO WIIS TO NETWORK ROUTERS—INTO THE WATER.
IT WAS PRETTY IMPRESSIVE—THE SOUND OF TONS OF TWISTING METAL, BREAKING GLASS, AND SNAPPING PLASTIC CASCADING DOWN THE HILLSIDE INTO A POND.
BUT THE BEST PART WAS WHEN NUMBER 5—WHO'D BEEN SILENT TILL NOW, NO DOUBT TRYING TO FIGURE OUT YET ANOTHER ESCAPE PLAN—SCREAMED LIKE THE WICKED WITCH OF THE WEST WHEN THE STUFF STARTED SPLASHING INTO THE WATER.
STOP!!
PUH-UL-LEASE! ST-OOP!!

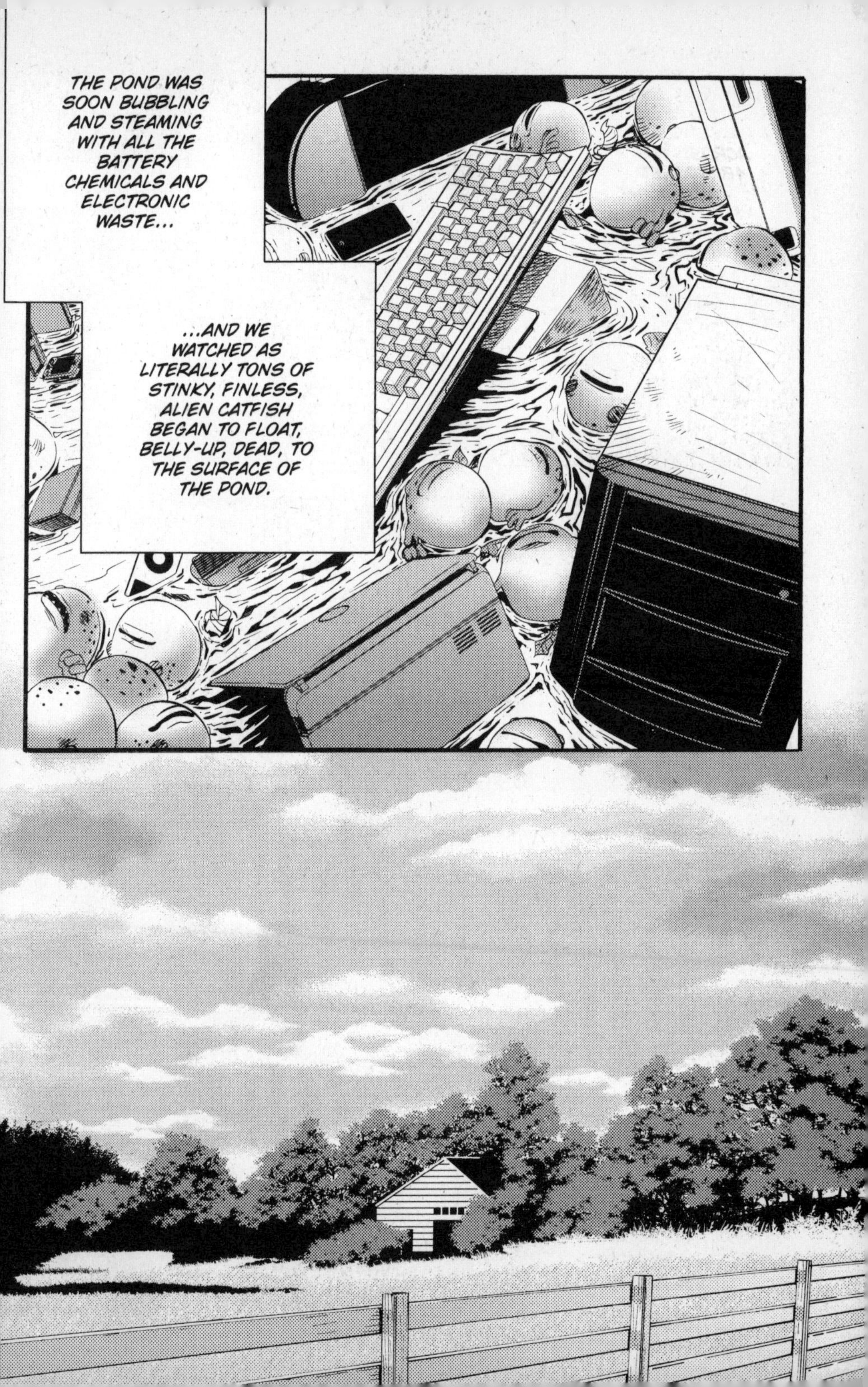
THE POND WAS SOON BUBBLING AND STEAMING WITH ALL THE BATTERY CHEMICALS AND ELECTRONIC WASTE...
...AND WE WATCHED AS LITERALLY TONS OF STINKY, FINLESS, ALIEN CATFISH BEGAN TO FLOAT, BELLY-UP, DEAD, TO THE SURFACE OF THE POND.

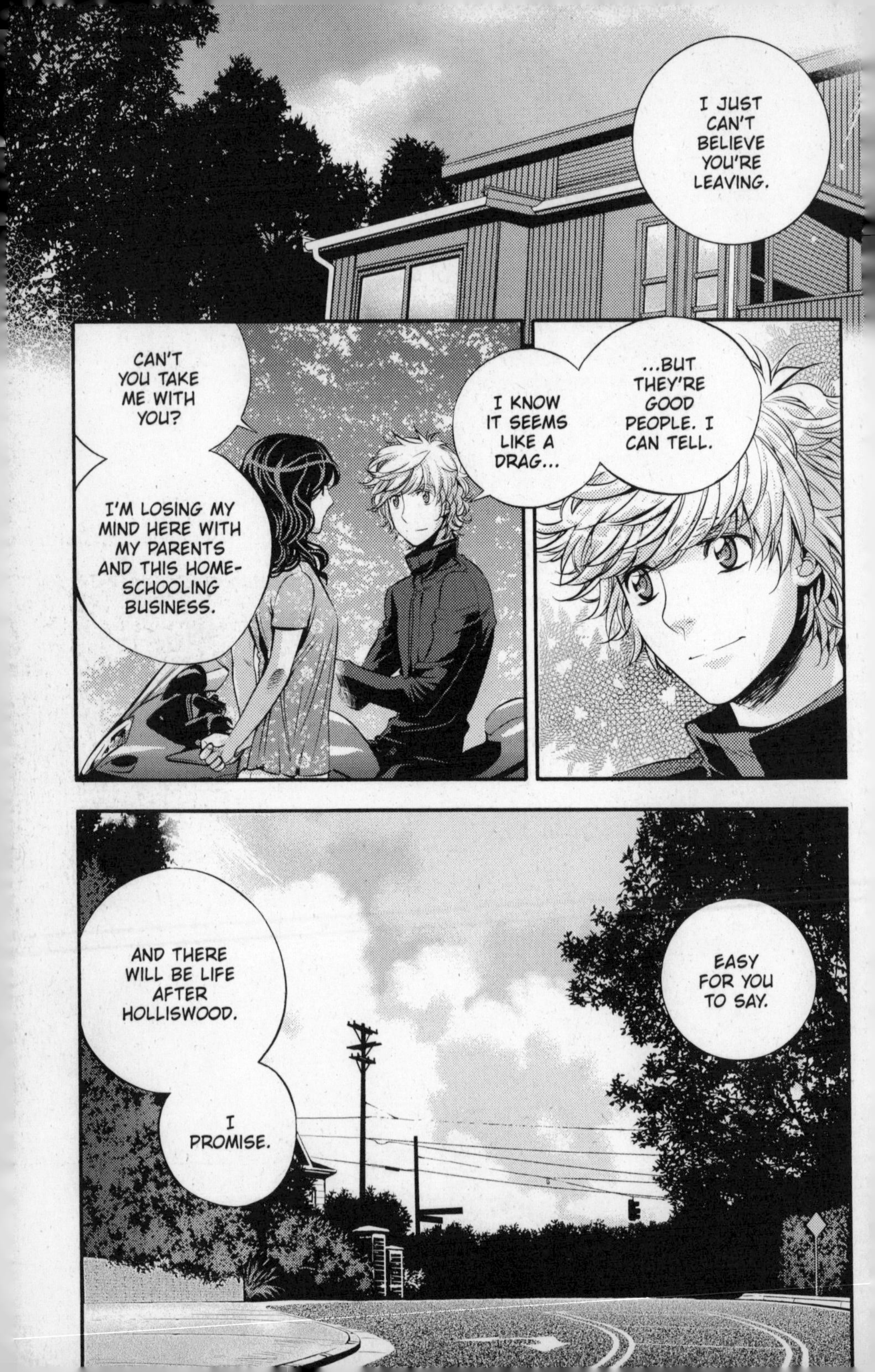
I JUST CAN'T BELIEVE YOU'RE LEAVING.
CAN'T YOU TAKE ME WITH YOU?
I'M LOSING MY MIND HERE WITH MY PARENTS AND THIS HOME-SCHOOLING BUSINESS.
I KNOW IT SEEMS LIKE A DRAG...
...BUT THEY'RE GOOD PEOPLE. I CAN TELL.
AND THERE WILL BE LIFE AFTER HOLLISWOOD.
I PROMISE.
EASY FOR YOU TO SAY.

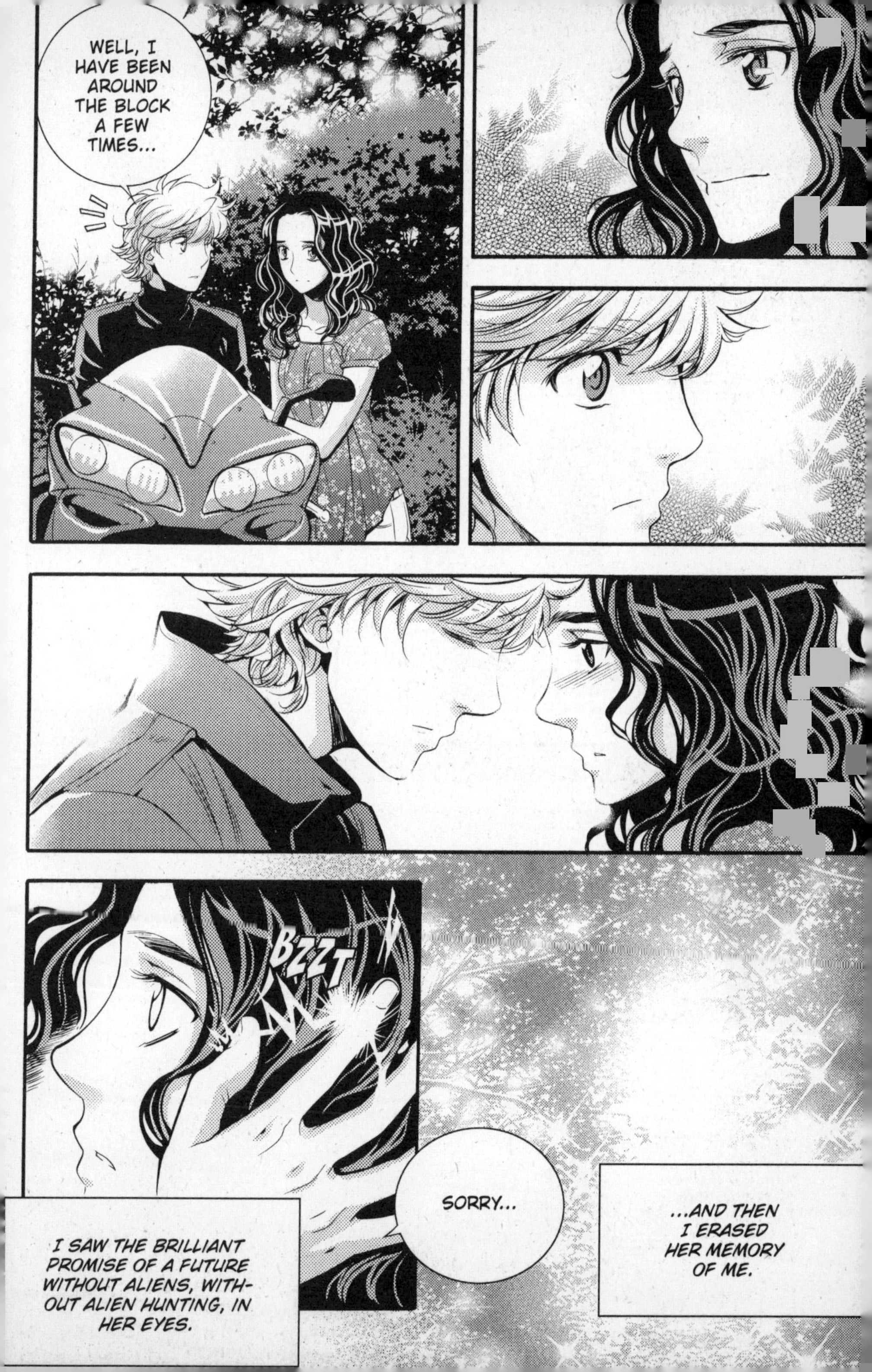
WELL, I HAVE BEEN AROUND THE BLOCK A FEW TIMES...
BZZT
I SAW THE BRILLIANT PROMISE OF A FUTURE WITHOUT ALIENS, WITH-OUT ALIEN HUNTING, IN HER EYES.
SORRY...
...AND THEN I ERASED HER MEMORY OF ME.

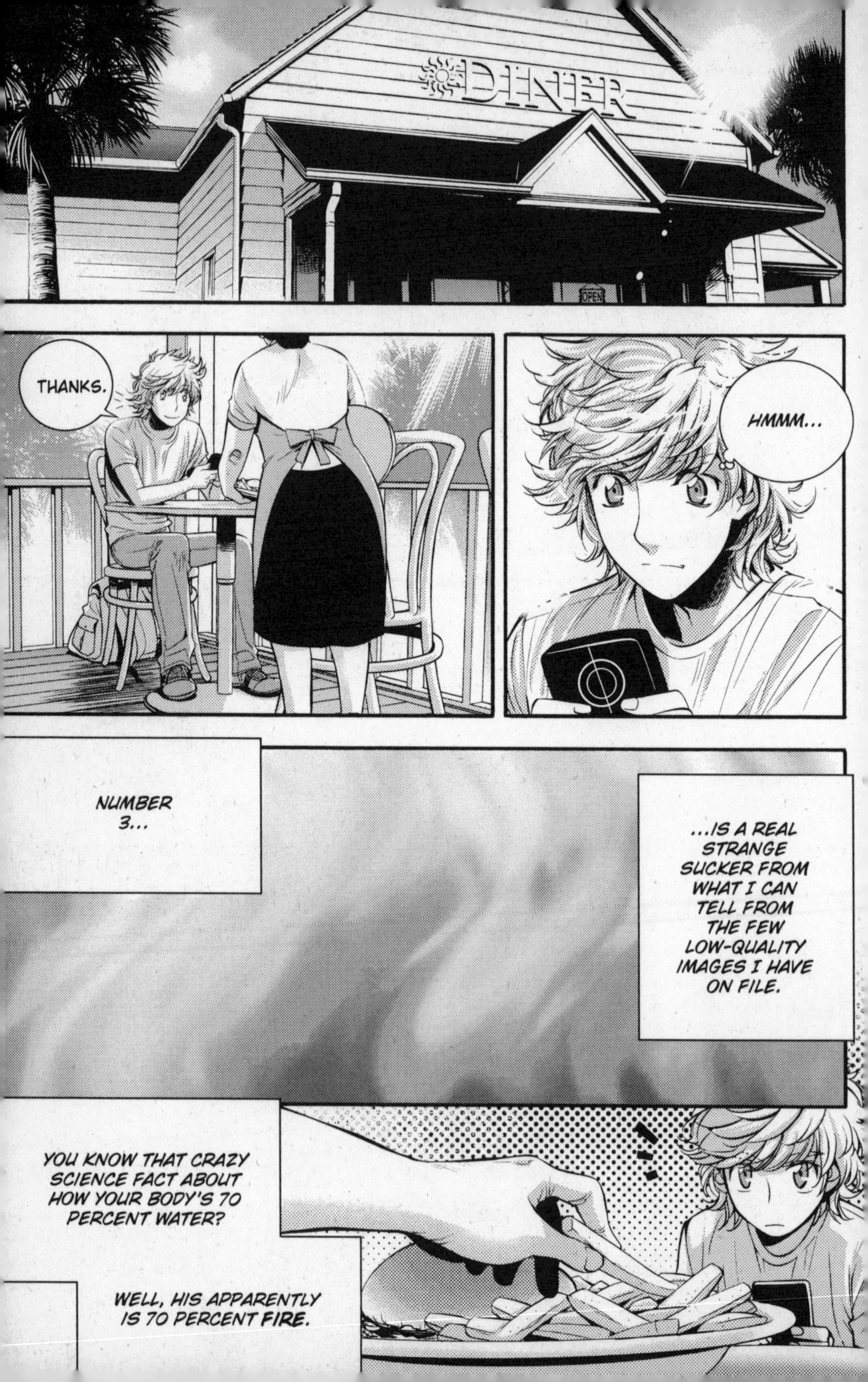
DINER
OPEN
THANKS.
HMMM...
NUMBER 3...
...IS A REAL STRANGE SUCKER FROM WHAT I CAN TELL FROM THE FEW LOW-QUALITY IMAGES I HAVE ON FILE.
YOU KNOW THAT CRAZY SCIENCE FACT ABOUT HOW YOUR BODY'S 70 PERCENT WATER?
WELL, HIS APPARENTLY IS 70 PERCENT FIRE.

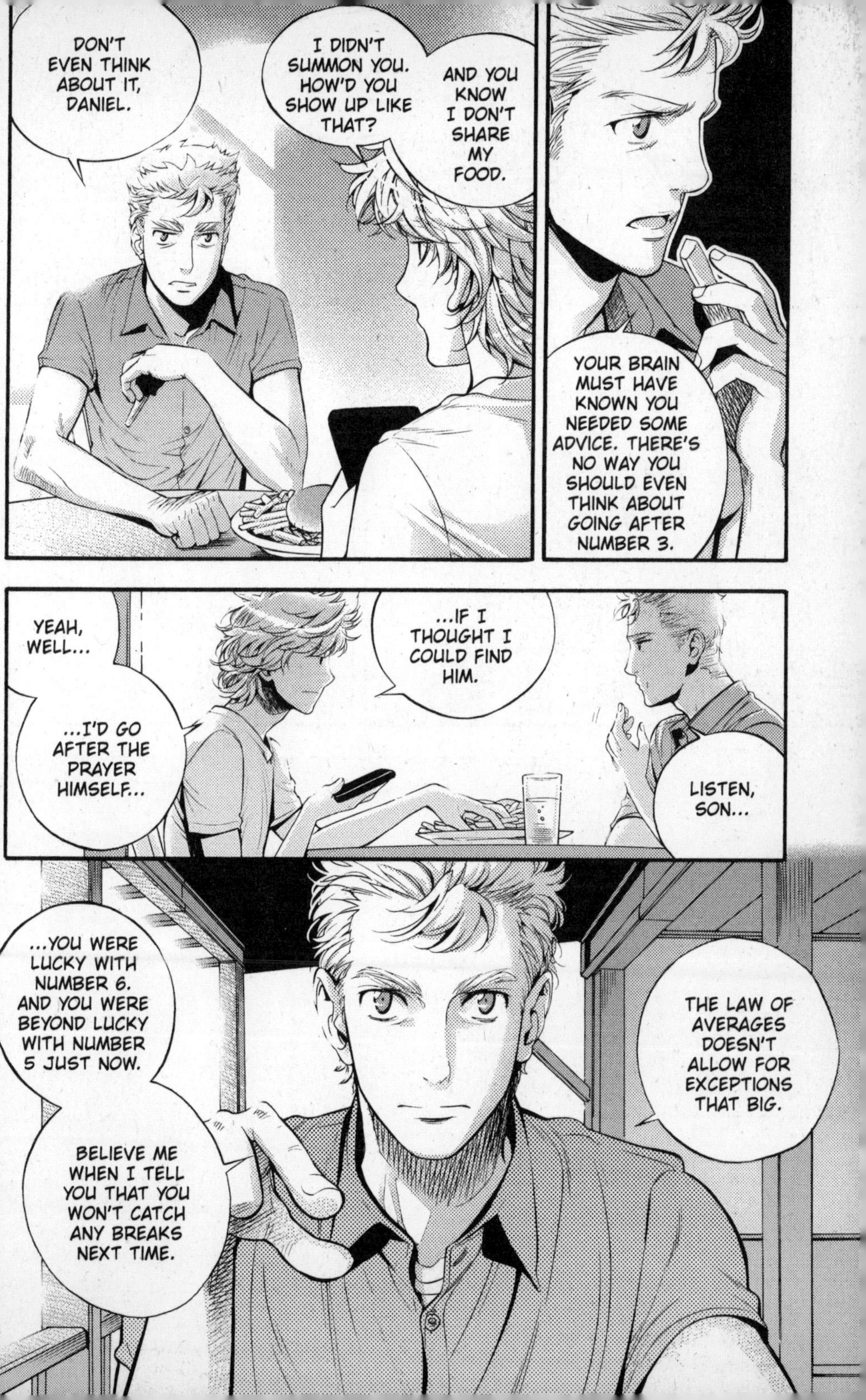
DON'T EVEN THINK ABOUT IT, DANIEL.
I DIDN'T SUMMON YOU. HOW'D YOU SHOW UP LIKE THAT?
AND YOU KNOW I DON'T SHARE MY FOOD.
YOUR BRAIN MUST HAVE KNOWN YOU NEEDED SOME ADVICE. THERE'S NO WAY YOU SHOULD EVEN THINK ABOUT GOING AFTER NUMBER 3.
YEAH, WELL...
...I'D GO AFTER THE PRAYER HIMSELF...
...IF I THOUGHT I COULD FIND HIM.
LISTEN, SON...
...YOU WERE LUCKY WITH NUMBER 6. AND YOU WERE BEYOND LUCKY WITH NUMBER 5 JUST NOW.
BELIEVE ME WHEN I TELL YOU THAT YOU WON'T CATCH ANY BREAKS NEXT TIME.
THE LAW OF AVERAGES DOESN'T ALLOW FOR EXCEPTIONS THAT BIG.

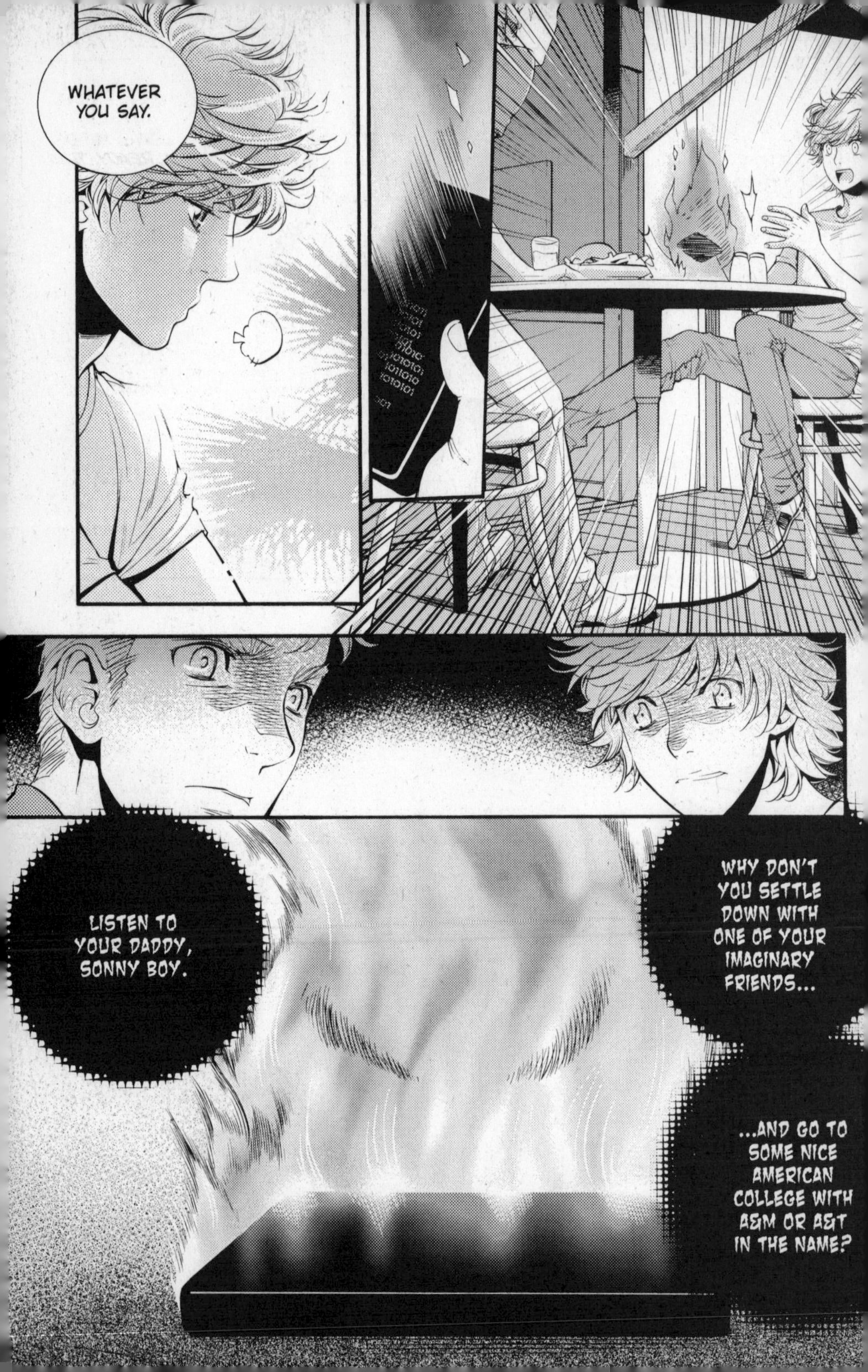
WHATEVER YOU SAY.
LISTEN TO YOUR DADDY, SONNY BOY.
WHY DON'T YOU SETTLE DOWN WITH ONE OF YOUR IMAGINARY FRIENDS...
...AND GO TO SOME NICE AMERICAN COLLEGE WITH A&M OR A&T IN THE NAME?

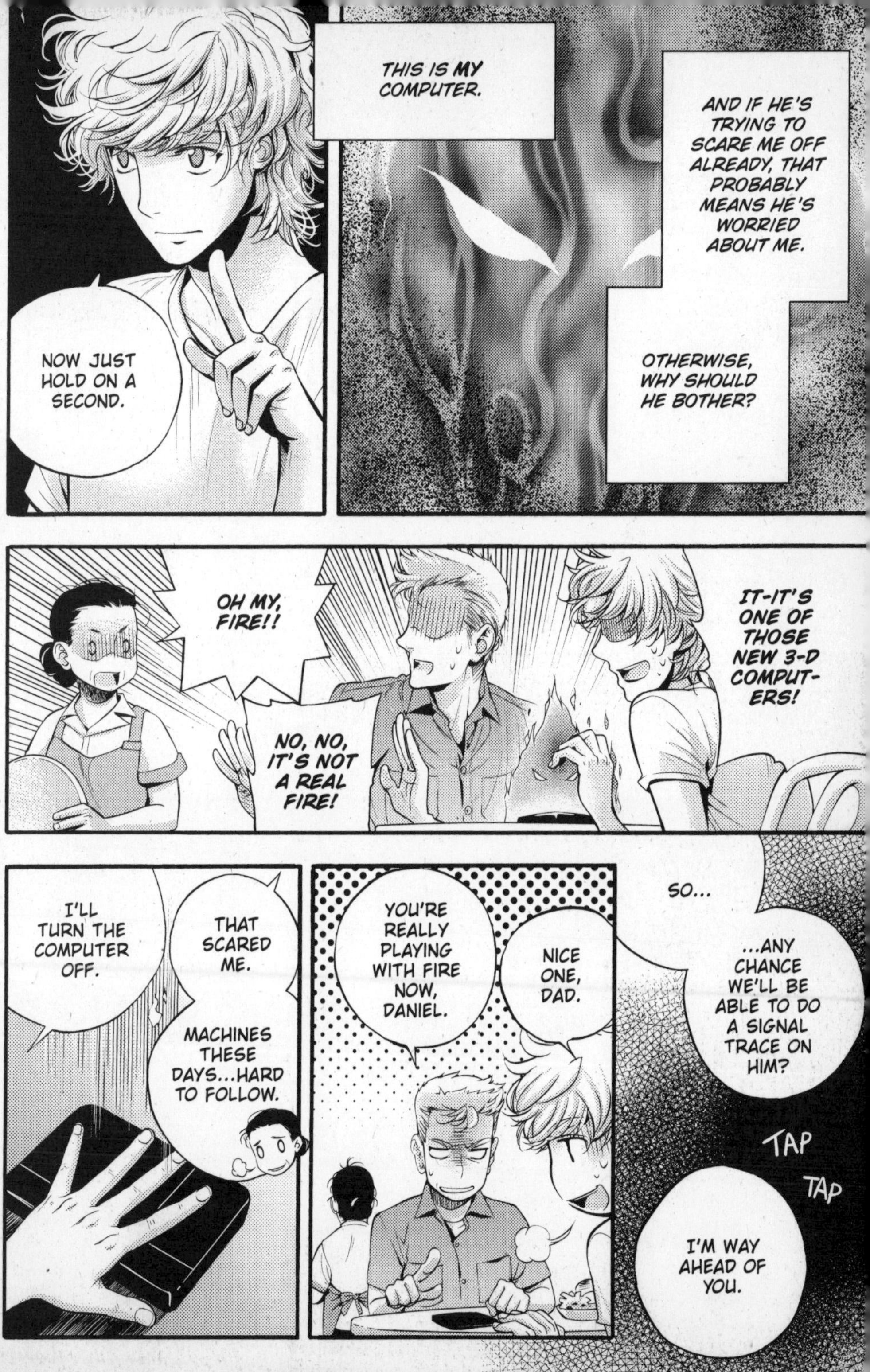
NOW JUST HOLD ON A SECOND.
THIS IS MY COMPUTER.
AND IF HE'S TRYING TO SCARE ME OFF ALREADY, THAT PROBABLY MEANS HE'S WORRIED ABOUT ME.
OTHERWISE, WHY SHOULD HE BOTHER?
OH MY, FIRE!!
NO, NO, IT'S NOT A REAL FIRE!
IT-IT'S ONE OF THOSE NEW 3-D COMPUT-ERS!
I'LL TURN THE COMPUTER OFF.
THAT SCARED ME.
MACHINES THESE DAYS...HARD TO FOLLOW.
YOU'RE REALLY PLAYING WITH FIRE NOW, DANIEL.
NICE ONE, DAD.
SO...
...ANY CHANCE WE'LL BE ABLE TO DO A SIGNAL TRACE ON HIM?
TAP
TAP
I'M WAY AHEAD OF YOU.

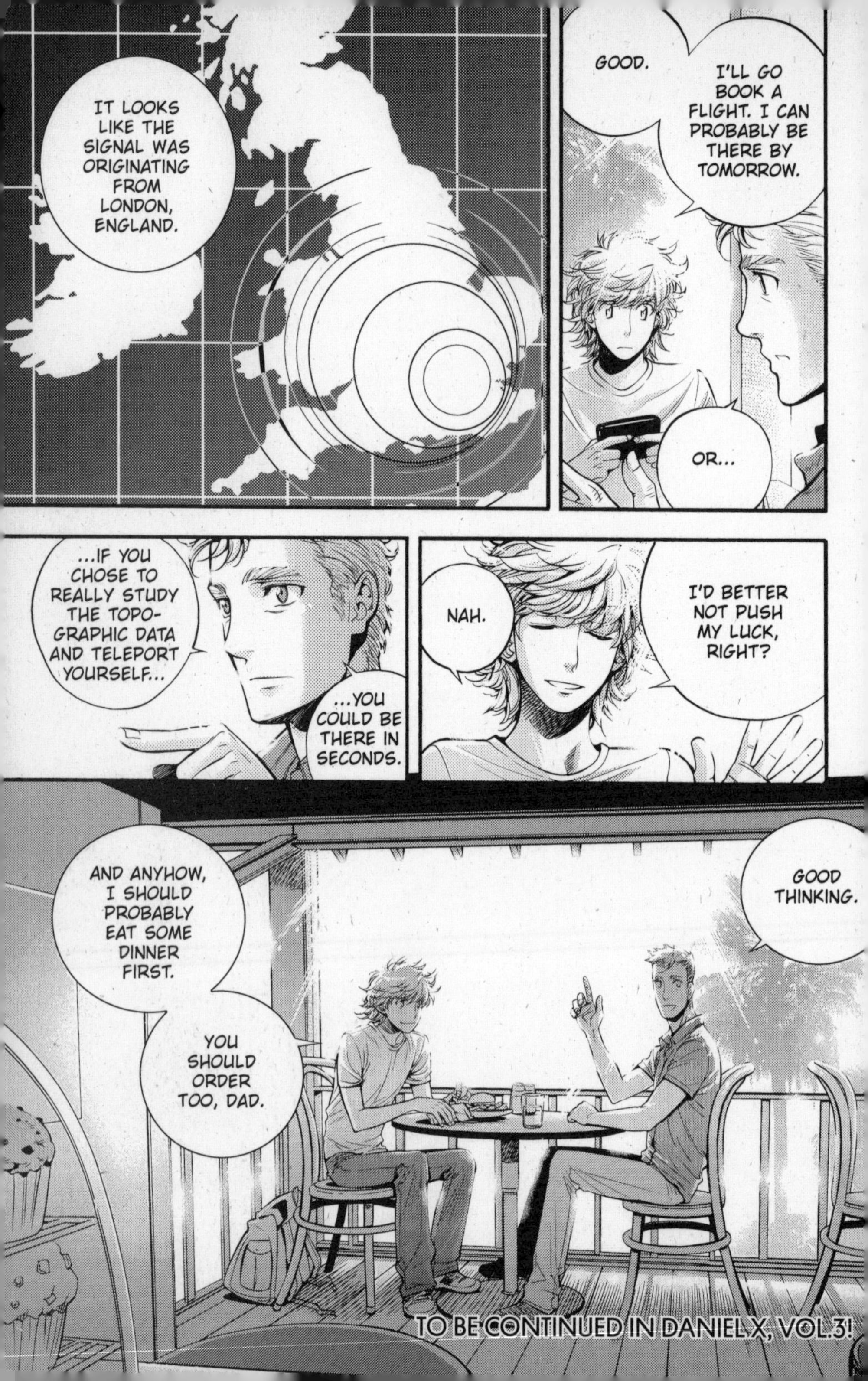
IT LOOKS LIKE THE SIGNAL WAS ORIGINATING FROM LONDON, ENGLAND.
GOOD.
I'LL GO BOOK A FLIGHT. I CAN PROBABLY BE THERE BY TOMORROW.
OR...
...IF YOU CHOSE TO REALLY STUDY THE TOPO-GRAPHIC DATA AND TELEPORT YOURSELF...
...YOU COULD BE THERE IN SECONDS.
NAH.
I'D BETTER NOT PUSH MY LUCK, RIGHT?
AND ANYHOW, I SHOULD PROBABLY EAT SOME DINNER FIRST.
YOU SHOULD ORDER TOO, DAD.
GOOD THINKING.
TO BE CONTINUED IN DANIEL X, VOL.3!

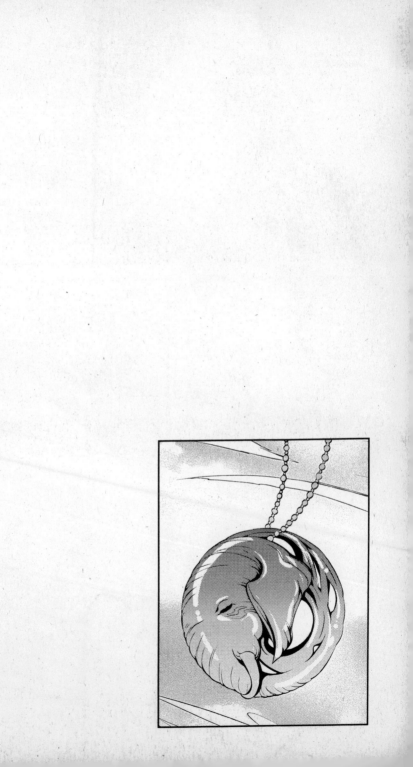

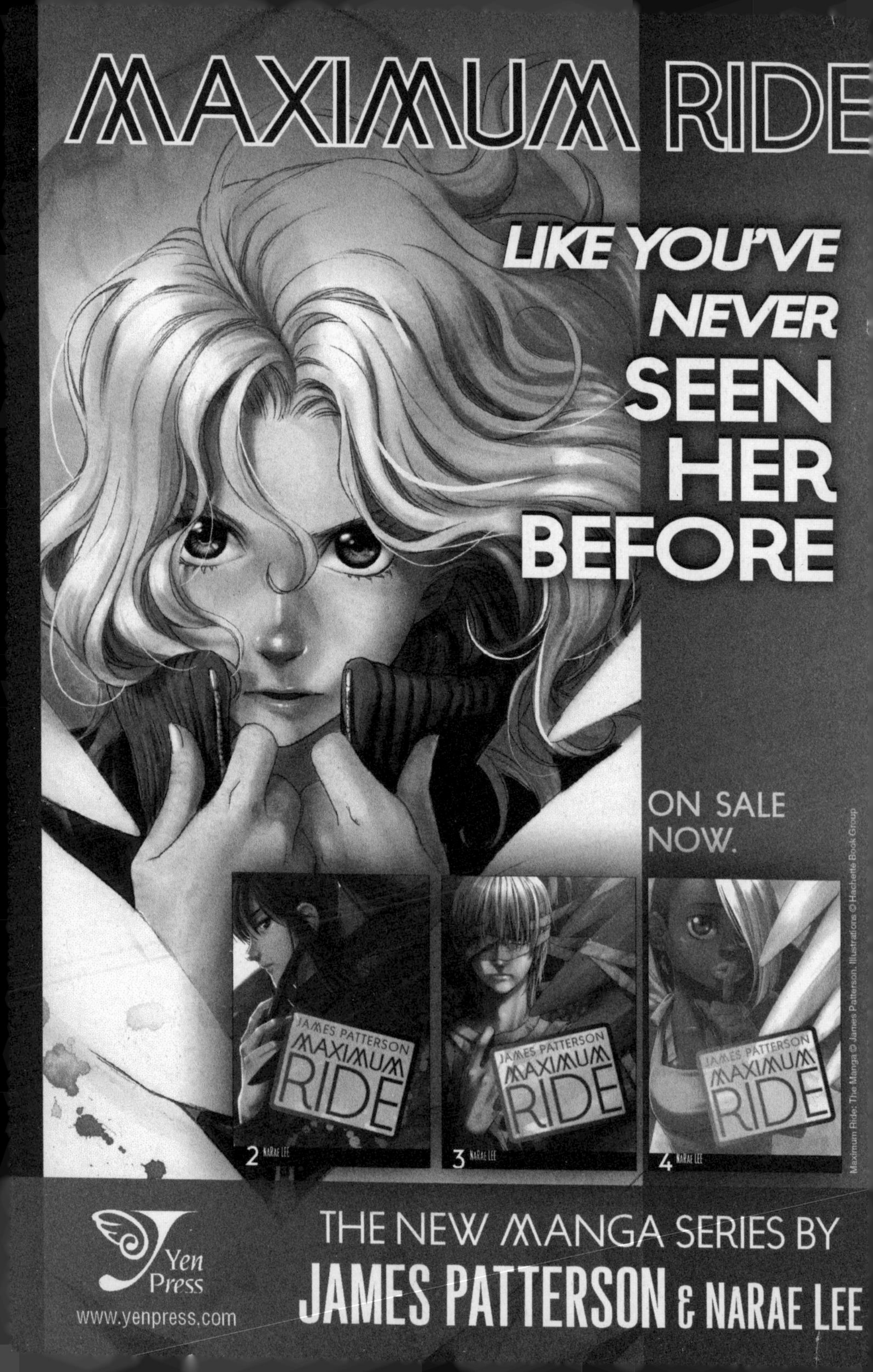
MAXIMUM RIDE
LIKE YOU'VE NEVER SEEN HER BEFORE
ON SALE NOW.
JAMES PATTERSON
MAXIMUM RIDE
2 NARAE LEE
JAMES PATTERSON
MAXIMUM RIDE
3 NARAE LEE
JAMES PATTERSON
MAXIMUM RIDE
4 NARAE LEE
Maximum Ride: The Manga © James Patterson. Illustrations © Hachette Book Group
Yen Press
www.yenpress.com
THE NEW MANGA SERIES BY
JAMES PATTERSON & NARAE LEE

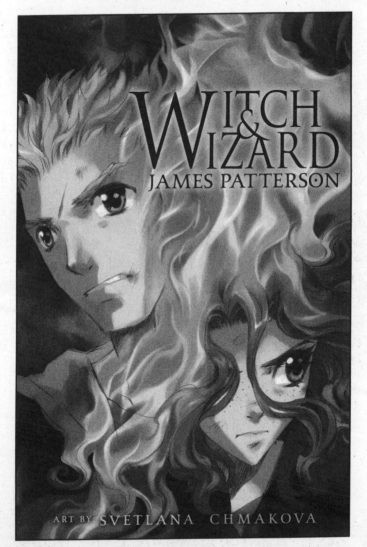

DANIEL X: THE MANGA②

JAMES PATTERSON
WITH NED RUST
& SEUNGHUI KYE

Adaptation and Illustration: SeungHui Kye

Lettering: JuYoun Lee & Abigail Blackman

DANIEL X, THE MANGA, Vol. 2 © 2011 by James Patterson

Illustrations © 2011 Hachette Book Group, Inc.

Yen Press
Hachette Book Group
237 Park Avenue, New York, NY 10017

www.HachetteBookGroup.com
www.YenPress.com

Yen Press is an imprint of Hachette Book Group, Inc. The Yen Press name and logo are trademarks of Hachette Book Group, Inc.

First Yen Press Edition: July 2011

ISBN: 978-0-316-07765-1

10 9 8 7 6 5 4 3 2 1

BVG

Printed in the United States of America